The Tri-unity of God Is Jewish

A Theological Study
on the Plurality and Tri-unity
of God in the Hebrew Scriptures

by
John B. Metzger, M.A.
April, 2005

i

Jewish Awareness Ministries
www.JewishAwareness.org
www.PromisesToIsrael.org

ISBN: 1-882324-32-3

Art work by
Amy Sheetreet
P.O. Box 44835
Haifa, Israel 31447

Printed by
Cenveo - Plus Communications
2828 Brannon Ave
St. Louis, MO 63139

Printing in the United States of America

Acknowledgements

To my Wife
Sharon
and her patience as I studied
for a year and a half
under a mountain of books
and typing on my computer
to write this book

To my Adviser
Dr. Robert Spender
at
Lancaster Bible College
Graduate School
For all his help in guiding me
through this process.

To my writing coach
Dr. Elaine Huber
For all her help and guidance
in writing this book

I would like to dedicate this book to four people:

Mabel Metzger
To my 96 year old mother
for all her encouragement over the years

Rev J Albert Ford
the first pastor of
McLean Bible Church
McLean, VA
who preached the whole Scripture:
Doctrine, Book Studies, Prophecy,
because of his ministry,
a love of the Word of God
and a love for Jewish people and Israel
took root in my life and gave me direction
as a teenager and for the rest of my life

Dr. Willis Bishop (retired)
Professor of Old Testament Studies
At
Washington Bible College
Lanham, MD
For his faithfulness in teaching over the years
and for giving me the foundation
for my Old Testament understanding

Dr. Arnold G. Fruchtenbaum
Founder & Director of Ariel Ministries
Tustin, CA
and
Camp Shoshannah
Keeseville, NY
For the understanding of the *Tanakh*
from a Jewish perspective.
God has used him to change my
life of ministry

Table of Contents

Preface

Words from the Author

I love the Jewish people and am deeply grieved by the atrocities that the "Christian" Church has committed against the Jewish people over the centuries. I intentionally set out to investigate what the Hebrew Scriptures say about the primary issue that separates Judaism from Christianity--an absolute monotheistic perspective of God that discredits the Christian perspective of God as indivisibly One and a plurality, or more specifically, a tri-unity.

Though I was well aware that the Jewish people have little historical and theological incentive to personally investigate the Christian "Jesus," as Christians lack clear perception that God's program for reaching the world is through the Jewish people. Judaism completely rejects with every ounce of strength the whole idea that God is a plurality, and that the Messiah could be God. I also knew that few Christians appreciate the evangelistic possibilities if God's Oneness and plurality (tri-unity) could be proven from the Hebrew Scriptures alone--without the aid of the New Testament. Therefore, I engaged in a two-year thesis study of the primary question, "Does the Old Testament clearly teach both monotheism and plurality or is that combination found only in the New Testament? This volume is an extension of that intensely researched answer.

I have become completely convinced that the Old Testament clearly presents God as both a monotheistic God and a plurality of three persons. Although the smallness of any human mind is incapable of logically explaining this Tri-unity, I have discovered that in the Hebrew Scriptures, God presents Himself as "One" God who is plural.

I passionately desire that the Jewish people--the most blessed nation on earth, the nation with some of the world's greatest intellects, the nation whose people consistently rise to the top in almost every field of endeavor--collectively and individually appropriate that giftedness by carefully considering the Hebrew Scriptures as God wrote them-- simply as *Hashem* Who longs to reveal Himself to them.

I was dismayed by a related but unexpected additional insight--that even many evangelical Christians do not want to see the Tri-unity of God in the Hebrew Scriptures-- that they perform biblical and secular "gymnastics" which is based on humanistic higher criticism with the Scriptures to discount the verbal plenary aspects of Inspiration. I discovered that many popular Christian commentaries ineffectively handle Scriptures related to the nature of God, especially the Trinity in the Hebrew Scriptures.

I acknowledge my limitations as a Hebrew scholar. But with contemporary Hebrew helps and available computer technologies, I am not a novice with the Scriptures. I am deeply passionate that this book encourage fundamental Bible believers to maintain their faith before it slips away in response to the pressures of Christian marketing that moves Christian "fluff" and error into the hearts and minds of believers. Steadfast believers need to turn the trend by countering that trend with solid Bible teaching and doctrine that encourages believers to hold firmly to the Scriptures and to walk in them.

Still, beyond that concern for Christian believers is my most intense prayer--that this study may challenge Jewish people to study the claims of *Hashem* Himself. He is, after all, G-d.

THE TRI-UNITY OF GOD IS JEWISH

The Statement of Purpose

Within Judaism and Christianity today the foundational belief that both hold in common is that God is one and that there are no gods besides Him (Deut 6:4; Isa 44:6; I Cor 8:6). However, Judaism and Christianity part company after that point. Judaism has an unmovable belief in monotheism, that God is one alone. Rabbi Stanley Greenberg of Temple Sinai of Philadelphia clearly contrasts the following statement of the Jewish belief in the oneness of God with the Christian belief of the tri-unity of God:

> Christians are, of course, entitled to believe in a Trinitarian conception of God, but their effort to base this conception on the Hebrew Bible must fly in the face of the overwhelming testimony of that Bible. Hebrew Scriptures are clear and unequivocal on the oneness of God . . . The Hebrew Bible affirms the one God with unmistakable clarity, Monotheism, an uncompromising belief in one God, is the hallmark of the Hebrew Bible, the unwavering affirmation of Judaism and the unshakable Faith of the Jew.
>
> Under no circumstances can a concept of a plurality of the Godhead or a trinity of the Godhead ever be based upon the Hebrew Bible.[1]

However, Christianity views God as a Trinity. The term "trinity" is an inadequate term to describe God because it only emphasizes the three persons and not the unity within the Trinity. Hence the term "tri-unity" will be used because it is the best term to unite the oneness or unity of God with the plurality of God.[2] But even tri-unity is not palatable in the mind of Jewish people.

Jacob Jocz, a Jewish believer in Messiah, states that the differences between Judaism and Christianity center around a person and who He is:

> At the center of the controversy between Church and Synagogue stands the Christological question. This is not a question whether Jesus is the Messiah, but whether the Christian understanding of the Messiah is admissible in view of the Jewish concept of God. Here lies the dividing line between Judaism and the Church. On this point neither can afford to compromise.[3]

This controversy lies at the heart of this book, not only who Jesus (*Yeshua*) is, but also how Scripture presents God and how Judaism and Christianity interprets those Scriptures.

---

[1] Arnold A. Fruchtenbaum, "Jewishness and the Trinity," n.p. [cited 18 November 2003]. Online: http://www.JewsForJesus.org/library.issue8 & [cited 19 July 2003] www.Messiahnj.org/af-tri-unity.htm.
[2] Paul Enns, *The Moody Handbook of Theology* (Chicago: Moody, 1989), 199.
[3] Jacob Jocz, "The Invisibility of God and the Incarnation," *CJT* 4, no. 3 (July 1958): 179-186.

Ancient belief in the oneness of God is a major reason that Jewish people have resisted the advance of the Gospel of Christ (Messiah) for over 20 centuries. They rejected *Yeshua* the Messiah,[4] the promised Messiah of Israel as God incarnate. In Old Testament times unbelief was demonstrated by turning to other gods. Both Israel, in 722 BCE[5] and later Judah in 586 BCE, suffered two great defeats, which resulted in the people being carried away into Assyria (Amos 7:10-17; Hos 4:1-6; 9:1-9)[6] and Babylon (2 Chr 34:14-28; Jer 2:5–3:10)[7] respectively. The beginning of the Diaspora,[8] or scattering around the world that Moses spoke of in Deuteronomy (28:15-68 with Jer 11:8; 30:1-10) had begun. These great defeats were a direct result of the Jewish people's unbelief and apostasy in relation to the Mosaic Law. They forsook God and His Law and worshipped false gods.

A second set of Jewish defeats (70 & 135 CE) which further contributed to the Diaspora, was not because they denied the oneness of God through idolatry as they had done previously, but because they had rejected their own Messiah. This denial and rejection was partially a result of their absolute belief in the oneness of God compounded by the rabbinic teaching also known as the Oral Law (Dan 9:26; Zech 11:1-17; 12;10; Matt 24:1-2; Mark 13:1-2; Luke 21:5-6; 20-24).[9] The Oral Law made an even greater division between the Hebrew text and what first century Pharisees taught in relationship to the Jewish concept of Messiah in the first century and what the Hebrew Scripture taught. That subject will not be dealt with here. For an informative study on the development of the Oral law read chapter seven in Arthur Kac's book (see appendix #4) to receive an insight as to the Jewish reasoning behind the Jewish people leaving the Written Law to obey the Oral Law.[10]

Because of that rejection the Church has unjustly persecuted the Jewish people for over 17 centuries in "Christian Europe." More recently, Islam has persecuted Israel

---

[4] Messiah: Messiah comes from the Hebrew word *Mashiach*, meaning "anointed." When translated into New Testament Greek, Messiah is *Christos* which becomes Christ in English.

[5] Common Era: These are alternate terms used as synonyms for the Latin adopted by the Church the birth of Christ. So BC and AD are the exact equivalent of BCE and CE.

[6] Andrew E. Hill and John H. Walton. *A survey of the Old Testament*, (Grand Rapids: Zondervan, 1991), 359.

[7] Hill and Walton, *A Survey of the Old Testament*, 329.

[8] Diaspora: The dispersion of Jews throughout the world beginning with Israel (722 BCE) and Judah (586 BCE) through the fall of the Second Temple (70 CE) and the defeat in the revolt in 135 CE. Refers to all Jews living outside the Land of Israel. Also known as the "Exile."

[9] Oral Law: Oral instruction beyond the written Torah, which was written down in the *Mishnah* around 220 CE (core of the Talmud) and is considered by Jewish people as authoritative, equal to the Scriptures. Rabbinic authorities use this argument to substantiate the Oral Law being as weighty as Scripture. They teach that Moses received more from God than the written Torah on Mount Sinai, that he received the Oral Law which was memorized, taught to Joshua, who taught it to the Judges, who then taught it to the Prophets and finally to the men of the Great Synagogue or the *Sophrim*. This Oral Law is the central reason why *Yeshua* and the Pharisees were at odds.

[10] Arthur W. Kac, *The Spiritual Dilemma of the Jewish People* (2nd ed. Grand Rapids: Baker, 1983), 62-82.

since the 7th century CE.[11]   Yet today there is no indication that the Jewish people have changed their view relative to Jesus being the Messiah of Israel, the promised God/man who is one with God.   There are Jewish people coming to faith in Messiah *Yeshua* today, but the percentages are quite small, even in Israel.   Even among some fringe Messianic groups there is no belief that *Yeshua* is God as is reflected in this quote from Uri Marcus:

> Myself as well as our entire congregation of Believers in *Ma'aleh Adumim*, completely reject the Trinitarian notions of plural unity, and will not acquiesce to any theology which challenges the ONEness of HaShem[12] in any fashion…. *Yeshua* is the Son of the living G-d, never G-d the son, in our view.[13]

That same belief is also seen in America by this statement of Joe Good:

> *Yeshua* was an attribute of the Father that was made flesh. But in being flesh, he was a man, totally man . . . *Yeshua* we do not see as being God when he walked here on earth. We see him as a man, a man anointed by God, sent by God to perform a function. Now in his resurrection, we do not see him as God. We see him as a man appointed by God and that has been restored back to what man was intended to be . . .. I once believed in the Trinity; now I obviously don't.[14]

In Judaism, without question, the issue of the plurality of God is not embraced, and it also has spilled over to some Jewish "believers." Christianity treats this topic by either affirming the tri-unity of God in the Hebrew Scriptures or by affirming that this doctrine is foreshadowed in the Old Testament (*Tanakh*).

The core belief today in Judaism, or more precisely Rabbinic Judaism,[15] is one primary underlying point, that God is "one" (Deut 6:4). Their rejection of Messiah resulted in the suffering of the Jewish people through the centuries. A related point to this is the fact that the Pharisees[16] believed the Messiah would be a Pharisee and that he would help them build up the Oral Law[17] that served as a fence about the Written

---

[11] To understand the significance of the Christian persecution of the Jewish people over the centuries, recommend reading from *Jews, God and History* by Max I. Dimont.

[12] HaShem: literally means "the name." Jewish people will refer to God as HaShem rather than mentioning the name of God.

[13] Richard Harvey, "Jesus the Messiah in Messianic Jewish Thought: Emerging Christologies," *Mishkan* (issue 39, 2003): 7.

[14] John Fischer, "Yeshua: The Deity Debate," *Mishkan* (issue 39, 2003): 23.

[15] Rabbinic Judaism: There are two Judaism's, first Biblical Judaism which is given in the Hebrew Scriptures without the Talmud, oral law and rabbinic commentaries, secondly Rabbinic Judaism with the oral law which is the heart of the Mishnah, which is the core of the Talmud. Rabbinic Judaism follows the interpretations of the rabbis to the neglect of the Scriptures.

[16] Pharisees: Pharisees were the most well known of several sects in Judaism in the first century There are the ones primarily responsible for the Oral Law, which are man made rules and regulations on how to keep the Law of Moses.

[17] Marc H. Tanenbaum and Marvin R. Wilson, eds., *Evangelicals and Jews in Conversation on Scripture, Theology, and History* (Grand Rapids: Baker, 1978), 60-61.

Law.[18] This fence was made up of man-made rules and regulations to protect the Written Law from being broken and the Jewish people from going into captivity. It was between the years of the first generation of scribes that followed Ezra the Scribe, to Judah Ha-Nasi in 220 CE when the memorized laws were written down into what is called the *Mishnah*.[19] The *Mishnah*, known as the fence that the rabbis built around the Written Law,[20] became known as the Oral Law which became equal to Scripture.[21] Their teaching in regard to the Messiah was that he would be a great man, a gifted leader[22] and warrior, but he would not be God,[23] which contradicts the very *Tanakh*[24] they said they believed. So when Jesus came on the scene and tore down the fence, the rabbis were incensed.[25] They could have considered Jesus as the Messiah, but not as God. Their theological position was based on the Oral Law and their reaction is clearly seen in Jn 10:32-33. The Messiah could not be God from their Pharisaic perspective.

Their suffering is not the result of believing in the unity and oneness of God. It is the failure to believe in the unity and oneness of God that presents Himself as a plurality of one God who could and did appear as a man in the Hebrew Scriptures (Genesis 18). However, because of that belief, they would not believe that *Yeshua* was one with the Father, and consequently they also could not believe that *Yeshua* was the long awaited promised Messiah of Israel.

The foundation for the plurality of the Godhead was laid out in the Hebrew Scriptures.[26] The leadership of Israel did not recognize that and consequently they rejected *Yeshua*, who clearly presented Himself as one with the Father. David Dockery's quote probably expresses the best way to view the tri-unity in the Hebrew Scriptures:

---

[18] J. Julius Scott, *Jewish Backgrounds of the New Testament* (Grand Rapids: Baker, 1995), 172-173.

[19] George Robinson, *Essential Judaism, a Complete Guide to Beliefs, Customs, and Rituals* (New York: Pocket Books, 2000), 341.

[20] A growing belief within Messianic Judaism is that in order to be a good Christian many Messianic Jews (and gentile believers) believe that the observance or the Written Law, or the Mosaic Law consisting of 613 laws is necessary. This is a dangerous position of mixing Law and Grace together. These positions are expressed in *Torah Rediscovered* (a book) and *First Fruits of Zion* (a magazine published by Ariel and D'vorah Berkowitz. This is a very dangerous book and magazine and is not for a theological novice or person ungrounded in the faith.

[21] Jacob Neusner, *An Introduction to Judaism* (Louisville, Kent: Westminster/John Knox, 1991), 168.

[22] Louis Goldberg, *Our Jewish Friends*. (Neptune, NJ: Loizeaux, 1983), 92-93.

[23] Emil Schurer, *A History of the Jewish People in the Time of Jesus Christ* (Peabody, Mass: Hendrickson, Division two, 1890), 2:160-162.

[24] Tanakh: the Hebrew Scriptures. The Hebrew term is an acronym derived from the three divisions of the Jewish Scriptures. The Hebrew words Torah, Nevi'im and Ketuvim or the Law, the Prophets and the Writings comprise the "*Tanakh*."

[25] This whole subject is beyond the scope of this paper but it does have a direct connection on why the Jewish leadership in Jesus' day rejected Him as the long awaited promised Messiah of Israel. There is a direct relationship between the Oral Law (fence) and its teaching with their rejection of Jesus.

[26] Hebrew Scriptures: This is the first 39 books of the Bible called the Old Testament. The term "Hebrews Scriptures" is used so as not to alienate Jewish people by saying Old Testament, which equates to them as being old, out of date or no longer in force.

God did not reveal Himself in clearly defined trinitarian terms in the Old Testament. However, the Old Testament prepared the faithful for the doctrine of the Trinity.[27]

The New Covenant truths are not intended to be understood in a vacuum. Rather, they are clearly rooted in the teachings of the Hebrew Scriptures. The *Tanakh* will not necessarily prove in dogmatic terms the tri-unity of the Godhead, but it will lay a strong foundation for the unity of God and the plurality of God. Benjamin Warfield presents the concept of the tri-unity in the Hebrew Scriptures in the following statement:

> The Mystery of the Trinity is not revealed in the Old Testament; but the mystery of the Trinity underlies the Old Testament revelation, and here and there almost comes into view. Thus the Old Testament revelation of God is not corrected by the fuller revelation which follows it, but only perfected, extended and enlarged.[28]

Dockery and Warfield express the fact that the tri-unity is in the Hebrew Scriptures. It is the intent of this book to go one step further, demonstrating that the plurality (and tri-unity) was revealed but not as fully developed as it is in the New Covenant. Would Abraham, Moses and David, to name a few, see the tri-unity and understand it; Probably they did not. But the Pharisees and Sadducees should have understood the fact of the plurality and unity of God in Jesus' day.

It has been the observation of this writer, over the last forty years, that the Pauline Epistles seem to be the fuel for most of the messages in the Church today. Yet even Paul makes mention of only one mystery which the *Tanakh* did not teach, and that mystery was the mystery of the Church (Rom 16:25-27; 1 Cor 2:7, 10; Eph 3:4-10; Col 1:26-27).[29] Because of the Jewish insistence on the oneness of God, to the exclusion of the unity or plurality of God, they missed their Messiah and fell prey to 46 false messiahs over the centuries.[30] A current example of a false messiah is seen within the ultra-orthodox Lubavitch Hasidic community, which believes that the late Rebbe Menachem Mendel Schneerson[31] is the Messiah.[32]

---

[27] David S. Dockery, *Biblical Illustrator* (Nashville: Sunday School Board of the Southern Baptist Convention, Vol. 17 No 4, Summer 1991), 27-30.

[28] Benjamin Breckinridge Warfield, *Biblical and Theological Studies* (Philadelphia: The Presbyterian and Reformed, 1968), 30-31.

[29] Robert L. Saucy, *The Church in God's Program* (Chicago: Moody, 1972), 59-60.

[30] James E. Smith, *The Promised Messiah*, (Nashville: Thomas Nelson, 1993), 470-474.

[31] Messianic Scriptures: (a) These tell us that the Messiah will be of Abraham (Gen 12:1-3), (b) that the scepter will not depart from Judah until He is revealed (Gen 49:10), (c) that He would be a prophet like Moses (Deut 18:15-19 with Num 12:5-8), (d) that He would be of the House of David (I Chr 17:10-14), (e) that He would be born in Bethlehem (Isa 9:5-6: Mic 5:2), (f) that He would have to come before the destruction of the second temple (Dan 9:24-27; Gen 49:10), (g) that He would die (Isa 53:10; Ps 22), (h) that He would be resurrected (Isa 53:10). Menachem Schneerson has failed to meet all these biblical criteria except for one; he was Jewish. He was born in Brooklyn, not Bethlehem, and since he has no idea what tribe he descended from he cannot lay claim to the tribe of Judah and the House of David. He not only was born in Brooklyn, but he was born 19 centuries after the destruction of the temple.

[32] David Berger, *The Rebbe, The Messiah and the Scandal of the Orthodox Indifference* (Portland:

Need for the Study

This most critical study cannot be separated from the eternal destiny of Jewish souls. One cannot separate the salvation that was provided in the Messiah from his or her belief in the oneness, unity of God and the plurality of God. Only their belief in the oneness of God is seen. Therefore, their belief in absolute monotheism rules out the whole redemptive plan of God, which was provided through the Messiah and includes the acceptance of the plurality of God. Since the Jewish people rejected *Yeshua ha Mashiach* as their Messiah, there is no possible way to deal with the question of sin and its separation from God, except by the substitutionary sacrifice of the Servant of the LORD,[33] the Messiah of Israel, on the tree.

Contrary to what Jewish rabbis and liberal Christian theologians would have Christians believe, the Mosaic Covenant[34] is not a saving covenant for the Jewish people.[35] Obedience to the Law cannot save. Habakkuk 2:4 says, "The righteous will live by his faith." There have been no offerings or sacrifices for sin because the temple was destroyed in Jerusalem in 70 CE by the Romans. With the possible exception of the years between 132-135 CE, during the second revolt against Rome led by Bar Kokhba[36] there has been no temple or sacrifice for 1,935 years. If the law was to be the covenant to give salvation, then God has made it completely impossible for the Jewish people to bring sacrifices to Him in Jerusalem at the Temple Mount. John Johnson expresses in a very clear and understanding way the development and belief of Dual Covenant theology.[37] The basic belief came out of the Holocaust and teaches that Jewish people are saved by observance of the Law and Gentiles are saved by their belief in Jesus. In other words Jewish people have the Mosaic Law and Gentiles have Jesus.[38]

The purpose of the Law was to provide a redeemed people with a rule of life in the areas of civil, religious and moral life.[39] Fruchtenbaum adds to Chafer's position by

---

Littman Library of Jewish Civilization, 2001), 20-25.

[33] Because Jewish people are very sensitive about writing or speaking the name of God, they will often refer to Him by using the terms *Adonai* (Lord) or *Ha Shem* (the Name). Because of the verity of names that the *Tanakh* uses for G-d, it is important to be correct when referring to the Hebrew Scriptures. This is being done to be precise not to be insensitive to Jewish People.

[34] Mosaic Covenant: God made five covenants with Israel. These covenants were divided into two groupings: conditional and unconditional covenants. Unconditional means that the Abrahamic, Land, Davidic and New Covenants were made by God and cannot be broken by man. By conditional we mean that Israel had a responsibility to keep their part of the covenant to receive the blessing of God. If Israel disobeyed, then God would not keep His part until they repented. This covenant is called the Mosaic Covenant.

[35] G. Jeffrey Macdonald, *Press Republican* (Plattsburgh, N.Y; September 13, 2002), A7.

[36] Rabbi Leibel Reznick, *The Holy Temple Revisited* (Northvale, N.J: Jason Aronson, 1993), 155-159.

[37] Dual Covenant Theology: This teaches that God's covenant (Mosaic Law) with the Jews hasn't been revoked and they are still in a saving covenant with God. In other words a good Christian is saved by being obedient to the New Testament and the Jew is saved by being obedient to the Mosaic Law. However, the Mosaic Law was never a saving covenant, no one was saved by obedience to the Law but by faith alone.

[38] John J. Johnson, "A New Testament Understanding of the Jewish Rejection of Jesus: Four Theologians on the Salvation of Israel." *JETS* 43, no. 2 (2000): 229-246.

[39] Lewis Sperry Chafer, *Systematic Theology* (Dallas: Dallas Seminary, 1948) 4:159-160.

holding that the sacrificial system was also a rule of life for the Old Testament saint. Its purpose was not for securing salvation but for the time when they would fail to keep the law. "Sacrifices were accepted as a means to restoration just as confession is for the believer today."[40] Fruchtenbaum has made two other observations. First, the 613 commandments derived from the Mosaic Law were issued as conditional. The conditional nature of the covenant is given in Exod 15:26[41] as well as in Deut 28:15. If the commandments were obeyed, abundant blessing was promised (vs. 1-14). But if they disobeyed, even more abundant cursing (vs. 16-68) would befall them. The second, the offering on the Day of Atonement did not remove sin (Hebrews 8-10). The Day of Atonement had its shortcomings because it was a temporary answer, not the permanent answer, for sin.[42] If it had, no further sacrifice on the Day of Atonement would have been necessary. Instead, the atonement provided only a covering for sin and restoration of fellowship but not the removal of the sin.[43] This Mosaic Law was fulfilled in the person of *Yeshua ha Meshiach*[44] for He became the sin bearer (Isa 53).

In the first century, as well as today, the core belief of Judaism teaches that God is one and not a unity of plurality. People need to have a good understanding of why Judaism believes that God is one (Deut. 6:4), not two or three, as Jewish people understand the teachings of Christianity. The Church believes in the tri-unity of the Godhead and can substantiate that from the Hebrew Scriptures. But the rabbis equally believe, from the same scriptures (and the Oral Law), that God is one and cannot be a man or God/man as is understood by Christians. How can Christians and Jews get two different readings from the same Scriptures? *Yeshua* was very clear on who He was, and that was clearly understood by the rabbinic leadership of Israel because *Yeshua* received a very strong, aggressive and negative response from the Pharisees and Sadducees (Jn 8:54-59;10:30-31).

A clear understanding of the phrase "unity of God" is important to comprehend and needs to be defined so both Jewish and Christian readers understand one another in this paper. Christians understand that God is a unity expressed in three persons, usually referred to as the trinity: God the Father, God the Son and God the Holy Spirit. They are indivisible (undivided) and equal in character and essence. However, the Jewish people understand that God is one, a unity, indivisible and, therefore hold only to God the Father. The term "indivisible" is used because in Old Testament history the pagan gods were able to be divided into multiple locations and gods. The multiplicity of deities is explained well by Jacobs:

> There is only one God and there are no others. Allied to this is the idea that God in His essence is indivisible. A deity like Baal could be split up, as it were, into various local deities, hence the plural form Baalim and Ashterot found in the

---

[40] Arnold A. Fruchtenbaum, *Israelology, the Missing Link in Systematic Theology* (Tustin, Calif: Ariel Ministries, 1989), 376.

[41] Fruchtenbaum, *Israelology, the Missing Link in Systematic Theology*, 588.

[42] Daniel Fuchs, *Israel's Holy Days* (Neptune, N.J: Loizeaux, 1985), 64-68.

[43] Fruchtenbaum, *Israelology, the Missing Link in Systematic Theology*, 588-589.

[44] The Hebrew name for Jesus the Christ.

7

Bible when speaking of the pagan gods. God is one and indivisible. He is Lord of all. He cannot be united syncretistically with other gods.[45]

The term "indivisible" accentuates the fact that God is not divided and is outside his creation, not part of it, nor is he divided into different locations competing with Himself. Christians would agree with the Jewish people in their understanding of God, except they recognize the plurality of God in the New Covenant as well as the multitude of references in the Hebrew Scriptures giving the foundation of the Christian teaching of the tri-unity. Therefore, in this study the unity of God is discussed from a Christian view with the plural concept, the tri-unity of God, will be in view unless stated otherwise.

Viewing the tri-unity from a Christian perspective is not helpful for the Jewish people because of their strong monotheistic heritage. Jewish believers in Messiah *Yeshua* uphold the tri-unity, but it is not their term of preference. The problem is how to define a doctrine that has no biblical terms. "Trinity" and "tri-unity" are not biblical terms. God is so overwhelming that He overflows or transcends our human notions of personhood. Anything beyond "one" or the "unity of God" is a problem for Jewish people. Jewish believers accept the tri-unity because they have examined the historical and biblical materials and concluded that it is correct even if the term is inadequate or gives the wrong concept to the Jewish mind. Michael Schiffman has a chapter in his book called "Messianic Jews & the Tri-unity of God" that would be very beneficial for Jewish and Gentile believers to read, to help gentile believers understand the frame of reference that Jewish people have.[46] Jewish people do not use creeds or councils like the Nicene Council in 325 CE. Instead of creeds, they use "testimonia" or "the quotation of Scriptures that supported their views."[47] Dwight Pryor further illustrates that there was no creedal usage of this doctrine when first century believers spoke of *Yeshua*.

> How do they explain theologically this devotion to a man and their veneration of him with God? They don't – to the frustration of our western minds! These Jewish believers expressed their monotheism in the same manner Israel had done from the beginning – in their worship. Not abstractly with theological speculations, but with actions demonstrating loyalty, veneration and service; not with propositional truths so much as with liturgical exclamations. For them the relationship of Jesus and God focused more on identify than divinity, and the truth was framed in textual associations more than theological affirmations. For example, scriptures that apply to *YHVH* are now, prerogatives of *Adonai*, such as creation and kingship are now extended to Jesus – not as some external, albeit divine agent, but as someone within the very identity and oneness of God himself. This is a crucial point. This veneration of *Yeshua* with and connected to *YHVH* is permissible only if he in some way is within the *echad* of God. Otherwise such attributions of scriptures, functions, authority, power, and

---

[45] Louis Jacobs, *A Jewish Theology* (West Orange, N.J: Behrman House, 1973), 21.
[46] Michael Schiffman, *Return of the Remnant* (Baltimore: Lederer Publications, 1992), 93-103.
[47] Fischer, Yeshua: The Deity Debate, *Mishkan* (issue 39, 2003), 20.

8

identity to him that apply exclusively to the God of Israel would violate the *Shema's* monotheism.[48]

That gives some idea of the Jewish frame of reference to the tri-unity and also how the early believers affirmed their belief in *Yeshua ha Mashiach*.[49]

Some Christian authors give little attention in showing the tremendous weight of Scripture the *Tanakh* provides not only in the oneness of God but His unity and plurality. Clearly, there is a need to synthesize and clarify in one book the foundations of the unity and plurality of the Godhead. This plurality also will be shown to be anchored to the *Torah*,[50] *Nevi'im*,[51] and *Ketuvim*[52] just as the oneness of God is anchored to the Hebrew Scriptures. Authors like Hodge[53] and Berkhof[54] add nothing or very little to the subject at hand. One reason is because they have not made it the emphasis or premise of their books or articles. Paul House in his *Old Testament Theology,* "summarizes its content and shows its theological significance in relationship to the whole of Old Testament Canon."[55] His theme is God and how He expresses Himself to Israel through the Hebrew Scriptures. Even though there are places where he speaks about the plural form for God, it is not the thrust of his book.[56] David Hinson's book, *Theology of the Old Testament*, deals with the oneness of God and quotes the *Shema* of Deut 6:4 without an adequate explanation of the word "one" or *echad*. In fact he says,

> It is the ordinary word used in counting, and fails to provide any single explanation of what the Jews meant when they said that "the LORD our God is one LORD."[57]

He later speaks of "the angel of the LORD" (*Yahweh*) without any reference to the fact that the angel of *Yahweh* is *Yahweh* and yet distinct from the LORD (*Yahweh*). He does state "that the angel is the LORD himself."[58] He does reference Gen 16:7-14 in con-

---

[48] Dwight A. Pryor, One god and Lord, *Mishkan* (issue 39 2003), 56.

[49] *Yeshua Ha Meshiach*: This is the Hebrew words meaning Jesus the Messiah. When it goes from Hebrew to Greek to English it becomes Jesus the Christ.

[50] The Torah: Also known as the Pentateuch, the first five books of the Bible. Meaning literally "teaching" or "instruction" or "guidance." Often translated as "the Law" in English Bibles, as in "the Law of the LORD is perfect" (Psalm 19:7 [v. 8 in Hebrew]). Torah in Judaism is an elastic term, which can also mean a single point of teaching to the whole of the Hebrew Bible, and the Oral Law.

[51] Nevi'im: This the second division of the Hebrew Scriptures called the Prophets (Joshua, Judges, 1 & 2, Samuel, 1 & 2 Kings, Isaiah, Jeremiah, Ezekiel, Hosea, Joel, Amos, Obadiah, Jonah, Micah, Nahum, Habakkuk, Zephaniah, Haggai, Zechariah, and Malachi).

[52] Ketuvim: This is the third division of the Hebrew Scriptures called the Writings (Psalms, Proverbs, Job, Song of Songs, Ruth, Lamentations, Ecclesiastes, Esther, Daniel, Ezra, Nehemiah, and 1 & 2 Chronicles).

[53] Charles Hodge, *Systematic Theology* (Grand Rapids: Eerdmans, 1970), 1:442-482.

[54] L. Berkhof, *Systematic Theology* (Grand Rapids: Eerdmans, 1941), 82-99.

[55] Paul House, *Old Testament Theology* (Downers Grove, Ill: InterVarsity, 1998), front cover.

[56] House, *Old Testament Theology*, 61-62.

[57] David Hinson, *Theology of the Old Testament* (London: Society for Promoting Christian Knowledge, 2001), 23-24.

[58] Hinson, *Theology of the Old Testament,* 60-61.

nection with Hagar, but he makes no use of examples to illustrate this from Gen 19:24 or Judg 2:1, which show that the angel of *Yahweh* is the LORD, yet distinct from God. Walter Brueggemann's *Theology of the Old Testament* deals with Israel's relationship to *Yahweh*. He makes good observations and statements on the Hebrew Scriptures but says little about the oneness or unity and plurality of the person of God. Thus, he does not deal with the formidable weight of evidence on how God is revealed in the Hebrew Scriptures.[59]

Books such as *Theological Word Book of the Old Testament*,[60] *All the Divine Names and Titles in the Bible*,[61] *The Names of God*,[62] *Dictionary of Old Testament Theology & Exegesis*[63] and *Names of God*[64] do reference the oneness or unity of God and the plurality of God. They speak of the origin and meaning of such terms as *El, Eloah, Elohim, YHVH, Adonai, Echad* versus *Yachid*, plus the plural descriptions of God. However, most of these books only lay out the basic facts of the unity and plurality of God and do not draw them together enabling the reader to get a full prospective of these plural terms of God in the Hebrew Scriptures and its weight as they stand together.

Another example is J. Barton Payne.[65] He touches on the names, titles and plurality of God but he does not give the depth of study beneficial to the Jewish audience. He discusses how the term *Elohim* developed during the time of Abraham to Moses rather than how it is used and understood throughout the Hebrew Scriptures. His understanding is that Abraham was a monolatrist rather than a monotheist.[66] His example of Abraham before Abimelech is lacking because nothing else in the Genesis text gives any reason to believe that Abraham was Monolatrist. Yet when coupling the biblical text together with archaeology, a better candidate for Monolatry is Balaam (Num 22:7-13). The *Bible and Spade*, a magazine of Associates for Biblical Research, gives the discovery of Balaam's name and prophecy on a pagan temple in present day Jordan.[67] Another possible candidate for Monolatry would be Jethro, Moses' father-in-law (Exod 18:11). Baker, in the *Dictionary of the Old Testament Pentateuch*[68] spends a considerable part of an article on the etymology of the names of God without showing how the names of God relate to each other or how the text of Scripture uses them in relation to each other. It is disappointing to see his short treatment of the plural noun

---

[59] Walter Brueggemann, *Theology of the Old Testament*. (Minneapolis: Fortress, 1997).

[60] Laird R. Harris, Gleason L. Archer, Jr. and Bruce K. Waltke, eds., *Theological Wordbook of the Old Testament* (2 vols; Chicago: Moody, 1980).

[61] Herbert Lockyer, *All The Divine Names and Titles in the Bible* (Grand Rapids: Zondervan), 1975.

[62] Andrew Jukes, *The Names of God* (Grand Rapids: Kregel, 1888).

[63] William VanGemeren, *Dictionary of Old Testament Theology & Exegesis* (Grand Rapids: Zondervan, 1997).

[64] Nathan Stone, *Names of God* (Chicago: Moody, 1944).

[65] Barton J. Payne, *The Theology of the Older Testament* (Grand Rapids: Zondervan, 1962), 125-127, 144-151.

[66] Monolatry is the worship of one god while recognizing there are other gods that can be worshipping them. Monotheism is the belief in one God and that no other gods exist.

[67] B.G. Wood, "Prophecy of Balaam Found in Jordan," *Bible and Spade* 6 (Autumn 1977): 121-124.

[68] Desmond Alexander and David Baker, *Dictionary of the Old Testament Pentateuch* (Downers Grove, Ill: InterVarsity, 2003).

Elohim. He does not even present the possibility of *Elohim* being anything beyond "a plurality of majesty, or royal plurals, as an intensification or claim to exclusivity, or as a honorific."[69]

The "plural of majesty", when referring to *Elohim,* means that when God addresses someone, He uses the plural "we" or "royal we", much as the Queen of England would use when addressing others in her presence. Baker's thoughts on the subject indicate a presupposition that the plurality of God does not play a part in his thinking.

This lack of attention to the tri-unity in the Hebrew Scriptures is also evident in evangelical theological journals. In 210 years of *Bib Sac, Westminster Theological Journal, JETS, Canadian Theological Journal, Grace Theological Journal* and *Master's Theological Journals,* almost nothing can be found on the tri-unity in the *Tanakh* unless it is embedded within another subject.[70]

It is not that Payne, Alexander and others, as mentioned above, do not speak of the issues of the names of God used in a singular and plural context, but they are scattered throughout their books. The purpose of this study is to put the references and insights of the unity and plurality of God all together and study them in more depth, in one place, so that a reader can get a fuller and unhindered view of the subject.

The understanding of the unity and plurality of God is the bottom line that must be dealt with before an "uncircumcised heart" of unbelief becomes a "circumcised" Jewish heart (Deut 30:6; Jer 9:25-26; Acts 3:11-19; 8:26-37). The unity and plurality of God is foundational to what Moses and the prophets wrote. Before the Jewish mind can embrace *Yeshua* as the Messiah, he must acknowledge God as one (a unity in plurality) and the Messiah as the God/man promised by the Hebrew Scriptures.

Scriptural and Theological Basis

This study of the unity (oneness) and plurality of God is based on how the Hebrew Scriptures treat the subject. A larger study of this issue would be to show the importance of this topic and how the rabbis have interpreted the Hebrew Scriptures by showing the background and importance of the Oral Law to that interpretation. This will have to be covered in a future study.

Robert Morey has made a very basic statement which is at the very heart of this paper. If God wanted to show that He was "multi-personal," then the student of the Word would be expected to find His plurality in the Hebrew Scriptures. The same is

---

[69] Alexander and Baker, *Dictionary of Old Testament Pentateuch,* 362.

[70] Bib Sac from 1945 to present, *Westminster Theological Journal* from 1960 to present, *JETS* from 1969 to present, *Canadian Theological Journal* form 1955 to 1970, *Grace Theological Journal* from 1960 to present, and *Masters Theological Journal* from 1990 to present.

true, if God wanted to show that He was "only one person," then that is what He would have written. Morey makes this statement:

> If the authors of the Bible believed that God was multi-personal, then we would expect to find that they would write about God in such a way as to indicate this idea to their readers. Thus, we must ask, "What would we expect to find in the Bible, if its authors believed that God was multi-personal?'
>
> On the other hand, if the authors of the Bible believed that God was only one person, i.e., they were classic Unitarians, then they would write about God in such a way as to indicate that idea. Thus, we are also warranted to ask, "What would we expect to find in the Bible, if Unitarians wrote it?"
>
> We will at times use the term "Unitarian" in its generic sense of anyone who denies the Trinity because he believes that God is only one person. This would include Jews, Muslims, Arians, and Modalists.[71]

This book will be looking at some of the names for God, such as God, Lord, LORD, and how they are used throughout the Hebrew Scriptures, as well as seeing how the authors of Scriptures reveal God to the reader. This study will also state how Christians view the core statement of Judaism (Deut 6:4) and how the word for "one" and the plurality of God is used throughout the Law, Prophets and Writings. Plural descriptions of God will then be discussed (such as Josh 24:19; Ps 149:2; Eccl 12:1; Isa 54:5) followed by a chapter on the Holy Spirit and lastly by passages that speak of the Messiah being divine in the *Tanakh*.

Two biblical positions underlie all discussions of the plurality and tri-unity of God in the Hebrew Scriptures progresses throughout this study. First, fundamentalist and evangelical believers affirm the inspiration of Scripture, which is the "breathing out of God" (God-breathed) through the Holy Spirit into men. This enabled them to receive and communicate divine truth, without error, making the speaker and/or writer infallible in the communication of God's truth. The Scriptures are God-breathed.[72] The second, tied very closely to inspiration, are two other related terms: verbal and plenary inspiration. By verbal, it is meant that every word of the original manuscripts of the Bible is given by inspiration of God. By plenary it is meant that it is full, complete, entire, extending to every part. So, every part of the Hebrew Scriptures and New Covenant is inspired equally by God.[73]

Since verbal and plenary inspiration is completely valid, then the words of Jesus as He taught regarding the subject of His divinity and the plurality of God should be highly regarded. He clearly states that Moses and the Prophets spoke of Him:

---

[71] Robert Morey, *The Trinity: Evidence and Issues* (Grand Rapids: World Publishing, 1996), 87.

[72] H. S. Miller, *General Biblical Introduction* (Houghton, N.Y: Word-Bearer, 1960), 17.

[73] Miller, *General Biblical Introduction*, 24.

> Search the [Hebrew] scriptures; for in them ye think ye have eternal life: and *they are they which testify of me.* (Jn 5:39)

> For had ye believed Moses, ye would have believed me; *for he wrote of me.* (Jn 5:46)

> Then he said unto them, O fools, and slow of heart to believe all that the prophets have spoken: Ought not Christ to have suffered these things, and to enter into his glory? *And beginning at Moses and all the prophets, he expounded unto them in all the scriptures [Hebrew] the things concerning himself.* (Lk 24:25-27)[74]

Jesus was not speaking irresponsibly by telling his disciples that Moses and the Prophets bear witness of Him. Or did He really mean that He, as the Son of God, was revealed in the Hebrew Scriptures and in order to do that He would have to be presented as God, and that God would then have to be in a plural form. The Pharisees had every right to reject Him if *Yeshua* taught in the New Covenant that He was divine, and the plurality of God was not taught in the Hebrew Scriptures. But if He was in the Hebrew Scriptures as He said, then the Pharisees rejected him for reasons beyond the claim of being divine, and they have been misinterpreting some very important Scriptures that God intended them to understand and believe. God would not have presented his Son in a vacuum, but the *Tanakh* would have given evidence of his divine nature. If the Father had not give ample witness of his plurality in the *Tanakh*, then He would have been setting up the Pharisees to reject Jesus, and all Israel has suffered over the centuries as a direct result of God's silence or deception on the subject of His plurality in the Hebrew Scriptures. The words of Jesus should not have been considered blasphemous as it was by the Sanhedrin (Jn 10:33; Matt 26:63-66; Lk 5:21) or belittled in reference to the doctrine of the tri-unity of God by Christian scholars in teaching the *Tanakh*. As the names of God, Theophanies, plural descriptions and the *Shema* of Deut 6:4 with *echad* vs *yachid*, of God are given, an interesting impression has developed. Have Christian theologians abandoned or abdicated the doctrine of the tri-unity of God to rabbinic Judaism?

The second biblical position coupled with a belief in verbal plenary inspiration is the belief in the literal method of interpretation. If the Scriptures are God-breathed, then God meant what He said without man's attempt to reinterpret what He said. David Cooper gives the following definition of this literal method of interpretation:

> When the plain sense of Scripture makes common sense, seek no other sense; therefore, take every word at its primary, ordinary, usual, literal meaning unless the facts of the immediate context, studied in the light of related passages and axiomatic and fundamental truths, indicate clearly otherwise.[75]

---

[74] *The Holy Bible*, King James Version (New York: Oxford University, 1996), 1281. All New Testament references are cited from the King James Version unless otherwise stated. For all Old Testament references see footnote 125. The italics are added for emphasis.

So when coming to the names of God, like *Elohim*, why do scholars want to argue against what God says about Himself? If verbal plenary inspiration of the Scriptures is believed by fundamentalist and evangelicals, then why do some of them try to make it plural of majesty?

Remembering clearly 35 years ago, the professors at Washington Bible College impressed upon their students when looking at Scripture to always look at the context, context, context! If a passage is not viewed within the context that God gave it, then one's study is vulnerable merely to the thoughts and intellect of man. That principle applies to a study of the relationship of *Elohim* to the plurality or tri-unity of God. Scholars and translators allow the context to determine whether it refers to pagan gods or the true God. Why are false gods recognized in the plurality (Isa 36:18-20), but when the same identical word (Exod 20:2-3), is used of the true God, (the vast majority of the time) the plurality of God is explained away by calling it a "plural of majesty?"

Limitations of the Research Project

The primary focus of this study is the oneness or unity and plurality of God and how the Hebrew Scriptures treat the subject. Therefore, it will not be the main purpose of this book to deal with the New Covenant proofs of the tri-unity. Erickson makes the comment that the *Tanakh* will lead us to a monotheistic belief, but as he said, what led the Church to move beyond the monotheistic belief was additional biblical witness (New Covenant).[76] The *Tanakh* did not need additional New Covenant revelation to substantiate the plurality or tri-unity of God, and this book will validate that. Nor will areas such as the Oral Law or rabbinic interpretation of the Law of Moses be dealt with. It will only be touched upon when it is necessary to understand the purpose of this paper.

Organization of Study

Names of God

Chapter two deals with the understanding and usage of the terms *El*, *Elim*, *Elohim* and *Eloah* and why *Elohim* is applied to two divine beings as in Ps 45:6-7. Some of these names are singular and some are plural according to how the Hebrew Scriptures use them. What does Hebrew grammar say in relation to *Elohim*, which is a plural term for one God? Consideration is also given to the usage of the term Lord, as *Adonai* and *Yahweh* (LORD) or *YHVH*, and why it is also applied to two divine beings

---

[75] David L Cooper, *The God of Israel* (Los Angeles: Biblical Research Society, 1945), 34-35.

[76] Millard J. Erickson, *Introducing Christian Doctrine* (Grand Rapids: Baker, 1992), 98.

in Gen 19:24; Zech 2:8-9. It appears that Christian theologians and scholars have abandoned or abdicated the tri-unity of God in the Hebrew Scriptures to Rabbinic Judaism's interpretation of God, which has been in complete control of the Jewish people for 2000 years. The difference is as great as day and night between Biblical Judaism and Rabbinic Judaism. One leads to truth and one to falsehood in relation to how the subject of the tri-unity is treated and understood. God, who is one, chose to reveal Himself with a multitude of plural references to Himself. Why, if God chose that course to reveal Himself, do Christian scholars who believe in the tri-unity in the New Covenant constantly force those plural references into singular interpretation in the Hebrew Scriptures? The outcome of how this subject is treated and understood by Christians from the Hebrew Scriptures determines the eternal fate of Jewish souls.

Theophany

Chapter three will deal with the understanding of the term "theophany" in the Hebrew Scriptures and how it is used. Jewish rabbis insist that God will not, has not and did not appear as a man in human history. Yet throughout the *Tanakh*, God did appear to Abraham, Jacob, Joshua and others in the form of a man. Jewish rabbis have that narrow unbiblical view because the incarnation of God cannot be entertained at all or rabbinic Judaism is finished. The term theophany involves such terms as "the angel of the Lord" and/or "the Captain of the Lord's Host," where God appeared in the form of a man with those names. *Yahweh* also said that He would send "My angel" (Exod 23:23) to lead them as they traveled through the wilderness. The second part of theophany is the *Shechinah* of God, which designates God's presence.[77] The presence of God, which appeared to Moses and Israel as the Glory of God, dwelt with Israel on Mount Sinai and then in the Holy of Holies of the tabernacle and later in the temple. If the theophanies of God are God Himself, then God is a plurality and the whole of Jewish understanding is at odds with the *Tanakh*, because in those theophanies God has chosen to show Himself as one God but as a plurality within His oneness.

Shema

Chapter four deals with the cornerstone and affirmation of the Jewish faith, the *Shema* of Deut 6:4. As far as Judaism is concerned this verse puts to rest, forever, the whole subject of the plurality or tri-unity of God. It specifically puts to rest the whole subject of the Incarnation of the Messiah in the Jewish mind because "*Yahweh* is one." This chapter focuses particularly on the words *Echad* and *Yachid* and the meaning of both. Maimonides, who is called the second Moses and who lived in the eleventh century C.E., changed the reading of the *Shema* in his second of Thirteen Articles to *Yachid*. It is necessary to understand why these two Hebrew words in his Thirteen Articles are so very important to the Jewish understanding of the *Shema* of Deut 6:4.

---

[77] Jacob Neusner and William Scott Green, *Dictionary of Judaism in the Biblical Period* (Peabody, Mass: Hendrickson, 1999), 577.

Once again, Christian theologians and scholars bypass studies on exactly how that word is used throughout the Hebrew Scriptures. Is God making a statement beyond his desire for Israel to love Him and commit to Him alone? Jewish Rabbis say no. But in this statement of belief, the *Shema* on the oneness of God, it is possible that God did have the unity or plurality of Himself in mind.

Plural Terms

Chapter five will deal with the plural pronouns used of God and other plural descriptions showing how they apply to the unity and plurality of God. God, in numerous places, used plural terms for Himself beyond the terms *Elohim*, angel of the *Yahweh* and the combination of terms for God both plural and singular of Himself. The plural personal pronoun "us" as in Gen 1:26, that God uses of Himself seven times in the Hebrew Scriptures will be studied. The four references in the *Tanakh* where these are found will make a strong statement toward understanding His person and the plural emphasis that God makes.

There are other descriptive terms that God uses to further strengthen His plurality, such as the plural attribute of "creator" in Eccl 12:1. Other descriptive plural words for God (*Elohim*) are located in Gen 20:13; 35:7, 2 Sam 7:23 and Psa 58:11.

Holy Spirit

This chapter will deal with the neglected area "spirit of the LORD" in the Hebrew Scriptures. While there are many references to His personal character in the New Covenant, the same is not as plentiful in the *Tanakh*. God did not just become a tri-unity in the New Covenant; He always was a tri-unity. But how is the "spirit of the LORD" and the fact that God is Spirit distinct in the *Tanakh*? The purpose of this chapter will be to substantiate that the Holy Spirit is active in the *Tanakh* and that He is represented often by His deeds or actions rather then always showing his personhood as is usually presented in the New Covenant.

Christian Cults and the Jewish people reject His personhood. To them He is merely the extension of God, or the presence of God, but not a separate distinct person. In Judaism there is no belief in a tri-unity of God. The person of Messiah usually takes center stage on the discussion of the plurality or tri-unity of God, and not the person of the *Ruah HaKodesh* (Holy Spirit). The absence of the argument of the Holy Spirit does not remove the importance of the ministry of the Holy Spirit in the Hebrew Scriptures.

Messiah is Divine

The purpose of this chapter with the background of the rest of this study is to show that the Messiah is God. This is contrary to everything that Judaism stands for. Here the specific purpose is to show the eternality of the Messiah. The term for "eternity" and "everlasting" are not as understood in the English language today. A complete understanding of the term and how they where used is the first area to be discussed. The second area is to show how the term "eternal" relates to the Messiah. Passages like 1 Chron 17:11-14, 2 Sam 7:10-14, Isa 9:6-7, Micah 5:2, and Jer 23:5-6 to prove His divinity. Also there are other verses with the main speaker being God or *Yahweh*, and with His own words describes what happened to Him. Those descriptions of Himself can only point to one person, the incarnation of God in the Person of *Yeshua*.

Summary and Conclusion

Chapter eight provides summary and conclusion. God revealed Himself to man through His Word, in a progressive manner. That revelation of Himself to man in Genesis 1 makes a statement of Himself as the pages, chapters, and books of the Scripture unfold His plurality before the reader until that final revelation is given in the incarnation of the Messiah to Israel. Both the plurality and the tri-unity of God can be proven in the Hebrew Scriptures. However, the tri-unity is not as well developed in the *Tanakh* as it is in the New Covenant. The *Tanakh*, as it adds one teaching point upon another throughout the Law, Prophets and Writings, [78] becomes a very formidable weight of evidence to prove the plurality of God. It is not just a plurality but the tri-unity that is in view when all is compiled.

The knowledge and understanding of this subject is very important in reaching Jewish people (as well as the various cults). Today, this people group is listed as one of the least reached groups in the United States of America.[79] Less than one percent of Jewish people embrace *Yeshua ha Meshiach* as their Redeemer, Saviour and Lord.[80] This study will be devoted to understanding the oneness, or the unity of God, and plurality of God as set forth in the Hebrew Scriptures by biblical, not rabbinic, interpretation.

---

[78] Law, Prophets and Writings: This is the Jewish designation for the three divisions of the *Tanakh*, or the Hebrew Scriptures.

[79] Patrick Johnstone and Jason Mandryk. *Operation World* (Waynesboro, Ga: Paternoster USA, 2001), 662.

[80] Jews For Jesus. "How many Jews of Jesus are there?" No pages. [Cited 12, January 2004]. Online: http://www.jfjonline.org/about/howmany.htm.

CHAPTER 2

NAMES FOR GOD

The nature and essence of God, as it relates to the revelation of the plurality or tri-unity of God in the Hebrew Scriptures, is an area of controversy between liberal theologians and Jewish Rabbis[81] on one side, and fundamental and evangelical theologians on the other. Even among conservative theologians there seems to be a tendency not to follow through on their beliefs from the New Covenant to the Hebrew Scriptures. The primary, authoritative source material that the New Covenant writers used was the Hebrew Scriptures. God did not just reveal Himself as the triune God out of a vacuum in the New Covenant. Rather, He started in Genesis 1 using clear statements of Himself in such terms as *Elohim* and "us." Geisler makes the following statements on these two terms:

> It is true that the very word for God in the Old Testament (*Elohim*) is plural in form; indeed, it can be translated "gods" (Ps 82:6). However, when used of God, it is plural grammatically, not ontologically. It is plural in literary form, but not in actual reality.
>
> The use of "we" or "us" of God is another literary form known as a royal or regal plural. It is used of royalty and of God in Semitic cultures.[82]

Geisler, though not seeing the plurality of God in the term *Elohim*, does see the tri-unity of God throughout the *Tanakh*. However, many of his references are looking back from the New Covenant to the *Tanakh*.[83] That is a questionable practice and yet easy thing to do. Scholars must not read New Covenant truth back into the Hebrew Scriptures. The Scriptures are inspired by God; every word, in every part of Scripture, is equally inspired. Man's logic and wisdom cannot reinterpret what God Himself said. The New Covenant (New Testament) was not written in a vacuum. The theological foundations and principles of all Church doctrines are rooted and anchored in the Hebrew Scriptures. The difficulty of dealing with the plurality or tri-unity of God in the Hebrew Scriptures is determining how much or if there is anything found in the *Tanakh*. There is seemingly endless insistence by Jewish rabbis that the plural of God in the *Tanakh* does not exist. They must insist that the plurality of God is non-existent or Rabbinic Judaism is finished. The difficulty lies with Christian scholars who appear to follow their lead. This chapter demonstrates the same basic argument as the rabbis, which minimizes the impact that the doctrine of the plurality or tri-unity of God could have in the *Tanakh*. The Hebrew Scriptures are more than just the foundation of Judaism. They are also the foundation for all doctrines that the Apostles taught in the New

---

[81] <u>Jewish Rabbis</u>: By placing Rabbis together with liberals, this does not mean to imply that Rabbis are liberal. Liberals and Rabbis may have the same conclusions, but they both arrive at them from totally different perspectives.

[82] Norman Geisler, *Systematic Theology* (Minneapolis: Bethany House, 2003), 2:277.

[83] Geisler, *Systematic Theology*, 278-290.

Covenant. Corroboration of this lies in the statements made by the Apostles Paul and Peter in 2 Tim 3:16 and 2 Pet 1:20-21 respectively:

> All scripture is given by inspiration of God, and is profitable for doctrine, for reproof, for correction, for instruction in righteousness.

> Knowing this first, that no prophecy of the scripture is of any private interpretation. For the prophecy came not in old time by the will of man: but holy men of God spake as they were moved by the Holy Ghost [Spirit].

These verses are directly referencing the Hebrew Scriptures. Paul and Peter, under the guidance and inspiration of the Holy Spirit (*Ruach haKodesh*), penned these words (2 Tim 3:16; 2 Pet 1:21) to express the fact that they were the foundational document for themselves, as well as for Luke, John and the other authors of the New Covenant.

אֵל *El*

El is used in the Hebrew Scriptures as a singular form for God about 238 times and is a very ancient Semitic term that was widely used.[84] In fact, it is said by Friedrich Oehler to be the oldest Semitic name for God.[85] In the Ugaritic Canaanite culture "*El*, the pagan god, was the proper name of the titulary head of the hierarchy of deities."[86] Preuss explains that *El* was "connected with the conception of a heavenly council. His titles include bull, ancient one, hero, king, and creator."[87] Although a particular definition of *El* may not be derived from Hebrew Scriptures, it contains material aids in understanding and has a direct relationship to Israel:

> *El* was considered the chief among the Canaanitic deities. Likened to a bull in a herd of cows, the people referred to him as "father bull" and regarded him as creator. *Asherah* was the wife of *El*.

> Chief among the seventy gods and goddesses that were considered offspring of *El* and *Asherah* was *Hadad*, more commonly known as *Baal*, meaning Lord.[88]

The etymology of *El*, when tracing all known historical information, makes it very difficult to come up with an original meaning. David Baker gives the following: (1) "The derivation or etymology of *El* and its related forms is unclear." He further adds that the term has to do with power.[89] James Smith also concurs with Baker in

---

[84] Harris, Archer, and Waltke, *Theological Wordbook of the Old Testament*, 1:42.
[85] Oehler, Gustave Friedrich, *Theology of the Old Testament*, (Grand Rapids: Zondervan, 1883), 87.
[86] Alexander and Baker, *Dictionary of the Old Testament Pentateuch*, 360.
[87] Horst Dietrich Preuss, *Old Testament Theology* (Trans. Leo G. Perdue: 2 vols.; Louisville: Westminster John Knox), 1:149.
[88] Samuel J. Schultz, *The Old Testament Speaks* (New York: Harper & Row), 92.
[89] Alexander and Baker, *Dictionary of the Old Testament Pentateuch*, 360.

saying that (2) "Most frequently mentioned suggestions for the original meaning are 'power' or 'fear,' but these are widely challenged and much disputed."[90]

The Hebrew Scriptures predominately use *El* as a generic term for God.[91] *El* is rarely used by itself. More often, it is used in combination with other words that further describe Him. An example would be Gen 16:13 where Hagar spoke of God as "*El* who sees."[92] Throughout the Torah (Law), Prophets and Writings of the Hebrew Scriptures, in both prose and poetry,[93] writers used *El* in at least three different ways. The following are some samples of how the authors of Scripture used this term.

El is used as a designation for *Elohim*. *El* is personal, showing His character of holiness, justice, might and that He is to be feared. The term *El* can be used by itself, without being combined with other terms, as is illustrated in the following examples. First, *El* is not a man (Num 23:19). Secondly, *El* brought Israel out of Egypt (Num 23:22). Thirdly, *El* made covenant promises to Abraham (Gen 17:1) and to Jacob (Gen 35:11). Fourthly, Moses pleads to *El* who is also identified as *Yahweh* for Miriam's healing from leprosy (Num 12:13). Fifthly, according to Deut 32:18, *El* is the one who birthed Israel. Lastly, when Jesus cried out to the Father on the cross, "*My El, my El why hast Thou forsaken me*," He was quoting from Ps 22:1.

The following combination of names shows *El* to be the same God as *Elohim* or *Yahweh*. *El* is combined with other terms to represent God in His various attributes such as *El Elyon*, The Highest God that Melchizedek refers to in Gen 14:18. *El Gibbor* or "Mighty God" is used as one of the names of the Messiah in Isa 9:6-7. *El Roe* means the "Lord that sees" in Gen 16:13-14. Moses refers to *El Olam* in Ps 90:2 meaning "God of Eternity." When speaking to Abraham God refers to Himself as *El Shaddai* or God Almighty, the All Sufficient God as in Gen 17:1.

The Hebrew Scriptures use numerous adjectives with *El*, showing the personal character of God, such as *El* of heaven (Ps 136:26) and the Most High *El* used by both Abraham and Melchizedek in Gen 14:18-20, 22. *El* is faithful in all that He says (Deut 7:9) and He also hides Himself (Isa 45:15). Jonah refers to God as a gracious *El* (Jonah 4:2) who can also be a great and dreadful *El* as is referenced in Daniel 11:36. *El* is the God of Jacob (Ps 146:5) and the *El* of Israel (Ps 68:35). *El*, which is used with LORD (*Yahweh*) and God (*Elohim*), show that *El* in the Scriptures is the God of Israel, the God of the Bible (Deut 4:31; Josh 22:22).

This word for God (*El*) is always used in the singular form. Most often it is used of the true God of Israel and is used of God by itself and with other descriptive words. The different words for God relate to each other. This word for God reveals a personal

---

[90] Harris, Archer, and Waltke, *Theological Wordbook of the Old Testament*, 1:42.
[91] Harris, Archer, and Waltke, *Theological Wordbook of the Old Testament*, 1:41.
[92] Payne, *The Theology of the Older Testament*, 145.
[93] John R. Kohlenberger III and James A Swanson, *The Hebrew English Concordance to the Old Testament* (Grand Rapids: Zondervan, 1998), 95-96.

God, a mighty God, a God to be feared, and a covenant making God.[94] Liddon observes that God used the words for Himself, with the singular verbs and plural nouns and pronouns. He says the following:

> When Moses is describing the primal creative act of God, he joins a singular verb to a plural noun. Language, it would seem, thus submits to a violent anomaly, that she may the better hint at the mystery of several Powers or Persons who not merely act together but who constitute a single Agent. The Hebrew language could have described God by singular forms, such as *El, Eloah*, and no question would have been raised as to the strictly Monotheistic force of those words. The Hebrew language might have amplified the idea of God thus conveyed by less dangerous processes than the employment of a plural form. Would it not have done so unless the plural form had been really necessary, in order to hint at the complex mystery of God's inner life, until that mystery should be more clearly unveiled by the explicit Revelations of a later day.[95]

This statement could be repeated under the sections of *Eloah* and *Elohim* a little latter in this book. God, through the pen of Moses, wanted to teach monotheism to Israel as an absolute truth, but He also wanted to give reference to His plurality. Moses had the words for God available to express the oneness of God only, but he did not choose to use them often.

אֵלִים *Elim*

Elim is the plural form of *El* but is used only four times in the Hebrew Scriptures (Exod 15:11; Ps 29:1; 89:6(7)[96]; Dan 11:36).[97] This word seems to bear no special significance. In fact, most books referred to do not even acknowledge the word. One text refers to the Exod 15:11 passage as it relates to pagan gods.[98] *Elim* is called, along with *Elohim*, a plural form of *El*.[99] However, others have taken the Psalm references of *Elim* and applied them to angels and sons of God or as heavenly beings.[100] Keil and Delitzsch also use the Psalm references and render them as sons of God or angelic beings.[101]

---

[94] Harris, Archer and Waltke, *Theological Wordbook of the Old Testament*, 1:42-43.

[95] J. Glentworth Butler, *Butler's Bible Works* (6 vols. New York: Funk & Wagnalls, 1889), 1:92.

[96] When a scripture reference appears as in Psalm 89:6[7], verse 7 in parenthesis means that in English translations it is found in v. 6 but in Hebrew Scriptures it would be found in v. 7.

[97] G. Johnannes Botterweck, Helmer Ringgren and Heinz-Josef Fabry. *Theological Dictionary of the Old Testament* (Grand Rapids: Eerdmans), 1:254.

[98] Alexander and Baker, *Dictionary of the Old Testament Pentateuch*, 361.

[99] Jenni and Westermann, *Theological Lexicon of the Old Testament*, 1:115.

[100] H. C. Leupold, *Exposition of The Psalms* (Grand Rapids: Baker, 1959), 250.

[101] C. F. Keil and F. Delitzsch, *Commentary on the Old Testament* (trans. James Martin; 10 vols.; Grand Rapids: Eerdmans, 1973). 5:368.

Elim seems to have no bearing on the subject of this study. Even though *Elim* is the plural of *El*, it is never used of the true God, thus making it a moot issue for the subject.

אֱלָה *Elah*

Elah is used 89 times in the Hebrew Scriptures. All but one of them (Jeremiah) are used during the time of the exile (Daniel) or post-exilic period (Ezra). Of those 89 references, at least 15 of them are to false gods.[102] *Elah* is the Aramaic form of *Eloah*, which is known as a verbal noun, "and is associated with the Hebrew verb *alah*, meaning to fear, to worship, to adore."[103] *Elah* indicates that the living and true God is identified with His people in captivity. It also carries a meaning of an oak, a tree symbolizing durability, a virtue characteristic of Him as being the Everlasting God.[104] It is also a singular word for God, and it is used in the same context as *Yahweh* (Ezra 6:18, 21-22).[105]

Elah is the same God as *El*, *Eloah*, *Elohim* and *Yahweh*. This word was used exclusively during the exile and post-exilic period, when the oneness of God needed to be taught and reaffirmed to Israel, after their displacement from the land by God for worshipping other gods. As Israel was once again being instructed under the leadership of Nehemiah and Ezra, the concept of monotheism was of utmost importance. The following question must be asked even though the answer cannot be known this side of life, but the observations and questions remain, which draws the student of the Scriptures to this unanswerable question. If, as the rabbis say, God is one alone with no plurality, how is it that an all-knowing God could not see down through the corridor of time and prevent this problem in the beginning? First, why isn't the singular form of God, *Elah*, used exclusively by Haggai, Malachi, Zephaniah, Zechariah or Ezekiel, exile or post-exilic writers, and not just in Ezra, and Daniel? Israel's worship of other gods was one of the major reasons for their displacement. If the urgency of teaching monotheism was so important, the observation once again is present. The second question is, since *Elah* is used to affirm monotheism to exiled and post-exilic Israel, why did Daniel and Ezra also use *Elohim*? The third question is, if God is one alone, a unity, why didn't the writers of Scripture, during that era, only use singular terms to remove all doubt and prevent future controversy? These questions are an argument from silence, to be sure, yet why the Hebrews used these words still remains a haunting question.

---

[102] George V. Wigram, *The Englishmans's Hebrew Concordance of the Old Testament* (Peabody, Mass: Hendrickson, 1996), 78-79.
[103] Lockyer, *All the Divine Names and Titles in the Bible*, 8.
[104] Lockyer, *All the Divine Names and Titles in the Bible*, 8-9.
[105] Samuel Prideaux Tregelles, *Gesenius' Hebrew and Chaldee Lexicon to the Old Testament Scriptures* (Grand Rapids: Eerdmans, 1957), 48.

Eloah occurs 57 times in the Hebrew Scriptures and may be the singular form of plural *Elohim*. Most of those references (41) occur in the book of Job.[106] The others are scattered mostly in the poetic portions of the Scriptures. *Eloah* first appears in Deut 32:15-17, then 2 Kings, 2 Chronicles, Nehemiah, Psalms, Proverbs, Isaiah, Daniel, and Habakkuk. Its use stretches from Job, believed by some to be the oldest book in the Hebrew Scriptures, to the post-exilic time of Nehemiah. In Job there are two references where God uses the term *Eloah*, of Himself: In 39:17 He relates to His providence and in 40:2 as the Almighty.[107] *Eloah* is unique in that it does not occur in combination with other divine names. *Eloah* is reaffirmed as God, in the singular, by this following observation:

> This term for God was usually clearly used for Israel's God, the true God. This is evident from the fact that the Levites in the post-exilic period used the term in quoting the descriptive revelation of God given in Exodus 34:6-7, where the original revelation to Moses had used *El* and *Yahweh* (Neh 9:17).[108]

VanGemeren says that the terms *Eloah*, *El* and *Yahweh* are interchangeable names of God.[109]

Eloah is used throughout the time period of the Hebrew Scriptures, along with *El*, as being singular for the name of God. But the writers of the Scriptures chose to use them sparingly in relation to the term *Elohim*. Noam Hendren speaks to the point when he says:

> The first hints of plurality are found in the terms used to designate God – "*Elohim*" and "*Adonai*" – both of which are plural forms of existing singular nouns. Had the biblical authors intended to assert the absolute (rather than compound) unity of the Godhead, they had readily available singular terms (*Eloah*, *Adoni*, as well as *El*) which would have avoided any confusion on this crucial point.[110]

Hendren points out that if the Hebrew writers wanted to show monotheism throughout the Scriptures, thus leaving no doors open for a plurality of God, they could have used *El, Elah* or *Eloah* in the place of *Elohim*, but they chose not to do that. Instead they chose to use a plural word for God the vast majority of the time rather than the singular form of God (*El, Elah, Eloah*), showing the plural nature of God. This reality is brought out by Barackman when he specifically says that "*Elohim*, the plural form

---

[106] Willem A. VanGemeren, *Dictionary of Old Testament Theology & Exegesis* (5 vols., Grand Rapids: Zondervan, 1997), 1:405.
[107] Harris, Archer, and Waltke, *Theological Wordbook of the Old Testament*, 1:43.
[108] Harris, Archer, and Waltke, *Theological Wordbook of the Old Testament*, 1:43.
[109] VanGemeren, *Dictionary of Old Testament Theology and Exegesis*, 1:405.
[110] Noam Hendren, "The Divine Unity and the Deity of Messiah," *Mishkan* (issue 39, 2003): 38.

indicates the plurality of Persons within the divine Trinity."[111] The authors of Scripture left the door open for the New Covenant's teaching of the tri-unity.

אֱלֹהִים *Elohim*

What is true of singular words for God (*El, Elah, Eloah*) is also true of the plural word *Elohim*. The etymology is, at best, uncertain.[112] Jack Scott presents three possibilities on the root of *Elohim*. First, he takes for granted that *'lh* is the assumed root of *El, Eloah* and *Elohim*, which means "gods" or "God." Next, he says "The view that the three Hebrew words come from one root is much disputed, and a final verdict is lacking." His third statement is "More probable is the view that *Elohim* comes from *Eloah* as a unique development of the Hebrew Scriptures."[113] Yet Payne makes further statements:

> *El*, seems to have arisen from the root *'ul*, the probable meaning of which is to be strong (cf. Gen 31:29 "power")."[114]

There is just no solid consistent information as to the etymology of *Elohim*.

The words being used: "assumed", "much disputed", "lacking," and "probable" indicate that there is nothing much here that is solid. There are words such as *Elohim* that scholars do not have enough information about to draw a strong conclusion. Since there is no consensus on the etymology of *Elohim*, the only alternative to help in understanding *El, Eloah,* and *Elohim* is to see how the Hebrew Scriptures use them and in what context they are used. But that is beyond the scope of this book. What is known and recognized is that *El, Elah, Eloah,* and *Elohim* are all nouns translated as "God" in the singular except for *elohim* when it references pagan "gods" in the plural. But when *Elohim* is translated as singular in the English text, there ought to be a note stating that *Elohim*, though used as a singular when translated is in fact a plural noun.

It is very important to see how *Elohim*, in particular, is used within the Hebrew text in relationship to *El, Eloah, Yahweh* and the Angel of *Yahweh*. First, *Elohim* is used 2600 times and is the second most frequent substantive in the Hebrew Scriptures following *ben* (son).[115] *Elohim* is introduced exclusively throughout the creation account of Gen 1:1-2:3 as the God of creation. *Elohim* is not a personal name but the general Hebrew word for deity.[116] Also, *Elohim* is often accompanied with *Yahweh*

---

[111] Barackman. *Practical Christian Theology* (Grand Rapids: Kregel, 1998), 66.
[112] Alexander and Baker, *Dictionary of the Old Testament Pentateuch*, 360.
[113] Harris, Archer, and Waltke, *Theological Wordbook of the Old Testament*, 1:41.
[114] Payne, *The Theology of the Older Testament*, 145.
[115] Jenni and Westermann, *Theological Lexicon of the Old Testament*, 1:116.
[116] Nahum M Sarna, *The JPS Torah Commentary, Genesis* (Philadelphia: The Jewish Publication Society, 1989), 5.

(יהוה) as in Gen 2:4-5; Exod 34:23; Ps 68:18 (19).[117]   In fact, *Elohim* and *Yahweh* are combined together 930 times throughout the Hebrew Scriptures in one of the following translated forms: "LORD thy God," "LORD God," "LORD our God," "LORD my God," "LORD your God," "LORD their God," "LORD his God."[118]   God, through the writers of Scripture, chose to use the plural form of Himself instead of using the singular form exclusively. He was teaching that He was a plurality. However, rabbinic Judaism wants to substantiate monotheism without plurality by trying to ignore the fact that God chose to use a plural description of Himself for one particular reason: He is a plurality (tri-unity).

God was revealing Himself to Israel by showing His indivisible oneness and at the same time showing His complex unity, being also a plurality. This is not acceptable to the Jewish mind because it is an antithesis and appears to go against the strict monotheism of Judaism.[119] *Yahweh* is combined with *El*, which is the singular form, and it is combined 21 times out of 258.[120]   *Elah*, the singular form, is never once used out of a possible 95 times.[121]   *Eloah* is used only once in Ps 68:31 out of 58 times.[122] All of these combinations are in the singular, which would show absolute monotheism. But the fact that *Elohim* is used in combination with *Yahweh* over 930 times is a significant amount more than the aforementioned group. God is showing to Israel that indeed He is one and that He is a unity and that unity is a plurality.

Elohim as a plurality is a person involved in the lives of His created beings. *Elohim* shows his personhood in a plural context. He is not distant, unconcerned or detached from human need. *Elohim* is used of God as the creator (Gen 1:1, 27; 2:3-4, 5:1). He interacts with humans (Gen 18; Deut 34:10 with Num 12:6-8) and walks with man (Gen 3:8; 5:24). He speaks to them (Gen 8:15; 9:8, 12, 17; 17:3, 23; 21:2; 35:15; 46:2) and listens to them (Gen 21:17; 30:17, 22; Exod 2:24). He provides for them (Gen 1:29, 2:8-9, 15; 4:25; 9:27; 22:8; 28:4; 30:18, 20) and protects them (Gen 31:7, 9, 16; 45:5, 7). He also makes covenants (Gen 9:16) and promises to man (Gen 17:9). *Elohim* is gracious and does good (Gen 50:20; Exod 1:20), but at the same time, He obligates man to keep certain responsibilities and commandments (Gen 2:16; 3:1, 3; 6:22; 7:9, 16; 17:9, 16; 21:4, 12; 31:16, 24; 35:1, 11; Exod 18:23).[123]   According to Scott, titles are attached to the noun *Elohim* that pertain to His work of Creation (Isa 45:18), His sovereignty (Isa 54:5), as well as focusing around His majesty or glory. But a far more frequent title is found in those passages that pertain to the Savior God.[124]   In *Elohim*, the plurality of God is expressed in ways which would minimally show the activity of God the Father and God the Son. He is also mighty, terrible and executes judgment as Deut 10:17-18 speaks of Him:

[117] Harris, Archer, and Waltke, *Theological Wordbook of the Old Testament*, 1:44.
[118] Robert Young, *Analytical Concordance to the Bible* (Grand Rapids: Eerdmans), 411-418.
[119] Schiffman, *Return of the Remnant*, 95.
[120] Young, *Analytical Concordance to the Bible*, 411.
[121] Young, *Analytical Concordance to the Bible*, 411.
[122] Young, *Analytical Concordance to the Bible*, 418.
[123] Alexander and Baker, *Dictionary of the Old Testament Pentateuch*, 362.
[124] Harris, Archer, and Waltke, *Theological Wordbook of the Old Testament*, 1:44.

For the Lord your God is God supreme, and Lord supreme, the great, the mighty, and the awesome God, who shows no favor and takes no bribes, but upholds the cause of the fatherless and the widow, and befriends the stranger, providing him with food and clothing.[125]

Elohim shows Himself in a multitude of ways. Unlike *El*, *Elah*, or *Eloah*, *Elohim* always appears as a plural, not in the singular, in the Hebrew Scriptures. This word for God is used of both God, as the true God predominantly, and of false pagan gods of the lands around Israel. Although a plural noun, associated verbs and descriptive terms are usually in the singular.[126] Since *Elohim* is plural, the term presents a paradox and attracts attention because the monotheistic God of Israel is representing Himself as a plurality. *Elohim* is used in the Hebrew text over 2600 times as a plural (2350 of them are in reference to the God of Israel), which is many more times than the singular usages of *El* (258), *Elah* (95), and *Eloah* (58) combined. *Elohim*, with singular nouns, verbs and descriptive terms, definitely shows monotheism, but it also can argue in favor of plurality, rather than against it.[127]

Arguments Against a Literal Understanding of *Elohim*

Jewish and/or Christian scholars do not object to the scriptural term *Elohim* that is used for God. The problem lies with how biblical scholars interpret *Elohim* in the context where *Elohim* is used by God of Himself or where others refer to Him as God in His revealed Word. There is no conscious effort, on the part of conservative Christian scholars, to undermine a doctrine of Scripture. In respect to Jewish scholars Paul says in Romans there is a spiritual blindness upon the hearts of Jewish people resulting in not being able to see the plurality of God (Amos 8:11-12). Paul, in Rom 11:10, is very clear as he quotes David in Ps 69:23: "Let their eyes be darkened, that they may not see, and bend down their back always."

Most of the authors (Jewish and Christian) cited agree that *Elohim* is plural and that it should be looked upon as a "plural of majesty" or an intensified form of the word. They, for the most part, do not think there is enough contextual evidence to warrant *Elohim* as a plural reference to God. However, they say that it is a foundation from which the New Covenant builds its doctrine of the trinity or tri-unity. Mathews states the following:

---

[125] Adele Berlin and Marc Zvi Brettler, *The Jewish Study Bible* (New York: Jewish Publication Society, 2004), 388. (All Old Testament references are cited from this translation unless otherwise noted) Three other translations are also used but not cited (1) Alexander Harkavy, *The Twenty-Four Books of the Old Testament* (2 vols., New York, N.Y: Hebrew Publishing , 1916), (2) Isaac Leeser, *The Twenty-Four Books of the Holy Bible* (New York: Hebrew Publishing, n.d.), (3) The Holy Bible, *The Orthodox Jewish Bible* (3rd edition, New York: Artists For Israel International, 2002).

[126] Sarna, *The Jewish Publication Society Torah Commentary: Genesis*, 5.

[127] Arnold A Fruchtenbaum, *Messianic Christology* (Tustin, Calif: Ariel Ministries, 1998), 103.

Why the plural was also used of the one God of Israel is uncertain, though most ascribe it to the use of the Hebrew plural that indicates honor or majesty. As a plural it is a literary convention that reflects special reverence.[128]

In the judgment of this author, this statement does not reflect a verbal plenary view of inspiration. Mathews states that its interpretation is uncertain and most scholars ascribe that there is not enough biblical evidence to support plurality. He continues:

> Since its plurality does not designate more than one entity, its morphological shape does not necessarily refer to the plurality of the Godhead. It is unreasonable to burden this one word *Elohim* with a developed view of the Christian Trinity. It is fair to say, however, that the creation account (1:2, 26-27) implies that there is a plurality within God (cf. 3:22; 11:7; 18:1ff.). But it is not until the era of the church that the Trinity is clearly articulated. New Testament tradition ascribes to Christ a role in creation (John 1:1-3; Col 1:15-17; Heb 1:2), but it is less clear about the role of the Spirit.[129]

Mathews hedges on the implications of *Elohim's* plurality and in the process explains away what God was intending readers to understand about Himself in the *Tanakh*. This researcher sees two things: First, the "burden" of a full blown development of the tri-unity is not being laid on one word. However, something is going on throughout the pages of the *Tanakh*. God, by His choice of terms, is saying that He, *Elohim*, is a plurality. The second thing, this whole argument has given this author a strong impression that Christian theologians have conceded the subject to Rabbinic Judaism.

Statements have been made by various authors on the plural aspect of *Elohim*. Louis Jacobs, a Jewish author, makes an honest statement when he says that the plural form of God has long been a puzzle to the rabbis. They are obliged, by Judaism, to defend it against "sectarians" (Christians) who say that the plural form is proof of more than one god.[130] Arnold Fruchtenbaum, a Jewish believer in Messiah *Yeshua*, says that the Hebrew grammar requires that when the plural form is used, as is the case with *Elohim*, the verbs agree with the associated nouns in both gender and number.[131] *Elohim* is plural and is used of the true God and the false gods as seen in Exod 20:2-3. When it is used of false gods, the verbs will also be plural, which is correct Hebrew grammar. When *Elohim* is used of the true God, the verbs, as in Gen 1:1 (*Elohim* created), are singular which shows the unity and oneness of God. But that singular construction can also imply that, even though *Elohim* is one, He is also a plurality in that oneness. Youngblood identifies the oneness and plurality of God in Genesis one.

> The first verse of Genesis itself provides us with a helpful cue. It tells us that "God created" (Gen 1:1). The noun "God" is plural in the Hebrew text, but the

---

[128] Kenneth A. Mathews, *The New American Commentary*. (vol. 1a. Nashville: Broadman & Holman, 2002), 1a:127.

[129] Matthews, *The New American Commentary*, 1a:127.

[130] Louis Jacobs, *A Jewish Theology* (West Orange, N.J: Behrman House, 1973), 138.

[131] Fruchtenbaum, *Messianic Christology*, 103.

verb "created" is singular in the Hebrew text. The Bible clearly teaches that God is one being, a unity (Deut 6:4; 1 Cor 8:4). At the same time, the Bible just as clearly teaches that the one God exists in three persons and is therefore also a trinity.[132]

Youngblood clearly sees and understands that God in His omniscience's chose to reveal Himself as one being and yet at the same time a unity of three persons. In reference to the oneness of *Elohim*, Hebrew grammar also demonstrates the plurality of *Elohim* as in Exod 20:3 and Deut 13:2. In both cases, when referring to *elohim* as false gods, it is correctly translated as "gods" by both Jewish and Christian scholars.

Numerous authors affirm the view that *Elohim* is to be understood as a "plural of majesty" and not as a reference to the plurality of God:

> The plural ending is usually described as a plural of majesty and not intended as a true plural when used of God. This is seen in the fact that the noun *Elohim* is consistently used with singular verb forms and with adjectives and pronouns in the singular.[133]

> The grammatical form of *Elohim* is that of an abstract plural of greatness or majesty, and not a true numeric plural.[134]

> The divine name, *Elohim* probably describes a plural of intensity or plural of majesty (simply "God" – an abstract plural).[135]

> The plural form may signify majesty or serve to intensify the basic idea. The preference for the use of *Elohim* in this chapter, rather than the sacred divine name *YHVH*, may well be conditioned by theological considerations; the term *Elohim*, connoting universalism and abstraction, is most appropriate for the transcendent God of creation.[136]

> Though morphologically plural, the word is regularly used as a singular when referring to Israel's God. This is shown by the regular use of singular verbs and adjectives in conjunction with the term. The purpose and meaning of the plural form is debated, with some seeing it as a plural of majesty, or royal plural as an intensification or claim to exclusivity, or as an honorific.[137]

Some scholars have held that the plural represents an intensified form for the supreme God; others believe it describes the supreme God and His heavenly court of created being. Still others hold that the plural form refers to the triune

---

[132] Ronald Youngblood, The Book of Genesis (2nd ed. Eugene, OR: Wipf and Stock Publishers, 1991), 23.
[133] Harris, Archer, and Waltke, *Theological Wordbook of the Old Testament*, 1:44.
[134] Payne, *The Theology of the Older Testament*, 145.
[135] Preuss, *Old Testament Theology*, 1:149.
[136] Sarna, *The Jewish Publication Society Torah Commentary: Genesis*, 5.
[137] Alexander and Baker, *Dictionary of the Old Testament Pentateuch*, 362.

God of Genesis 1:1-3, who works through Word and Spirit in the creation of the world. In any event, *Elohim* conveys the idea that the one Supreme Being, who is the only true God, is in some sense plural.[138]

Collectively, the consensus of these scholars is that the term *Elohim* is not a true plural, and it does not represent the plurality of God in the *Tanakh*. Their arguments are centered around these thoughts: *Elohim* is a "plural of majesty," and secondly, Hebrew grammar of the plural noun is followed by a singular verb when speaking of the true God, showing that God is one alone. They are reaffirming the belief, by the use of Hebrew grammar, that false gods, which always have plural verbs, show only the plural concept of pagan gods, such as Baal. This is a Jewish rabbinic argument whose views are different on inspiration[139] from that which is held by fundamental and evangelical scholars. Also, they generally do not use the literal interpretation of the Scriptures, or as Renald Showers calls it, the historical-grammatical method.[140]

Arguments For a Literal Understanding of *Elohim*

In the preceding section, no flexibility was shown toward the proposition that God could be revealing Himself by using the same Hebrew grammar to show exceptions in the language. God is affirming His oneness and plurality while protecting the teaching of the Hebrew Scriptures against polytheism. Israel was surrounded by polytheistic Canaanite nations, as well as the Amorites, Moabites and the Egyptians.

When *Elohim* is modified by a singular word, both Jewish and Christian translators want it to be understood as God, when God meant it to be understood as a plural representation of Himself with the singular modifier to show His oneness. Cooper expresses the same thing when he asks:

> Why should the grammar be ignored and the word be translated as if it were a singular noun when it refers to Israel's God, since the facts are that it is a plural noun and means more than one?[141]

According to Hebrew grammar, if *Elohim* is plural, it is not grammatically correct for singular verbs to follow. So the Hebrew construction breaks down with the pattern of Hebrew grammar. However, there are several instances where plural verbs follow *Elohim*, the true God, which is grammatically correct as in 2 Sam 7:23:

---

[138] Ronald F Youngblood, *New Illustrated Bible Dictionary* (Nashville: Thomas Nelson, 1995), 504.

[139] Jewish Inspiration: Based on Numbers 12:5-8 you have three tiers of Inspiration. First because God spoke to Moses face to face in the Torah (Law), that is the most inspired. Secondly, God spoke to Prophets in visions and dreams, so they are less inspired then the Law. Thirdly, the leased inspired are the Writings.

[140] Renald E. Showers, *There Really is a Difference!* (Bellmawr, NJ: Friends of Israel Gospel Ministry, 1990), 53.

[141] Cooper, *The God of Israel*, 24-25.

And who is like Your people Israel, a unique nation on earth, whom God went and redeemed as His people, winning renown for Himself.

literally it says;

And what one nation on the earth is like Thy people Israel, whom God [*Elohim*] they went to redeem for themselves.[142]

Robert Morris, a Jewish believer in *Yeshua*, speaks to the fact that Jews for Judaism[143] teaches that the Doctrine of the Trinity is a pagan concept.[144] Yet 2 Sam 7:23 says that more than one *Elohim* redeemed Israel.

In dealing with arguments for *Elohim* being a unity, the first concept to consider is a complex unity. God did introduce Himself as a plurality and tri-unity in the *Tanakh*. An example can be given from Gen 2:24 of a complex unity when God took two separate identities (man and woman) and put them together as a complex unity of one. This concept is difficult for Jewish people to comprehend in relation to *Elohim*. Stan Rosenthal, a Jewish believer in Messiah *Yeshua*, tells how they view it:

Jewish people often object to the tri-unity of God because of what they believe is taught in the *Shema* . . . The accepted premise among Jewish people views this as saying that God is indivisibly one. Consequently, the objection is raised: I cannot believe in this person, Jesus, whom Christians claim to be God. For them the *Shema* appears to have silenced forever the argument which embraces the historic Christian belief in the deity of Jesus.[145]

Rosenthal is simply saying that the *Shema*, to the Jewish people, teaches that God is indivisible, and because of that, Jesus is another god. Hence, they reject Jesus as God, as well as God's substitutionary sacrifice for sin. The *Shema* has become the watch word in Judaism, and they use it to show that *Elohim* (God) is indivisible, one. In this section, the object is to show that God is indivisible, one, and yet plural. The argument that *Elohim* represents a "plural of majesty" is a foreign concept in the *Tanakh*. The Hebrew kings never spoke of themselves as a "plural of majesty," so there is no background for this concept in the Hebrew Scriptures, which the following statement expresses:

But that is to read into Hebrew speech a modern mode of address. So far as our biblical records can help us, the kings of Judah and Israel are all addressed in the singular.[146]

---

[142] Fruchtenbaum, *Messianic Christology*, 104.

[143] <u>Jews for Judaism</u>: Jews for Judaism is an anti-missionary organization against Christian missionaries to Jewish people who strongly try to reconvert new Jewish believers in Messiah back to rabbinic Judaism.

[144] Robert Morris, *Anti-Missionary Argument: The Trinity* (Irvine, CA: HaDavar Messianic Ministries), 1.

[145] Stanley Rosenthal, *One God or Three*? (Bellmawr, NJ: Friends of Israel Gospel Ministry, 1978), 17-18.

[146] George A.F. Knight, A *Christian Theology of the Old Testament* (Carlisle, UK: Paternoster Publishing, 1998), 54.

So in the Hebrew text the kings of Judah and Israel never used a "plural of majesty" in speaking of themselves. This is echoed by Grudem when he says:

> In Old Testament Hebrew there are no other examples of a monarch using plural verbs or plural pronouns of himself in such a "plural of majesty," so this suggestion has no evidence to support it.[147]

The closest thing to the idea of "plural of majesty" is in Isa 7:13-14 when God speaks of the House of David. However, that is a collective statement about the House of David, not a "plural of majesty." Nathan Stone echoes the fact that the term "plural of majesty" is an expression unknown to the kings of Israel:

> They say that the plural is only a plural of majesty such as used by rulers and kings. But such use of the plural was not known then. We find no king of Israel speaking of himself as "we" and "us."[148]

Although the Queen of England uses the "plural of majesty," England is a western Gentile nation, whereas Israel is a Middle Eastern Semitic nation, now 20 centuries removed from modern England. This has been observed and answered by Stuart Briscoe:

> Some commentators suggest that the plural words are used to give a sense of intensity and majesty to God (in much the same way that the Queen in her official pronouncements uses the "royal we"). But a clear statement about the Trinity becomes apparent when the "Us" and "Our" and the plural *Elohim* are considered alongside the statement about the "Spirit of God" being active in creation.[149]

Henry Smith says that the "plural of majesty" cannot be accepted today because "such plurals of majesty, however, are without parallel in Hebrew."[150] Then he draws an inaccurate conclusion by saying that the only plausible view is that the word originally was narrowed down to apply to One and that vestiges of a belief in a group of divine beings have survived even in our present Bible. He then cites Gen 1:26: "Let us make man in our image" and 3:22 where God takes counsel with His associates, or as in 6:2 with the "sons of God." Smith uses human logic instead of letting Scripture interpret Scripture. It appears that since he does not accept a high view of Scripture, he attempts to find some natural human answer rather than accepting the plurality of God. Towner uses similar logic by stating that "plural of majesty" is not likely, but then goes on to state that because the plural personal pronoun is used rarely by God, it must be a heavenly council:

---

[147] Wayne Grudem, *Systematic Theology* (Grand Rapids: Zondervan, 1994), 227.

[148] Nathan Stone, *Names of God* (Chicago: Moody, 1944), 16.

[149] Stuart Briscoe, *The Communicator's Commentary* (vol. 1. Waco, Tex: Word, 1987), 34.

[150] Henry Preserved Smith, *The Religion of Israel* (New York: Charles Scribner's Sons, 1914), 14.

Is God using the "plural of majesty," and speaking in the manner of the queen of England or the pope? Not likely! If anyone has the right to make self-references in the plural (especially considering that God is, at least from a Christian point of view, a Holy Trinity), it would surely be God. However, this plural usage happens again only very rarely (Gen 3:22; 11:7; Isa 6:8). Surely, if God were thinking majestically, the plural would be used more consistently than that. We are left, then, with the heavenly council as the only likely way of explaining this use of the plural in verse 1:26.[151]

The fact is that God did use first person plural pronouns only in four passages. But to conclude that it must be a heavenly council merely on that basis, is ignoring the abundance of other plural references that not only show Him to be a plurality but a tri-unity.

Interpreting Scripture must always be done within its immediate and distant context, whether in the *Tanakh* or the New Covenant. If the Hebrew Scriptures do not use a "plural of majesty," why do scholars force a reading into the text? The Scriptures, as a whole, are the writings of God Himself to reveal Himself to mankind. The only viable way to develop that concept, when studying the Scriptures, is to let God reveal Himself rather than reading into the text what God never intended. God is intending man to understand from Genesis 1, that He is a plural compound One. This concept of a complex unity is not "plural of majesty" or intensity but a complex unity of the tri-unity of God. Complex unity is expressed well by Robert Morris:

> Philosophically, the idea of a complex, indivisible unity is not foreign to the Bible. The nation of Israel is a complex indivisible unity (one nation made up of 12 tribes), the Law of Moses is a complex, indivisible unity (one law made up of 613 commandments), and marriage is a complex, indivisible unity (a one flesh relationship consisting of man and woman). Is it inconsistent if the God of the Universe is a complex, indivisible unity as well?[152]

Is God a complex unity? Yes. Can he reveal Himself in a tri-unity? Yes. To force the fully developed doctrine of the tri-unity from the New Covenant into Genesis 1 or the word *Elohim* is completely exegetically improper. What can be seen is that God is a plurality, not a "plural of majesty," which is a foreign term to the *Tanakh*. It can also be seen that God is a complex compound unity. It is the strong opinion of this author that God has given ample evidences of His unity, as well as His plurality.

It's not that Israelite people did not know how to use the word "we," they did use it, but kings didn't use it when they were functioning as kings. There is only one consistent use of the "we" that so many scholars want to see as plural of majesty. But it is just not present in the Hebrew text in relation to the kings of Judah or Israel. One predominate way that the word "we" is used is in prayers of confession before God.

---

[151] W. Sibley Towner, Westminster Bible Companion: Genesis (Louisville, KY: Westminster John Knox Press, 2001), 24-25

[152] Morris, *Anti-Missionary Arguments – The Trinity*, 3.

Some of the great men of God confessed their sins and the sins of the nation before God using "we." They have used the plural "we" but not as a plural of majesty as seen in the following references from Isaiah, Daniel and Nehemiah:

Isaiah:

53:2   He had no form or beauty that *we* should look at him:

53:3   No charm, that *we* should find him pleasing

53:4   Yet it was our sickness that he was bearing, Our suffering that he endured. *We* accounted him plagued, smitten and afflicted by God;

53:5   But he was wounded because of our sins, crushed because of our iniquities. He bore the chastisement that made us whole, and by his bruises *we* were healed.

Daniel:

9:5   *We* have sinned; *we* have gone astray; *we* have acted wickedly; *we* have been rebellious and have deviated from Your commandments

9:8   The shame, O LORD, is on us, on our kings, our officers, and our fathers, because *we* have sinned against You.

9:9   To the Lord our God belong mercy and forgiveness, for *we* rebelled against Him,

9:11   All Israel has violated Your teaching and gone astray, disobeying You; so the curse and the oath written in the Teaching of Moses, the servant of God, have been poured down upon us, for *we* have sinned against Him.

9:13   All that calamity, just as is written in the Teaching of Moses, came upon us, yet *we* did not supplicate the LORD our God, did not repent of our iniquity or become wise through Your truth.

9:14   Hence the LORD was intent upon bringing calamity upon us, for the LORD our God is in the right in all that He has done, but *we* have not obeyed Him.

9:15   Now, O Lord our God, You who brought Your people out of the land of Egypt with a mighty hand, winning fame for Yourself to this very day, *we* have sinned, *we* have acted wickedly.

9:18   Not because of any merit of ours do *we* lay our plea before You but because of Your abundant mercies.

Nehemiah:

1:6   Let Your ear be attentive and Your eyes open to receive the prayer of Your servant that I am praying to You now, day and night, on behalf of the Israelites, Your servants, confessing the sins that *we* Israelites have committed against You, sins that I and my father's house have committed.

1:7   *We* have offended You by not keeping the commandments, the laws, and the rules that You gave to Your servant Moses:

"We" is used in the confession of sin but it is never used in the context of a king speaking in reference to himself and his court. Nor do you find the king speaking of himself and the people as "we". When he speaks it is within the context of "I am the king."

Getting back to the plural word *elohim*, Cooper states that the regular ending for a plural noun in the masculine gender and plural number is ם‎ֹ *(im)* and that with this grammatical structure no one would disagree.

> Since this word has the plural ending and is listed by all lexicographers and grammarians as a noun in the plural number, we must accept this connotation in every instance unless there are facts in the context showing a departure from the ordinary, usual literal meaning.[153]

Previously cited authors say that *Elohim* is not a true plural word. Yet when the plural Hebrew ending is present, it is consistently treated as a plural until God describes Himself. This is an observation anyone can make. Observe in either the *Tanakh* or an Hebrew/English interlinear, אֱלֹהִים‎ (*Elohim*) is consistently translated as God in the singular. The plural Hebrew ending is ם‎ֹ (*'im'*), as in *Cherubim, Seraphim* or *Shedhim* (demons). Whenever the ending *'im,'* is used, it is translated in the plural, except for *Elohim*. It is the view of this author that many of the previously cited authors want to explain away the plural *'im'* ending rather than accept it for what it is, a plural.

The plural personal pronouns of God which will be covered under a later chapter are relevant here. What does God say about Himself? *Elohim* is making a statement early in human history (3 of the 4 times in Genesis) that He is a plurality by using the plural personal pronoun "us" before the time of Abraham. The references are: "Let US make man" (Gen 1:26). When Adam and Eve sinned, God said "They have become one of US" (Gen 3:22). Also, at the tower of Babel God said, "Let US go down" (Gen 11:7). The other plural pronoun reference is found in the call of Isaiah when God said, "Who will go for US?" (Isa 6:6). Isaiah hears pronouns in the singular and plural, simultaneously, from the very "lips" of God.[154]

The argument of what God has written cannot be expressed too strongly. He was revealing Himself to His people. Why do scholars explain the plurality of *Elohim* in ways that do not seem to be in harmony with the context of how God has chosen to reveal Himself to His people? Jack Scott, in *Theological Wordbook of the Old Testament*, states that the word *Elohim* is not to be understood as a true plural:

> The plural ending is usually described as a plural of majesty and not intended as a true plural when used of God. This is seen in the fact that the noun *Elohim*

---

[153] Cooper, *The God of Israel*, 34.
[154] Knight, *A Christian Theology of the Old Testament*, 55.

is consistently used with singular verb forms and with adjectives and pronouns in the singular.[155]

In agreement with Scott, Page Kelley says that "אֱלֹהִים (*Elohim*) is plural in form but normally functions as a singular noun."[156] Contrary to Scott's and Kelley's statements, if they base their view on verbal plenary inspiration and the literal method of interpretation of the Scriptures, it is impossible to arrive at that conclusion. This author believes that if *Elohim* is viewed by verbal plenary inspiration, using the literal method of interpretation, the conclusion must be that God is using the term *Elohim* of Himself to strongly state that He, as God, is presenting Himself in a plural context. Not only must scholars be consistent in their view of inspiration, but they must also be consistent in using the literal method of interpretation. Otherwise scholars become the authority and God is reduced to just a point of argument.

Jesus (*Yeshua*) expected the Pharisees to know and understand the plurality of *Elohim* when He equated Himself with God, the Father, as in Jn 10:30. The fact that Hebrew grammar is broken, when a singular verb is used with the plural noun [*Elohim*], should immediately attract the attention of the reader. It can be argued that God is revealing Himself as a plural God who is, in essence, one. Why turn and explain away the conclusion that *Yeshua* expected the Pharisees to see?

Another important observation is that often *Elohim* and *Yahweh* are used together denoting the same God, as was previously mentioned at the beginning of the section entitled *Elohim*. *Yahweh* and *Elohim* are combined showing unity and plurality, and *Elohim* and *Yahweh* are both individually applied to two divine personalities, distinct and separate from each other, yet a unity of one, a compound unity. *Yahweh* in Hos 1:2, 7 is applied to two separate and distinct *Yahweh*s who is their *Elohim*s. It is pointed out by Fruchtenbaum that Hosea is saying there are two *Yahweh*s which are separate and distinct from each other, yet a unity:

> When the LORD first spoke to Hosea, and the LORD said to Hosea, Go, get yourself a wife of whoredom . . . . But I will have compassion on the house of Judah. And I will give them victory through the LORD their God [*Elohim*], I will not give them victory with bow, and sword and battle, by horses and riders.[157]

Fruchtenbaum says that the speaker is *Elohim* who will save them by *Yahweh*, their *Elohim*. Fruchtenbaum is correct, except for the fact that *Elohim* is not the speaker. *Yahweh* is the speaker. Here the speaker is the LORD, or *Yahweh*, communicating to Hosea rather than *Elohim* saying that He will send another LORD, or *Yahweh* who is their *Elohim*, to save them. So *Yahweh*, the speaker, the personal God of Israel, is going to send another *Yahweh*, who is their *Elohim*, to save them. Here the text is dealing with two *Yahweh*s rather than two *Elohim*s, and the one being sent is their

---

[155] Harris, Archer, and Waltke, *Theological Wordbook of the Old Testament*, 1:44.
[156] Page H. Kelley, *Biblical Hebrew: An Introductory Grammar* (Grand Rapids: Eerdmans, 1992), 32.
[157] Fruchtenbaum, *Messianic Christology*, 105.

Elohim. A second example of two *Elohims*[158] is found in Ps 45:6-7[7-8] where *Elohim* is applied to two separate and distinct *Elohim*s:

> Thy throne, O God, is for ever and ever: the scepter of thy kingdom is a right scepter. Thou lovest righteousness, and hatest wickedness: therefore God, thy God, hath anointed thee with the oil of gladness above thy fellows.   KJV

Dr. Arnold Fruchtenbaum has noted that in Ps 45:6-7 the first *Elohim* is being addressed, and the second *Elohim* is the God of the first *Elohim*. Here are two distinct *Elohims*. *Elohim's Elohim* has set *Elohim* above His fellows and Has anointed him with the oil of joy or gladness.[159]

Another source of evidence to show the plurality of *Elohim* is the plural verbs and modifiers that follow *Elohim*. Normal Hebrew grammar says that following the plural *Elohim* with a plural verb or modifier is correct grammar.

> אֱלֹהִים [*Elohim*] is plural in form, but normally functions as a singular noun. However, it may also function as a plural noun, accompanied by plural modifiers and plural verb forms. This usually occurs when reference is being made to the "gods" of the nations.[160]

In most places throughout Scripture *Elohim* is followed by a singular verb or modifier, which breaks the Hebrew grammatical construction. But there are four verses with *Elohim* and four plural verbs, or modifiers that apply to the true *Elohim*. This coincides with normal Hebrew grammatical construction. The impact of this is that *Elohim* is a true plurality of God, and these four examples help to further show that plurality. First, in Gen 20:13 Abraham says, "When God (*Elohim*) caused me to wander from my father's house."   Literally it says, "God (*Elohim*) they caused me to wander." The second in Gen 35:7 Jacob says, "And he built there an altar and called the place El-beth-el: because there God appeared unto him, when he fled from the face of his brother." Again, it literally says, the God (*Elohim*) revealed Themselves. The third is in 2 Sam 7:23. David said, "And what one nation in the earth is like thy people, even like Israel, whom God went to redeem for a people to himself"? Literally, again David said, "whom God (*Elohim*) they went to redeem for Themselves." Lastly, in Ps 58:11[12], the psalmist says, "So that a man shall say, verily there is a reward for the righteous: verily there is a God that judgeth in the earth." Literally it means, "God (*Elohim*) They judge on earth!" So here the testimony of Abraham, Jacob, David and the Psalmist refer to God in the plural.

---

[158] Grudem, *Systematic Theology*, 227.
[159] Fruchtenbaum, *Messianic Christology*, 104.
[160] Kelley, *Biblical Hebrew: An Introductory Grammar*, 32.

Sadly, in their separate systematic theologies Hodge,[161] Bancroft,[162] Buswell,[163] Barackman,[164] Grudem,[165] Berkhof,[166] and Erickson[167] do not cover or recognize these four verses (Gen 20:13, 35:7, 2 Sam 7:23, and Ps 58:11). Only *Strong's Systematic Theology* refers to Gen 20:13 and 35:7 as plural descriptions of *Elohim* the true God.[168] In these systematic theologies that pastors, theological students and lay people refer to, they find a completely inadequate treatment of the plurality and tri-unity of God in the Hebrew Scriptures.

Lastly, all of the preceding arguments for the plurality or tri-unity of *Elohim* in the Hebrew Scriptures are not new to the New Covenant, and the Church is not witnessing the birth of something new. Plurality has been firmly established and reflected throughout the pages of the *Tanakh*. The *Tanakh* and New Covenant are Trinitarian to the very heart. This tri-unity of God in the New Covenant has its foundations clearly in the *Tanakh*. This doctrine does not appear in the making in the New Covenant, it has already been made.[169] Warfield gives a very logical argument for the foundation of the tri-unity in the word *Elohim* as he introduced it to us in the following statement:

> It was the task of the Old Testament revelation to fix firmly in the minds and hearts of the people of God the great fundamental truth of the unity of the Godhead; and it would have been dangerous to speak to them of the plurality within this unity until this task had been fully accomplished. The real reason for the delay in the revelation of the Trinity, however, is grounded in the secular development of the redemptive purpose of God: the times were not ripe for the revelation of the Trinity in the unity of the Godhead until the fullness of the time had come for God to send forth His Son unto redemption, and his Spirit unto sanctification."[170]

Warfield is saying that in Genesis 1, or even in the *Torah*, God did not present a full-blown revelation of Himself because of the rampant polytheism in the ancient world. He was a triune God from the beginning, but used progressive revelation to unfold His tri-unity until the full revelation was given in the New Covenant. That does not eradicate the fact that His plurality (and tri-unity) is presented in the *Tanakh* through numerous avenues. David L. Cooper also expresses why God revealed Himself, both as a unity (one) and as a plurality:

---

[161] Hodge, *Systematic Theology*, 1:442-482.

[162] Emery H. Bancroft, *Christian Theology* (Grand Rapids: Zondervan, 1964), 71-73, 83-85.

[163] James Oliver Buswell, *A Systematic Theology of the Christian Religion* (Grand Rapids: Zondervan, 1962), 1:102-129.

[164] Floyd H. Barackman, *Practical Christian Theology* (Grand Rapids: Kregel, 1998), 60-68.

[165] Grudem, *Systematic Theology*, 226-261.

[166] Berkhof, *Systematic Theology*, 82-99.

[167] Erickson, *Introducing Christian Doctrine*, 96-105.

[168] Augustus H Strong, *Systematic Theology* (Westwood, N.J: Fleming H. Revell, 1965), 318.

[169] Benjamin Breckinridge Warfield, *Biblical and Theological Studies* (Philadelphia: The Presbyterian and Reformed. 1968), 32.

[170] Warfield, *Biblical and Theological Studies*, 33-34.

What is the reason for the use of this plural noun referring to the Divine Being with the verb in the singular number? There can be but one true explanation which is that, while emphasizing the distinct personalities of the God-head, the ancient writers were anxious to refute polytheism and to assert the unity and the oneness of these divine personalities. Thus this peculiar grammatical usage is an affirmation of both the unity and plurality of the Divine Being.[171]

A Jewish believer expresses why the tri-unity of God is not fully revealed in the Hebrew Scriptures:

The reason a formal trinitarian concept does not exist in the Old Testament is not because it is borrowed from Hellenism, as some suggest, but because as the revelation of God is progressive, so as with the nature of the Messiah Himself, a full enough revelation did not exist in Jewish scripture until the New Covenant.[172]

Due to the fact that the singular verbs or modifiers follow *Elohim*, God was showing the Jewish people the plurality of Himself and the fact that the combination of the plural and singular lends support to the plurality of God. In the Soncino Commentaries rabbis try to say the opposite, that it can only mean the unity of God:

The Hebrew has the plural form, the plural of majesty; but no idea of plurality is to be read into the word, because the verb created is in the singular (E).[173]

As illustrated, *Elohim* denotes the oneness of God, the fact that He is indivisible, but is at the same time plural. "Plural of majesty" does not apply because "plural of majesty" is not used by Hebrew kings as the leadership in Israel, within the *Tanakh*. Contrary to Abraham Ibn Ezra's above quote, the plurality can be read into *Elohim* because God used it in revealing Himself. Cooper further states that writers of the *Tanakh* used all three names of God: *El, Elah, Eloah* in the singular and *Elohim* in the plural. Cooper demonstrates that the writers of the *Tanakh* had ample words to express the singular, absolute oneness of God but, in the majority of cases chose the plural *Elohim* instead:

The English word which is translated 'God" in the Hebrew Scriptures in the majority of cases is אֱלֹהִים *Elohim*. This term is in the plural number, as everyone who knows Hebrew admits. Moses and the prophets referring to -- idols in the plural -- invariably used this same form. Since it connoted a plurality of idols, it certainly indicates a plurality of the divine personalities subsisting in the one divine essence when applied to the true God. Frequently, however, Moses and the prophets used אֵל *EL*, in referring to the Divine Being, which is in the

---

[171] David L Cooper, *God's Gracious Provision for Man* (Los Angeles: Biblical Research Society, 1953), 114.

[172] Schiffman, *Return of the Remnant*, 94.

[173] A Cohen, *The Soncino Chumash, the Five Books of Moses with Haphtaroth* (London: Soncino, 1993), 1.

singular number and means only one. Occasionally they used אֱלוֹהַ *Eloah*.
Beyond controversy this also is in the singular number. If the Divine Being
were simply a single personality, the sacred writers could have used either of
these words in the singular to convey that idea. In Joshua 22:22 however appear
both the singular and plural forms, which combination amounts to an affirmation
regarding the unity of the divine personalities constituting the one God: יְהוָה
אֵל אֱלֹהִים יְהוָה אֵל אֱלֹהִים "God, Gods, Jehovah, God Gods, Jehovah."[174]

Cooper's argument on the names of God is well done, and his reference to Josh
22:22 is quite convincing. In this text Joshua repeats, twice for emphasis, that *El*
(singular), *Elohim* (plural) and *Yahweh* (singular) are both singular and plural terms for
God. In this verse the God of Israel is called by all three names, and one of them is in
the plural. When the *Ruach haKodesh* of God wrote the Scriptures, every word was
inspired (verbal plenary), because He knew exactly what He wanted to say.

The authors of Scripture use the plural forms of *Elohim* that denote pagan gods
only in context that Israel does not worship plural gods as the heathen do. They
worship a plural God who is a complete complex unity, indivisibly one and completely
equal in nature, character and essence. The greater portion of the 2600 uses of *Elohim*
refers to the God of Israel; only about 250 of them refer to pagan gods. The writers of
Scripture use the term as a contrast between plural pagan gods and the plural indivisible
God of Israel.

Moses from Genesis through Deuteronomy was God's human author who
composed the whole of the Pentateuch. Moses uses the term *Elohim* throughout his
writings of the true God. *Elohim* met with Abraham, Isaac, Jacob, Moses and was the
one who guided the children of Israel through the wilderness to the Promised Land.[175]
The creator God of Genesis one is the same God throughout the Torah who does refer to
Himself in the plural. Throughout the Torah God is identified as not just *Elohim*, but
Yahweh, *Adonai*, the Messenger (Angel) of the LORD, and the *Shechinah* of God. Psa
96:5 in reference to the creator God calls Him LORD.

Dual Plurality

Hebrew nouns have another quality that impacts the study, and that quality is
number. Number is the singular and plural aspect as it relates to nouns. Another
number used in Hebrew is the "dual," which indicates plurality, but only in the sense of
"a pair or two." Ross, in his Hebrew grammar, clarifies that "Hebrew nouns have three
numbers, singular, plural and dual. Dual is a special kind of plural ending used to
indicate a pair, or two of something."[176] Examples of dual nouns are: two ears (אָזְנַיִם),
two days (יוֹמַיִם), two horses (סוּסַיִם), two mares (סוּסָתַיִם), two hands (יָדַיִם), two feet

---

[174] Cooper, *What Men Must Believe* (Los Angeles: Biblical Research Society, 1943), 105.

[175] John H. Sailhamer, *The Expositor's Bible Commentary* (Grand Rapids: Zondervan, 1990), 2:20.

[176] Allen P. Ross, *Introducing Biblical Hebrew* (Grand Rapids: Baker Academic, 2001), 71.

(רַגְלַיִם), two horns (קַרְנַיִם). Rendsburg states that dual forms are not as rare as would be expected when he says:

> Although most grammars have not recognized them, dual forms are not as rare in Hebrew as one might expect.[177]

He goes on in his article to illustrate the dual is used more often than normally seen such as in Ruth 1:22 when the text says concerning Ruth and Naomi "and they (c. dual) came to Bethlehem."[178] D. L. Cooper adds insight that dual is never used of God, which would simply mean that if *Elohim* is a plurality; He must be more than two.

> Usually this form of noun was employed when a pair of objects was mentioned. When, for instance, a Hebrew wished to speak of a person's hands, he put the noun in the dual number. The same thing was true with reference to eyes and feet. By the use of this form the writer indicated that there were but two. If there had been only two personalities in the Divine Being and the prophets had wished to emphasize that fact, they could have put the word of God in the dual number. But not one time did they resort to any such method. On the contrary, as we have already seen, they used a word for God in the singular and another in the plural number, which facts show that there were at least three personalities constituting the Divine Being. The noun in the singular number doubtless stressed the unity of God, whereas the one in the plural laid emphasis upon the plurality of the Almighty. In the original the plural word for God is used with a verb in the plural number in Genesis 20:13 and 35:7. Evidently, since the Scriptures are infallibly inspired, there was a very definite reason why the noun for God, *Elohim*, is used here with a plural verb."[179]

Observations and insights such as these should not be ignored and minimized because the *Tanakh* is God's book, and He is revealing Himself to Israel and mankind. A Christian Arab from the west bank area of Israel draws a parallel between Arabic and Hebrew in relation to dual plurality:

> Our Arabic verbs and pronouns are very different from many other languages. The Old Testament, written in Hebrew, has similar verbs and pronouns. Arabic has a singular, a dual, and then a plural verb. "He ate" would be *Akal*. "They (two) ate" would be *Akalou*. In the Semitic language, the verb frequently identifies the number of persons involved in the action. "You" in English can refer to one, two, or a million, but not so in Arabic or Hebrew.[180]

Shorrosh affirms that the tri-unity is assumed in the very first chapter in Genesis (1:26 and 3:22) in the Hebrew Scriptures. Barackman states that God is one (Deut 6:4) but that *Elohim* indicates a plurality of persons (Gen 1:1) coupled with the "us" passages

---

[177] Gary Rendsburg, "Dual Personal Pronouns and Dual Verbs in Hebrew." *JQR* 73, no. 1 (1982):38-58.
[178] Rendsburg, "Dual Personal Pronouns and Dual Verbs in Hebrew." 40.
[179] Cooper, *What Men Must Believe*, 105-106.
[180] Anis A. Shorrosh, *Islam Revealed: A Christian Arab's View of Islam* (Nashville: Nelson, 1988), 239.

(Gen 1:26).[181] *Elohim* clearly indicates more than two because it always has a plural ending and never has a dual ending. He also says that God is a tri-unity because of passages such as Isa 48:16, which is a representation of three persons.[182]

Special uses of *Elohim*, in a plural sense, serve as a powerful argument for His plurality. In Gen 3:5 Satan says to Eve, "You shall be as *Elohim* (plural), knowing good and evil." Why would Satan be using that plural descriptive word so early in human history? There were no other gods or idols at that point to be worshipped. There was nothing! Adam and Eve were in innocence of paradise at that stage of history; no sin was yet in the world. Could it be that Satan used *Elohim* because, as one of the *cherubim*, he served in the immediate presence of God and knew God to be a plurality? Charles Baker expressed the impact of *Elohim* in relation to Adam and Eve:

> Satan told Eve that she and her husband would be as gods, knowing good and evil, it would appear that Eve at this time could not have known of any false gods or others who could be called gods, and it would therefore make better sense to make *Elohim* here refer to the one true God. There is nothing in this verse to make the first occurrence of *Elohim* (translated God- verses 1 & 3) to be different person from the *Elohim* at the end of the verse (translated gods).[183]

Baker's observation has merit and insight into understanding the probable situation in the temptation scene of Genesis 3.

In Psa 138:1 David says that before the gods he will sing praise unto you (God). David was not a polytheist, and yet David praised God before the *Elohims*, and *Elohim* is translated from the Hebrew Scripture as gods![184] Why do all these translations (ASV 1901, NASV, KJV, NKJV, NIV, RSV) use "gods?" How is this to be understood? Did David praise *Elohim* because he understood something about the plural nature of *Elohim*? Or is David praising *Elohim* before the judges in Israel (Exod 21:6; 22:8, 9, 28)? Both are real possibilities, but the second one is more likely. *Elohim* is translated as "God" with a marginal note saying "to the judges" in the *Tanakh* of the Jewish Publication Society.[185] Obviously, David was praising *Elohim* in the "holy temple," not before false gods, but before the judges. Baker makes the following observation:

> Of course, David could have had in mind praising God before some great ones in the earth, but it is unlikely that he was thinking about standing in an idol temple to praise God. It seems more likely that he was simply reiterating what he had said in the first part of the verse; "I will praise thee with my whole heart: before *Elohim* will I sing praise unto thee."[186]

---

[181] Barackman, *Practical Christian Theology*, 63.

[182] Barackman, *Practical Christian Theology*, 66.

[183] Charles F Baker, *A Dispensational Theology* (Grand Rapids: Grace Bible College, 1971), 143.

[184] The following translations all use gods: ASV 1901, NASV, KJV, NKJV, NIV, RSV.

[185] Tanakh: *The Holy Scriptures*, (Philadelphia: The Jewish Publication Society, 1985), 117.

[186] Baker, *A Dispensational Theology*, 143.

Since Adam and Eve knew nothing of polytheism, understanding the Gen 3:5 reference as a plurality of God would fit into their frame of reference. David was a monotheist in his worship of God, and the Psalms reference that he was worshipping God in His holy temple "before the judges" makes more sense. It is hard to believe that God would move the writers of the *Tanakh* to select a name for God from polytheistic terminology, since that same Hebrew Scripture completely condemns polytheism. If God did breathe His Word through Moses, David and the prophets, it seems more logical to believe that He led them to use the plural noun with singular verbs and adjectives to reveal something of His true nature as a tri-unity. This truth would only be fully revealed after the incarnation of His Son, the Messiah of Israel.[187]

Exod 21:5-6, illustrates the Scriptural text translated correctly to reflect the context of the passage:

> And if the servant shall plainly say, I love my master, my wife, and my children; I will not go out free: Then his master shall bring him unto the judges [*elohim's*].[188]

The NASB uses the word "God," but in the footnotes it says "or judges." Clearly *Elohim* is translated in the plural when it refers to God's representatives, the judges, but not when it is translated for the true God. In Ps 97:7 *Elohim* is used again and translated "gods," but the text is referring to angels who are called to worship God.[189] So *Elohim* is made plural when the text demands it, but when it is used of God, authors switch to "plural of majesty." Attempting to change the meaning by interpreting plural as singular is not "rightly dividing the word of truth" (2 Tim. 2:15). Have Christian theologians conceded or abdicated the tri-unity of God to Rabbinic Judaism?

Clearly, scriptural usages of *Elohim* indicate that the plurality of God, as well as the tri-unity of God, was present in the beginning of God's revelation of Himself. Over the years of interacting with this world's perspective, there seems to be the consensus that religion evolved from polytheism to monotheism. Some authors, like Jacobs,[190] allude to the fact that monotheism developed in an evolutionary manner from polytheism[191] over the centuries, to henotheism,[192] and then to monotheism,[193] which Israel embraced. He further states that this is a matter for biblical scholarship, contrasted to Payne who says:

> Historically, however, this truth was only progressively revealed by God and grasped by fallen man. Before the fall Adam knew God, but most of his descendants became polytheists (Josh 24:2).[194]

---

[187] Baker, *A Dispensational Theology*, 142.
[188] Alexander Harkavy, *The Twenty-Four Books of the Old Testament* (2 vols., New York, N.Y: Hebrew Publishing , 1916), 123.
[189] Cooper, *The God of Israel*, 35.
[190] Jacobs, *A Jewish Theology*, 22
[191] Polytheism: The belief in many gods.
[192] Henotheism: The worship of one god without denying the existence of other gods.
[193] Monotheism: The belief that there is but one God.
[194] Payne, *The Theology of the Older Testament*, 125.

Dyrness references Payne's statement as well, saying that Israel had no clear understanding of monotheism.[195] Israel, as a group, may have lost that concept because of the idolatry in Egypt, but not everyone in Israel lost monotheism. Niehaus, in his book, *God At Sinai*, reflects on the Apostle Paul's statement (Rom 1:18-32), which is the reverse of Jacob's premise. God had revealed Himself to mankind from the beginning. But man chose, from the beginning, to turn his back on God and worship images of mortal man, birds, animals and reptiles:

> Those pagan religions-characterized by polytheism (or henotheism at best) and idolatry-represent a weltanschauung that is degraded from the truth. The apostle Paul put pagan religion in perspective when he portrayed it as a result of the Fall. According to Paul, humanity knew God from the beginning but chose not to glorify him or give thanks to him, and as a result, "their foolish hearts were darkened" and "they became fools and exchanged the glory of the immortal God for images made to look like mortal man and birds and animals and reptiles (Rom 1:21-23)."[196]

The concept that *Elohim* revealed Himself, from the beginning, is continued by Henry Thiessen: "We assert that monotheism was the original religion of mankind."[197] That concept of God did not evolve from polytheism to monotheism but rather degenerated from monotheism to polytheism. What better reason and convincing proof can be given than these scriptural uses of *Elohim* where God revealed Himself to Adam and Eve as one God in a plurality of unity? This is further suggested by Jack Scott:

> However, a better reason can be seen in Scripture itself where, in the very first chapter of Genesis, the necessity of a term conveying both the unity of the one God and yet allowing for a plurality of persons is found (Gen 1:2, 26).[198]

So *Elohim* opens the door for God's revelation of Himself in a plural manner. He is one God. He has revealed Himself to mankind as a plurality of unity, indivisible. He is revealed as a tri-unity, which the Hebrew word *Elohim* represents by being translated as a plurality. The Rabbinic argument affirms the oneness of God, which preserves their rejection of Jesus as the God/man, Who is equal, in essence, with the Father, Who is *Elohim* a plurality, yet one.

From the time of Moses through the exile, Israel struggled with worshipping *Elohim*, alone, as God. Joshua, at the end of his life, challenged Israel to choose who they are going to serve (Josh 24:14-15). He told them to put away the gods (*elohim*) which their fathers served. In Judges 2, where the cycle of sin is given, the first step to bondage was the worship of Baal (v. 11). The worship of other gods (*elohim*) was Israel's stumbling block throughout the pages of the *Tanakh*, but Israel knew that their God was *Elohim*, *Yahweh*, and that He demanded complete exclusive worship. As

---

[195] Dyrness, *Themes in Old Testament Theology*, 48.
[196] Jeffrey J Niehaus, *God At Sinai* (Grand Rapids: Zondervan, 1995), 82.
[197] Henry C. Thiessen, *Lectures in Systematic Theology* (Grand Rapids: Eerdmans, 1979), 38.
[198] Harris, Archer, and Waltke, *Theological Wordbook of the Old Testament*, 1:44.

Isaiah 44 points out so clearly, the other gods (*elohim*) were not gods (*elohim*) at all but mere objects of wood and stone or heavenly bodies, all lifeless, created by the imagination of man's mind and with his hands.

אֲדוֹן *Adonai*

The word *adonai*, translated "Lord," is plural of *adon* (lord) in the Hebrew Scriptures and is consistently in the plural when used of God.[199] The word is used by itself 134 times and connected to *Yahweh* 315 times.[200] That is an additional 449 plural references with *Elohim* and other plural descriptions (discussed later) to show the plurality of God. However, Jenni calls *adonai* a majestic plural as seen with *Elohim*.[201] Alden affirms *adonai* as a plural usage as is true with *Elohim*, but also equates it with "plural of majesty" as is often done with *Elohim*.[202] This is the same argument used with *Elohim* in trying to make it a "plural of majesty" instead of accepting it as God used it. The Scripture, God's revelation of Himself, speaks for itself. If He chose to use the plural *adonai* for Lord as He spoke of Himself, who are scholars to say that He cannot speak of Himself in that manner? Barackman also says of *Adonai*, that "the plural form indicates the plurality of Persons."[203] Even more significant is the statement from a Jewish dictionary:

> *Adon* means lord, master when applied to persons in authority (Gen 45:8-9; Deut 10:17; Judg 19:26-27; I Sam 29:8), and is occasionally used for God (Exod 23:17; 34:23; Josh 3:11, 13). *Adonai*, on the other hand, is a plural form based on *Adon*, but is used exclusively for God and is often used as a parallel to *YHVH* (Gen 15:2, 8; Josh 7:7; Isa 25:8) or as a substitute for it (Isa 13:17; Amos 7:7-8, 9:1; Ezek 18:25).[204]

The plural usage of *Adonai* in connection with, or in place of, *Yahweh*, which further makes the point that *Yahweh*, as "one," and within that oneness is plurality, adds more weight for the plurality of God in the *Tanakh*.

Adonai and *Yahweh* were equally used of God as divine names before 300 BCE, after that period of time, *adonai* gradually came into use more than *Yahweh*. Finally, around the time of Christ, *adonai* completely replaced *Yahweh* in the spoken language.

---

[199] Fruchtenbaum, *Messianic Christology*, 105.

[200] Botterweck, Ringgren, and Fabry. *Theological Dictionary of the Old Testament*, 1:62.

[201] Jenni and Westermann, *Theological Lexicon of the Old Testament*, 1:24.

[202] Harris, Archer, and Waltke, *Theological Wordbook of the Old Testament*, 1:13.

[203] Barackman, *Practical Christian Theology*, 66.

[204] Neusner and Green, *Dictionary of Judaism in the Biblical Period*, 389.

יהוה *Yahweh*

Although *Yahweh* is Israel's personal name for God, the correct pronunciation was lost sometime during the Middle Ages. During the late second temple period, this name was regarded as unspeakably holy and therefore unsuitable for use in public. However, although it was used privately in the synagogue and Temple,[205] by the Middle Ages its pronunciation was lost.[206] *Yahweh* was replaced by the word *Adonai* for Lord sometime before the end of the second temple period.

Yahweh is made up of the Hebrew consonants יהוה or [*yhwh*], which are called the Tetragrammaton.[207] No consensus exists in relation to the structure and etymology of *Yahweh*. The name is generally thought to be a verbal form derived from the root *hwy*, later *hyh*. The meaning of the word is not completely certain, but the general consensus is "to be, happen, become" or "be at hand, exist, come to pass."[208] *Yahweh* seems to be native to Hebrew, since there seem to be no references to the word among the other nations before the time of Moses.[209] The primary explanation of *Yahweh* occurs in Exod 3:13-15, where God reveals His name to Moses. Those verses state that He is the one who exists (Exod 3:14); He is with his people; (v.12), and He wants to be known by them (v. 15).[210] In Exod 6:3, God told Moses that Abraham, Isaac and Jacob knew Him as *El Shaddai* (God Almighty), but *Yahweh* was His name even in the times of the patriarchs. Moses, as he records the history of man, the call of Abraham and his descendents in Genesis, starts using God's name (*Yahweh*) in chapter 2:4. *Yahweh*, which is used 6,828 times, is the second most used word in the Hebrew language[211] in the singular form,[212] which lays a very strong foundation for monotheism in the Scriptures.

Gen 21:33 clearly identifies *Yahweh*, who is called upon and is connected with *El* of eternity or everlasting. *Yahweh* is identified with *Elohim* in Lev 19:2, where the people are to be "holy, for I, the LORD (*Yahweh*) your God (*Elohim*) am holy." *Yahweh*, in combination with *Elohim*, is significant because the two are equated with each other. The difference in meaning, with the combination of these names, is that *Yahweh* is their personal God and *Elohim* is more removed from the creation as expressed here:

> In the Pentateuch . . . The name *Yahweh* is employed when God is presented to us in His personal character and in direct relationship to people or nature; and *Elohim*, when the Deity is alluded to as a Transcendental Being who exists completely outside and above the physical universe.[213]

---

[205] Neusner and Green, *Dictionary of Judaism in the Biblical Period*, 259.

[206] Stone, *Names of God*, 25.

[207] Botterweck, Ringgren, and Fabry, *Theological Dictionary of the Old Testament*, 1:71.

[208] Botterweck, Ringgren, and Fabry. *Theological Dictionary of the Old Testament*, 5:500.

[209] Alexander and Baker, *Dictionary of the Old Testament Pentateuch*, 363.

[210] Alexander and Baker, *Dictionary of the Old Testament Pentateuch*, 363.

[211] Enns, *The Moody Handbook of Theology*, 197.

[212] Chafer, *Chafers Systematic Theology*, 6:17.

[213] Walter A Elwell, *Evangelical Dictionary of Theology* (Grand Rapids: Baker, 1986), 466.

While *Yahweh* and *Elohim* are called holy in Lev 19:2, holy is a very special statement which only applies to *Yahweh*. In Isa 6:3 *Yahweh* is addressed as "Holy, Holy, Holy is *Yahweh* of hosts." In Deut 5:9 Moses also spells out that *Yahweh*, *El* and *Elohim* is a jealous God. "For I, the LORD (*Yahweh*) your God (*Elohim*), am a jealous God (*El*)." These three words are used as synonyms for the same God.

Yahweh's name is also combined with other words, making compound forms of His name to describe certain aspects of His person. Such as *Yahweh-jireh*: "The LORD will provide" (Gen 22:14) and *Yahweh-Nissi* "The LORD our banner" (Exod 17:15). Other compound forms are *Yahweh-Shalom*: "The LORD is peace" (Judg 6:24) and *Yahweh-Sabbaoth*: "The LORD of hosts" (1 Sam 1:3). The last compound form is *Yahweh-M'Kaddesh* and it means "The LORD thy sanctifier (Exod 31:13)," a reference to the Messiah, *Yahweh-Tsidkenu*: "The LORD our righteousness (Jer 23:6)." The only discussion or question with *Yahweh* is the root word for the name of God. Everything else seems to be in agreement in relationship to His singularity and oneness.

Yahweh is singular in the Hebrew text, yet plural terms of God are connected with His name. *Yahweh*, *El* and *Elohim* are used together as the same God, a plural and singular designation of God. There are plural references to *Yahweh* (LORD) in the English text which is not always seen by the causal reader of the Scriptures.

Two *Yahwehs* in the *Tanakh*

Yahweh is the name of Israel's personal God, and the word substantiates that God is one alone. His oneness is borne out in many passages of the Hebrew text (Gen 21:33; Exod 20:2; Lev 19:2; 20:26; 21:8; Deut 4:24; 5:9, 6:4; Isa 41:4, 44:6, 45:5, 14, 18, 21; 48:12; Jer 2:5, 11). Yet God, in His revelation of Himself, continues to identify Himself (*Yahweh*) with plurality, as presented in the following Scriptures:

Genesis 19:24

In Genesis 18-19 three men visit Abraham, and he recognizes them simply as men. The promise is given of Isaac's birth in verse 9, but the text does not begin to identify the men until verse 13, where the one man identifies Himself as *Yahweh*. The other two men are identified as angels going to Sodom (Gen 19:1). The focus of this section of Scriptures is not the two men who left but the one who identified Himself to Abraham as *Yahweh*. In verses 13-23 Abraham is having a dialogue with *Yahweh*, the LORD. Rabbis say that God cannot become a man in human form. Yet, here *Yahweh* appeared in human form, and He even had a meal with Abraham. This passage of Scripture goes against what Rabbinic Judaism teaches about the nature of God as seen in this quote by Weiss-Rosmarin:

> The Unity of God, sacred to Judaism beyond all else, is utterly irreconcilable
> with the Christian idea of the divisibility of the Divine Being and, above all,

with the belief in incarnation. According to Jewish belief God is pure spirit, eternally transcendent and divorced from even the slightest vestige of corporeality. Christianity, on the other hand, asserts that God became man in Jesus, a teaching which is contrary to the very spirit of Judaism.[214]

Weiss-Rosmarin says that Judaism is "irreconcilable" to what Christians believe about *Yeshua* and the incarnation. To him, God is pure spirit and in no way can He be placed in a corporal body. Yet in Genesis 18, God did come in a corporal body and even ate a meal with Abraham. Weiss-Rosmarin's statement is in complete conflict with the statements of Moses, who records what Abraham saw and heard. Weiss-Rosmarin continues with two short statements:

> Is not this contrary to all Jewish teachings of God which emphasize and stress that God is not like man and can never become man or even resemble man? Judaism has always fought, and with all weapons at its disposal, against the Christian idea of incarnation, that is to say, of God's coming into human life. The thought that "God was made man" is shocking beyond words to the Jew who believes that God is One and Unique, and that this Uniqueness consists also in His utter difference from anything and everything in existence and anything and everything man can possibly fashion in his mind to label "God." Christian Trinity which divides the Unity of God into three, namely, God the Father, Jesus the Son and the Holy Spirit?[215]

Where, in the *Tanakh*, does God say He cannot become a man or even resemble man? Christianity does not teach that God can be divided into three. Nor does it teach tritheism, which is what Rabbinic Judaism teaches concerning Christianity, but not Biblical Judaism. Weiss-Rosmarin continues:

> Jewish monotheism is not only the negation of the many gods but also the Rejection of the personification of God on the one hand and of the deification of human beings on the other. Judaism's refusal to worship Jesus is therefore not only due to its repudiation of the doctrine of incarnation, the belief that God became a person, but equally so to its defiant resistance to all and any attempts of according Divine qualities and honors to mere mortals.[216]

Weiss-Rosmarin's perspective is tainted by the writings of Rabbinic Judaism. If Rabbinic Judaism were to acknowledge even the possibility of the plurality of God, then rabbinic Judaism would fall like a sandcastle on the seashore. Yet, contradictory to what Weiss-Rosmarin said, *Yahweh* did appear in human form as a man to Abraham, the Father of the Jewish people, and to Jacob as he wrestled with the angel of *Yahweh* (Gen 32:24-30; Hos 12:3-5) and to Joshua before the attack of Jericho (Josh 5:13-15). In Genesis 18, the one man who identifies Himself eight times between verses 13-33 is

---

[214] Trude Weiss-Rosmarin, *Judaism and Christianity, the Differences* (Middle Village, NY: Jonathan David, 1997), 21.

[215] Weiss-Rosmarin, *Judaism and Christianity, the Differences*, 21-22.

[216] Weiss-Rosmarin, *Judaism and Christianity, the Differences*, 21-23.

Yahweh. In this section of Scripture *Yahweh* is in human form and eating a meal with Abraham after he had washed the visitors' feet. Fruchtenbaum comments on Gen 19:24 by saying that *Yahweh,* the one who was talking with Abraham, rains down fire from *Yahweh* in heaven. Clearly there are two distinct *Yahwehs* showing plurality:

> The first *YHVH* is on earth and is said to be raining down fire from a Second *YHVH* who is in heaven. Two distinct persons are called *YHVH* in the same text.[217]

So not only are there two *Yahwehs,* but one of them is in a human form and is called the Angel of the LORD.

Zechariah 2:8-9

In this passage one *Yahweh* will be sent to Israel, and Israel will recognize that He was sent by another *Yahweh.* Bob Morris, a Jewish believer in Messiah, says *Yahweh* is presented as two distinct *Yahwehs,* one sending the other:

> In verse 12 of the *Tanakh* (verse 8 in English), *YHVH* #1 is the speaker. He speaks about the value of Israel using the word picture of the pupil of the eye. Israel is personal and valuable and protected by God as the eye of a man is personal, valuable and protected by him. He is extremely personal here using the term "My eye." Then in verse 9, *YHVH* #1 says that He is being sent to accomplish a task by *YHVH* #2. One *YHVH* is sending another *YHVH* to perform a task.[218]

Walter Kaiser, also referring this passage of Scripture, sees the same thing as Morris noted above: "Mystery of mysteries, *Yahweh* is Lord, yet He was also sent."[219]

Hosea 1:1-7

In Hos 1:1-7 not only are there two *Yahwehs,*[220] but an additional factor is added in verse 7. *Yahweh,* who spoke in verses 2, 4, and 6, will deliver Israel by sending another *Yahweh* who is Israel's *Elohim.* This passage is even more interesting because of that additional factor.[221] Not only are there two *Yahwehs,* but the second *Yahweh* that is being sent is their *Elohim,* plural God.

---

[217] Fruchtenbaum, *Messianic Christology*, 105.
[218] Morris, *Anti-Missionary Arguments - The Trinity*, 6.
[219] Walter C. Kaiser, Jr. *The Communicator's Commentary: Micah - Malachi* (21vols. Waco, Tex: Word, 1992), 21:315.
[220] Grudem, *Systematic Theology*, 228.
[221] Cooper, *The God of Israel*, 27.

Isaiah 44:6

In this passage of Isaiah there is another reference to two distinct *Yahwehs*. One called Himself "*Yahweh* the King of Israel," and then refers to a second as "His Redeemer, the *Yahweh* of hosts." It can be clearly seen in this verse that there are two distinct *Yahweh*'s. God throughout the *Tanakh*, shows His plurality, but it is especially seen in the book of Isaiah (discussed further in chapter 5).

What is clearly seen is that *Yahweh* speaks of Himself and then of another *Yahweh*, but at the end of the verse He states: "and beside me there is no God" (KJV) or *Elohim*. *Yahweh* refers to two *Yahwehs* and then states there is no other *Elohim*. *Yahweh* emphasizes His oneness and unity, and *Elohim* emphasizes His plurality in unity. There is one additional point concerning the Angel of *Yahweh*, which also shows His plurality, but this will be developed in the next chapter under Theophanies. That chapter will be dedicated to showing God's plurality through two kinds of theophanies, the Angel of *Yahweh* and the *Shechinah* glory of God.

In Scripture *Yahweh*, though singular, is also seen as a plurality, but in that plurality He is never combined with a female counterpart, such as *Asherah* (1 Ki 15:13; 2 Ki 17:10; 2 Chr 19:3; 33:19; Mic 5:14), a female counterpart of *Baal*, the pagan gods of Canaan. One author says:

> The fact that *Yahweh* never had a female counterpart is of great fundamental value. The Hebrew language does not even have a native word for goddess![222]

Yahweh expresses God's oneness and unity as well as two equal beings called *Yahweh*. Even the plurality of *Yahweh* is evident as it is clearly presented from the above mentioned Scriptures.

This chapter examined the names of God (*El*, *Elah*, *Eloah*, *Elohim*, Lord and LORD), and concluded that God used both singular and plural names for Himself. God also used singular verbs or adjectives with the plural noun *Elohim* to draw attention to Himself as the monotheistic God who in essence is plural. Particular attention was given to *Elohim* and *Yahweh* (LORD), which shows that God did reveal Himself as a plurality in unity.

---

[222] Th. C. Vriezen, *An Outline of Old Testament Theology* (Newton, Mass: Charles T. Branford Company, 1970), 327.

CHAPTER 3

THEOPHANIES

This chapter further affirms the plurality of God by validating that theophany speaks and shows the unity and plurality as *Yahweh*, yet is distinct from *Yahweh*. Theophany is the appearance of God in both a human form, as well as the appearance of His glory. Theophany is not a biblical term.[223] It is a theological term used to refer to the visible or auditory manifestations of God.[224] In other words, a theophany is a manifestation of God to the physical senses.[225] God becomes visible so that man can actually interact with Him. It is a Greek word that is derived "from two Greek terms, *theos* (God) and *phaino* (shine, give light), but in the passive the verb means to appear or to be revealed."[226] Hence, the appearance of the "captain of the host of the LORD" before Joshua, or as the glory (*Shechinah*) of God that appeared before all Israel on Mount Sinai was a theophany of God.

God always takes the initiative. He never reveals Himself completely, only in a temporary way. There is only one permanent manifestation of God, and this was the incarnation of Messiah when He dwelt on the earth for approximately 36 years.[227] In Exodus 24:9-11 there is a unique appearance of *Yahweh* before Moses, Aaron and his two sons, as well as the 70 elders of Israel. At this point, seventy-four men literally "saw" the God of Israel in a human form. Morey points out that not only did they see the God of Israel (v. 10), but they stared at God (v. 11). Morey makes the following observations:

> That the men saw God in human form is clear from the fact that, in verse 10, the form had "feet" (Heb. רַגְלָיו and Gk. πόδας) and God was "standing before them as opposed to "sitting" on the throne before them (cf. Isa 6:1).

> It is impossible to escape the fact that the appearance which they saw had feet. and, if God had feet, then He had legs. And if He had legs, then He had a torso, etc.

> This passage cannot be dismissed on the basis that it was a dream. What happened to these seventy-four men was not a dream because, (1) the men were not asleep and, (2) dreams are never group events. Throughout the Bible, only individuals had dreams (Gen 20:3; 31:10; 37:5; Judg 7:13; Dan 2:3).

> Neither can we dismiss this passage as a vision. The Biblical authors had no problem identifying when visions took place (Gen 15:1; Num 12:6; Ezek 1:1).[228]

---

[223] Tenney, *The Zondervan Pictorial Encyclopedia of the Bible*, 388.

[224] Elwell, *Evangelical Dictionary of Theology*, 1087.

[225] Enns, *The Moody Handbook of Theology*, 258.

[226] Bromiley, *The International Standard Bible Encyclopedia*, 4:827.

[227] Elwell, *Evangelical Dictionary of Theology*, 1087.

[228] Morey, *The Trinity: Evidence and Issues*, 123.

What the seventy-four men saw and stared at was the God-Man standing before them identified both as the God of Israel and *Yahweh*. What they saw was a theophany of God.

This discussion on theophany is divided into two sections. First is the Angel of *Yahweh* where He speaks audibly and appears in human form. The second appearance is the *Shechinah* glory of God where He appears in His glory with fire, cloud and smoke, as on Mount Sinai.

Theophany – The Angel of the LORD

Theophanies, in the Hebrew Scriptures, could appear to men in one of four forms so that God could magnify and authenticate His revelation of Himself to His servants.[229] The term is used to indicate how God appeared in these four different forms with four basic purposes.

1. He appeared in human form to Abraham (Gen 18) and to Joshua (Josh 5).
2. He appeared in a non-human form in Exod 3.
3. He appeared as an angel in Exod 23:20-23.
4. He spoke audibly in Gen 3:8; 1 Kings 19:12, and Matt 3:17.

Theophanies had four basic purposes:

1. God appeared to initiate/ratify a covenant with Abraham (Gen 15) and later with Moses and the Israelite nation at large (Exod).
2. God appeared to instruct, or correct, his covenant partner, Israel (Josh 5:13-15; 1 Kgs 18:20-40).
3. God appeared to commission or encourage prophets (Isa 6; Ezek 1; 1 Kgs 18:9-18).
4. God appeared to the nation to bring covenantal judgment on his rebellious subjects (Lev 9:23-10:2; Num 11:1-2; 12:2).[230]

Theophany is viewed by Christians and by the Jewish people differently. What is quite clear according to Morey is that:

As a man, God walked, talked, ate and fellowshipped with other men. During these times God could be seen by the human eye, touched by the human hand, and heard by the human ear. God was literally manifested in the flesh and dwelt among us. The Invisible became Visible and the Immaterial became Material without ceasing, at any time, to be true deity.[231]

---

[229] Tenney, *Zondervan Pictorial Encyclopedia of the Bible*, 5:720.
[230] Alexander and Baker, *Dictionary of the Old Testament Pentateuch*, 860.
[231] Morey, *The Trinity: Evidence and Issues*, 106.

Christians often look at the passages that deal only with the Angel of *Yahweh*. For example, Chafer seems to focus on that narrow view of theophany:

> Theophany usually is limited to appearances of God in the form of man or angels, other phenomena such as *shekhinah* glory not being considered a theophany.[232]

However, the Scriptures indicate a broader view, which includes the above mentioned four categories.

The Angel of *Yahweh*

There are numerous times in the Hebrew Scriptures that *Yahweh* is associated with, and is distinguished from, the Angel of *Yahweh* (LORD – *YHVH*). A careful study of the Hebrew Scriptures will clearly show that God and the Angel of the LORD are two different persons and that they both differentiate Themselves from each other as Reymond expresses:

> A careful analysis of the relevant passages will disclose that God differentiates himself from this Angel by the very title itself as by the fact that he refers to him in the third person and may even address him in the second person in 2 Sam 24:16, and yet the Angel in his speeches, while also often distinguishing himself from God, lays claim to divine attributes and prerogatives, indeed, to identity with God.[233]

These distinctions between the Angel of *Yahweh* and the LORD will be examined, but before these examples from Genesis 22, Judg 2:1 and Zech 3:1-10 are viewed another matter in the *Tanakh* needs to be cleared up.

Before describing the appearances of the Angel of the LORD, the term angel needs clarification due to the unbiblical imagery that has been attached to the term angel from the Middle Ages to the present time. Today when people think of angels, they picture in their mind angels as created beings with wings, wearing a halo, both male and female and sitting on a cloud playing harps. These mental pictures are not biblical and give an incorrect picture of angels, and in particular, the Angel of the LORD.

The word מַלְאָךְ is the Hebrew word for angel. The word, when translated correctly, is "messenger" and not angel. Anyone who took a message to someone else and delivered that message is called a מַלְאָךְ in Hebrew, or messenger. It would include both a human messenger, such as a prophet who delivers a message from God, to an individual, king or nation. It also would include a heavenly messenger (angel) that God sends to bear messages to His earthly servants. There are both human and

---

[232] Chafer, *Chafer Systematic Theology*, 5:31.
[233] Robert L. Reymond, *Jesus: Divine Messiah* (Ross-shire, Scotland: Mentor Imprint, 2003), 72.

heavenly messengers, but both are very distinct. Man is man, and heavenly spirits (angels) are not human beings. This word is used hundreds of times in the Hebrew Scriptures and is understood as "messenger." There is nothing mystical or magical about the word.[234]

How did the Hebrew word "messenger" become angel in our Bibles today? Morey gives a brief history or evolution of the word:

> If the word מַלְאָךְ simply meant "messenger," then where did we get the word "angel?" The mistake was made during the Middle Ages. The Greek word α"γγελος was used in the Septuagint (LXX) for מַלְאָךְ because it also meant messenger. It was a real and proper translation from Hebrew to Greek.
>
> This is in contrast to the Latin Bible where the Greek word α"γγελος is merely transliterated into Latin and becomes *angelus*. Thus, instead of translating the words and α"γγελος as "messenger," the Latin Bible transliterated the Greek word α"γγελος into the Latin word *angelus*.
>
> This error was further compounded when the Latin Bible was translated into English. Instead of translating the Latin word *angelus* as "messengers," it was transliterated into the English word "angel." They did not translate it most of the time, but simply retained the Latin transliteration.[235]

Morey continues by illustrating Matthew 11:10 where the Greek word α"γγελος is translated "messenger" and not angel. This meant that the English translators knew the difference but most of the time chose to transliterate instead of translate the Hebrew (מַלְאָךְ) and Greek (α"γγελος) words.[236] In order to be consistent with the Scriptures throughout the rest of this book, the term "messenger" will be used instead of angel.

The first example comes from Gen 22:11-12 with the broader context in verses 1-19. In verse one *Elohim* gave Abraham instructions for offering his son as a sacrifice to Him. When Abraham is about to offer his son, the Messenger (Angel) of *Yahweh* stops him in verses 11-12. Then the Messenger of *Yahweh* said "for now I know that you fear God," *Elohim* who initially instructed Abraham. But here in verse 12 the Messenger of *Yahweh* uses the personal pronoun "Me," which refers back to verse one as *Elohim*. The Messenger (Angel) of *Yahweh* equates Himself equally with *Elohim* by using the personal pronoun "Me."

In this section of Scripture God identifies Himself four ways: first, as *Elohim* (vs 1), second, as the Messenger (Angel) of *Yahweh* (v. 11), and third as Me (v. 12), referring back to the first two terms for God, and the fourth, as *Yahweh* (vs 16).

---

[234] Morey, *The Trinity: Evidence and Issues*, 138.
[235] Morey, *The Trinity: Evidence and Issues*, 139.
[236] Morey, *The Trinity: Evidence and Issues*, 139.

In this text (Gen 22), *Elohim* (plural) the Godhead is speaking and then one of the Godhead speaks separately, as the Messenger (Angel) of *Yahweh*, who also represents Himself as *Yahweh* in verse 16. This Messenger (angel) of *Yahweh* identifies Himself as the one who swore to Abraham earlier, which reflects back on the Abrahamic Covenant of Genesis 12 and 15. Here the Messenger (Angel) of *Yahweh* has identified Himself with *Elohim* and also spoke as *Yahweh*, yet He is distinct from *Elohim*.

The second example is found in Judg 2:1, which is a fascinating reflection of the distinctiveness of the Messenger (Angel) of *Yahweh* from *Yahweh*. Notice, first of all, that the Messenger does not introduce His speech to the nation of Israel by "Thus says *Yahweh*," which was the practice of the prophets as in Judges 6:8. Here the Messenger (Angel) of *Yahweh* speaks in the first person as God Himself, the One who brought them out of Egypt into the land that was promised to their fathers.[237] According to Morey some Jewish commentaries, such as "*Targum of Jonathan*", have the words, "Thus says *Yahweh*", but the phrase does not appear in any Hebrew manuscripts or the Septuagint.[238] The person speaking in verse one is the Messenger (Angel) of *Yahweh* who makes reference to four things. First (1), He says that He brought Israel out of Egypt. Notice in connection with *Yahweh* and His reference to this messenger:

> I am sending an angel before you to guard you on the way and to bring you to the place that I have made ready. Pay heed to him and obey him. Do not defy him, for he will not pardon your offenses, since My Name is in him; but if you obey him and do all that I say, I will be an enemy to your enemies and a foe to your foes. When My Angel goes before you and brings you to the Amorites, the Hittites, the Perizzites, and Canaanites, the Hivites and the Jebusites, and I will annihilate them. Exod 23:20-23

In these verses *Yahweh* speaks of "an (Messenger) angel" in (v. 20) and "My (messenger) angel" in (v. 23), and He equates Him as one with Him when He says, "My Name is in him." In Isa 42:8 and 48:11 *Yahweh* makes these statements:

> I am the LORD, that is My name; I will not yield My glory to another, nor My renown to idols.

> For My sake, My own sake, do I act – lest My name be dishonored! I will not give My glory to another.

Vine connects God's glory with the name of God (*Yahweh*):

> This is a ratification of the significance of His Name. His glory is the manifestation of His nature, attributes and power.[239]

---

[237] Morey, *The Trinity: Evidence and Issues*, 156.
[238] Morey, *The Trinity: Evidence and Issues*, 157.
[239] V. E. Vine, *Isaiah* (Grand Rapids: Zondervan, 1946), 108.

Yahweh makes this connection. He, *Yahweh*, will not give or yield His glory (*Shechinah*) to another. Yet in Exod 23:20-23 *Yahweh* says that His name is in the angel. The Messenger of *Yahweh* appears numerous times as He leads them to the Promised Land as the *Shechinah* of God. So who is the Messenger? In Exod 32:34 and 33:2-3, *Yahweh* adds more information on the messenger:

> Go now, lead the people where I told you. See, My angel shall go before you. But when I make an accounting, I will bring them to account for their sins.

> I will send an angel before you, and I will drive out the Canaanites, the Amorites, the Hittites, the Perizzites, the Hivites, and the Jebusites – a land flowing with milk and honey. But I will not go in your midst, since you are a stiffnecked people, lest I destroy you on the way.

Twice *Yahweh* says that He will send "My (messenger) angel" or "an (messenger) angel" before you to lead you. *Yahweh* clearly states that He will not go up with them. So who is that Messenger? Exod 33:14-16 seems to contradict the other passages that say He didn't go with them. In this dialog between Moses and the LORD (*Yahweh*), Moses requested that the *Yahweh*'s presence go with them, and *Yahweh* consented because Moses has found favor and knows his name. The word "presence" in the Hebrew is פָּנַי (*panim*) meaning "face," which is also a plural.[240] It is the view of this author that the Messenger of *Yahweh* (Judg 2:1) is also called the "messenger of His Presence" in Isa 63:9 who would be the Second Person of the Godhead rather than God the Father going up with them. It is also interesting to note that the *Jewish Study Bible* recognizes the messenger as divine. Judg 2:1 clearly answers that question by stating the "Angel (Messenger) of *Yahweh*" brought them up from Egypt. In verses 4 and 5 notice the response of the people: "The people broke into weeping. So they named that place Bochim, and they offered sacrifices there to the LORD." Their response was that the Messenger of *Yahweh* was equal too and yet distinct from *Yahweh*.

The second (2) point of reference that the Messenger of *Yahweh* makes is that He brought them into the Promised Land. Exod 33:2-3 expresses the same thing as Judg 2:1. The third (3) point of reference of Judg 2:1 is that the Messenger of *Yahweh* says that, "I had promised on oath to your fathers." That is a direct reference to the Abrahamic Covenant in Genesis 15 as the same one that walked between the cut animals. The Messenger of *Yahweh* made the Covenant with Abraham. The fourth (4) point of reference is that He says "I will never break My covenant with you." So in Judg 2:1 the Messenger (Angel) of *Yahweh* is clearly distinct from *Yahweh*, yet He is equal to Him and He speaks as God.

The third and last example comes from Zech 3:1-10. This is the last reference to the Messenger (Angel) of *Yahweh* in the *Tanakh*. In verse one the Messenger (Angel) of the *Yahweh* is introduced. In verse two the NASB uses the name "*Yahweh*," but in the Jewish Publication Society Version (JPS), it has in brackets "the (Messenger) angel

---

[240] Harris, Archer, and Waltke, *Theological Wordbook of the Old Testament*, 2:727.

of" *Yahweh*.[241]   In verse four this Messenger (Angel) of *Yahweh* is able to remove iniquity, which only God can do. Again in verse five the JPS version understands the messenger as the Messenger (Angel) of *Yahweh*. In verse six the Messenger (Angel) of *Yahweh* charges the High Priest, Joshua, and then speaks in verse seven as the "Lord of Hosts."   Also in verse seven the Messenger (Angel) of *Yahweh* commands them to "walk in MY ways. [242] Here again the Messenger of *Yahweh* speaks as *Yahweh*, showing not only that He is equal and one with *Yahweh* but also that He is distinct from *Yahweh*. Listed in the footnotes are the other passages in the *Tanakh* of the Messenger (Angel) of *Yahweh*.[243]

Yahweh Is Distinct From The Messenger (Angel) Of The LORD

Yahweh is the personal God of Israel. However, when He communicates with Israel in person, He does so through the Messenger (Angel) of the LORD (*Yahweh*), also called the Messenger of God (*Elohim*). As discussed in the previous section, *Yahweh* and the messenger of the LORD (*Yahweh*) spoke as God, and both are distinct personalities, yet both speak as God (Gen 32:24-30; Exod 3:4-5; Josh 5:14-15; Judg 2:1; 6:11-24; 13:2-24).[244]

Hengstenberg meticulously demonstrates that *Yahweh* and the Messenger (Angel) of the LORD (*Yahweh*) are two distinct personalities.

> Sound Christian Theology has discovered the outlines of such a distinction betwixt the hidden and the revealed God, in many passages of the Old Testament, in which mention is made of the Angel or Messenger of God.[245]

> There is no substantial difference betwixt the passages in which Jehovah Himself is mentioned, and those in which the Angel of Jehovah is spoken of.[246]

Like Hengstenberg, Payne expresses the point that the Messenger (Angel) of the LORD (*Yahweh*) is distinct from God and yet is God.[247] He also maintains that in Exod 14:9

---

[241] Adele Berlin and Marc Zvi Brettler, *The Jewish Study Bible* (New York, Oxford, 2004), 1253.

[242] Charles Feinberg, *God Remembers* (New York: American Board of Missions to the Jews, 1965), 54-58

[243] Other references of the Messenger of *Yahweh* are: (a) Gen 16:7, 13 in connection with Hagar. Abraham (b) has visitors in Genesis 18, one of them is the Messenger of *Yahweh*. (c) Gen 31: 11-13; 32:24-30 deals with two examples with Jacob. (d) Moses with his initial contact with the Messenger of *Yahweh* in Exod 3:2-15 when he is commissioned. (e) Josh 5:14-15 before the battle of Jericho is confronted by the Captain of the Host. (f) Gideon is confronted with the Messenger of *Yahweh* in Judg 6:11-24 and (g) Manoah and his wife in Judg 13:2-24. (h) Also during the time of Hezekiah as the Messenger of the *Yahweh* destroys 185,000 Assyrian soldiers in 2 Kings 19:35. (i) The last occurrence is in Zechariah 1:12-14, 3:6-8.

[244] Buswell, *A Systematic Theology of the Christian Religion*, 122.

[245] E. W. Hengstenberg, *Christology of the Old Testament* (Grand Rapids: Kregel, 1956), 1:116.

[246] Hengstenberg, *Christology of the Old Testament*, 1:119.

[247] Payne, *The Theology of the Older Testament*, 167-168.

and Num 20:16 the messenger leads, while other passages say God leads.[248] In fact, Payne even lays out the possibility that there may be other appearances that have not yet been seen:

> It is indeed possible that when visible appearances of God occur elsewhere in the Scriptures the actual subject may again be the *Malakh Yahwe*,[249] even though the term itself may not be used.[250]

Notice in the above statement that Payne said it was possible that *Elohim* or *Yahweh* have revealed Themselves in other passages not yet known or understood at this point. It is an open question. Payne sums up his argument about the Messenger (Angel) of the LORD (*Yahweh*) by saying that:

> Old Testament revelations of the unique angel of the Testament can be appreciated only when understood as pre-incarnate appearances of Jesus Christ the Second Person of the Trinity and the one Savior of mankind.[251]

Chafer argues for two distinct personalities since God, at times, spoke as the Messenger (Angel) of *Yahweh* and at other times as *Yahweh* Himself:

> The fact is that the Angel of Jehovah is at times One other than Jehovah, and at other times He is Jehovah Himself.[252]

Clearly, the Messenger (Angel) of the LORD (*Yahweh*) is recognized as the Second Person of the tri-unity of God. He is distinct from the Father and yet one in unity with God. Both being distinctive Hebrew terms, the Messenger (Angel) of the LORD (*Yahweh*) and *Elohim* give very strong evidence that the plurality, or tri-unity of God, is indeed in the Hebrew Scriptures. In other words, the Messenger (Angel) of the LORD (*Yahweh*) was clearly God Himself.[253]

Throughout the *Tanakh*, both *Yahweh* and the Messenger (Angel) of *Yahweh* are in the singular form for God. The Messenger (Angel) of *Yahweh* and *Yahweh* both, without question, teach the oneness of God because they are always in the singular form. What must be identified is that the Messenger (Angel) of *Yahweh*, who is distinct from *Yahweh*, speaks as *Yahweh*. This is an inescapable fact when these passages are studied. These facts also show plurality within *Yahweh*, because the Messenger (Angel) of *Yahweh* is distinct from *Yahweh*. The Messenger (Angel) of *Yahweh* and *Yahweh* relate to Israel as a monotheist God. Yet in the revelation of Themselves, they do so in a compound or complex unity as the *Shema* in Deut 6:4 will confirm in the next chapter.

---

[248] Payne, *The Theology of the Older Testament*, 168.

[249] The Hebrew noun *malakh* means "messenger" or "angel."

[250] Payne, *The Theology of the Older Testament*, 168.

[251] Payne, *The Theology of the Older Testament*, 170.

[252] Chafer, *Chafers Systematic Theology*, 1:299.

[253] Merrill C Tenney, *The Zondervan Pictorial Encyclopedia of the Bible* (Grand Rapids: Zondervan, 1975), 5:389.

Shechinah

Earlier in the introduction of Theophanies, they were divided into two sections, the Messenger (Angel) of the *Yahweh* and the *Shechinah* or glory of God's presence. The Hebrew word for *Shechinah* is שׁכינה, literally means "the dwelling," as in Gen 9:27. The definition is "the majestic presence or manifestation of God which has descended to 'dwell' among men."[254] Rabbi Nahmanides (1194-1270) considered it the essence of God as manifested in a distinct form.[255] The *Shechinah* as a theophany includes the non-human appearances of God through fire, cloud and smoke. The Jewish people called that revelation of Himself the *Shechinah* of God or the glory of God.

According to VanGemeren the word *Shechinah* does not occur in the *Tanakh*. VanGemeren continues by stating that:

> The root *skn* occurs not only in the verb ("dwell"), but also in the noun *miskan* ("dwelling place," "tabernacle") and the name Shecaniah ("*Yahweh* dwells"; e.g., 1 Chron 3:21f.).[256]

Fruchtenbaum concurs with VanGemeren and adds some practicality to the above statement:

> The usual title found in the Scriptures for the *Shechinah* Glory is the glory of Jehovah, or the glory of the Lord. The Hebrew form is *Kvod Adonai*, which means "the glory of Jehovah" and describes what the *Shechinah* Glory is.
>
> Other titles give it the sense of "dwelling," which portrays what the *Shechinah* Glory does. The Hebrew word *Shechinah*, from the root *shachan*, means "to dwell." The Greek word *Skeinei*, which is similar in sound as the Hebrew *Shechinah* (Greek has no "sh" sound), means "to tabernacle."[257]

The Hebrew word for glory, כָּבוֹד (kavod), as in the "glory of the LORD filled the tabernacle" in Exod 40:34, is not the term *Shechinah*, but glory. Over the years through Israel's contact with Hellenism, the glory of the LORD was equated with *Shechinah*. Post-exilic Jews, and later Christians,[258] understood the term *Shechinah* as "to dwell" or "to reside."[259] The apostle John picks this up in Jn 1:14 where he says, "The Word was made flesh, and dwelt (tabernacled or *shekhinah*) among us." *Shechinah* first appears in the *Targums*[260] and rabbinic literature.

---

[254] Singer, *The Jewish Encyclopedia*, 11:258.

[255] Singer, *The Jewish Encyclopedia*, 11:259.

[256] Geoffrey W. Bromiley, *The International Standard Bible Encyclopedia* (Grand Rapids: Eerdmans, 1988), 4:466.

[257] Arnold G. Fruchtenbaum, *The Footsteps of the Messiah: A Study of the Sequence of Prophetic Events* (Tustin, CA: Ariel Ministries, 2003), 599.

[258] Unger, *Unger's Bible Dictionary*, 1009.

[259] Orr, *The International Standard Bible Encyclopedia*, 4:2758.

[260] <u>Targum</u>: This is an Aramaic paraphrase of the Hebrew Scriptures from the first century BCE into the

Niehaus takes the theophanies of God back to Genesis 1 to the creation account, as well as to the fall of man in Genesis 3, including the judgment account of Genesis 6, and labels them pre-Sinai theophanies.[261] The fact is that God did communicate to Adam and Noah, but it does not indicate how. God, in Gen 3:8 did communicate directly with man in the Garden, by his voice, but no further information is given about how He walked with them. With Noah, it simply says in Gen 6:13 that God spoke to him, but it does not say how He communicated the information. In the biblical text there is not enough evidence to say, with authority, how God communicated in these instances.

Whether God reveals His presence as plurality to the nation of Israel as *Yahweh*, the Messenger (Angel) of *Yahweh*, or as *Shechinah* glory of God, that presence is the Second Person of the Godhead. That is rarely disputed among fundamental and evangelical scholars.

The first undisputed *Shechinah* is recorded in Gen 15:9-18.[262] In these verses God made a covenant with Abraham by walking between the carcasses of slaughtered animals.

> When the sun was set and it was very dark, there appeared a smoking oven, and a flaming torch which passed between these pieces. (vv. 17-18)

This pre-Sinai theophany introduces smoke (smoking oven) and fire (flaming torch), two non-human elements that are part of the Mount Sinai theophanies. These are characteristic of the *Shechinah* of God that appeared to Israel and to some of the prophets. In Judg 2:1 the Angel (Messenger) of *Yahweh* identifies Himself as the covenant maker with Abraham which was confirmed in the pre-Sinai theophany of Genesis 15. There is little doubt that the *Shechinah* of God and the Messenger (Angel) of *Yahweh* were the same persons.

The second notable *Shechinah* was the burning bush that attracted Moses' attention when he was shepherding sheep on Mount Sinai (Exodus 3). Verse two makes it clear that it was the Messenger (Angel) of *Yahweh* who appeared to Moses in a blazing fire from a bush that was not consumed. This Messenger (Angel) told Moses to remove his shoes because he was standing on holy ground, in the presence of God. Then, He referred to the Abrahamic Covenant (Gen 15:12-18) and the predicted deliverance that was going to take place. Moses was His deliverer. When asked his name, the Messenger (Angel) of *Yahweh* responded, "I AM WHO I AM." This "I AM" is undoubtedly the same person as the Messenger (Angel) of *Yahweh*, the *Shechinah* of God, in the burning bush. This appearance to Moses led to a personal relationship between Israel and their God.

---

first century of the CE. The "*Targums* regarded the *Shechinah* as God himself." It was first used in the *Targums* to avoid the anthropomorphic references to God as in Gen 9:27 - "let him [God] dwell in the tents of Shem" to "may the Glory of his shekhinah dwell in the midst of the tents of Shem."
[261] Niehaus, *God At Sinai*, 142-171.
[262] Niehaus, *God at Sinai*, 172-180.

In the third notable *Shechinah*, God traveled with Israel by giving them a pillar of cloud by day and a pillar of fire by night (Exod 13:21-22). As the Egyptian army advanced against Israel, at the shore of the Red Sea (Sea of Aquaba),[263] that evidence of God's glory became a wall between them. According to Exod 40:36-38 this cloud and fire led them throughout the wilderness wanderings. Up to this point God had appeared only to individual patriarchs and Moses. Now He was appearing to the nation of Israel at large. However, God could not completely reveal Himself because the holiness of His very nature required that He conceal Himself from the presence of man in the form of a thick, dark cloud.[264]

In this appearance of the *Shechinah* of God, the pillar of cloud and fire moved between the Egyptian army and the Israelites. Exod 14:19 says, "The Angel (Messenger) of God, who had been going ahead of the Israelite army." Here the *Shechinah* is identified as the Messenger of *Elohim*.[265] The use of *Elohim* is significant in that it identifies the *Shechinah* of God, or the theophany of God, within a plural context. It does so in the plural form of *Elohim* rather than as *El, Elah* or *Eloah* in the singular. Then, as if such proofs were insufficient, verse 24 declares that this Messenger (Angel) of *Elohim* was *Yahweh* looking down from the pillar of cloud and fire. Clearly, the plural *Elohim* and the singular *Yahweh* were the same persons. It is also noted that the phrase "Angel (Messenger) of God" is used (seven times) alternately with the "Angel (Messenger) of *Yahweh*."[266]

The fourth notable *Shechinah* is God's appearance before the whole nation of Israel at the foot of Mount Sinai. The human reaction to the *Shechinah* of God that appeared before Israel was one of fear and terror.[267] Deut 18:16 expresses the fear and terror of the people as they heard and saw His glory or *Shechinah*. The *Shechinah* of God rested on Mount Sinai, and a cloud covered it (Exod 24:16) to conceal His full glory. As *Yahweh* spoke from the midst of the fire and cloud, Israel "heard the sound of words, but saw no form, only a voice" (Deut 4:12). Deut 5:22 adds that the Lord spoke "from the midst of the fire, of the cloud and of the thick gloom, with a great voice." Exod 19:16-20 adds more descriptive words: "thunder and lightning flashes," "thick cloud," "very loud trumpet sound," "so that all the people . . . trembled," "smoke because the *Yahweh* descended upon it in fire," "its smoke ascended like the smoke of a furnace, and the whole mountain quaked violently," ". . . sound of the trumpet grew louder and louder." The *Shechinah* of God, the Second Person of the Godhead, was the pre-incarnate Messiah as He established the Mosaic Covenant with Israel.

The fifth notable *Shechinah* appearance was when God took his place in the Holy of Holies in the Tabernacle. Since the Glory of God cannot be seen by man, God

---

[263] Campus Crusade for Christ. *The Exodus Revealed, Search for the Red Sea Crossing.* (Irvine CA: Discovery Media Productions, 2001), videotape.

[264] Alexander and Baker, *Dictionary of the Old Testament Pentateuch*, 861.

[265] Arthur W. Kac, *The Messiahship of Jesus* (Grand Rapids: Baker, 1986), 200-201.

[266] Botterweck, Ringgren, and Fabry. *Theological Dictionary of the Old Testament*, 1:281.

[267] Alexander and Baker, *Dictionary of the Old Testament Pentateuch*, 863.

covered his glory, or *Shechinah*, with a thick dark cloud that filled the tabernacle as He took up residence (Exod 40:34-35).[268]

The sixth notable *Shechinah* appearance was the pillar of fire by night and the cloud by day that followed Israel as they traveled for 40 years through the area of the Sinai Peninsula and part of western Arabia. The *Shechinah* of God appeared at numerous times as He met with Moses, but He also appeared to judge individuals or the nation. The following are six examples of individual and corporate judgments that was given to Israel for their rebellion in the wilderness. These judgments (Exod 23:23; 32:34; 33:3) were not carried out by *Yahweh* because He did not go with them, rather, the messenger carried out these judgments as He took Israel through the wilderness and into the Land. So all of the following examples are the Messenger (Angel) of *Yahweh*, equal, yet distinct from *Yahweh*, showing plurality:

(1) Nadab and Abihu offered strange fire before the Lord[269] in Lev 10:1-2, and fire came from the presence of *Yahweh* and consumed them. Leviticus 9:23-24 shows that it was the glory of *Yahweh* that was present and that fire proceeded from *Yahweh*.

(2) In Num 11:1-2, at Taberah, Israel murmured before God, and He responded to their sin: "The fire of the LORD burned among them and consumed some of the outskirts of the camp."[270]

(3) In Num 12:2-5 the *Shechinah* of God appeared at the "doorway of the tent of meeting" in judgment of Aaron and Miriam for their sin against Moses, their brother, and condemned their sin and caused Miriam to be leprous.[271]

(4) Num 14:10 says that the *Shechinah* of God appeared before Israel "in the tent of meeting" to quell the riot against Moses after the report of the ten unbelieving spies. Verse 23 gave the verdict that Israel will not "see the land which I swore to their fathers." This act of rebellion, their refusal to believe "by faith" in Him, was an unpardonable sin (Num 14:11). This was an "evil congregation," (vv. 27, 35; cf. Matt 12:31-45) and as a result, He condemned them to wander in the wilderness for 38 years until they all died.

(5) Later Korah, a Levitical family, not of the family of Aaron, rebelled against Moses and Aaron as they gathered the congregation against Moses and Aaron at the door of the tent of meeting. There the glory of the *Yahweh* appeared to the congregation. He opened the earth and swallowed up all the families of Korah, Dathan and Abiram and sent fire to consume 250 men offering incense (Num

---

[268] Elwell, *Evangelical Dictionary of Theology*, 1010.
[269] Niehaus, *God at Sinai*, 208.
[270] Niehaus, *God at Sinai*, 210.
[271] Niehaus, *God at Sinai*, 211.

16:1-40). This was not their God given responsibility.[272] They were usurping responsibilities reserved for the Aaronic priests.

(6) Even after such a devastating judgment, Israel grumbled against Moses and Aaron saying that they were the cause of the death of these men. Again, the *Shechinah* of God appeared with a plague upon the people so that 14,700 died (Num 16:42, 49). As mentioned earlier in this section, the *Shechinah* of God is the pre-incarnate Messiah of Israel.

Each one of these six examples of the *Shechinah* glory of God shows that these persons are one, yet distinct. Exod 23:20-23 clearly states that *Yahweh* did not go with Israel, but that He sent His Messenger (angel), which establishes the fact that *Yahweh* and His Messenger in these *Shechinah* glory references are equal and distinct. Clearly, these *Shechinah* references establish the plurality of God. through the *Shechinah* glory of God references are seen without question in these passages.

The seventh notable *Shechinah* appearance occurred when the presence of God filled the new Solomonic Temple in Jerusalem.[273] In 1 Kgs 8:10-11; 9:3 and 2 Chr 7:1 the *Shechinah* of God, the glory of *Yahweh*, filled the Temple, and as in the Mount Sinai appearance, this also was with a cloud. Solomon (1 Kgs 8:12) refers to the cloud as a thick cloud. Not only did the *Shechinah* of God fill the temple, but fire came down from heaven and consumed the burnt offerings and sacrifices.

The eighth notable *Shechinah* appearance that could be called post-Sinai appearances, occurred when Isaiah and Ezekiel received their commissions as prophets.[274] In chapter 6 Isaiah saw the Lord sitting on His throne. Verses 1-3 give a description of God that very few have seen. Verse 4 has two examples of a theophany: "The foundations of the thresholds trembled at the voice of him . . . the temple was filling with smoke." This theophany marks the call of Isaiah into his prophetic ministry by God recalling to memory Israel's Mount Sinai experience and the consecration of Solomon's temple.[275]

Isaiah's vision was awesome, but Ezekiel's vision was indescribable. Certain theophanic pictures are seen in Ezekiel 1, such as: "a great cloud with fire flashing continually (v. 4)." Ezekiel 1 is filled with things like nothing else in the Hebrew Scriptures. This theophany is also Ezekiel's call found in chapter 2:3.[276]

Ezekiel chapters 8-11 describe the sin of the religious and political leaders of Israel in their worship of pagan deities in the temple. Not only is Israel's sin described in these chapters, but the *Shechinah* of God is in the process of leaving the temple of God to return to heaven (Hos 5:15; Matt 23:37-39). Neusner, in giving a rabbinic

---

[272] Niehaus, *God at Sinai*, 214-215.

[273] Niehaus, *God at Sinai*, 243.

[274] Isidore Singer, *The Jewish Encyclopedia*. (New York: Funk and Wagnalls, 1906), 12:137.

[275] Niehaus, *God at Sinai*, 249-254.

[276] Niehaus, *God at Sinai*, 254-279.

Jewish response, says that in 70 AD the *Shechinah* of God went into exile with the captives.[277] Passages in Ezekiel document that the *Shechinah* of God left the temple in 592 BCE (Ezek 8:1) in several stages (9:3; 10:18; 11:23). Singer also states that the *Shechinah* of God was one of five things missing in the second temple.[278] Also, according to Josephus, neither the Ark of God nor the *Shechinah* was present in 63 BCE when Pompey, the conquering Roman general, entered the temple and the Holy of Holies.[279] So the *Shechinah* did not go into exile with the captives but left the temple and the nation over 600 years earlier and returned to heaven. Proof of the absence of God's tangible glory from the temple is that Pompey was not struck dead upon penetrating the veil as Jewish authors like Singer,[280] and Schurer[281] attest. Christian authors also validate those Jewish authors, such as Pfeiffer,[282] Moeller,[283] Sloan,[284] and Sacchi.[285]

The last possible reference to the theophany of God is found in Dan 5:5 when the hand of God wrote on the wall in the banquet hall in Belshazzar's palace. Some background information must be given to lead up to the Daniel reference. Deut 9:10 (cp. Exod 31:18; 32:15-16; 34:1) refers to the *Shechinah* of God who wrote the Ten Commandments with "the finger of God." This event was part of the *Shechinah* of God's activities on Mount Sinai. In the New Covenant "Jesus stooped down and with his finger wrote on the ground (Jn 8:6)." Jesus, the Messiah of Israel, and the *Shechinah* of God, was the pre-incarnate Messiah, who now, with His *Shechinah* glory veiled in flesh, does not speak immediately but wrote with his finger, the "finger of God (Deut 9:10)," in the ground. Did He stoop and write the seventh commandment as He wrote with his finger on Mount Sinai? That will never be known, but the Jn 8:6 text does have strong implications.

The fingers of God are mentioned in three other places. One is found in Ps 8:3 (not a theophany), where David says, "When I consider Thy heavens, the work of Thy fingers." The second reference is a metaphor used for God by Pharaoh's magician as they reacted to the plagues in Exod 8:19. The third reference is the one now under consideration. More evidence for a theophany is found in Dan 5:5 where "suddenly the fingers of a man's hand" appeared before Belshazzar on the banquet hall wall. This was a theophany, and the reason for that conclusion is because it was a supernatural event. The context involves the temple vessels being defiled by a proud and obstinate king

---

[277] Neusner, *God at Sinai*, 577.

[278] Singer, *The Jewish Encyclopedia*, 11:260.

[279] Flavius Josephus, *Josephus Complete Works* (trans. William Whiston. Grand Rapids: Kregel, 1978), 436.

[280] Singer, *The Jewish Encyclopedia*, 10:123.

[281] Emil Schurer, *A History of the Jewish People in the Time of Jesus Christ*. 5 vols. (trans. John Macpherson. Peabody, MA: Hendrickson, 2003), 1:322.

[282] Charles F. Pfeiffer, *Old Testament History* (Grand Rapids: Baker), 586.

[283] Henry Moeller, *The Legacy of Zion: Intertestamental Texts related to the New Testament* (Grand Rapids: Baker, 1977), 126.

[284] W. W. Sloan, *Between the Testaments* (Paterson, NJ: Littlefield, Adams & Co.), 58.

[285] Paolo Sacchi, *The History of the Second Temple Period* (Sheffield, England: Sheffield Academic Press, 2000), 270.

who evidently learned little from his grandfather, Nebuchadnezzar. This was the hand of God, not a lesser being, who wrote with his fingers.

In summary, all of the aforementioned references of the *Shechinah* glory of God reflect the conclusion that the *Shechinah* and the Messenger (Angel) of *Yahweh* are equal to, and yet distinct from, *Yahweh*. God appeared as a man (Genesis 18) and in the burning bush (Exodus 3) as the Messenger (Angel) of *Yahweh*. These two points are important, but the main emphasis is that God's personal presence was revealed. In other words, as the passages are examined, the terms for *Yahweh* and the theophanies of God are distinct from each other. The big question is: "Who is the Angel (Messenger) of *Yahweh*?" If God appeared in a localized place, then who was He? Christian scholars maintain that the Messenger (Angel) of *Yahweh* and other disclosures of God were the Second Person of the Godhead, God the Son, Jesus Christ. For example, Walvoord points out four reasons why the Messenger (Angel) of *Yahweh* is Messiah *Yeshua* and not the Father or the Holy Spirit:

1. The Second person is the visible God of the New Covenant (Jn 10:30).
2. The Angel of *Yahweh* no longer appears after the incarnation (Jn 5:36-38).[286]
3. Both the Angel of *Yahweh* and Messiah are sent by the Father.
4. In the process of elimination it could not be the Father, for the Father is the sender. Angel of *Yahweh* appears in a bodily form usually in human form: the Holy Spirit never has appeared in human or bodily form.[287]

When observing the theophanies of God, the words of John the Baptist in Jn 1:18 come to remembrance in relation to who has seen the Father:

No man hath seen God at any time; the only begotten Son, which is in the bosom of the Father, he hath declared him.

The words of *Yeshua* in Jn 14:9-11 declares that He is the exact representation of the Father, which parallels the author of Hebrews (1:1-3) who states that God has spoken through His Son. Because He was the Son being equal to the Father, on the Mount of Transfiguration, His glory was veiled in flesh at the time of His incarnation (Matt 17:1-8). The *Tanakh*, through the theophanies, is a rich source of information on the plurality of God. Minimally, with this rich source of biblical information from the *Tanakh*, the rabbis should have recognized the plurality of *Yahweh* as He presented Himself as different persons, equal, indivisible, yet a plurality.

---

[286] Isa 48:16 and Zech 2:8-9 say that Angel of *Yahweh* is sent by *Yahweh*. In John's gospel *Yeshua* clarifies that the Father sent Him; 3:34; 4:34; 5:23-24,30, 36-38; 6:29, 38-39, 44, 57; 7:16, 18, 28-29, 33; 8:16, 18, 26, 29, 42; 9:4; 10:36; 11:42; 12:44-45, 49; 13:20; 14:24; 15:21; 16:5, 27; 17:3, 8, 18, 21, 23, 25. These 40 references document that the Father sent Messiah into the world.
[287] John F. Walvoord, *Jesus Christ our Lord.* (Chicago: Moody, 1969), 44-46.

When the character and essence of God is examined in light of Lk 24:25-27, 44-48, it is clear that *Yeshua*, when speaking to the two disciples on the Emmaus Road, the Law, Prophets and Writings referred to Him:

> And beginning at Moses and all the Prophets, he expounded unto them in all the scriptures the things concerning himself (vs 27).

> These are the words which I spake unto you, while I was yet with you, that all things must be fulfilled, which were written in the law of Moses, and in the prophets, and in the psalms, concerning me. Then opened he their understanding, that they might understand the scriptures (vs 44-45).

Perhaps today, in this intellectual age, scholars have retreated from what *Yeshua* taught to His disciples on that eventful day. These verses apply to all that was said of *Yeshua* in the Law, Prophets and Writings. One of the many things that *Yeshua* would have related from the *Tanakh* was to show the disciples that He was the Messenger (Angel) of *Yahweh*, the *Shechinah* of God, as well as *Yahweh* and *Elohim*, the Creator and covenant-making God with Israel. What an awesome view of *Yeshua* in the Hebrew Scriptures that must have been. Based on the New Covenant, these persons in the Theophanies, in the form of man, Messenger (Angel) of *Yahweh*, *Shechinah* or God, are the pre-incarnate Messiah of Israel.[288]

All of the references of the *Shechinah* Glory of God, with the Messenger (Angel) of *Yahweh* references, amount to a heavy weight in substantiating the plurality or tri-unity of God. The Father and the Holy Spirit are never revealed in a physical form. Only the Second Person of the tri-unity appeared in human form as a theophany or as the *Shechinah* Glory of God.

---

[288] Enns, *The Moody Handbook of Theology*, 216.

CHAPTER 4

SHEMA

Hear, O Israel! The LORD is our God, the LORD alone. You shall love the LORD your God with all your heart and with all your soul and with all your might. Take to heart these instructions with which I charge you this day. Impress them upon your children. Recite them when you stay at home and when you are away, when you lie down and when you get up. Bind them as a sign on your hand and let them serve as a symbol on your forehead; inscribe them on the doorposts of your house and on your gates. [Deut. 6:4-9]

The *Shema* provides a statement of unity to both Jewish and Christian believers. God is one, indivisible, He is Israel's God and their full attention and worship is to be directed to Him alone. The focus of attention is verse four, "Hear, O Israel! The LORD is our God, the LORD alone (is one). But on occasion the *Shema* of Deut 6:4 presents conflict and disagreements on the nature of God. Whether *Yahweh* is "one" alone as Judaism believes, or whether *Yahweh* is a unity or tri-unity as Christianity believes, there is much contention in relation to the Hebrew word, *echad*. Even though Christianity accepts the belief in the tri-unity of God, many scholars as documented in this chapter, do not see the plurality or tri-unity of God in Deut 6:4.

Resolving the difficulty of this text calls for a five-fold analysis: (1) the Jewish view of God and how Judaism views the *Shema* in relationship to Christianity; (2) Christianity's struggles with the proper meaning of *echad*; (3) comments by Christian authors as to why or why not *echad* should be taken as one alone or as a tri-unity; (4) the significance of *yachid* in relationship to *echad*; (5) this writer's conclusions and observations on *echad*.

Judaism

The *Shema* of Deut 6:4-9 is the cornerstone of the Jewish faith. In studying the *Shema*, verse four in particular, the word translated "one" from the Hebrew אֶחָד (*echad*) must be analyzed. The Jewish concept of the unity of God is grounded on a particular understanding of this word, *echad*, in the *Shema*.

Judaism is emphatic about the unity and oneness of God. God is pure spirit, an incorporeal being and cannot, in any way, become a man. They see Christians as Tri-theists, dividing God into three persons. Making the incarnation of God as a man is irreconcilable in their mind. For example Jacobs a Jewish author states:

There is only one God and there are no others. Allied to this is the idea that God in His essence is indivisible. A deity like Baal could be split up, as it were, into various local deities, hence the plural form Baalim and Ashterot found in the Bible when speaking of the pagan gods.[289]

The polytheistic deities were thought of as separate beings, frequently in conflict with one another, each having a part of the universe for his or her domain. Monotheism denies the existence of such beings.[290]

Gerald Root comments that pagan mythology portrays each god as doing his or her own thing. However, there is no such conflict when there is one God. If there were many gods there would be no uniformity in the universe, whereas with *Yahweh* there is no such conflict. For example: If *Yahweh* is in charge today, and He has made light to travel at 186,000 miles per second, and if tomorrow another god is in control and he wants light to travel at 50,000 miles per second, the whole universe would be in complete chaos. That is only one example of untold myriads of possible illustrations. God must be God, with no rivals.[291]

Jacobs continues to state along with Weiss-Rosmarin the perception of Jewish scholars:

For many of them the idea of God's unity embraced the further idea that there is no multiplicity in His Being, that, as they expressed it, His was an "absolute simplicity."[292]

The Unity of God, sacred to Judaism beyond all else, is utterly irreconcilable with the Christian idea of the divisibility of the Divine Being and above all, with the belief in incarnation. According to Jewish belief God is pure spirit, eternally transcendent and divorced from even the slightest vestige of corporeality. Christianity, on the other hand, asserts that God became man in Jesus, a teaching which is contrary to the very spirit of Judaism.[293]

Is not this contrary to all Jewish teachings of God which emphasize and stress that God is not like man and can never become man or even resemble man?[294]

How, then, can the Jewish and Christian ideas of God be reconciled, or how can it be said that the "two religions are truly, basically one"? Is the One and Unique God, the absolute Unity – unknowable, indefinable – really the same as the Christian Trinity which divides the Unity of God into three, namely, God the Father, Jesus the Son and the Holy Spirit? Is the Jewish transcendent

---

[289] Jacobs, *A Jewish Theology*, 21.
[290] Jacobs, *A Jewish Theology*, 22.
[291] Gerald Root. "*A Critical Investigation of Deuteronomy 6:4*" (B.D. thesis, Grace Theological Seminary, 1964), 42.
[292] Jacobs, *A Jewish Theology*, 27.
[293] Weiss-Rosmarin, *Judaism and Christianity*, 21.
[294] Weiss-Rosmarin, *Judaism and Christianity*, 21.

and purely spiritual belief in a God in Whom there is no trace of matter and Who can never become corporeal really the same as Christian belief which glories in God "who made man?"[295]

Sometimes Christian authors like Erickson, make confusing statements that appear to support the Jewish concept of Christianity that God is divisible, a plurality. Erickson says that, "He (God) is an organism, that is, a unity of distinct parts."[296] Christianity has never embraced God as being three parts of a whole. Judaism cannot accept God becoming man, and equally Judaism cannot accept placing upon man divine qualities. This is reflected in Weiss-Rosmarin statements:

> Jewish Monotheism is not only the negation of the many gods but also the rejection of the personification of God on the one hand and of the deification of human beings on the other. Judaism's refusal to worship Jesus is therefore not only due to its repudiation of the doctrine of incarnation, the belief that God became a person, but equally so to its defiant resistance to all and any attempts of according Divine qualities and honors to mere mortals.[297]

> Catholicism as well as Protestantism worships persons and the images of persons. However, while Catholicism venerates in addition to Jesus a large and still expanding pantheon of Saints and their relics, besides devoting a special cult to the worship of the "Mother of God."[298]

Generally speaking, Jewish people view Christianity from the theological background of Roman Catholicism because it was the Church, under Roman leadership, that they primarily had to deal with in the past. It is primarily the Catholic Church's corrupt teaching that has dealt with them so treacherously over the centuries, but Protestants equally are not free from guilt in the negative treatment of Jewish people. To Judaism, God is a pure spirit being and it is inconceivable that a man could be God or that God would become man. Judaism holds, with unwavering dogmatism, that man is nothing more than man. Christians would completely agree with their assertion of man but differ in the Christian belief that God can become a man.

> To Judaism man is man and God is God and shall remain God in unequalled and eternal majesty.[299]

> The man Moses has been its watchword through the ages; thus it has warded off all attempts to enthrone any mortal as God. With equal consistency it has refused to admit the possibility of any man's sharing in God's perfection, or the incarnation of God in any human being.[300]

---

[295] Weiss-Rosmarin, *Judaism and Christianity*, 21-22.
[296] Erickson, *Introducing Christian Doctrine*, 100.
[297] Weiss-Rosmarin, *Judaism and Christianity*, 23.
[298] Weiss-Rosmarin, *Judaism and Christianity*, 24.
[299] Weiss-Rosmarin, *Judaism and Christianity*, 26.
[300] Weiss-Rosmarin, *Judaism and Christianity*, 27.

During the Middle Ages the Jewish assertion of God's unity became an explicit denial of the Christian dogma of the Trinity, a total disavowal of the thesis that God, though one, is somehow at the same time three persons, "co-eternal and co-equal."[301]

These statements reveal the antagonism of Judaism towards the Christian teaching on the Trinity, and rightly so, because of the unbiblical, anti-Semitic positions that the Church has held. The Church, through the Church Fathers, laid the foundation for the anti-Semitism that was practiced against the Jews for 1500 years.[302] One long quote suffices to reflect the hatred of the Jew by the Church, and even by great men of the Reformation. Martin Luther's quote is enough to point out the anti-Semitism of Christendom:

> First, he urged, "their synagogues should be set on fire, and whatever is left should be buried in dirt so that on one may ever be able to see a stone or cinder of it." Jewish prayer-books should be destroyed and rabbis forbidden to preach. Then the Jewish people should be dealt with, their homes "smashed and destroyed" and their inmates put under one roof or in a stable like gypsies, to teach them they are not master in our land". Jews should be banned from the roads and markets their property seized and then these "poisonous envenomed worms" should be drafted into forced labour and made to earn their bread "by the sweat of their noses."[303]

This is enough to set the tone for the unbiblical attitudes and actions of the Church for centuries. More could be written, but that is not the purpose of this book. The Jewish position, which was firm to begin with, became a granite rock. In summary, God is one to the Jewish people, period! To them, belief in the incarnation is inconceivable.

Christianity

Judaism views Paul, the Hellenized Pharisee, rather than *Yeshua*, as the founder of Christianity. Pryor points out that the New Covenant letters provide impressive evidence that the early first century believers in (Jewish) church had the highest Christology.[304] Peter was very clear in his letters that *Yeshua* is God (1 Pet 1:1-25; 2:21-24; 4:11; 2 Pet 1:16, 18) the Saviour, Redeemer and resurrected Lord. James spoke of himself as the "bond-servant" of *Yeshua* (1:1) and challenged his readers to "hold your faith in our glorious Lord Jesus Christ (2:1)." Jude is clear that *Yeshua* is Saviour: "be glory, majesty, dominion and authority, before all time and now and forever (v. 25)." John, in the first chapter of both his Gospel and in his First Epistle, clearly states that *Yeshua* is God. The theme of the writer of Hebrews is that *Yeshua* is better than the angels, Moses, priesthood and sacrifices. James, Peter, Jude, John and

---

[301] Milton Steinberg, *Basic Judaism* (New York: A Harvest/HBJ Book, 1947), 45.
[302] Stan Telchin, *Abandoned* (Grand Rapids, Baker Book House, 1997), 51-72.
[303] Paul Johnson, *A History of the Jews* (New York, HarperCollins, 1987), 242.
[304] Pryor, "One God and Lord," *Mishkan*, no. 39 (2003), 55.

the writer of Hebrews, who knew Paul, did not just copy Paul's theology, because they rarely saw each other. The early Jewish church knew who *Yeshua* was by living, teaching, and dying for their belief that *Yeshua* was the Messiah of Israel, the God/man.

The understanding of Deut 6:4, through the eyes of Christianity will differ depending on how the tri-unity of God is viewed in the Hebrew Scriptures. *Echad* has become somewhat of a difficult word to interpret, or has it been given a narrow restricted definition by Judaism because of the impact of Christian witness.

First, in considering verse four in the Hebrew, the *Shema* revolves around four words -- יְהוָה אֱלֹהֵינוּ יְהוָה אֶחָד (*LORD* our God, *LORD* is One). There is no problem in belief or interpretation with "*Shema* Israel." Nor is there a problem in belief or interpretation with יְהוָה אֱלֹהֵינוּ ("LORD our God") except the way *Elohenu* is viewed ("our Gods" or "God"). *Yahweh* is Israel's personal name for their God *Elohim*, who is the Creator and the covenant maker! The major problem lies with יְהוָה אֶחָד ("LORD is one,") that God is "one" in regard to interpretation which will effect belief. *Yahweh* is One, but the difficulty is what is meant by "one."

Although Herbert Wolf suggests that the lexical and syntactical difficulties of יְהוָה אֶחָד ("LORD is one") are evident in numerous translations, all aspects of the challenge can be represented by four common translations. The "LORD is one" is translated four different ways, which incorporates each specific aspect of their interpretation.

The first view of Deut 6:4 is "the LORD is our God, the LORD alone."[305] His explanation of his option above is that it has in its favor both the broad and immediate context of the book of Deuteronomy. The *Shema* serves as the introduction to motivate Israel to keep the command to love the LORD (v. 5). This notion suits this command in v. 5 very well because the LORD is Israel's unique God Who stands alone, along with Israel's obligation to love that God.

The second view of Deut 6:4 expresses the interpretation as LORD our God: LORD is unique (only one).[306] Lohfink and Bergmann state that *echad* should be understood as "only one," or "unique one." This is one God who led them, loved them (Deut 5:10) and gave them the law. God did it without the help of foreign gods (Deut 32:12). The *Shema* saw Israel's obligation to respond to this unique God in love by being obedient to the Law or Decalog. Points one and two seem to be very close in their views.

The third view of Deut 6:4 of looking at the *Shema* is "the LORD our God, the LORD is one." Jenson points out that:

---

[305] Harris, Archer, and Waltke, *Theological Wordbook of the Old Testament*, 1:30.
[306] Botterweck, Ringgren, and Fabry. *Theological Dictionary of the Old Testament*, 1:196.

The syntax of the verbless sentence is disputed, but analogy with other uses of "LORD our God" in Deut suggests that the traditional syntax should be retained ("The LORD our God, the LORD is One").[307]

He points out further that "one" is not a title or name of God but an adjective of quality. The correlation between the two halves of Deut 6:4 suggests that the interpretation of *Shema* is not pointed against the polytheism of the day or to a non-abstract monotheism, but it is a claim to Israel's total obedience to the exclusion of all others.

The last view of Deut 6:4 says, the LORD our God, the LORD is a unity of one.[308] The essence of oneness is linked to the *Shema*, and the *echad* is a compound or complex unity, a united one. This view not only includes the uniqueness and oneness of God but also the unity of God expressed in three persons. This oneness, yet a compound unity, possesses the summation of all divine attributes which in their essence are undivided. These three persons of the tri-unity do not act independently of one another.

All four of the above positions hold to a basic truth that God is "one alone," "unique one," the only one to be loved and worshipped. The last one agrees with the other three but adds the dimension that all that was said of the other three is true. It adds that God is a compound or complex unity, and the word *echad* expresses that interpretation (Gen 1:5, 2:24).

McConville gives the same points for possible interpretation but says nothing concerning the unity of God of how the word *echad* is used. However, he does give two additional helpful points in determining how the word is used but again with not conclusions:

> Between the other renderings the chief difference concerns whether to translate *echad* as an adjective, "one," or an adverb "alone."

> It differs from the First Commandment (Deut 5:7) in that the emphasis falls heavily on the word "one."[309]

He states that the problem of how *echad* is to be translated, whether as an adjective or as an adverb is at the center of the question, but he gives no conclusion. But he also admits that the emphasis, the thrust, the focus of the verse is on *echad*. This does not conclude the unity of God and plurality, but he does reinforce the fact that this word *echad* is the focus of attention by Moses. This author believes the key to understanding the verse is to see just how this word *echad* is used first by Moses and then by the rest of the *Tanakh* (See appendix 2 concerning the usage of *echad* in the Torah).

---

[307] VanGemeren, *Dictionary of Old Testament Theology and Exegesis*, 1:350.
[308] Enns, *The Moody Handbook of Theology*, 199-200.
[309] J. G. McConville, *Apollos Old Testament Commentary: Deuteronomy* (Downer Grove, IL: InterVarsity, 2002), 140-142.

In the preceding paragraphs it was observed that *echad* is interpreted four ways. Now the usages of this word will be observed. *Echad* is used 970 times throughout the Hebrew Scriptures.[310] What is meant by this word? Does the word indicate one of unity, one alone, or one of uniqueness? Smith says that the precise meaning is unclear.[311] That is seen from the previous paragraph with the four possible usages of *echad*. Do those who believe in the tri-unity read too much into *echad*? The immediate context of the word in the book of Deuteronomy requires that *Yahweh* is the one and only God and Israel's personal God.[312] Both Judaism and Christianity would not disagree with this view. Evans has noted that *echad*, which expresses the unity of the Godhead, is not simple but compound and is always used to describe a divine unity.[313]

According to Payne the *Shema* teaches that:

This passage does not primarily concern a divine unity of simplicity; that God constitutes a unity within Himself, in contrast, for example, with Baal, who was splintered up so as to exist separately in countless individual plots of ground (hence the plural, the Baalim). It concerns rather the divine unity of singularity; that God constitutes the sole deity, as opposed to others, which is the essence of monotheism.[314]

Verse five, which says to "Love the LORD thy God with all thine heart," is only relevant because God is the only one.[315] The *Tanakh*, as it recorded the Prophets and the Writings, affirms the fact of Moses' monotheism. The people, however, as a whole, did not love the Lord because they worshipped other gods and did not worship God alone.

Usages of *Echad*

Janzen's article, is devoted to the *Shema*, but fails to show the importance of *echad* in the *Shema*. The *Shema* is the most significant verse that *echad* appears in and the question is how is it interpreted in the *Shema*? Other references to *echad* throughout the *Tanakh* should be analyzed in relation to its immediate context so that the Deut 6:4 passage can be clearly understood as to whether it is one or a compound unity. Upon reading Janzen's article, this most important word (*echad*) is not dealt with in relation to the issue of oneness and/or compound unity as it relates to the *Shema*. He refers to *echad* in several passages in the *Tanakh* without any relationship to the immediate context (Deut 6:4). He does seem to embrace *echad* as being one "alone." He consistently refers to the broader context of Deut 6:4-5. Janzen's article lacks evidence of a

---

[310] Jenni and Westermann, *Theological Lexicon of the Old Testament*, 1:79.

[311] Ralph L. Smith, *Old Testament Theology its History, Method, and Message* (Nashville: Broadman and Holman, 1993), 226-227.

[312] Botterweck, Ringgren, and Fabry. *Theological Dictionary of the Old Testament*, 1:196.

[313] William Evans, *The Great Doctrines of the Bible*. (Chicago: Moody, 1974), 26-27.

[314] Payne, *The Theology of the Older Testament*, 126.

[315] Payne, *The Theology of the Older Testament*, 126.

biblical study of the word *echad* and how it is used in the *Tanakh* and in the *Shema* and elsewhere.[316]

An analysis of the Hebrew Scriptures uncovers three distinct usages of the term *echad*. The word *echad* is first used as a compound unity.[317] It is two separate persons becoming an *echad*, a unity in Gen 2:24 which says, "Therefore shall a man leave his father and his mother, and shall cleave unto his wife; and they shall be one (*echad*) flesh." Gen 11:1 applies the same concept to language: "And the whole earth as of one (*echad*) language, and of one speech." All humanity had *echad* speech. The spies, upon returning from Canaan in Num 13:23, brought with them a cluster (*echad*) of grapes. Exod 24:3, Judg 20:1 and Ezra 3:1 picture the nation of Israel answering God with one (*echad*) voice and gathering before the Lord as one (*echad*) man. In Ezek 37:17, 19, 22, Ezekiel is told by God to put together two sticks as an *echad* stick, "And join them one to another into one (*echad*) stick . . . even with the stick of Judah, and make them one (*echad*) stick, ... and I will make them one (*echad*) nation in the land." The two sticks represented the houses of Israel and Judah being joined together, in the future, as one *echad* nation. Other references that support two separate units becoming one are found in Gen 34:22, Exod 25:36, Num 14:15, Josh 10:42, 1 Sam 11:7b, 1 Kgs 22:13b, 2 Chr 5:13, 30:12, Neh 8:1, Prov 1:14, Jer 32:39 and Mal 2:10. Although this "unity" concept of *echad* is used the least in number of all three divisions mentioned at the beginning of the paragraph, yet it has become the focal point in discussions of Deut 6:4.

A second way *echad* is used is to show things or persons in relationships that do not require a compound unity, as in the first category.[318] However, it is still within a plural context, as in Exod 17:12: "But Moses' hands were heavy; and they took a stone and put it under him, and he sat thereon; and Aaron and Hur stayed up his hands, the one (*echad*) on the one side, and the other (*echad*) on the other side and his hands were steady until the going down of the sun."

The same *echad* is also applied to offerings. In Lev 12:8, for example, sacrificial animals are considered *echad*: "And if she be not able to bring a lamb, then she shall bring two turtledoves, or two young pigeons; the one (*echad*) for the burnt offering and the other (*echad*) for a sin offering." Samson, in Judg 16:29, also uses the context of plurality where it says he "took hold of the two middle pillars upon which the house stood, and on which it was borne up of the one (*echad*) with his right hand, and the other (*echad*) with his left." After David's sin with Bathsheba, Nathan comes before David with the story in 2 Sam 12:1 of two men in a city, "one (*echad*) was rich and other (*echad*) poor." These references are all illustrated in the context of plurality but not in a compound unity. Other references show the same concept (Gen 21:15; Exod 25:19; Num 6:11; Deut 21:15; Josh 4:2; 1 Sam 1:2; 1 Kgs 3:25; 2 Kgs 6:5; 1 Chr 29:1 and 2 Chr 3:17). This usage of *echad* is used more frequently than the other two.

---

[316] J. Gerald Janzen, "On The Most Important Word In The Shema (Deuteronomy VI 4-5)," *Vetus Testamentum* 37, 3 (1987): 280-300.

[317] Harris, Archer, and Waltke, *Theological Wordbook of the Old Testament*, 1:30.

[318] VanGemeren, *Dictionary of Old Testament Theology and Exegesis*, 1:349.

A third way *echad* is used is to indicate the separateness, individuality, of a thing or person. This division will be reflected in three parts and the first denotes one standing by itself.[319] The second as in Joshua demonstrates a cardinal 'one' as he enumerates the kings one by one (Josh 12:9-24). The third is used as an ordinal (first or first one) number as seen in Exod 40:17 when the Tabernacle was set up on the *echad* or first day of the first month.[320] Additional passages that demonstrate this third type of *echad's* include: (Gen 33:13; Exod 23:29;Lev 23:18; Num 7:13-82; Deut 17:6; Josh 12:9-24; Judg 9:53; 1 Sam 26:8; 2 Sam 12:3; 1 Kgs 2:16; 11:13; 2 Kgs 8:26; 2 Chr 18:7). An interesting factor is that even when *echad* is used as an individual one, its context often is dealing with two or more of something. The term is usually referring to a singular object, but it is also used in the context of many. In the three passages of Num 7:11-82 (85), 29:1-38 (24) and Josh 12:9-24 (32) the cardinal one is mentioned a total of 141 times in an individual sense.

With these three factors in mind, how do scholars interpret *echad* in Deut 6:4? It seems that the oneness of God is not the question, but the compound unity and plurality of God is the area of discussion.

Comments by Christian Authors on *Echad*:

This section is divided into two parts: those who do not see and those who do see the plurality (or tri-unity) of God in Hebrew Scriptures, and in particular, Deut 6:4. Christian authors are divided over the interpretation of the term *echad*, except that Moses is affirming the oneness, uniqueness, and the unity of God. Only with a passing notice do they say that *echad* may mean a compound one of unity. Herbert Wolf states that *echad* is singular, but the usage of the word *echad* in the *Shema* allows for the New Testament teaching of the Trinity. The doctrine of the Trinity is foreshadowed in the Hebrew Scriptures, but this verse concentrates on the fact that God is one and that Israel owes its exclusive loyalty to Him (Deut 5:9; 6:5).[321] Wolf merely speaks of compound unity, along with other possible usages of the word.

Echad not seen as Compound Unity

Lohfink and Bergman basically say that Deut 6:4 is to be regarded as a reiteration of the love motif in Deut 5:10 which states, "but showing kindness to the thousandth generation of those who love Me and keep My commandments:"

> The demand for love is itself one of the many formulations of the fundamental demand made on Israel to worship *Yahweh* alone and not any of the other gods.[322]

---

[319] Harris, Archer, and Waltke, *Theological Wordbook of the Old Testament*, 1:30.
[320] VanGemeren, *Dictionary of Old Testament Theology and Exegesis*, 1:349.
[321] Harris, Archer, and Waltke, *Theological Wordbook of the Old Testament*, 1:30.
[322] Botterweck, Ringgren and Fabry. *Theological Dictionary of the Old Testament*, 1:196.

These two scholars continue by saying that Deut 6:4 can be interpreted as two nominative sentences in sequence. This means that *"Yahweh our God,"* is taken and pressed to mean that God, though plural, is to be taken as singular, and the second half of the passage, *"Yahweh is one"* is used to express this God as being one. They also mention that it could be taken as one nominative sentence, with three different possibilities, as to subject and predicate:

> That Deuteronomy 6:4 contains a 'mono-Yahwistic' statement: a statement made in opposition to dividing *Yahweh* into many local individual *Yahwehs*.[323]

Lohfink and Bergman do not even discuss the possibility of a compound unity. They emphasize only the oneness, uniqueness, and unity of God.

Philip Jenson refers to five usages of *echad* in the Hebrew text. He claims that the *Shema* is not intended to do three things as referenced in the statement below, but that it does affirm monotheism. However, no hint is even given to the placement of the *Shema* into the category of a compound unity in his summary statement:

> The correlation between the two halves of the sentence and the following verses suggests that this is not so much an abstract monotheism as a claim to Israel's total obedience and the exclusion of any other (cf. 5:7). The immediate context does not suggest that it is directed against polytheism or different ideas of *Yahweh* found in local cults. Nor is this idea used to support the Deut. program of the centralization of worship. However, in the broader context of Deut and the OT it can imply unity, uniqueness, and monotheism.[324]

Sauer, in *Theological Lexicon of the Old Testament*, says that Deut 6:4 may refer to God as a cardinal one. He gives two possible translations to the last phrase: *"is one Yahweh"* or *"Yahweh is one* (alone)." His summary statement says that this passage "most clearly expresses *Yahweh's* unity and exclusivity" and that the statement "is embedded in the commandment to love this unique LORD."[325]

While the authors have helpful information, they do not interact with the relationship between *Yahweh* and *Elohim* or *echad* with *Yahweh* and *Elohim*. They look at *echad* within the larger context of the Hebrew Scriptures to determine its possible usage in Deut 6:4. They all affirm the unity, oneness and uniqueness of God. But in the opinion of this author, they do not even give *echad* a look as to the possibility of the plurality of God within their interpretations.

Other authors say little, either pro or con. Enns, as an example, simply states that the essence of God is linked to Deut 6:4 with *echad* being a compound unity or united one. There is no real explanation of how he arrived at that position.[326]

---

[323] Botterweck, Ringgren and Fabry. *Theological Dictionary of the Old Testament*, 1:197.
[324] VanGemeren, *Dictionary of Old Testament Theology and Exegesis*, 1:349-350.
[325] Jenni and Westermann, *Theological Lexicon of the Old Testament*, 1:79.
[326] Enns, *The Moody Handbook of Theology*, 199-200.

Peter Craige speaks to the fact that *echad* can be rendered in a number of different ways, stating that one could be a title or name of God. He affirms the uniqueness and unity of God but says nothing about the possibility of *echad* being a compound one.[327]

Eugene Merrill does not deal with *echad* as a compound unity. But he makes this interesting observation of the text:

> The Divine Name should be construed as a nominative in each case and the terms "our God" and "one" as parallel predicate nominatives.[328]

This statement is saying that "LORD," in both cases, is nominative and "our God" and "one" is the predicate. The predicate describes the LORD as (1) *Elohim* and (2) as one. The two words describe, or are reflective of, the nominative. He drops the statement at that point and does not explain what he was trying to establish. This subject and explanation is again discussed at the end of this chapter.

David Hinson does not deal with *echad* as a compound unity. He simply affirms the concept of God being a unity. However, Hinson raises an interesting question:

> But is there any evidence that people of Old Testament times began to share in thoughts which would gradually lead to the New Testament doctrine of the Trinity? Did God provide them with experiences which would prepare the way for belief in the Trinity? Were they, without full realization, experiencing God the Trinity?[329]

Hinson follows up the previous remarks with three sections on wisdom, the Word of God and the Spirit of God, which is helpful information. But it was also very disappointing because he does not deal with *Elohim*, *El*, *Eloah*, *Yahweh*, and Lord in their relationship to each other. His defining statement is:

> Some readers may ask why God's revelation of himself in Old Testament times omitted the idea of the Trinity. The answer seems to be that the Jews needed first to grasp the truth about the Unity of God.[330]

The whole point of the *Tanakh* is that God did not omit the idea of the plurality and tri-unity from the pages of the Hebrew Scriptures.

Reginald Fuller clearly reveals his mockery and unbelief in relationship to the Scriptures. However, he does make one very helpful statement concerning Judaism moving toward recognizing distinction within the Godhead:

---

[327] P. C. Craigie, *The New International Commentary on the Old Testament: The Book of Deuteronomy*; Grand Rapids: Eerdmans, 1976), 168-169.
[328] Eugene Merrill, *The New American Commentary*. (vol. 4. Nashville: Broadman & Holman, 1994), 4:163.
[329] Hinson, *Theology of the Old Testament*, 50.
[330] Hinson, *Theology of the Old Testament*, 49.

But already the Judaic tradition was moving to the direction of recognizing distinctions within the activity of God. These activities included creation, revelation/redemption, and indwelling presence. It was also moving in the direction of distinctions within the being of God, distinctions corresponding to these activities, ascribing them to the Wisdom of Word (logos) and the Spirit of God. Judaism did not go very far in this direction, but the direction was certainly established. The Christian community was impelled to move much further, though still in the same direction. Thus it eventually developed the doctrine of the Trinity. This development was not a deviation from the Hebrew Scriptures but a continuation of a process already begun. On the other hand, those who remained under the first covenant backtracked from this line of development.[331]

His comments on Judaic tradition moving in the direction of recognizing distinctions within the activity of God would be an extremely interesting subject to follow through. What did Fuller see in his research that prompted his remarks? That will have to be a future study. The first century believers in Messiah did clearly see the distinctions in the Godhead.

Marvin Wilson gives some valuable information on the *Shema* and its background from the Intertestament period and during the life and times of *Yeshua*. Wilson is strong on the unity of God but not on the compound unity. His defining statement is:

In the Old Testament *echad* usually refers to a single unit, such as a person. Certain interpreters have insisted, however, that *echad* may also be used to designate a collective unit (Gen. 1:5; 2:24; Num. 13:23), a diversity with unity. Thus some Christian scholars have found room for trinitarian monotheism in the *echad* of Deuteronomy 6:4. So interpreted, God is seen as a complex unity, not simply as numerically one. It must be remembered, however, that the main focus of the *Shema* in its original setting – ancient Near Eastern polytheism – is clearly upon the fact that there is one God. (Deut. 4:39).[332]

It is true that the original setting was clearly to promote monotheism, but to say that it rules out the possibility of a compound or complex unity is unwarranted.

Although Paul House states that *Yahweh* is unique and possesses a unified character, he makes no mention of God being a compound one.[333]

Ernest Wright, in the *Interpreter's Bible*, holds the *Shema* to be a statement of "Israel's exclusive attention, affection, and worship and is not diffused, but single."[334] He affirms the unity and oneness of God.

---

[331] Reginald H. Fuller, "The *Vestigia Trinitatis* in the Old Testament," in *The Quest for Context and Meaning* (ed. Craig A. Evans and Shemaryahu Talmon, Leiden, Netherlands: Brill, 1997), 507.

[332] Marvin R. Wilson, *Our Father Abraham*. (Grand Rapids: Eerdmans, 1989), 125.

[333] House, *Old Testament Theology*, 178.

[334] George Arthur Buttrick, *The Interpreter's Bible*. (Nashville: Abingdon, 1953), 2:372-373.

The *Shema* is of great importance, not just for the Jewish people and the whole discussion of the oneness and unity of God, but also for Christians discussing the theological impact of this verse, "Hear, O Israel! The LORD is our God, the LORD alone." It is surprising that many Christian scholars do not generally acknowledge as a legitimate argument that *echad* is a compound or complex unity of God. Apparently these scholars deem *echad*, and the truth of God as being a compound or complex unity to be unimportant, based on their concept of how *Elohim* and the tri-unity of God is treated, in general, by many Christian scholars, as has been pointed out earlier in this book.

Echad Seen As Compound Unity

Some authors do acknowledge that the *Shema* presents God simultaneously as both "one" and a compound unity. A select group of scholars openly acknowledge the fact of the compound unity of God and even state that emphatically, but it is often without support. Gerald Root, in his thesis on Deut 6:4, makes several statements that only deal with the unity of God.

> The answer is this: the verse emphasizes the unity of God rather than the Trinity, but it does not deny God's Triunity. The verse does not concern itself with the question and neither affirms nor denies the Trinity.[335]

> If God is One, in what sense is He One? He is one (אֶחָד) God but three Persons. The normal usage of this word allows such an interpretation.[336]

In referring to Gen 2:24; 11:6; and Exodus 24:3 which all deal with *echad* as being a compound unity, he says:

> It is evident that that word cannot be restricted to the sense of only or alone.[337]

Root is not avoiding the compound unity of God, but he does not come out strongly for it, even though he goes much further than the previous texts cited. Here is his statement of summary for his position:

> It was God's choice of the word to lead Israel away from idolatry and emphasize His unity, and yet elastic enough to permit a far greater revelation of Himself at a later time. Nor could the argument be used that this word has not as of this time obtained this particular meaning, for it was used long before and after God's revelation in Deuteronomy 6:4.[338]

---

[335] Root, "*A Critical Investigation of Deuteronomy 6:4*," 38.
[336] Root, "*A Critical Investigation of Deuteronomy 6:4*," 38.
[337] Root, "*A Critical Investigation of Deuteronomy 6:4*," 39.
[338] Root, "*A Critical Investigation of Deuteronomy 6:4*," 40.

Root presents the oneness of God very strongly and the compound unity of God in an open meaningful manner, but without commitment.

When speaking of *echad*, Thomas A. Thomas strongly presents not just the unity of God, but the compound unity of God. He points out that there are two ways to look at *echad*:

> There are at least two senses in which the word one can be used; namely, first of all, in the sense of a compound unity, or, in the second place, in the sense of a single unit; that is, either more than one object composing a whole, or the whole being made up of only a single object. The question, then, is, in which of these two senses is the word אֶחָד to be taken?[339]

He discusses Gen 2:24, Num 13:23 and Judg 20:1 as examples to support a compound unity. His defining statement is:

> It is clearly the term used to express compound unity. Consequently, then, it is quite possible that when Moses declares in Deuteronomy 6:4 "Hear, O Israel: the Lord our God is one (אֶחָד) Lord" he is using the term in this sense. God is one, it is true, but why not in the sense that a man and his wife are one, and the cluster of grapes is one, or as the whole congregation of Israel is one? There is no internal reason why it could not be so used.[340]

Lewis Sperry Chafer clearly raises the two possible views of *echad*: First, he states that God is One and there is no other. Secondly, he cites Gen 1:5; 2:24 as a possibility that *echad* is a compound unity.[341] Chafer simply raises the issue and then drops it, without further explanation.

Jim Nixon points out that Deut 6:4 allows for the plurality of God. He further says that it does not teach the tri-unity of God but the plurality of God.[342] His position is that the *Shema* teaches exclusive monotheism, the total denial of any other, as well as being plural.[343]

Henry Heydt, former president of Lancaster School of the Bible, states very clearly his position on the *Shema* by affirming the oneness and compound oneness with *echad* in the following statement:

> The Jew does not understand the Christian doctrine of the Trinity (tri-unity) because he does not understand the teaching of his own Scriptures on unity.

---

[339] Thomas A. Thomas, *"The Trinity in the Old Testament"* (Th.M. thesis., Dallas Theological Seminary, 1952), 4-5.

[340] Thomas, *"The Trinity in the Old Testament,"* 7.

[341] Chafer, *Chafer Systematic Theology,* 1:266-267.

[342] Jim Nixon, *"The Doctrine of the Trinity in the Old Testament"* (Th. M. thesis., Dallas Theological Seminary, 1974), 11-12.

[343] Nixon, *"The Doctrine of the Trinity in the Old Testament,"* 22-23.

There are two kinds of oneness, absolute oneness and compound oneness, and the Hebrew has two words to express these. The word for absolute oneness is *yachid*.[344] (Gen. 22:2, 12, 16)

Stan Rosenthal,[345] Lewis Goldberg,[346] Arnold Fruchtenbaum[347] and Robert Morris[348] take Deut 6:4 and show it as a compound unity of God in the Hebrew Scriptures. They see *Elohim* as a plurality of God and *echad* as a complex or compound unity of God. The next three authors were the only three men who dealt with the issue of the plurality of God in a concrete detailed manner. The others have said either nothing or only elude to a compound unity, or made strong statements in its favor. But even those who made strong statements of belief did not give a comprehensive study of *echad*.

In dealing with two Jewish objections to the tri-unity of God, Michael Brown presents Deut 6:4 in a detailed apologetic format, on the plurality and tri-unity of God in conjunction with *echad*.[349] One example shows some of the interpretative problems that come with absolute oneness, which is the rabbinic approach:

> The rabbis spoke much about the *shekhina*, the Divine Presence, corresponding also to the feminine, motherly aspects of God. They taught that the *Shekhina* went into exile with the Jewish people, suffering with "her" children in foreign lands. According to this concept, God cannot be "whole" again until his people return from their physical and spiritual wanderings and the Temple is rebuilt. The rabbis based this idea on verses that spoke of God being with his people (corporately or individually) in their trouble, distress, and exile.[350]

This explanation of the Jewish people says that God is divisible and will not be whole again until Israel, as a nation, is re-gathered from every nation on earth and reestablished in the Land. So much for God being a unity and indivisible! If God is not a complex unity, how can He be one when He is divided?

David L. Cooper presents a strong, detailed and comprehensive case for the tri-unity of God in the Hebrew Scriptures and for *echad* being a compound unity. He believes in verbal plenary inspiration. Therefore he deals with the Hebrew text by letting Scripture, interpret Scripture, letting God reveal Himself as He chose. In Cooper's book, *What Men Must Believe*, the chapter on "The Unity of the Divine Personalities," gives a biblical argument for the tri-unity of God, as well as the *Shema*, not only proving monotheism but compound unity as well. Cooper illustrates, with *Elohim*, one of the other words used in Deut 6:4. Moses knew that *Elohim* is plural, so

---

[344] Henry Heydt, *Studies in Jewish Evangelism* (New York: American Board to the Jews, 1951), 124.
[345] Rosenthal, *One God or Three?* 17-26.
[346] Goldberg, *Our Jewish Friends*, 80-83.
[347] Fruchtenbaum, *Messianic Christology*, 108.
[348] Morris, *Anti-Missionary Arguments: The Trinity*, 14-16.
[349] Brown, *Answering Jewish Objections*, 2:3-37.
[350] Brown, *Answering Jewish Objections*, 2:12.

why didn't he use *El* or *Eloah* instead of *Elohenu* (אֱלֹהֵינוּ), "our Gods?" *Elohim* is grammatically incorrect as it is in many places when it is followed by singular verbs.[351]

Robert Morey compares the Unitarian and Trinitarian viewpoints of the Scriptures in relationship to God. He observes that if God is one, a solitary person, then it would be expected that the authors of Scripture would use the Hebrew word יָחִיד (*yachid*). If that were the case, it would be very damaging to the Trinitarian view. However, what is found is that the word for God is never used with יָחִיד.[352] Instead, what is found is that אֶחָד (*echad*) is used in connection with God. Morey states that אֶחָד is the only available Hebrew word they could use to express the idea of compound or complex one.[353] So, once again, if the authors of Scripture believed God was a plurality or tri-unity, then one would be expected to find the usage of אֶחָד to express a multi-personal God over against a God who was one alone.

If, in the *Shema*, Moses was teaching monotheism alone, as Judaism states, then why didn't Moses do one of the following in his presentation of God? (1) Why didn't he use correct grammar by using the correct singular forms for God by using *Yahweh* our *El* or *Eloah*? Was the use of *Elohim* a mistake or was Moses guided by the *Ruach haKodesh* as he penned the *Shema*? (2) Why did Moses choose to use a plural concept for one rather than a singular concept of God?

Yachid - יָחִיד

The differences between *echad* and *yachid* are significant in the *Tanakh, echad* minimally means unity, a unity involving a plurality. Whereas *yachid*'s meaning is to express absolute oneness, one standing by itself, alone. *Yachid* suits that purpose very well. *Yachid* יָחִיד appears 12 times in the Law, Prophets and Writings of the Hebrew text. It is used five times in reference to an only son (Zech 12:10), three times in reference to a child (Judg 11:34), twice in reference to being "lonely" (Ps 68:6), and twice in reference to "your precious life" (Ps 22:20).[354] Paul Gilchrist says that this word "basically refers to an only child," and its basic meaning is "only begotten son, beloved, with secondary meanings of isolated and lonely."[355] In reference to life, Brown, Driver and Briggs say:

> My only one, for my life, as the one unique and priceless possession which cannot be replaced.[356]

---

[351] Cooper, *What Men Must Believe*, 113.
[352] Morey, *The Trinity: Evidence and Issues*, 88.
[353] Morey, *The Trinity: Evidence and Issues*, 89.
[354] John R. Kohlenberger III and James A. Swanson, *The Hebrew English Concordance to the Old Testament* (Grand Rapids: Zondervan, 1998), 697.
[355] Harris, Archer, and Waltke, *Theological Wordbook of the Old Testament*, 372.
[356] Francis Brown, S. R. Driver, and Charles A. Briggs, *A Hebrew and English Lexicon of the Old Testament* (Oxford: Clarendon Press, n.d.), 402.

The word *yachid* comes into play because of Moses Maimonides (1135-1204 CE), who is also called Rambam. He was a philosopher, a Torah and Talmud scholar who wrote many commentaries as well as practiced medicine. One of the things that Maimonides wrote was the 13 principles of the Jewish faith.[357] The second principle is as follows:

> I believe with perfect faith that God is one. There is no unity that is in anyway like His. He alone is our God – He was, He is, and He will be.[358]

As Maimonides (Ramban) wrote the second principle of faith, he substituted *yachid* for *echad* in Deut 6:4 of the Hebrew text. He clearly recognized that *yachid* contradicted the Christians use of *echad* to prove the tri-unity of God. A Jewish believer in Israel reflects on Ramban's thoughts and why he replaced *echad* with *yachid*:

> For Rambam, the term *echad* allowed for elements of personal complexity within the Godhead which he had excluded a prioi for philosophical reasons. As used in the *Tanakh*, *echad* is the word of choice to express the unification of two or more elements to form one entity. Whether it is "the evening and the morning" combining to form "one day," (Gen 1:5) male and female becoming "one flesh" (Gen 2:24), or Ezekiel's two sticks becoming "one stick" in his hand (37:17), a compound unity is the result.

> Thus, by describing the Lord as *echad*, the *Shema* does not exclude complexity within the essential divine unity. As Rambam understood, the term falls far short of asserting an absolute philosophical unity.[359]

It is also important to note the comment by Robinson "that his (Maimonides') attempts to unite Aristole and Torah had a profound influence on his Christian contemporaries."[360] Did men like Maimonides and Rashi (1040–1105 CE)[361] have an impact on Christianity by obscuring the full significance of *Elohim* and *echad*? It is known that Rashi did change the interpretation of the Suffering Servant and His relationship to the Jewish understanding of Isaiah 53. Today the Jewish position on Deut 6:4 is that God is *yachid*, an absolute one. If Moses was teaching complete absolute monotheism, then Deut 6:4 should have the following reading:

> *Yahweh* our *Eloah* or *El* [God], *Yahweh* is *yachid* (absolute one), instead of *Yahweh* our *Elohenu* [our Gods], *Yahweh* is *echad* (compound unity)

The first statement reflects the meaning taught by Maimonides. The second statement reflects the meaning as taught by Moses. There is quite a difference. Moses was

---

[357] Robinson, *Essential Judaism*, 415-421.

[358] Robinson, *Essential Judaism*, 416.

[359] Noam Hendren, "The Divine Unity and the Deity of the Messiah," *Mishkan*, no. 39 (2003), 38.

[360] Robinson, *Essential Judaism*, 420.

[361] Rashi (Rabbi Shelomo Yitzkhaki): was an extraordinary Torah and Talumdic scholar. He was fluent in many languages, an accomplished poet, and a skilled philologist. He wrote many commentaries on the Torah. Today his commentaries are part of the Talmud itself.

guided by the *Ruach haKodesh* in what he wrote; Maimonides was not! The consequential differences between *echad* and *yachid* are made quite clear by scholars like Chafer,[362] Rosenthal,[363] Heydt,[364] Goldberg,[365] Brown,[366] Fruchtenbaum,[367] Cooper,[368] Benach,[369] and Criswell.[370] As the result of studying the Hebrew language and making *aliyah* to Israel, Moshe Golden shared the invaluable insight that in Modern Hebrew *yachid* is a compound "one" and *echad* is an absolute "one," which is just the opposite of the Hebrew Scriptures. So the true meaning of Scripture is once again obscured from the modern Jewish reader.

Author's Position on *Echad*

A careful analysis of *echad* in the Hebrew Scriptures clarifies that the term signifies unity in the context of plurality. The context of Deuteronomy and the *Torah*, as a whole, is to present God as one. Yet sprinkled throughout the text of the *Torah* and the *Tanakh*, monotheism is conceptualized as a unity of persons equal in nature and essence but with differing activities. Interwoven throughout the *Tanakh* are clear instances with abundant evidence of the plurality of God. Abundant evidence of that plurality is found in repeated instances of the plural word *Elohim*, as well as theophanies, and the Messenger (Angel) of *Yahweh* and the *Shechinah* of God. Included are personal pronouns and plural descriptions that God uses of Himself, which are discussed in the next chapter.

Walter Zimmerli confirms the use of plural unity of the verb *echad* in Ezekiel 21 (16) by stating that the only way this word makes any sense in the context of Ezekiel 21:21 is to see it as a plural compound of unity.[371] He simply says that it "gives no satisfactory sense unless understood from אֶחָד (*echad*)"[372] It was noted earlier in chapter two that one possible way of interpreting *Shema* is to see *Yahweh* in Deut 6:4, as a nominative, while *Elohim* and *echad* are predicates of the nominative, or descriptive of the nominative.[373] If *Elohim* is a plural description of God, as was pointed out in chapter two, then it makes complete sense that *echad*, being a compound unity, also expresses a plurality. The text would look like this:

---

[362] Chafer, *Systematic Theology*, 1:267.

[363] Rosenthal, *One God or Three?* 21.

[364] Heydt, *Studies in Jewish Evangelism*, 125.

[365] Goldberg, *Our Jewish Friends*, 81-82.

[366] Brown, *Answering Jewish Objections*, 2:4.

[367] Arnold A. Fruchtenbaum, *The Trinity – Manuscript #50*, (Tustin, Cal: Ariel Ministries, 1983), 11-12.

[368] Cooper, *The God of Israel*, 44-57.

[369] Henry Benach, *Go To Learn* (Chattanooga: International Board of Jewish Missions, 1997), 20-22, 48-50.

[370] W. A. Criswell, *The Criswell Study Bible* (Nashville: Nelson, 1979), 233.

[371] There is a discrepancy with some translations between finding it in verse 16 or verse 21.

[372] Walter Zimmerli, *Ezekiel 1* (Philadelphia: Fortress Press, 1979), 430.

[373] Merrill, *The New American Commentary*, 4:162-163.

Monotheism, singular (*Yahweh*) our plurality (*Elohim*), plural
Monotheism, singular (*Yahweh*) is a compound one (*echad*), plural

Elohim reflects back to *Yahweh* and *echad* reflects back to *Yahweh*. The God of Israel is a compound unity. This author believes that the *echad* of the Shema is a compound unity, but recognizes that there is far stronger evidence to show that *echad* is minimally a plurality (See Appendix 2). Because *Elohim* is never presented as a dual personality, yet still as a plurality, He has to be more than two, at least three, but never more than three. In the Hebrew Scriptures the Father speaks to the Son (Psa 2:7) and the Son speaks to the Father (Zech 1:12).[374] Also the Holy Spirit came upon and filled Bezaleel (Exod 35:30-31), the spirit of wisdom filled Joshua (Deut 34:9), the spirit came upon (1 Sam 11:6) and left (1 Sam 16:14) Saul, as well as came upon David when he was anointed by Samuel (1 Sam 16:13). The Hebrew Scriptures and the New Covenant, together or separately, never present more than three. Although the tri-unity is not explicitly presented in the Hebrew Scriptures, yet it is present.[375] Otherwise, Jesus was making false claims of His divinity to the Jewish nation to whom He was presenting Himself as the Messiah and God. Lewis Goldberg sums up this issue of the plurality of God in relation to Deut 6:4 by saying:

> We need to be scriptural even though we may never completely understand
> the scriptural concept. We never completely understand the scriptural concept.
> We see from the wording of Deuteronomy 6:4 that it was not Moses' intent to
> avoid a composite description of God. Rather, he was led to express God's
> nature in this way to allow for the future unfolding of the truth it contains.[376]

---

[374] Geisler, *Systematic Theology*, 2:288-289.
[375] Geisler, *Systematic Theology*, 2:289-290.
[376] Goldberg, *Our Jewish Friends*, 82.

CHAPTER 5

PLURAL DESCRIPTIONS

This chapter focuses on the personal pronouns attributed to God, and other plural descriptions of God, which is a significant area of debate and controversy between Christian and Jewish scholars. Initial discussion involves four passages where God refers to Himself by using plural pronouns (Gen 1:26, 3:22, 11:7; Isa 6:8).

Pronouns

In the Hebrew text, the plural term for God is *Elohim*. From Genesis 1 through Gen 2:3 *Elohim* is the only one identified and the only one doing the action of creating. God (*Elohim*) chose to reveal Himself by not predominately using the singular forms for God (*El, Elah, Eloah*) which were available for His use. Those who subscribe to verbal plenary inspiration must also affirm that the text's use of a plural descriptive term refers to God as a plural compound, complex unity. Therefore, at least two persons are involved in the creation of the world, a fact that makes null and void such counter-arguments as "plural of majesty," or "plural of deliberation," remnants of polytheism, "heavenly court" and "angels." It is the view of this author that these counterarguments that Jewish and Christian theologians force unnaturally upon the text do an injustice to God and how He chose to reveal Himself. Jamieson, Fausset and Brown make clear that all such counterarguments are "contrary to the whole tenor of Scripture."[377]

Understanding the plurality of reference in the earlier cited Genesis and Isaiah passages requires a clear grasp of the significance of the seven plural Hebrew pronouns in these passages.

All of the verbs are first person common plural forms in the Qal Imperfect tense. The suffixes attached to the prepositions are also first person common plural forms. They indicate a plurality of persons acting and making decisions.

Gen 1:26   נַעֲשֶׂה אָדָם בְּצַלְמֵנוּ כִּדְמוּתֵנוּ
         Let us make man – Verb Qal Impf 1 c p
         In image of us – Prep ncms const suffix 1 c p
         In likeness of us – Prep ncfs const suffix 1 c p

Gen 3:22   כְּאַחַד מִמֶּנּוּ
         Like one of
         From us – Prep + 1 c p suffix

---

[377] Robert Jamieson et al., *A Commentary: Critical, Experimental and Practical on the Old and New Testaments* (6 vols. Grand Rapids: Eerdmans, 1945), 1:8.

Gen 11:7   נֵרְדָה וְנָבְלָה

         Let us go down – Verb Qal Impf 1 c p

         And let us confuse – Verb Qal Impf 1 c p

Isa 6:8   יֵלֶךְ־לָנוּ

         He will go – for us - Prep + 1 c p suffix[378]

To illustrate in Gen 1:26 the verb "make" is an imperfect first person common plural with the pronoun "us" which is also first person common plural. In this passage the person speaking is plural and the verb of action is in agreement. From this point on the English equivalent, "us" and "our" of the Hebrew plural pronouns will be used.

Genesis 1:26

> And God said, Let us make man in our image, after our likeness. They shall rule the fish of the sea, the birds of the sky, the cattle, the whole earth, and all the creeping things that creep on the earth.

In this verse *Elohim* makes a clear statement of intent, "Let us make man." This is a unique statement in two ways. First, throughout this chapter, *Elohim* said, "Let there be" (vv. 3, 6, 9, 14, 20). Then in v. 26, with the creation of mankind, He says, "Let us make man." Hamilton relates these two phrases this way:

> The shift from the consistent use of the verb in the jussive (e.g., "Let there be") to a cohortative ("Let us make") is enough to prepare the reader for something momentous on this sixth day.[379]

There is a significant difference when the verb on the other days of creation is, "Let there be" but on the sixth day the verb "make" is grammatically plural.[380] Indeed, *Elohim* is not going to just create man. He is going to create man uniquely by doing and saying, "Let us make man in Our image, after Our likeness." *Elohim* used the personal plural pronoun "Us," which obviously references two or more persons. The pronoun "Us" describes *Elohim* when about to create man, in "Our image" and "Our likeness." According to Owens the two Hebrew words בְּצַלְמֵנוּ -- כִּדְמוּתֵנוּ translated "in Our image" -- "in Our likeness," have plural suffixes.[381] Miller states that the words "image" (*selem*) and "likeness" (*demut*) are in the singular.[382] Clearly, the uniqueness of the plural personal pronouns in Gen 1:26 draws attention to *Elohim*'s choice of specific words to indicate specific actions. For example, in Gen 1:1 it is *Elohim* who

---

[378] Taken from Gramcord software and Owens, *Analytical Key to the Old Testament*, 5, 13, 41; Kohlenberger, *The Interlinear NIV Hebrew-English Old Testament*, 1:3, 8, 24, 4:13.

[379] Victor P. Hamilton, *The New International Commentary on the Old Testament: The Book of Genesis, Chapters 1-17*, 134.

[380] Mathews, *The New American Commentary: Genesis 1:11:26*, 1a:161.

[381] John Joseph Owens, *Analytical Key to the Old Testament* (4 vols. Grand Rapids: Baker, 1989), 1:5.

[382] Paul A Miller, *Gramcord* (Vancouver, Wash: Gramcord Institute, 1999), www.gramcord.org.

creates. Because the term *Elohim* is plural, it declares God as plural. The singular verb "created," shows *Elohim*'s unity. In v. 26 the pronoun "Our" is tied to two singular words "image" and "likeness" showing the one speaking as being plural while at the same time confirming His unity. The above observation is important because there is no justification for forcing onto the text interpretations like consulting with "heavenly court" or "angels" which Loewen and Towner do in their articles in relation to Gen 1:26:

> The example that is sometimes given, "let us make man in our image," probably does not refer to a plurality of Gods, but rather to some kind of 'heavenly council' with which God is represented as being in consultation.[383]

> We are left, then, with the heavenly council as the only likely way of explaining this use of the plural in verse 1:26. Even in the latest hand to contribute to the final form of the Pentateuch – the Priestly writer – we come smack up against the feeble remnants of polytheism. God is speaking for the entire divine court.[384]

One thing becomes very clear. Mankind was not created in the image of angels. *Elohim* is omnipotent, omnipresent, and omniscient, He does not need to consult angels. The "Our" is not *Elohim* speaking to angels but *Elohim* speaking to equal partners in the Godhead.[385] Clearly, there is a consultation with a divine council, but that divine council is the tri-unity of God, which at this point is only reflective of God's plurality. Mathews makes a good observation that the first hearers did not understand tri-unity but did understand plurality:

> The first audience could not have understood it in the sense of a trinitarian reference. Although the Christian Trinity cannot be derived solely from the use of the plural, a plurality within the unity of the Godhead may be derived from the passage.[386]

Mathews' position on the plurality of God is visible in his comments on Genesis 1, but the tri-unity is not visible. The plurality of God does leave the door open for the progression of revelation to the tri-unity of God, but Genesis 1 does not show the tri-unity. Other passages in the Hebrew Scriptures, such as Psa 2:7, 45:7, 110:1 and Isa 48:16 record members of the God-head speaking to each other.[387] Cassuto also gives three valued points on why *Elohim* has no reason to consult angels. He says:

> Against this interpretation it can be contended: (1) that it conflicts with the central thought of the section that God alone created the entire world; (2) that

---

[383] Jacob A. Loewen, "The Names of God in the Old Testament," *The Bible Translator* 35, no. 2 (1984): 201-207.

[384] Towner, *Westminster Bible Companion*, 25.

[385] Henry M. Morris, *The Genesis Record* (Grand Rapids, Mich: Baker, 1976), 72.

[386] Mathews, *The New American Commentary: Genesis 1:11:26*, 163.

[387] Morris, *The Genesis Record*, 72.

the expression 'Let us make' is not one of consultation; (3) that if the intention was to tell us that God took counsel, the Bible would have explicitly stated whom He consulted, as we are told in the other passages that are usually cited in support of this theory (I Ki 22:19; Isa 6:2-8; Job 1 and 2).[388]

Cassuto's three points make it evident that *Elohim* did not consult anyone besides Himself. However, Cassuto is not consistent with the Gen 1:26 text because he improperly applies "plural of exhortation." For example when a person exhorts himself to do a given task, he uses the plural: "Let us go!" "Let us rise up!" "Let us sit!" and the like.[389] Again, the explanation ignores the plain sense of what *Elohim* said. Leupold dogmatically sees the tri-unity in the Genesis 1 account,[390] but only because he has read tri-unity into the text. The tri-unity is not revealed in the Genesis 1 account.[391] *Elohim* did consult with Himself, equal partners of the Godhead before time:

> The Lamb had, in the determination of these councils, been slain before the foundation of the world; the names of the redeemed had been written in His book of life before the foundation of the world; and God called those who were to be saved by His grace, before the world began. (1 Pet 1:20; Rev 17:8; 2 Tim 1:9)[392]

Kac observes that the plural verb "let us make" and the two nouns with plural suffixes make it obligatory to translate the text as saying: "And *Elohim* said, Let Us make man in Our images and Our likenesses." Kac points out that up to verse 26, *Elohim* alone is the Creator, but in v. 26, with the creation of mankind, a double plural appears.[393] There is no need to stretch both the word *Elohim* and other personal pronouns to say something *Elohim* did not intend.

Another aspect of the plurality and unity of *Elohim* is evident in v. 27. Although *Elohim* makes a statement of intent in v. 26, He immediately follows that through with projected action in v. 27. He uses several singular words in v. 27 to express and emphasize His unity in the creation of man. *Elohim* used "created" three times, which is singular in expressing His creation of mankind. This emphasizes His oneness and unity by stating that "in His (singular) image, the image of God (*Elohim*) He created him (man).". While v. 26 clearly pinpoints the plurality of *Elohim*, the singularity of *Elohim* in v. 27 further demonstrates that *Elohim* is a unity of one, and a plurality. Mathews confirms that view:

> Our passage describes the result of God's creative act by both plural and singular pronoun "his image" in v. 27. Here the unity and plurality of God are in view. The plural indicates an intradivine conversation, a plurality in the Godhead, between God and his Spirit.[394]

---

[388] U. Cassuto, *A Commentary on the Book of Genesis: Part One* (Jerusalem: Magnes Press, 1961), 54.

[389] Cassuto, *A Commentary on the Book of Genesis: part one*, 54.

[390] Leupold, *Expositions of Genesis*, 86.

[391] Youngblood, *The Genesis Debate*, 123.

[392] Morris, *The Genesis Record*, 73.

[393] Kac, *The Messiahship of Jesus*, 165.

[394] Mathews, *The New American Commentary: Genesis 1-11:26*, 1a:163.

Taking into account all that has been said, it is not difficult to understand that God chose to reveal Himself as *Elohim*, Who is plural. He engaged with the other members of the Godhead to create man in Their image. The other lines of reasoning such as "plural of majesty," "plural of deliberation," "heavenly courts or councils" that Christians and Jewish scholars use to interpret the Hebrew Scripture, fall short of the context that God, in His wisdom, gave to reveal Himself to mankind. Youngblood clearly and precisely states what the human finite mind on the issue of the triune God will not grasp and yet is taught:

> Though a mystery, the uniplurality of God's nature is taught consistently throughout Scripture.[395]

Genesis 3:22

In Gen 3:22 God again uses the personal plural pronoun "Us" in the biblical text. First observe the verse:

> And the LORD God said, "Now that the man has become like one of us Knowing good and bad, what if he should stretch out his hand and take also from the tree of life and eat, and live forever!"

In the first half of this verse, the words LORD God (*Yahweh Elohim*), and the phrase "man has become like one of us," God used name distinctions to focus attention on His personal name, essence and plurality. *Yahweh* (singular) and *Elohim* (plural) use the personal plural pronoun "us" to designate Himself. Morris adds some further insight by saying that there is a "heavenly council" so to speak as was also observed in Gen 1:26, but that heavenly council is the inner council of the tri-unity of God:

> Verse 22 gives a brief insight into the inner councils of the triune Godhead as in Genesis 1:26, such a council was recorded relative to the decision to create man, so now the council decrees his expulsion from the garden and the tree of life. In both passages, the divine unity is stressed ('And the LORD God said') and also the divine plurality ("us.")[396]

God, in His tri-unity, says that man is like one of "us." How did man become like God? It was only in the sense that now man can know good and evil, not as some who indicate that man was upgraded to become like a divine being or angel. Merrill makes the point that in some way man is becoming like God:

> That is, man in some sense has become like God. Surely the divine lament is not that man has become like an angel or some other creature.[397]

---

[395] Youngblood, The Book of Genesis, 30.
[396] Morris, *The Genesis Record*, 131.
[397] Youngblood, *The Genesis Debate*, 122.

Only in one regard did man become like God. After the fall man knew good and evil.[398] Man is not and can not be like divine beings or angels. It would be a promotion to be like an angel. Man became degenerate and enslaved to sin. Merrill continues his statement with a contrast. The creator of the universe does not need the assistance of lesser beings.

> Again, it is hardly conceivable that the Lord is invoking the assistance of the angels or anyone else. It is He alone who creates, commands, and judges his creation. It is he alone who speaks and who does so on occasion as a subject described by grammatically plural terminology.[399]

Merrill is correct. It is inconceivable that God would be comparing man with divine beings like angels. As the great I AM, He does not need the assistance of any creature in judging man that He, Himself, had created to serve Him.

In Gen 3:22 and 1:26 *Elohim* was showing His plurality, along with His unity. However, in Gen 3:22 there is one difference. *Yahweh*, which is singular, shows oneness and plurality in unity, while *Elohim* is showing plurality in oneness.

One further observation on this passage which continues to show plurality is in these words for Gen 3:22:

> And the LORD God said, Now that the man has become like one of us, knowing good and evil.

In appendix #2 a detailed chart is given on the word *echad*, meaning one, and how it is used in the Torah or the Five Books of Moses. The overwhelming conclusion of the study is that *echad* is used within a plural context almost exclusively by Moses. In Gen 3:22 God states that man has become like *echad*, "one" of us. Here God uses a plural word (*echad*) to represent Himself, along with the plural personal pronoun "us." The plurality of God is very strong in Gen 3:22 in the following three words, "LORD God (*elohim*)," "one (*echad*)" and "us." If verbal plenary inspiration is believed, then the only conclusion to this passage is that God is revealing Himself as a plurality.

Genesis 11:7

> Let us, then, go down and confound their speech there, so that they shall not understand one another's speech.

---

[398] David A. Hubbard and Glenn W. Barker, *World Biblical Commentary: Genesis 1-15* (52 vols.; Waco, Tex: Word Books, 1987), 85.
[399] Youngblood, *The Genesis Debate*, 122.

92

In Gen 11:7, *Yahweh*, not *Elohim*, says, "Let us go down" to confuse the language of the people. The point in Gen 1:26 is that *Elohim* says, "Let Us make man," but in Gen 3:22 it is *Yahweh Elohim* saying that "man has become one of Us." In Gen 1:26 *Elohim* (plural) says "let us," whereas in 3:22 Israel's personal name for God, *Yahweh*, is combined with *Elohim* to indicate that these names for God are interchangeable. The name *Yahweh*, which emphasizes unity and oneness, is combined with *Elohim*, which is a plurality. Observe the progression of the names of God in Gen 11:7, God simply uses His personal name, *Yahweh*, when saying, "Let Us go down." The signi-ficant shift in the nouns from *Elohim* to *Yahweh Elohim* to *Yahweh* are significant because the plural personal pronoun "us" is used each time to designate the plurality of God. Whether God uses *Elohim*, *Yahweh Elohim* or *Yahweh*, it points to the same reality, that God is a unity of one, yet plural.

Speiser's argument on "grammatical plural," states that the phrase "Let us go down" in 11:7, is "grammatically plural; or this may be a plural of majesty."[400] Emphasizing the fact that even though this is grammatically plural it is to be interpreted in reality as a singular statement. Speiser also uses the same explanation of the "let us" in Gen 1:26. This view raises the question of one's priority and methods of interpretation of Scripture. Since the terms "let us" are grammatically plural, it does not have to be changed to mean singular because plurality does not fit a certain theological perspective. Because God by inspiration, in the very first chapter of His revelation to mankind, does not give the names of the tri-unity, there is no reason to remove, delete, or discount the use of the plural noun and plural pronouns to describe His personhood. Speiser makes this statement to defend his view on grammatical plural being changed in reality to a singular meaning:

> For the singulars "my image, my likeness" Heb. employs here plural possess-ives, which most translations reproduce. Yet no other divine being has been mentioned; and the very next verse used the singular throughout. The point at issue, therefore is one of grammar alone, without direct bearing on the meaning.[401]

Speiser argues that *Elohim* is a grammatical plural because He used singular modifiers.[402] Thus the singular aspect of grammar would take precedent over the interpretation when God chose to use a personal plural pronoun. If that is Speiser's implication, then the word *Elohim* would simply translate as a singular, which is what all translations do. If that argument be the case, God is a very poor communicator, being completely ineffective with language to convey His essence to mankind.

There is one other observation of the text in Gen11:3-4, which, to this author, shows the inconsistency of scholars. When man uses "let us," the phrase is considered plural, but when *Yahweh* uses "let us," the same phrase is considered singular. The people at Babel said "Let us make bricks" and "let us build for ourselves" they used

---

[400] E. A. Speiser, *The Anchor Bible: Genesis* (Garden City, NY: Doubleday, 1964), 75.
[401] Speiser, *The Anchor Bible: Genesis*, 7.
[402] See chapter two, section under *Elohim*.

plural personal pronouns. This observation about the people in the land of Shinar is never argued. Yet when *Yahweh* uses "Let us go down," all of a sudden scholars, like Speiser, take the same "let us" and then attempt to say that *Yahweh* is not speaking in a plural. The grammar in vv. 3-4 is the same as v. 7. All of the usages of "let us make" or "let us go down" are first person common plural (1 c p), yet Speiser would make the reference to God (v. 7) which he says is a grammatical plural to be taken as a singular, but the references to the people are taken literally:

Gen 11:3 נִלְבְּנָה לְבֵנִים וְנִשְׂרְפָה
Let us make – Verb Qal Cohortative 1 p
bricks
and let us bake - Verb Qal Impf 1 c p

Gen 11:4 וְנַעֲשֶׂה־לָּנוּ
So let us make – Verb Qal Impf 1 c p
For us – Prep 1 c p

Gen 11:7 נֵרְדָה וְנָבְלָה
Let us go down – Verb Qal Cohortative 1 p
And let us confuse – Verb Qal Cohortative 1 p

Morris so aptly gives his contrast between Nimrod and God. Nimrod's council meets saying "let us" and God's "council" meets saying "let us." God's council is the equal members of the triune God:

> But as Nimrod and his cohorts had held a council of conspiracy and aggression on earth, so God now called a "council," as it were, in heaven, to institute formal action to prevent the accomplishment of Nimrod's plans. Such a divine council is indicated by the plural pronoun in verse 7, "let us."[403]

Yahweh uses the plural personal pronoun "us," as He refers to His divine council of the Godhead, when They went down and confused the language of the people. One other observation deserves attention in Gen 11:1, 6. As was discussed in chapter four (and appendix #2), *echad* in the *Shema* of Deut 6:4 minimally has to be viewed within a plural context. In verses 1 and 6 *echad* is used not only in a plural context, but in the context of a unity as seen in verses 1 and 6:

> Everyone on earth had the same (*echad*) language and the same (*echad*) words.

> And the LORD said, If as one (*echad*) people with one (*echad*) language for all, this is how they have begun to act.

The whole context of this passage is dealing with plurality, whether it is the plurality of man acting together because they have one language so that they can accomplish their

---

[403] Morris, *The Genesis Record*, 273.

act of rebellion against God, or whether it was God Himself referring to Himself in plurality. When Scripture is taken literally as God intended it to be, there is only one conclusion a student of the Scriptures can come to, and that is that God is a plurality.

Isaiah 6:8

> Then I heard the voice of my Lord saying, "Whom shall I send? Who will go for us?' And I said, "Here am I; send me."

In this passage *Adonai* uses two personal pronouns ("I" and "us") as He invites Isaiah to his prophetic ministry by saying, "Whom shall I send? Who will go for us?" First, Isaiah says that he "beheld my Lord (*Adonai*) seated on a high and lofty throne." Obviously, *Adonai* in verse one is God Almighty. The Seraphim who minister before God continuously say, "Holy, Holy, Holy, is the LORD (*Yahweh*) of hosts" (Isa 6:3). Then "the House (heavenly temple) kept filling with smoke," which is a reference to the *Shechinah* of God (6:4). After which Isaiah speaks of his sinfulness and says, "My own eyes have beheld the King LORD (*Yahweh*) of Hosts" (v. 5). Then Isaiah heard the voice of *Adonai* saying, "Whom shall I send? Who will go for us?" (v.8). *Yahweh* and *Adonai* are used interchangeably with one notable distinction. *Yahweh* is singular and *Adonai*, when used of God, is plural.[404]

From the time of Isaiah to the time of *Yeshua*, about 700 years, the word *Adonai* (plural) slowly began to replace *Yahweh* (singular) as the name of God, and that is significant. That actually occurred sometime before the end of the second temple period. *Yahweh* and *Adonai* are the same person, and even though the Seraphim are in the context serving *Yahweh*, it is *Adonai* (plural) who asks the question (v. 8) for the triune God in Isaiah's presence. The major names of God are all used with the personal plural pronoun "us," *Elohim* (Gen 1:26), *Yahweh Elohim* (Gen 3:22), *Yahweh* (Gen 11:7) and *Adonai* (Isa 6:8)

Opposition to Plural Pronouns

God is one alone and yet a plurality, for He refers to Himself in the context of plurality by using plural pronouns. God is one; with that no one would disagree. While the Hebrew Scriptures give a plural description, others, both Jewish and Christian theologians, do not see these plural pronouns as referring to the plurality of God. Hasel, in his article, clarifies the extent of the disagreement:

> What does the plural "us" in this enigmatic phrase indicate? Should it be changed to the singular or does it indeed have a plural meaning? If it has a plural meaning, is its intention to express an address between gods, or between

---

[404] Neusner and Green, *Dictionary of Judaism in the Biblical Period*, 389. See chapter two, section under Adonai.

95

God and heavenly beings, or between God and the earth or earthly elements? Is it a plural of majesty, a plural of deliberation, or a plural of fullness? These suggestions and their supporting arguments will receive critical consideration with an attempt to evaluate their cogency.[405]

Christian and Jewish scholars agree that the "us" cannot represent plurality. Their views express how the plural "us" should be treated. In the following paragraphs these views will briefly be discussed.

In the Hebrew Scriptures there are four references to plural personal pronouns where God uses them of Himself to indicate plurality. Of these four references, three of them are found in Genesis: in the creation account (Gen 1:26), the fall of man (Gen 3:22), and the confusing of the language at the tower of Babel (Gen 11:7). The remaining plural pronoun is found in Isaiah 6:8. These four references to the personal plural pronouns support the plurality of God. However, it seems that the greatest controversy swirls around the disagreement about the plural pronouns in Gen 1:26. Often authors refer back to the Gen 1:26 passage when dealing with the other passages on plural pronouns (Gen 3:22, 11:7; Isa 6:8). These four passages on the plural pronouns will be examined in two ways: (1) from the perspective of Jewish and Christian scholars who oppose them as references to the plurality of God and (2) from Christian authors who affirm the plurality of God in these passages.

Four common proposals surface to be discussed. A number of Jewish and Christian scholars seek to discredit the plural personal pronouns by using one or more of the four different lines of argument: (a) The first line of argument is when *Elohim* used the words "us" and "our," He was referring to His "heavenly court" which included angels, sons of God, and Seraphim. (b) The argument is "plural of majesty," (c) and the third line of reasoning is the "plural of deliberation" argument. (d) And the fourth line of argument is that *Elohim* is referencing the earth to assist Him which He had just created.

The following comments reflect the Jewish interpretation of the plural personal pronoun "us" in the *Tanakh*. Sarna refers to *Elohim* and the pronoun 'us" by saying:

This is an Israelite version of the polytheistic assemblies of the pantheon mono-theized and depaganized.[406]

Sarna gives his resistance to the plural personal pronouns by saying:

Elohim is a comprehensive term for supernatural beings and is often employed for angels.[407]

---

[405] Gerhard F. Hasel, "The Meaning of "Let Us" in Genesis 1:26," *AUSS* 13 (1975): 58-66.
[406] Sarna, *The JPS Torah Commentary on Genesis*, 12.
[407] Sarna, *The JPS Torah Commentary on Genesis*, 25.

Sarna asserts that in Gen 35:7 angels are seen as divine beings.[408]   Another Jewish response is by Slotki, in the Soncino series, whose source of authority is Rabbis Abraham Ibn Ezra (1092-1167) and David Kimchi (1160-1235).[409]   He states that the "us" (Isa 6:8) represents the angelic host. These interpretations are widely held views in Judaism from both modern and ancient scholars as represented by Sarna and Slotki on how the plural personal pronouns that God uses of Himself are interpreted by the Jewish scholars.

Christian authors refer to other Jewish writers to understand their claims, as was just spoken about in connection to the plural personal pronouns of God. Driver asserts that most Jewish thought is that these reflect God and His "heavenly court" who He is consulting:

> General Jewish interpretation and some Christians (notably Delitzsch) is that God is represented as including with Himself His celestial court (I Kgs 22:19), and consulting with them before creating the highest of His works, man.[410]

Fruchtenbaum, a Jewish believer, illustrates from Rashi concerning the activity of angels in the creation of mankind, man was not created by angels but was created in the image of angels. According to Rashi, God was being polite, or showing good manners and humility, by asking permission of the lower beings, angels, to create man in their image.[411]   Merrill also references Rashi in a journal article concerning the "let us" of Gen 1:26 in the following quote from Rashi:

> We will make man – Although they did not assist Him in forming him and although this [use of the plural] may give the heretics an occasion to rebel, yet the passage does not refrain from teaching proper conduct and the virtue of humbleness, namely, that the greater should consult, and take permission from the smaller; for had it been written, "I shall make man," we could not, then, have learned that He spoke to His judicial council but to Himself. And as a refutation of the heretics it is written immediately after this verse "And God created the man," and it is not written "and they created."[412]

Rashi's whole statement is an assumption that he makes with absolutely no precedent in the *Tanakh* of *Elohim* showing humbleness by consulting the lesser (angels) before He creates man. Ryle, who also references Jewish explanation that God was addressing the inhabitants of heaven, adds this statement in connection to Gen 1:26 by saying:

> Old Jewish explanation that God is here addressing the inhabitants of heaven. In the thought of the devout Israelite, God was one, but not isolated. He was

---

[408] Sarna, *The JPS Torah Commentary on Genesis*, 241.

[409] I. W. Slotki, *Isaiah* (New York: Soncino Press (1983), 30.

[410] S. R. Driver, *Westminster Commentaries, the Book of Genesis*, (London: Methuen & Co, 1911), 14.

[411] Arnold A. Fruchtenbaum, *Genesis* (27 tapes, Tustin, Calif: Ariel Ministries, n.d.), tape 1, chapter 1:26.

[412] Eugene H Merrill, "Rashi, Nicholas De Lyra, and the Christian Exegesis," *WTJ* 38 (1975): 66-79.

surrounded by the heavenly host (I Ki 22:19), attended by the Seraphim (Isa 6:1-6), holding His court with "the sons of God (Job 1:6)."[413]

Ryle also points out the same thing just quoted in relation to the Jewish interpretation of Gen 3:22.[414]

Among Christian scholars, Hamilton replicates the Jewish argument that the pantheon of gods was replaced by the heavenly court concept:

In the biblical adaptation of the story the pantheon concept was replaced with the heavenly court concept. Thus, it is not other gods, but to the angelic host, the "sons of God," that God speaks.[415]

Westermann speaking of Gen 3:22 states that many modern scholars refer to the heavenly court as polytheistic in intent:

Namely whether the phrase 'like one of us' means 'the higher spiritual beings,' or the heavenly court (H. Gunkel and the majority of recent interpreters), or whether God includes the other gods with himself, the phrase being actually polytheistic in intent.[416]

Driver uses ancient Babylonian accounts to support his argument that presents the idea that the biblical account arose out of a pantheon of gods in a pre-Israelite background:

There is force in these considerations; and probably the ultimate explanation has to be sought in a pre-Israelite stage of the tradition (such as is represented by the Babylonian account; where a polytheistic view of man's origin found expression). This would naturally be replaced in a Heb. recession by the idea of a heavenly council of angels, as in I Kings 22; Job 1:38; Daniel 4:14; 7:10.[417]

It has been regarded as a survival of polytheism, and has been compared with "*Elohim*," a plural word for "God" which some regard as a relic of polytheism.[418]

Some Christian scholars such as Davidson are very clear in their meaning that God's plurality is not represented by pagan polytheism. God is representing Himself as a true plurality in unity as Isa 6:8 and Gen 1:26 affirm:

---

[413] Herbert E. Ryle, *Cambridge Bible: the Book of Genesis* (London: Cambridge University, 1914), 19.
[414] Ryle, *Cambridge Bible: the Book of Genesis*, 19.
[415] Hamilton, *The New International Commentary on the Old Testament: The Book of Genesis, Chapters 1-17*, 133.
[416] Claus Westermann, *Genesis 1-11, A Continental Commentary* (trans. John J. Scullion: Minneapolis, Minn: Fortress Press, 1994), 272-273.
[417] S. R. Driver et al., eds., *A Critical and Exegetical Commentary on Genesis* (Edinburgh: T & T Clark, 1930), 31.
[418] Ryle, *Cambridge Bible: The Book of Genesis*, 18.

There is no vagueness or obscurity in either of the passages referred to. If God, who speaks in these passages, uses the word "us" of Himself, there is a perfectly clear statement to the effect that the Godhead is a Plurality.[419]

Davidson is open to the idea that *Adonai* did include the plurality of *Elohim*. However, he also opens the door to the angels being included:

> The point, however, is whether the Divine speaker uses the word "us" of Himself, i.e. of the Godhead alone, or whether He does not rather include others, e.g. His heavenly council along with Him. The opinion of most expositors is to the latter effect.[420]

Clearly, Jewish scholars will avoid the plural personal pronouns by referring to polytheism as just stated above of the pantheon of gods, which were monotheized and depaganized at a later time. Jewish scholars will also assert the argument of "heavenly court" and "angels" being involved in the "us" passages. Driver equates that the passage Gen 1:26 account refers back to ancient pagan Babylonian accounts of a pantheon of gods. According to this line of argument, the "heavenly host" are one and the same thing with this concept of polytheistic relics of gods that have remained in the biblical text. It will also be noted that some authors intertwine the "heavenly court" and "angels," with pagan origins so that the phrase "let us" becomes a relic of polytheism carried over from paganism[421] rather than a clear presentation of God's plurality.

It is clear, to this author, that when the plain sense of Scripture is used and left to speak for itself, there is no problem with the understanding of these texts. The danger of perverting the text is when a person has a preconceived belief and cannot see the plurality of God. As creator of the universe, God was always a plurality and is understood in the New Covenant as a tri-unity. Scholars, both Jewish and Christian, may be taking liberties with the Scripture in an attempt to understand it, but in reality they are perverting it. The reality is that God in the presentation of His Son to Israel as their Messiah and to mankind as the Saviour from sin, would not present a new doctrine of plurality or tri-unity. God would not, in the middle of His redemptive plan for Israel and the world, present the central figure of Scripture without a foundation being laid in the *Tanakh*. The *Tanakh* minimally presents the plurality of God

The second line of argument is the view of "plural of majesty." The "plural of majesty" argument given by both Jewish and Christian scholars contends that God was speaking as a western monarch, as the Queen of England would speak to her subjects.[422] The Haftorah, in speaking of Gen 3:22, refers to the "us" as a "plural of majesty," and as a consequence of the fall, man became "as one of the angels; or 'us' is a "plural of

---

[419] A. B. Davidson, *The Theology of the Old Testament* (New York: Scribner's, 1928), 129.

[420] Davidson, *The Theology of the Old Testament*, 129.

[421] G. Herbert Livingston, *The Pentateuch in Its Cultural Environment* (2nd ed. Grand Rapids: Baker Book House, 1987), 140.

[422] Briscoe, *The Communicator's Commentary: Genesis*, 1:34.

majesty."[423]   Rabbi Hertz, editor of the Haftorah follows the logic to its natural conclusion that:

> Man is become as God – omniscient. Man, having through disobedience secure-
> ed the faculty of unlimited knowledge, there was real danger that his knowledge
> would outstrip his sense of obedience to Divine Law.[424]

That interpretation of "us" making it a "plural of majesty" puts *Elohim* in the same class of beings that are ministering spirits (angels) and to man.   The "plural of majesty" is echoed again by Sarna in his commentary on Gen 11:7.[425] The rabbis say that *Elohim* is speaking like a Western monarch who uses the royal "we."[426]   Authors, such as Ryle, Hamilton, Westermann, and Skinner, advocate or have cited others who raise the possibility that these arguments of "plural of majesty," "heavenly court" could be a reference to a pantheon of gods with a polytheistic reference to God. What is notable is that frequently "plural of majesty" and "heavenly court" are linked to a pantheon of gods or a survival of polytheism, as it relates to these four plural personal pronoun texts.

> On the plural, "we will go down," cf. comments on 1:26 and 3:22. One is not to
> assume as background remnants of polytheistic talk or the idea of the heavenly
> court (as do many modern exegetes, like G.A. Cooke, F.M. Cross, H.
> Schmidt).[427]

Westermann points out clearly that these plural personal pronouns in Genesis are not to be understood from a background of polytheism as some modern exegetes have done.

The third line of reasoning is the argument of "plural of deliberation," or God thinking something over within Himself, as if saying, "let me or I will make man". "Plural of deliberation" means that the speaker is conferring or consulting with himself. Reyburn and McG. Fry refer to Isa 6:8 as an example of God consulting Himself before acting.[428] Westermann uses grammar to further his argument in pressing for "plural of deliberation:"

> The grammatical construction is a plural of deliberation. In favor of a plural of
> deliberation in 1:26 is the fact that in Isaiah 6:8 the plural and the singular are
> used in the same sentence with the same meaning; similarly in 2 Samuel 24:14
> where it is a question of one and the same conclusion: "...Let us fall into the
> hand of the Lord... but let me not fall into the hand of man." ... A clear example

---

[423] Sarna, *The JPS Torah Commentary on Genesis*, 13.
[424] Hertz, *The Pentateuch and Haftorahs*, 13.
[425] Sarna, *The JPS Torah Commentary on Genesis*, 39.
[426] For more information on "plural of majesty" refer back to *Elohim* in chapter two.
[427] Westermann, *Genesis 1-11, A Continental Commentary*, 552.
[428] William D. Reyburn and Euan McG. Fry, *A Handbook on Genesis* (New York: United Bible Societies, 1997), 50.

of this type of deliberation occurs in Genesis 11:7; "Come let us go down . . .," has shown that this usage perseveres right down to the present day.[429]

But Westermann misses the point of his own examples. When David say "us" he means the nation, but when *Yahweh* (singular) say "let us go down" it is the one God who expresses his plurality. Turner, in his book on Genesis, is in agreement and refers to Westermann that this passage should be treated as a "plural of deliberation."[430] Ryle points out that in Gen 11:7 God is either announcing His purpose by using a deliberative first person plural, or that He is addressing the powers of heaven that attend to and minister to Him.[431] The Haftorah, which references Gen 1:26, states that the "Scripture represents God as deliberating over the making of the human species." The phrase "Let us make man" is a "Hebrew idiomatic way of expressing deliberation as in 11:7; or, it is the 'plural of majesty,' royal commands, being conveyed in the first person plural."[432] Then Hamilton also states that these plural personal pronouns are *Elohim* deliberating with Himself:

> This verse is a deliberation. God dialogues with himself and observes that man has become "like one of us" in "knowing good and evil."[433]

It is highly improbable that an all knowing and all powerful *Yahweh Elohim* would talk with Himself; rather *Elohim* is to be understood minimally as a plurality. Christian scholars seem to be forcing an interpretation on the text that is not there. God is not deliberating with Himself. There is no need to because He is plural, yet a unity of one, indivisible. The "plural of deliberation" is not needed when God is a plurality. Cooper states:

> Such an expression as this, God could not use in speaking to a created being. The language unquestionably implies the equality of the speaker and the ones addressed.[434]

The fourth line of argument is that *Elohim* is referencing the earth that He had just created. Rabbi Ramban or Nachmainides, a 13th century rabbi, says of Gen 1:26 that the phrase "let us make" in "our image" refers to "the aforementioned earth."[435] Payne Smith refers to 12th century rabbi Maimonide's view that God took counsel with the earth, for the earth supplied the body of man and *Elohim* provided the soul of man.[436] This point does not show up as a Christian argument, even though the earth is

---

[429] Westermann, *Genesis 1-11, A Continental Commentary*, 145.

[430] Laurence A. Turner, *Genesis* (Sheffield, England: Sheffield Academic Press, 2000), 23.

[431] Ryle, *Cambridge Bible, the Book of Genesis*, 148.

[432] Hertz, *The Pentateuch and Haftorahs*, 5.

[433] Hamilton, *The New International Commentary on the Old Testament: Genesis chapters 1-17*, 208.

[434] Cooper, *The God of Israel*, 28.

[435] Moshe ben Nachman, *Ramban (Nachmanides), Commentary on the Torah – Genesis* (trans. Charles B. Chavel: New York: Shilo Publishing House, Inc. 1999), 52.

[436] Charles John Ellicott, *The Handy Commentary, Genesis* (London: Cassell & Company, n.d.), 79.

in the context of Genesis 1. Rabbi Moshe Ben Nachman (1195–1270) gives the following reason for the usage of the earth in the creation of man:

> The correct explanation of *na'aseh* (let us make) [which is in the plural form when it should have been in the singular] is as follows: It has been shown to you that G-d created something from nothing only on the first day, and afterwards He formed and made things from those created elements. Thus when He gave the water the power of bringing forth a living soul, the command concerning them was *Let the water swarm.* The command concerning cattle was Let the earth bring forth. But in the case of man he said, Let us make, that is, I and the aforementioned earth, let us make man, the earth to bring forth the body from its elements as it did with the cattle and beasts, as it is written, and the Eternal G-d formed man of the dust of the ground, and He, blessed be He, to give the spirit from His mouth, the Supreme One, as it is written, And He breathed into his nostrils the breath of life. And He said, In our image, and after our likeness, as man will then be similar to both. In the capacity of his body, he will be similar to the earth from which he was taken, and in spirit he will be similar to the higher beings, because it [the spirit] is not a body and will not die. In the second verse, He says, In the image of G-d He created them, in order to relate the distinction by which man is distinguished from the rest of created beings.[437]

The only problem with his interpretation is that in verses 3, 6, 9, 14, 20, 24 there is not a plural personal pronoun in connection to the "Let the" or "Let there" as on the other days of creation. Only in verse 26 with the creation of man is there a plural personal pronoun. Nachmanides uses a logical argument except when he includes the earth as a partner in the creation of man, that is not a rational statement. Material things do not have intelligence to understand or emotion to feel, let alone a will to make a choice. The earth simply is there because God placed it there. The only thing that the rabbis can point to is the statement that, if they do not obey the Law (Deut 4:26; 30:19; 31:28), God promises to call heaven and earth to witness against them. In conclusion, Isa 40:13 is quite clear that God does not have to be informed by any counselor, whether it be the material earth or with created beings.

In summary, arguments are given for both the reality of the plurality of God in the plural personal pronouns in the *Tanakh* and the arguments against these pronouns being understood as plural statements by God. Alan Hauser, who does believe in the tri-unity in the New Covenant, claims that both Genesis 1 and the *Tanakh*, as a whole, do not present the plurality of God:

> The issue of whether the doctrine of the Trinity is implied in Genesis 1 does not have any substantive impact on the broader issue of the validity of the doctrine.[438]

---

[437] Nachman, *Commentary on the Torah – Genesis*, 52-53.
[438] Ronald Youngblood, *The Genesis Debate* (Nashville: Nelson, 1986), 110.

However, the plurality of God does have an impact on witnessing to Jewish people. Mankind and Jewish people, according to Romans 1, stand before God in judgment, condemned. However, Jewish people were worshipping the one true God, not idols, but they still missed their Messiah (God incarnate) because they didn't recognize the plurality of God in the *Tanakh*. Hauser also makes a strong statement to totally discredit the tri-unity in the *Tanakh*:

> Furthermore, when one looks at the Old Testament it becomes clear that there are no discernible references to the Trinity. Claimed allusions to the Trinity became perceptible by hindsight only after the Church councils had defined the doctrine. Without perspective of the Church councils and the Church Fathers who formulated the creeds, it is inconceivable that we could even speak of a doctrine of the Trinity in the Old Testament. In other words, it would not be possible to state the doctrine even in skeleton form on the basis of passages chosen only from the Old Testament.[439]

God did give ample testimony of His plurality, in Genesis 1, of the *Torah*, as well as the rest of the *Tanakh*. Every Jewish person who had contact with *Yeshua* in that day was responsible for rejecting or accepting Him as the God/man. The fact is that Israel, as a nation, rejected Him (Matt 12:22-42) and turned Him over to the Romans for crucifixion. They also stand condemned because God did reaffirm His plurality in the *Tanakh*. Contrary to the above quote, the doctrine of the tri-unity does have substantive impact on the broader issue of the doctrine. If the plurality of God was not given in the *Tanakh* then *Yeshua* would also have been taking unjustified liberties with the *Tanakh* when He insisted that the Law, Prophets and Writings spoke of Him. Hauser contends that the development of the doctrine of the tri-unity, after the Church councils, was an act of hindsight. There is one major problem with Hauser's above quoted view. Almost 300 years before the council of Nicea in 325 CE, the tri-unity of God had already been recognized and was being taught by the first century church. The first century believers, such as Matthew, Mark, Luke, John, Paul, James, Peter, Jude and the author of Hebrews, did not need the councils to make creeds (which were made because of error in the church) to have and hold to the tri-unity of God. They were eyewitnesses of the Glory of God. As John says, "our hands have handled, of the Word of Life (1 Jn 1:1)." As stated earlier in this paper, God did not present Messiah in a vacuum. Hauser sums up his writing with this summary of the doctrine of the tri-unity:

> Thus we conclude that these plurals can be understood to refer to the different persons of the Trinity only if that concept is read into the passage and only if the plurals are made to carry meanings and implications that run counter to similar usages elsewhere in the Old Testament.[440]

If believers only had the *Tanakh* to study, the conclusion minimally would be that God is one, but is somehow more complex than the word "one" normally conveys, He is a

---

[439] Youngblood, *The Genesis Debate*, 111-112.
[440] Youngblood, *The Genesis Debate*, 123.

plurality. Even without any exposure to the New Covenant, that belief would be a minimal understanding of the Hebrew Scriptures.

Plural Verbs Used With *Elohim*

There are other passages in the Scriptures (Gen 20:13; 35:7; 2 Sam 7:23; Psa 58:11) that throw light on the plurality of God in the *Tanakh*. Hebrew grammar requires that verbs agree with associated nouns in both gender and number. When *Elohim* is used of the true God, these rules are normally broken because the plural noun is almost always followed by a singular verb except in the four verses cited in the beginning of this paragraph. With the plural noun *Elohim* a singular verb should attract attention. Likewise, the plural verbs that follow *Elohim* should equally attract attention. Even though the grammar is normal, this is an unusual combination because of its infrequent use in the *Tanakh*. Fruchtenbaum expresses the significance well:

> It is also said that while *Elohim* is plural, the verbs used with it are always singular when applied to the true God, and plural for false gods. The rules of Hebrew grammar require that verbs agree with the associated nouns in both gender and number. When *Elohim* is used for pagan gods, these rules are always followed and a plural verb is always used. When *Elohim* is used of the one true God, however, these rules are normally broken - the plural noun *Elohim* is usually followed by a singular verb. While it is true that this is most often the case, it is not always the case. There are several places in the Hebrew text where *Elohim*, speaking of the God of Israel, is followed by a plural verb.[441]

The following passages are four rare incidents where the noun *Elohim* and the verb are plural in reference to the true God.

Genesis 20:13

> So when God made me wander from my father's house, I said to her Let this be the kindness that you shall do me: whatever place we come to, say there of me: He is my brother.

Because the plural noun *Elohim* with plural verb "cause (me) to wander" is so unusual in connection to *Elohim*, Reyburn, Driver as well as the Haftorah attempt to explain away the plural reference to the true God. For example, Driver's assertion that Abraham was adapting the above quoted reference of his speech to a pagan (Abimelech), he was accommodating Abimelech's polytheistic outlook who believed in many gods, states the following:

---

[441] Fruchtenbaum, *Messianic Christology*, 103-104.

The verb is plural, perhaps, in conversation with a heathen, from accommodation to a polytheistic point of view. *Elohim*, even when used of the true God, is occasionally construed with a plural, for reasons which cannot always be definitely assigned.[442]

This is also the same argument given in the Haftorah.[443] Reyburn's own argument contends that the plural noun *Elohim* and the plural verb "wander" "is probably best to take the plural usage in a singular sense, since this usage occurs elsewhere."[444] Wenham says that this verse speaks of the true God, but because of the plural verb as seen by Reyburn, *Elohim* should be rendered "gods" instead of "(*Elohim* or God) they caused me to wander," for the interpretation "gods" better accommodates Abimelech's polytheistic outlook.[445] However, because this is considered an anomaly,[446] many scholars want it to read as stated above. If this plural verb, with the plural noun *Elohim*, is an anomaly, how is it that in Hebrew grammar it is the norm? The plural noun *Elohim* and the singular verb are the exception and not the grammatical rule. The rule is that all plural Hebrew nouns have plural verbs.[447] The fact that Christian scholars consider the plural noun, *Elohim*, and plural verb as correct usage, is an anomaly of its own according to Hebrew grammar. God chose to give this representation of Himself, and it does not need to be changed. The reason for changing its interpretation is because it does not meet a prescribed view that God can use a plural verb to affirm His plurality, if He chooses to do so.

Westermann indicates that it is quite unlikely that Abraham adapted to Abimelech's polytheism, because the God of Abraham also spoke to Abimelech and gave him instructions.[448] The context of this passage does not warrant Abraham accommodating a heathen (20:1, 17).[449]

Simply stated, according to the biblical text, *Elohim* (they) caused me to wander is the literal rendering. Because God chose the wording through inspiration, there is no reason to alter the meaning as Reyburn, Driver and the Haftorah prescribe.

Genesis 35:7

There he built an altar and named the site El-bethel, for it was there that God had revealed himself to him when he was fleeing from his brother.

---

[442] Driver, *Westminster Commentaries, the Book of Genesis*, 208.

[443] Hertz, *The Pentateuch and Haftorah*, 71.

[444] Reyburn and McG. Fry, *A Handbook on Genesis*, 455.

[445] Gordon Wenham, *Word Biblical Commentary: Genesis 16-50* (Waco, Tex: Word, 1987), 72.

[446] Anomaly: a deviation from the common rule, irregular.

[447] There are two other words that would also have this in common with *Elohim*, there are "waters" and "heavens."

[448] Westermann, *Genesis 12-36, A Continental Commentary*, 327.

[449] For additional comments on these passages (Gen 20:13, 35:7, 2 Sam 7:23 and Psa 58:11), see pages 14, 42, 49-50.

This passage clarifies that upon Jacob's return to Canaan, *Elohim* revealed Themselves to Jacob after he built the altar. True to Hebrew grammar, the plural *Elohim* is followed by a plural verb "revealed," which carries the interpretation that *Elohim* revealed Themselves, and that is God demonstrating His plurality. Westermann uses the same argument as in Genesis 20:13 that even though "revealed" is plural, it should be treated as a singular.[450] Speiser says that the verb "revealed" is plural but that it should be rendered "divine beings."[451] Reyburn discusses the text and includes nothing about a plural verb. Driver points out that the plural verb (revealed) "suggests that the sentence preserves a more polytheist version of the Bethel-legend than Gen 28:12."[452]

Hamilton recognizes the plural verb and sees *Elohim* referring to the true God, for two reasons. First, *Elohim* should have the same meaning as in vv.1, 5, where it clearly refers to the true God. Secondly, the text gives no evidence that the messengers (angels) revealed themselves to Jacob.[453] However, since God is the actual author of the infallible, inspired Scriptures, He had Moses record the specific personal pronouns and/or verbs that convey the clear meaning of plurality and/or tri-unity. Therefore, *Elohim* revealed Themselves to Jacob showing the plurality in the Godhead.

2 Samuel 7:23

> And what one nation in the earth is like thy people, even like Israel, whom God went to redeem for a people to himself, and to make him a name, and to do for you great things and terrible, for thy land, before thy people, which thou redeemedst to thee from Egypt, from the nations and their gods? (NASB)

This verse is the third example of God using a plural verb (redeemed) with his name (*Elohim*). Kohlenberger translates "they went out and redeemed," as being plural.[454] He shows that the plural reference grammatically clearly refers back to *Elohim*. Gramcord also treats the phrase as a plural referring back to *Elohim*.[455] Keil and Delitzsch state that the plural phrase refers to the true God.[456] Through the use of correct grammar, *Elohim* accomplishes the same result as when He violated correct grammar by bringing attention to His plurality. Hence, this plural verb can literally be translated "whom *Elohim* they went to redeem for Themselves." It has been observed by all the authors investigated that the reverse is never true. No one has addressed the issue of a singular verb with an obvious passage that deals with false gods.

---

[450] Westermann, *Genesis 12-36, A Continental Commentary*, 552.
[451] Speiser, *The Anchor Bible: Genesis*, 270.
[452] Driver, *Westminster Commentaries, The Book of Genesis*, 424.
[453] Hamilton, *The New International Commentary on the Old Testament: Genesis 18-50*, 377.
[454] John R. Kohlenberger III, *The Interlinear NIV Hebrew-English Old Testament* (Grand Rapids: Zondervan, 1987), 2:270.
[455] Miller, *Gramcord Institute*, CD Rom.
[456] Keil and Delitzsch, *Commentary on the Old Testament*, 2:352.

Psalm 58:11(12)

> Men will say, "There is, then, a reward for the righteous; there is, indeed, divine justice on earth."

> And men will say, "Surely there is a reward for the righteous; Surely there is a God who judges on earth!" (NASB)

In this verse, *Elohim* and the modifier, "judge," are in the plural. Lange says that this is the same usage as in Gen 20:13 and 2 Sam 7:23.[457] Both Beale[458] and Owens[459] identify the word "judge" as being plural. There is not much discussion in commentaries on the plural aspect of the word "judge" with *Elohim*. This verse could be translated literally as *"Elohim* they judge on earth!" Thus, Fruchtenbaum states that this and other "plural verbs in reference to the true God support the idea of plurality in the Godhead.[460]

Other Plural Descriptions

The next eight additional Hebrew Scriptures describe God as plural. Each is significant, but there will only be a very brief statement about each one.

Deuteronomy 5:23

> For what mortal ever heard the voice of the living God speak out of the fire, as we did and lived?

Weinfeld says that both words in the phrase "living God" are in the plural. *Elohim* is plural for God and "living" is a plural adjective (also found in 1 Sam 17:26, 36; Jer 10:10; 23:36).[461] As a plural adjective, "living" is a description of *Elohim* that gives added weight to God's plurality. Yet according to Gerleman, there are other passages that are translated "living," but they are in the singular (Josh 3:10; Hos 1:10; Ps 42:3; 2 Kgs 19:4, 16 with Isa 37:4, 17; 2 Sam 22:47 with Ps 18:47).[462] Though this term is not used in every case as a plural adjective there are five passages cited where *Elohim* uses them as a plural description of Himself.

---

[457] John Peter Lange, *Lange's Commentary on the Holy Scriptures* (trans. Philip Schaff; 12 vols. Grand Rapids: Zondervan, 1960), 5:353.
[458] Todd S. Beale, William A. Banks, and Colin Smith *Old Testament Parsing Guide: Job-Malachi*, 2:45.
[459] Owens, *Analytical Key to the Old Testament*, 3:356.
[460] Fruchtenbaum, *Messianic Christology*, 104.
[461] Moshe Weinfeld, *The Anchor Bible: Deuteronomy 1-11* (New York, NY: Doubleday, 1991), 320-321.
[462] Jenni and Westermann, *Theological Lexicon of the Old Testament*, 1:415.

Deuteronomy 10:17

For the Lord your God is God of gods, and Lord of lords, a great God, a mighty, and a terrible, which regardeth not persons, nor taketh reward.[463]

Moses uses several different names for the same God, as seen more clearly in the NASB:

For the LORD [*Yahweh*] your God [*Elohim*] is the God [*Elohim*] of gods [*Elohim*] and the Lord [*Adonai*] of lords [*Adonai*], the great, the mighty, and the awesome God [*El*] who does not show partiality, nor take a bribe. (Brackets are author's inserts.)

This verse could be translated as, "For *Yahweh* (singular) your *Elohim* (plural) is the *Elohim* (plural) of *Elohim* (plural) and the *Adonai's* (plural) of *Adonai's* (plural)[464] the great, the mighty, and the awesome *El* (singular)."   Cooper comments not only on the divine personalities of God but also on the polytheistic error that must be avoided:

These expressions echo the plurality of divine personalities of the one Sovereign Being. But to avoid the error of polytheism, He asserts their unity using the word *El*, God, in the singular number. Then He differentiates Himself from idols by asserting His absoluteness in greatness, power and terribleness-He is the almighty sovereign.[465]

Cooper expresses the cautions that God took in giving a clear picture of His plurality while protecting His unity with the use of *El*.

Joshua 24:19

Joshua, however, said to the people, "You will not be able to serve the LORD, for He is a holy God."

As Joshua gives an unusual speech to Israel at the end of his life, he speaks of *Elohim* as being a "holy God" as well as a jealous God. Both Kohlenberger[466] and Miller[467] acknowledge the word "holy" as a plural adjective. Lange says that it is a plural adjective and also cites 1 Sam 17:26 with Josh 24:19.[468] Both Cooper[469] and Fruchtenbaum[470] agree that "holy" should be translated "holy Gods." By the inspiration

---

[463] Harkavy, *The Twenty-Four Books of the Old Testament*, 1:307.

[464] Cooper, *The God of Israel*, 33.

[465] Cooper, *The God of Israel*, 34.

[466] Kohlenberger, *The Interlinear NIV Hebrew English Old Testament*, 70.

[467] Miller, *Gramcord Institute*, "CD Rom".

[468] Lange, *Lange's Commentary on the Holy Scriptures*, 2:185.

[469] Cooper, *The God of Israel*, 29.

[470] Fruchtenbaum, *Messianic Christology*, 107.

of the Spirit of God, Joshua chose to use another plural descriptive adjective to further add weight in describing the plurality of God.

Ecclesiastes 12:1

> Remember also your Creator in the days of your youth, before the evil days come and the years draw near when you will say, "I have no delight in them." (NASB)

In this passage, without the term *Elohim* or God mentioned, Solomon makes an interesting statement: "Remember now thy creator in the days of thy youth (KJV)." There is a range of views on the meaning of "creator" in this passage. Ogden and Zogbo state:

> "Your creator" is the object of the imperative 'remember.' The form here is plural (literally "those who created you").[471]

Ogden and Zogbo recognize it as a plural as does Leupold.

> *Bore'ekha* is the plural form *bore'im* plus a suffix and means literally "creators." Along with these plural affirmations of "creator" it is also unique because this word is also a plural adjective, which Kohlenberger translates as "Ones-Creating you."[472] Longman says the difficulty with the word "creator" is that it is plural, meaning that the literal reading is "your creators."[473] However, there is no difficulty because if inspiration of Scripture means anything, then God can represent Himself as a plural. Jamieson, Fausset and Brown state that clearly when they say:

> The Hebrew is Creators, plural, implying the plurality of persons, as in Genesis 1:26.[474]

If grammatically "creator" is a plural, why attempt to change what God, in His infinite wisdom, gave in His word?

However, the JPS version replaces "creator" with an alternate interpretation of this word. That version says, "So appreciate your vigor in the days of your youth." [475] The omission is significant because "creator" appears in the Hebrew Scriptures. Because some authors feel that this interpretation is not the best as one author said:

---

[471] Graham S. Ogden and Lynell Zogbo, *A Handbook on Ecclesiastes* (New York: United Bible Societies, 1997), 418.

[472] Kohlenberger, *The Interlinear NIV Hebrew English Old Testament*, 588.

[473] Longman III. Tremper, *The New International Commentary on the Old Testament: Ecclesiastes*, 264.

[474] Jamerison, Fausset, and Brown. *A Commentary: Critical, Experimental and Practical on the Old and New Testaments*, 3;541.

[475] Berlin and Brettler, *The Jewish Study Bible*, 1620.

Some commentaries think the text as we have it may have been damaged in transmission.[476]

This means there must be alternative readings to the Masoretic Text.[477] So three views[478] have arisen, of which one is reflected in the JPS version. The three views are first that it has a possible meaning of "your well" which is a metaphoric reference of a man's wife.[479] The second possible meaning is "your grave" or "your pit" which reflects death. The third possible meaning is "your vigor" which reflects mans health and strength.

The Hebrew text tells the reader that man is to remember his "creator" in the days of his youth. Others want to depart from it to an alternate non-Masoretic reading. The fact remains that "creator" is plural and because often in the wisdom literature God is referred to as Creator.

Psalm 149:2

Let Israel rejoice in its maker; let the children of Zion exult in their king.

Israel is to sing a new song to *Yahweh*, and Israel is to "rejoice in its maker." "Maker" is also a plural adjective and when literally translated would say, "Let Israel be glad in his makers." Keil and Delitzsch refer to "Maker" as "The Creator of Israel"[480] in the plural form. Dahood also notes that "maker" is a plural and even ties it in with Isa 54:5.[481] The interesting point is that Owens[482] recognizes "maker" as a plural adjective but refuses to acknowledge the plurality of God in this passage. Clearly, with *Elohim* and the "Let Us" personal pronouns of Genesis as well as other plural descriptive words as "creator," "maker," God presents Himself as a plurality by the use of a variety of plural terms for God.

Isaiah 54:5

For He who made you will espouse you—His name is "LORD of Hosts."
The Holy One of Israel will redeem you –He is called "God of all the Earth."

[476] Ogden and Zogbo, *A Handbook on Ecclesiastes*, 418.
[477] Longman III, *The New International Commentary on the Old Testament: Ecclesiastes*, 267.
[478] James L. Crenshaw, *The Old Testament Library, Ecclesiastes* (Philadelphia: Westminister Press, 1987), 184-185,
[479] Robert Gordis, *Koheleth, The Man and His World, A Study of Ecclesiastes* (New York: Schocken Books, 1968), 340.
[480] Keil and Delitzsch, *Commentary on the Old Testament*, 5:412.
[481] Mitchell Dahood, *The Anchor Bible: Psalms 101-150* (Garden City, NY: Doubleday, 1970), 357.
[482] Owens, *Analytical Key to the Old Testament*, 3:519.

> For your husband is your Maker, Whose name is the LORD of hosts; and your
> Redeemer is the Holy One of Israel, Who is called the God of all the earth.
> (NASB)

The plural descriptions in this verse present some very good images of God's relationship to Israel. There are four words to be noted in this verse: *Yahweh*, *Elohim*, "husband" and "maker." First, *Yahweh* is the personal name of Israel's God, in the singular. *Elohim*, being plural, is second and is used to name God and to affirm plurality. And finally, two plural adjectives, "maker" and "husband," literally mean that Israel has "Makers" and "Husbands." Keil and Delitzsch confirm this usage and also refer to some of the same passages previously discussed in this chapter (Josh 24:19; 1 Sam 17:26; Gen 20:13; 35:7 and 2 Sam 7:23).[483] Vine briefly combines "maker" and "husband" with *Elohim*[484] to affirm that *Elohim*, of Genesis 1, is the creator (Eccl 12:1) and is Israel's "husband" and "maker" when He made the covenant with them on Mount Sinai. Both "husband" and "maker" are plural adjectives describing *Yahweh*, which is in the singular. Young basically makes application of this passage to God and the Church rather than to God's relationship to Israel.[485] That raises another theological issue that will not be discussed in this book, the differences between Covenant[486] and Dispensational theology.[487] In Isa 54:4-5 Young does recognize the plural adjectives but attributes them to "plural of majesty." The impact of this verse is that Israel has "Makers" and "Husbands" whose name is *Yahweh* of hosts. *Yahweh* is Israel's Redeemer, the Holy One of Israel, whose name is *Elohim*. Once again, these verses show a plural affirmation of His being.

Isaiah 50:1-6

> Thus said the LORD: . . . The Lord God gave me a skilled tongue, to know how to speak timely words to the weary. Morning by morning, He rouses, He rouses my ear to give heed like disciples. The Lord God opened my ears, and I did not disobey, I did not run away. I offered my back to the floggers, and my cheeks to those who tore out my hair. I did not hide my face from insult and spittle.

Walter Kaiser recognizes these verses as a "Servant of the LORD" passage and along with three other passages (Isa 42:17; 49:1-6; 50:4-9; and 52:13-53:12) as the pre-

---

[483] Keil and Delitzsch, *Commentary on the Old Testament*, 7:344.

[484] V. E. Vine, *Isaiah* (Grand Rapids: Zondervan, 1946), 174.

[485] Edward Young, *The Book of Isaiah* (Grand Rapids: Eerdmans, 1972), 3:364.

[486] Covenant Theology: Covenant Theology teaches that the Church has replaced Israel and that now the Church is the Israel of God. Therefore, because God has no place for Israel in the future, the Church assumes all the promises to Israel. Israel can expect only the cursings. Covenant Theology sees only the dispensation of Grace, which involves all of time from Adam to present.

[487] Dispensational Theology: Acknowledges seven dispensations during which salvation is by faith alone. It recognizes Israel and the Church as two distinct groups that God has chosen to work through. During the Dispensation of Grace (Acts 2 through the Rapture of the Church) God is working with the Church, both Jewish and Gentile believers and not the nation of Israel at this time. However, because of His covenant promises to Abraham, God will again establish Israel and the Messiah will reign on the world from Jerusalem.

incarnate Messiah.[488] There are three basic explanations as to who the "Servant of the LORD" are in these passages.[489] First, Rashi, the renowned rabbi from the Middle Ages, taught that the servant was Israel.[490] The second is David Kimkhi, another renowned rabbi of the 12th and 13th century taught that "the servant is said to be Isaiah himself."[491] Briggs taught that this is not a reference to the Messiah, and like Kimkhi taught that it probably refers to Isaiah.[492] The third basic explanation is that the Servant of the LORD is the Messiah, Jesus.[493]

Arnold Fruchtenbaum observes in this passage the plurality of God, whereas no one else seems to. According to Fruchtenbaum, *Yahweh* (Isa 50:1) is the first person of the plurality to be mentioned. However, in v. 4 a second person of the plurality is mentioned in the phrase "the Lord God hath given me."[494] The "me" is the speaker identified in v. 1 as *Yahweh*. In v. 4 *Yahweh* speaks of *Adonai Elohim*, who gave Him the tongue of the learned. Who are these personalities of plurality? Verses 5-6 identify the person, not by name, but by the actions He voluntarily receives. The description is a preview of the flogging and mocking of the Messiah (Matt 27:26, 30-31).[495] In v. 6, Young gives a good insight into the volunteer beatings that the Messiah received before the crucifixion:

> There is majesty in the description, as though the servant were in full control of the situation. He sets himself forth as one who acts. Instead of saying that men beat him he declares that he himself gave his back to those who struck him. He either voluntarily yielded himself to flogging, or he offered himself thereto.[496]

Therefore, v. 4 and following identifies the speaker as *Yahweh*, the Servant of the LORD, who refers to the "Father" as *Adonai Elohim*. Here again, there are two members of the Godhead present, God the Father and God the Son.

Zechariah 11:4-14

> Then I said to them, "If you are satisfied, pay me my wages; if not, don't." So they weighed out my wages, thirty shekels of silver. The noble sum that I was worth in their estimation. The LORD said to me, "Deposit it in the treasury." And I took the thirty shekels and deposited it in the treasury in the House of the LORD. (vv. 12-13)

---

[488] Walter C. Kaiser, Jr. *Toward an Old Testament Theology* (Grand Rapids, Zondervan, 1991), 215.

[489] There are several other authors that can be studied as to the three basic views on the Servant of the Lord passages in Isaiah: (1) Victor Buksbazen, *Isaiah's Messiah* (Bellmawr, NJ: Friends of Israel Gospel Ministry, 2002). (2) David Baron, *The Servant of Jehovah* (Jerusalem: Keren Ahvah Meshihit, 2000). (3) Michael L. Brown, *Answering Jewish Objections to Jesus* (vol. 3. Grand Rapids: Baker, 2003), 40-49.

[490] Slotki, *The Soncino Books of the Bible, Isaiah*, 247.

[491] Slotki, *The Soncino Books of the Bible, Isaiah*, 247.

[492] Charles A Briggs, *Messianic Prophecy* (Peabody, MA: Hendrickson, 1988), 356.

[493] Edward J. Young, *The Book of Isaiah* (Grand Rapids: Eerdmans, 1972), 3:301.

[494] Fruchtenbaum, *Messianic Christology*, 50-51.

[495] Herbert Wolf, *Interpreting Isaiah* (Grand Rapids: Zondervan, 1985), 210.

[496] Young, *Isaiah*, 3:300.

Although this passage shows that the speaker is *Yahweh*, yet what happened to *Yahweh* never happened to God the Father, but to God the Son. Numerous scholars agree on the identity of *Yahweh* in Zech 11:12-13 as *Yeshua* the Messiah of Israel (Keil and Delitzsch;[497] Unger;[498] Merrill;[499] Baron;[500] Kaiser;[501] Smith;[502] Hengstenberg;[503] Feinberg;[504] Henderson;[505] Laetsch.[506] It has already been noted that the *Tanakh* records two *Yahwehs* (Gen 19:24, Isa 44:6, Hos 1:4-7, Zech 2:8-9).[507] In this passage the LORD (*Yahweh*) is presented as the good Shepherd as Zechariah acts out the symbolic action of receiving the LORD's wages from the people.[508]

One thing about the verse stands out clearly. The LORD (*Yahweh*) was speaking and used the term "I" repeatedly to reaffirm throughout this passage that it was He who spoke (vv. 4, 6-10, 12-14). Verses 4 and 13 identified LORD (*Yahweh*) as the speaker, whereas in the other verses He uses the first person pronoun "I." In v. 12, *Yahweh* asks for His wages through Zechariah, who was acting out the role of the good Shepherd. The good Shepherd's (Messiah) request is not compulsory. The wages that *Yahweh* was looking for was Israel's love, obedience and devotion to God their Shepherd.[509] However, instead of giving Him the internal or spiritual wage of their repentance, Israel gave Him a monetary wage, which was a deliberate insult.[510] Israel could have refrained from paying wages altogether, but instead insulted the good Shepherd with 30 pieces of silver, which according to the Law, is the price of a dead slave (Exod 21:32).[511] Merrill clarifies that *Yahweh*, rather than Zechariah, is the one being appraised as unworthy (Zech 12:13).[512] The one who was sold out for 30 pieces of silver was the LORD [*Yahweh*], the personal God of Israel, in this case, the Messiah *Yeshua*. Matt 23:37 takes on greater meaning when it is understood that *Yeshua* is speaking as God the Father or as LORD (*Yahweh*), from the *Tanakh*:

> O Jerusalem, Jerusalem, thou that killest the prophets, and stonest them which are sent to thee, how often would I have gathered thy children together, even as a hen gathereth her chickens under her wings, and ye would not!

---

[497] Keil and Delitzsch. *Commentary on the Old Testament in Ten Volumes*, 10:368.

[498] Merrill F. Unger, *Zechariah: Prophet of Messiah's Glory* (Grand Rapids: Zondervan, 1963), 199.

[499] Eugene H. Merrill, *An Exegetical Commentary: Haggai, Zechariah, Malachi* (Chicago: Moody, 1994), 298.

[500] Baron, *The Visions and Prophecies of Zechariah*, 380, 403-407.

[501] Walter C. Kaiser, Jr. *The Communicator's Commentary: Micah – Malachi* (vol. 21, Waco, TX: Word, 1992), 394.

[502] Smith, *The Promised Messiah*, 444.

[503] Hengstenberg, *Christology of the Old Testament*, 4:35.

[504] Charles L. Feinberg, *The Minor Prophets* (Chicago: Moody, 1952), 328.

[505] Ebenezer Henderson, *Thornapple Commentaries: The Twelve Minor Prophets* (Grand Rapids: Baker, 1980), 420.

[506] Theodore Laetsch, *The Minor Prophets* (St. Louis: Concordia, 1956), 474.

[507] See chapter two, section entitled *Yahweh*.

[508] Baron, *The Visions and Prophecies of Zechariah*, 380.

[509] Feinberg, *The Minor Prophets*, 328.

[510] Hengstenberg, *Christology of the Old Testament*, 4:35.

[511] Smith, *The Promised Messiah*, 444.

[512] Merrill, *An Exegetical Commentary: Haggai, Zechariah, Malachi*, 298.

Tri-unity in Isaiah

Isaiah was an eighth-century prophet, a contemporary with Micah. His presentation of the Emmanuel (Isa 7-12), Servant of the LORD (Isa 42, 49, 50, and 53), and the future restoration of Israel (Isa 54, 60-66) makes this book one of the greatest treasures in the *Tanakh.* Isaiah prophesied the captivity of Israel and the fall of Babylon to the Medes and Persians, as well as God anointing Cyrus, who would permit Jewish people to return home, back to the land of Israel. Isaiah prophesied the birth of the Messiah, His message, His rejection and His sufferings. Isaiah was a great prophet, a man who received an abundance of prophecies from the Lord concerning His people and His Messiah. Last of all, Isaiah brings all three members of the unity of God together in at least three chapters (Isa 48:12-16, 61:1, 63:7-14). These chapters provide the best evidence for the tri-unity of God in the Hebrew Scriptures.

Isaiah 48:12-16

> Listen to Me, O Jacob, Israel, whom I have called: I am He—I am the first, and I Am the last as well. My own hand founded the earth, My right hand spread out the skies. I call unto them, let them stand up. (vv. 12-13)

> Draw near to Me and hear this: From the beginning, I did not speak in secret; from the time anything existed, I was there. And now the Lord God has sent Me, endowed with His spirit. (v. 16)

The passage begins with a familiar word, *Shema*, the same word used in Deut 6:4. It becomes obvious that God wants Israel to hear because He uses the term listen (*Shema*) in vv. 12, 14, and 16. Yet in v. 18 *Yahweh* says that Israel did not hear or obey His commandments. In v. 12, the speaker is establishing that He called them by saying, "Listen (*Shema*) to me, O Jacob, Israel, whom I called." According to Judg 2:1, the Messenger (Angel) of *Yahweh* called Israel where He references the Abrahamic Covenant in Genesis 15. All three references reflect the same person. *Yahweh* continues speaking by saying, "I AM He, I AM the first, I AM the last." That phrase simply means that *Yahweh* was before time and will be after time is no more. *Yahweh* continues in v. 13 reflecting back to Genesis 1 by identifying Himself as *Elohim* the Creator whose "own hand founded the earth, My right hand spread out the skies. I call unto them, let them stand up." Verses 14 and 15 refer to Cyrus, the Mede, who will judge Babylon and allow Israel to return. In v. 16 it is as if *Yahweh* was calling Israel to come close and hear (*Shema*). He makes one point: "I did not speak in secret" or He did not hide His thoughts from them. From the time of your calling, even the calling of Cyrus, He was there. Young accurately states that from the beginning God spoke openly and clearly to His people:

Beginning refers to the time when God first began to give prophetic revelations. From the moment that God first spoke to man through the prophets He did not speak in secret but openly and clearly.[513]

Up to this point, in these verses there is general agreement among scholars that it is *Yahweh* who is speaking. However, in the last part of this verse there is no unanimity among scholars as to who is speaking.

There are two contradictory views concerning the identity of the speaker in Isaiah 48:16c, "And now the Lord God has sent me, endowed with His spirit." A footnote in the JPS version says that it literally reads "and His spirit."[514] Slotki says that according to Rabbi David Kimchi (1160-1235), the "sent one" is the prophet who was present, and he would be sent with His Spirit within him.[515] According to Slotki, "Bible critics" have come to the conclusion that there are three Isaiah's who wrote the book of Isaiah and the second (Deutero-) Isaiah would be the prophet represented in verse 16.[516] Others in the same frame as Slotki say that there are two Isaiah's. These scholars want to change speakers and insert Isaiah or an anonymous "Second Isaiah."[517] Yet still others believe that the speaker is *Yahweh* Himself. Wolf summarizes the two views as to the speaker:

> The phrase the Sovereign LORD has sent me, with his Spirit, either means that God sent Isaiah to speak these words through the power of the Holy Spirit or that God would send the Servant as another of the new things He would perform (v. 6).[518]

Webb points out that the speaker in Isa 48:16c must be the Servant of the LORD (*Yahweh* the Messiah) due to the context in which the statement is placed. Webb gives his thoughts on the subject that *Yahweh* is speaking before and immediately following this phrase in question. So since *Yahweh* is speaking before and after the phrase "And now the Lord God has sent Me, endowed with His spirit," it makes no logical sense to say that someone else is speaking:

> With this issue hanging heavily in the air, the scene is set for the Servant of the LORD to take center stage again in chapter 49. In fact it is more than likely that his voice has already been heard here in chapter 48. For who else can it be who announces his presence in verse 16 with the words, And now the Sovereign LORD has sent me, with his Spirit?

---

[513] Young, *The Book of Isaiah*, 3:258.
[514] Berlin and Brettler, *The Jewish Study Bible*, 882.
[515] Slotki, *The Soncino Books of the Bible, Isaiah*, 237.
[516] Slotki, *The Soncino Books of the Bible, Isaiah*, Introduction x.
[517] Barry G. Webb, *The Message of Isaiah* (Downers Grove, IL: Inter-Varsity, 1996), 192.
[518] Wolf, *Interpreting Isaiah*, 204.

But the reference to the Spirit pointedly recalls the presentation of the Servant in 42:1, I will put my Spirit on him. And the voice we hear in the Sovereign LORD has sent me sounds remarkably like the voice we are about to hear again in 49:1: before I was born the LORD called Me.[519]

Vine does not even make reference to the comment that there is another speaker in v. 16c. He points to the speaker as being the Messiah. He very clearly states his view:

The close of verse 16 brings before us a striking instance of the work of the Trinity: and now the Lord God hath sent Me and His Spirit. That Christ is the Speaker, and not the prophet is to be gathered from a comparison with 61:1. His words are undoubtedly a prelude to what He is about to declare of Himself in chapter 49:5-6.[520]

To the contrary, Young points out that the Lord and the speaker are two different persons:

Who is the speaker in the third clause? Obviously it cannot be the Lord, for a distinction is made between the speaker and the Lord.

The speaker is the Servant par excellence, already introduced in 42:1, and about to be brought more prominently into the picture in chapters forty-nine, fifty, and fifty-three.[521]

The point of this whole discussion is to discover who is in view in v. 16. There are two sides with completely opposing views. If the speaker is not *Yahweh*, minimally the plurality of God is still present with the "Lord God" and "His Spirit." But if *Yahweh* (Me) is the speaker, from v. 12 onward, the tri-unity of God is present. This is significant, if *Yahweh* is the speaker. The one who called Israel (Abrahamic Covenant), also identified Himself as the I AM (Ex 3:14), the first and last, and the creator in Genesis 1. Verse 16c gives three distinct personalities in the Godhead. The reference of "Me" is distinct from the Lord God (*Adonai Elohim*) and is distinct from the Holy Spirit. Simply put, the Lord God (Father) sends Me (Son) and the Holy Spirit. It is not a coincidence that in the Gospel of John, over 40 times *Yeshua* refers to the fact that the Father sent Him, which collaborates with Isa 48:16 as well as Zech 2:6-11. In Isa 48:16 there is a very clear presentation of the tri-unity of God, which is supported by Barackman, Strong, and Berkhof. Strong's position is clear when he states that "there are three who are implicitly recognized as God."[522] Berkhof, in referencing the tri-unity of God in Isa 48:16, says that in the Hebrew Scriptures God speaks to other members of the Godhead and the Messiah speaks of God the Spirit:

---

[519] Webb, *The Message of Isaiah*, 192.
[520] Vine, *Isaiah*, 139.
[521] Young, *Isaiah*, 3:258-259.
[522] Strong, *Systematic Theology*, 317-318.

God is the speaker, and mentions both the Messiah and the Spirit, or the Messiah is the speaker who mentions both God and the Spirit, Isa. 48:16; 61:1; 63:9, 10. Thus the Old Testament contains a clear anticipation of the fuller revelation of the Trinity in the New Testament.[523]

Likewise, Barackman specifically states that Isaiah 48:16 is a reference to the tri-unity of God in the Hebrew Scriptures:

> The Trinity consists of more than two Persons is indicated by the plural noun "God" (Heb. Elohim in Gen 1:1) and the plural pronoun "us" (Gen 1:26; 3:22; 11:7; Isa 6:8). The three Persons of the Trinity are seen in Isaiah 48:16 and 61:1, with the Son (the Messiah) speaking in both passages.[524]

In summary, the evidence is there, from numerous sources, that Isa 48:16 is a reference to the triune God of the Hebrew Scriptures.

Isaiah 61:1-2a

> The Spirit of the Lord God is upon me, because the LORD has anointed me; He has sent me as a herald of joy to the humble, to bind up the wound of heart, to proclaim release to the captives, Liberation to the imprisoned; to proclaim a year of the LORD's favor.

This passage is a well-known passage from the New Covenant because *Yeshua* quoted it when He read from the scroll of Isaiah in the synagogue in Nazareth (Lk 4:16-22). The only thing the Soncino Commentary series has to say about the verse is that the anointing is to be taken metaphorically because only kings and priests were anointed.[525] However, it seems unlikely that *Yeshua* would have been anointed since He was neither an earthly king nor a priest. So how was He anointed? According to Isa 11:2 and 42:1, *Yeshua* by the Holy Spirit will be anointed for service. Matt 3:16 says exactly the same thing as Isa 61:1, that He was anointed, not with oil, but with the Holy Spirit.

The tri-unity of God is clearly enunciated in Isa 61:1. Kaiser speaks to the point by saying:

> *Yahweh* appoints the Servant and the Spirit anoints him, thereby making one of the earliest constructs of the doctrine of the Trinity. Rather than being anointed with oil as many the priests and kings in the OT, this Servant is anointed by the Holy Spirit himself.[526]

---

[523] L. Berkhof, *Systematic Theology*, 86.

[524] Barackman, *Practical Christian Theology*, 63.

[525] Slotki, *The Soncino Books of the Bible, Isaiah*, 298.

[526] Walter C. Kaiser, *The Messiah in the Old Testament* (Grand Rapids: Zondervan, 1995), 183.

Vine states firmly that "this passage speaks of the Trinity."[527] Young echoes that point by saying that Isa 61:1 is Trinitarian in content and that the speaker is the Messiah.[528] Berkhof recognizes all three passages as representing the tri-unity of God (Isa 48:16, 61:1, 63:7-10).

Isaiah 63:7-14

In Isa 48:16 and 61:1, Isaiah emphasizes the tri-unity of God. Previously, it was all in one verse, but here it is spread out over several verses. Isaiah himself is speaking on behalf of *Yahweh*. He refers to *Yahweh* in v. 7. The "Angel of His presence" (Exod. 23:20-23) in v. 9, who saved Israel from their affliction, was the Messenger (Angel) of *Yahweh* that appeared throughout biblical history in the *Tanakh*, who led them out of Egypt, through the wilderness and into the Promise Land, Canaan. Then in vv. 10, 14 Isaiah references the Holy Spirit. Once again, the tri-unity of God is present.

---

[527] Vine, *Isaiah*, 199.
[528] Young, *The Book of Isaiah*, 3:459.

CHAPTER SIX

HOLY SPIRIT רוּחַ קָדוֹשׁ

The men who penned the New Covenant clearly perceived the Holy Spirit to be as much "God" as they did *Yeshua* (Jesus). However, it is still slightly challenging. People of a Unitarian belief only see the Holy Spirit as an impersonal power or influence of God. Once again, can it be determined from the Hebrew Scriptures alone that the Holy Spirit is indeed God, equal in His nature and essence with God the Father and God the Son. The distinctions – first, second, and third person – are not believed to be a reference to rank because all three persons are equal in power and honor.[529] The New Covenant has abundant references to the person of the Holy Spirit, and because of this abundance, many authors rely heavily on the New Covenant to prove the personality of the Holy Spirit. In dealing with progressive revelation, in relationship to Messiah, the Son of God, and the Holy Spirit, they are not as clearly stated as in the New Covenant. But they are there and He is active in the *Tanakh*.

Difficulties with the Term "Spirit" רוּחַ

One of the difficulties with the Holy Spirit is how to determine if He is distinct from God the Father because the Father is also Spirit. Erickson states the problem of understanding the term "Spirit" as it relates to God:

> It is often difficult to identify the Holy Spirit within the Old Testament, for it reflects the earliest stages of progressive revelation. In fact, the term "Holy Spirit" is rarely employed here. Rather, the usual expression is the "the Spirit of God."[530]

Louis Goldberg, a Jewish believer in Messiah, draws attention to a basic understanding scholars must have as they deal with the distinction between God, who is a spirit, and the Holy Spirit. He states the following:

> Of course, our Jewish friends do not acknowledge the Spirit as One in the tri-unity of God; the term Spirit is recognized as a synonym for God.[531]

John Feinberg also expresses the difficulty of determining whether a certain text is speaking of the Father's spirit or the Holy Spirit:

> The OT also frequently refers to the Spirit of God. Though in some passages such as Gen 6:3 ("My spirit shall not strive") and Ps 139:7 (the psalmist asks

---

[529] Leon J. Wood, *The Holy Spirit in the Old Testament* (Eugene, OR: Wipf and Stock Publishers, 1998), 13.

[530] Millard J. Erickson, *Christian Theology*, 2nd Ed, 881.

[531] Louis Goldberg, *Our Jewish Friends*, 83.

God, "Where can I go from thy Spirit?") it is not entirely clear whether the Spirit is a distinct personage or rather a reference to God the Father's Spirit, there are many passages in which the Spirit is distinct.[532]

This study has proved the reality of Goldberg and Feinberg's observations. Verses that refer to the Spirit of God are difficult to prove there is a distinction between the Father and the Holy Spirit. Hildebrandt echoes Feinberg's explanation that the Hebrew Scriptures reveal the "Spirit" but that the focus is different than in the New Covenant when he says:

> But the main difficulty in presenting the personhood of the Spirit in the OT is due to the OT focus on the deeds of the Spirit in relation to humankind. Thus, non-personal words and phrases are used to describe the Spirit as divine energy, as a wind and fire, as light and space.[533]

Some authors, such as Erickson, see clearly the Third Person of the God-head in the Hebrew Scripture but also recognize the difficulties in distinguishing His person. He points out that the words "Spirit" and "God" are two nouns and that many times the reader could not distinguish between the two different persons as seen in the following quote:

> Most Old Testament references to the Third Person of the Trinity consist of the two nouns *Spirit* and *God*. It is not apparent from this construction that a separate person is involved. The expression "Spirit of God" could well be understood as being simply a reference to the will, mind, or activity of God. There are, however, some cases where the New Testament makes it clear that an Old Testament reference to the "Spirit of God" is a reference to the Holy Spirit. One of the most prominent of these New Testament passages is Acts 2:16-21, where Peter explains that what is occurring at Pentecost is the fulfillment of the prophet Joel's statement, "I will pour out my Spirit on all people" (2:17).[534]

These authors express the same concerns that this author sees on how the term "spirit" is used in connection with God. However, T. S. Caulley goes too far when he makes a definite statement that the Holy Spirit is not mentioned, as a person, in the Hebrew Scriptures. He states:

> The OT does not contain an idea of a semi-independent divine entity, the Holy Spirit. Rather, we find special expressions of God's activity with and through men. God's spirit is holy in the same way his word and his name are holy; they are all forms of his revelation and, as such, are set in antithesis to all things human or material.[535]

---

[532] John Feinberg, *No One Like Him*, 454.

[533] Wilf Hildebrandt, *An Old Testament Theology of the Spirit of God* (Peabody, MA: Hendrickson, 1995), 89.

[534] Millard J. Erickson, *Christian Theology*, 2nd Ed, 882.

[535] Walter A. Elwell, *Evangelical Dictionary of Theology* (Grand Rapids, MI: Baker, 1984), 521-522.

Caulley leaves the impression that the Holy Spirit is not a separate entity from the other members of the God-head. Caulley further confirms that impression when he states:

> Holy Spirit: In the NT, the third person of the Trinity; in the OT, God's power. In the OT the spirit of the Lord is generally an expression for God's power, the extension of himself whereby he carries out many of his mighty deeds.[536]

Caulley seems to deny the personality of the Holy Spirit in the *Tanakh*. J. H. Raven is quoted by Erickson who reflects the same view as Caulley, when he states the following:

> There is here no distinction of persons in the God-head. The Spirit of God in the Old Testament is God himself exercising active influence.[537]

That statement is not acceptable, as will be seen later in this chapter, because the *Tanakh* does make a distinction between "God" and the "Spirit." God, as the greatest communicator in the universe who reveals Himself as a plurality in the Hebrew Scriptures, would not reveal His nature and essence in an incomplete manner. The writers of the New Covenant completely understood the concept of the plurality of God, including the Holy Spirit, as the third person of the God-head. How did they come to understand that concept? It was through the *Tanakh*! Some scholars do not see the Holy Spirit and verses that speak of the spirit, which admittedly is sometimes difficult or hard to determine how to interpret them. Consequently, only the verses that show, without question, that the Holy Spirit, is a person, will be dealt with in this chapter.

The Use of the Term "Spirit"

The basic idea of *ruah* (Gr. *Pneuma*) is "air in motion" from air which cannot come between a crocodile's scales (Job 41:16) to the blast of a storm (Isa 25:4; Hab 1:11). The Hebrew word רוּחַ or *ruah* is used 387 times in the Hebrew Scriptures.[538] Wood says that *ruah* is used in a noun or verb form 388 times. Wood further states that it is used in the following ways:

> It is used to designate the human spirit, God's Holy Spirit, and several other entities such as "wind," "breath," "odor," and "space." Surprisingly, its most basic meaning seems to have been "wind."[539]

Ruah is used in all portions of the *Tanakh* as Hildebrandt gives the divisions of each section of the Hebrew Scriptures. It is used 38 times in the Torah (Law) while in the

---

[536] Walter A. Elwell, *Evangelical Dictionary of Theology*, 521.
[537] Millard J. Erickson, *Christian Theology*, 2nd Ed, 882. Erickson quotes J.H. Raven from his work called the History of the Religion of Israel (Grand Rapids, MI: Baker, 1979), 164.
[538] William A. VanGemeren, *Dictionary of Old Testament and Exegesis*, 3:1073.
[539] Leon J. Wood, *The Holy Spirit in the Old Testament*, 16.

Prophets 201 times (47 in former Prophets and 154 in the latter Prophets), 139 times in the Writings and is used in the Aramaic portions of Daniel 11 times.[540] Of the 387 times that *ruah* is used 136 times the term is applied to God and 129 times to man or animals. The basic meaning is physical "wind" or "breath."[541]

Ruah has different uses for spirit as expressed in emotions of aggressiveness (Isa 25:4) or anger (Jud 8:3; Prov 29:11). *Ruah* or breath is further used to signify activity and life (Job 17:1), a "second wind," and he "revives" (Judg 15:19; 1 Sam 30:12; Gen 45:27). The breath of mankind is in the hands of God (Job 12:10; Isa 42:5). Also, *ruah* is used of angelic beings as in "a spirit from God."[542] Other examples of this usage of *ruah* is: as the wind shakes the trees (Isa 7:2), or as in the "cool" of the day (Gen 3:8), or as the breath which the Lord gives to the people (Isa 42:5), or even as bad breath (odor) as in Job 19:17 where the literal rendering is "my breath is strange to my wife."[543] In the *Dictionary of Old Testament Theological and* Exegesis, it is divided into six areas (wind, compass point, breath, disposition, seat of cognition and volition and spirit) to help show the usage of *ruah*. Under wind:

(1) *Ruah* is used to refer to the force of nature, commonly known as wind (Exod 10:13; Num 11:31; 1 Kgs 18:45; 2 Kgs 3:17; Psa 48:7 [8]; Isa 7:2; 41:16; Jer 18:17; Ezek 17:10; Hos 13:15; Jonah 4:8).

(2) *Ruah* was used as four compass points, as in "every wind" or as in every direction (Ezek 5:10-12; 12:14; 17:21; Jer 49:36; Ezek 37:9 Zech 2:6 [10]; Dan 7:2).

(3) *Ruah* is also rendered as breath, which is similar to wind, in that both denote the movement of air. It is used to "refer to the life-sustaining function called breathing or breath. This breath is the essence of life (Gen 6:17; Job 12:10; Isa 38:16; 42:5; Ezek 37:5-14; Mal 2:15-16)."

(4) *Ruah* is used to show "a person's or group's disposition, attitude, mood, inclination, as an approximate synonym of *nepel*, appetite, disposition, person (Gen 26:35; Exod 6:9; 1 Kgs21:5; Job 21:4; Prov 14:29; Isa 19:3; Ezek 3:14)."

(5) *Ruah* denotes the seat of cognition and volition, those activities involved in thinking, aptitude, and decision-making. The knowledge and ability to perform a particular task is one clear example of this use of *ruah* (I Chr 28:12; Isa 29:24; Ezek 11:5-6; 20:32; 38:10).

---

[540] Wilf Hildebrandt, *An Old Testament Theology of the Spirit of God* (Peabody, MA: Hendrickson, 1995), 2.

[541] William Dyrness, *Themes in Old Testament Theology* (Downers Grove, IL: InterVarsity Press, 1977), 86.

[542] Harris, Archer, and Waltke, *Theological Wordbook of the Old Testament*, 836.

[543] William Dyrness, *Themes in Old Testament Theology*, 86.

(6) Lastly, in the *Tanakh* the most significant usage of *ruah* involves its representation of the metaphysical or numinous, specifically the "Spirit of God/ the LORD." The expression "Spirit of God" actually appears only 11 times (Gen 1:2; Psa 104:29; Job 33:4), "Spirit of the LORD" 25 times (Judg 9:23; 1 Sam 16:14-16, 23; 18:10; 19:9), and Holy Spirit 3 times (Psa 51:11 [13]; Isa 63:10-11).[544]

Personality and Work of the Holy Spirit in the *Tanakh*

Many scriptures deal with *ruah* in a non-personal manner. But the focus of this paper is on the ways in which the term reflects the personality of the Holy Spirit and that He is distinct from the Father and the Son. The Holy Spirit did operate in the New Covenant as a person, but it is different in the *Tanakh* in that He did his work in the form of acts without using a personal description of Himself.

The Holy Spirit is a Person

If the plurality of God is true and it can stand on its own in the *Tanakh* without the well documented New Covenant, then the tri-unity of the New Covenant should also be able to stand on its own in the Hebrew Scriptures, in relation to the Holy Spirit. Morey uses the same logic to argue that whatever biblical evidence is used to show the Son must be taken the same way in relation to the Holy Spirit:

> The Biblical evidence that convinced us that the Father and the Son are Persons, is the exact same kind of evidence that demonstrates that the Spirit is a Person. Thus, to deny the evidence when we apply it to the Spirit, but to accept it when we apply it to the Father or to the Son is sheer hypocrisy as well as being self-refuting. If the evidence is valid for One, then it is valid for all Three.[545]

Passages that affirm the Holy Spirit's personality will be examined first. Both David Cooper and Robert Morey express this point:

> Turning back to our original passage, Isaiah 63:8-10, we see God who becomes the Saviour of Israel (vs. 8). In verse 9 the angel of His presence saved her in that He carried out the actual plan of the Almighty. Then in verse 10 we note the Holy Spirit whom she grieved and against whom she rebelled. Thus in these three verses we see three divine personalities.[546]

First, Isaiah says that קָדְשׁוֹ "His Holy Spirit" was וְעִצְּבוּ "grieved to the point of being provoked." The word וְעִצְּבוּ is a waw consecutive participle of עָצָב and

---

[544] Willem A. VanGemeren, *Dictionary of Old Testament and Exegesis*, 3:1073-1076.
[545] Morey, *The Trinity: Evidence and Issues*, 188.
[546] Cooper, *The God of Israel*, 80.

means to feel profound hurt, pain, and grief. For example, the word עָצָב was used to describe the inward pain felt by David when he heard that his son Absalom was dead (2 Sam 19:1-2). His weeping reveals how deeply he felt the pain. It was even used of God in Gen 6:6, where we are told, "He was grieved in His heart." Secondly, only a Person can be grieved by מְרִי "rebellion" against Him. Thus, the Holy Spirit is a Person and not an impersonal force.[547]

Walvoord agrees with Cooper and Morey that the Isa 63:10 passage expresses the personality of the Holy Spirit.[548] Here the Holy Spirit is not only recognized as a person but as a distinct person from the other members of the tri-unity.

In Micah 2:7 the author expresses the fact that the Holy Spirit is capable of being impatient. Being impatient is a quality of a person. A wind or force does not have the personal capacity to be annoyed or be impatient. Morey states that fact:

> The word translated "impatient" is הֲקָצַר which is a qal perfect of the word קָצַר which means to be impatient. It is used in this sense in such places as Num 21:4; Judg 10:16; 16:16, etc. The question, "Is the Spirit of the LORD impatient?" reveals that the Jews believed that the Holy Spirit was a Person capable of becoming annoyed with the sin of man.[549]

Further statements on the personality of the Holy Spirit are given by Payne in referring to Moses. Payne states that God said to Moses, the Spirit, not My Spirit, which would not indicate the Spirit of the Father, but the Spirit who is distinct from Himself:

> The personality of the Spirit was first revealed to Moses. Specifically, God informed Moses relative to the seventy elders who were to assist him in government: "I will take of the Spirit who is upon you and I will place [Him] upon them, so they may bear the burden of the people with thee" (Num 11:17). This statement indicates that the Spirit is distinct from *Yahweh*, that He is personal (giving judicial advice), and that He is divine (guiding Israel).[550]

Payne's statement shows the distinctness between two members of the tri-unity. It also shows that the Holy Spirit will guide, which is something that a person does, as He guides the 70 elders in administering judicial advice to the people of Israel. Payne also references Isa 48:16 ("and the Lord God has sent Me and His Spirit") and shows the Holy Spirit to be a personality that is distinct from the Father.[551] Kirkpatrick also affirms the personality of the Holy Spirit in referencing some of the same passages already cited:

---

[547] Robert Morey, *The Trinity: Evidence and Issues*, 189.
[548] John Walvoord, *The Holy Spirit* (Findlay, OH: Dunham Publishing, 1958), 7.
[549] Robert Morey, *The Trinity: Evidence and Issues*, 190.
[550] Barton Payne, *The Theology of the Older Testament* (Grand Rapids, MI: Zondervan, 1962), 173.
[551] Barton Payne, *The Theology of the Older Testament*, 173.

Passages like these which imply that the spirit of Jehovah personally acts, prepare the way for the New Testament revelation concerning Him, and can be used in the fullest Christian sense.[552]

A further confirmation on the personality of the Holy Spirit is seen in creation with the act of intelligence in relation to creation of the world. To be involved in the creation of the universe and the creation of man shows a tremendous complex mind far beyond human understanding. Ryrie refers to Job 26:13 and 33:4 where Job references the Spirit of God as the creator.[553] In Psalm 104:30 the psalmist says; "Thou dost send forth Thy Spirit, they are created; and Thou dost renew the face of the ground." Lockyer states the following in relation to this verse:

> It is evident from the immediate context that the "all" and the "they" refer to the living creatures of the whole world, and to beasts, birds, and fish in particular.[554]

Enns expresses the personality of the Holy Spirit in showing His omnipotence and omnipresence in Job 33:4 and Psalm 139:7-10.[555]

Not only does the "Spirit" guide and show intelligence, but in 2 Samuel 23:1 David, when on his deathbed, makes a very fascinating statement when he said that the Holy Spirit spoke by him which is another act of personality:

> These are the last words of David: The utterance of David the son of Jesse, the utterance of the man set on high, the anointed of the God of Jacob, the favorite of Songs of Israel: The spirit of the LORD has spoken through me, His message is on my tongue.

How much of the tri-unity of God did David understand? That may never be known. But this text and others clarify that David minimally understood the plurality of God. Morey makes a summary statement in relation to the Holy Spirit as a person speaking through David:

> The personhood of the Spirit is as certain as the inspiration of the Psalms of David. Notice that it is the Spirit's word which is the word of God. Only a Person can speak the word of God. Only a self-conscious living, person speaks.[556]

Once again in Nehemiah 9:30 the personality of the Holy Spirit is given in that He testified against rebellious Israel. Morey makes a firm statement that only a person has the capability of "testifying" or giving witness:"

---

[552] A. F. Kirkpatrick, *The Book of Psalms* (Cambridge: The University Press, 1914), 2:293.

[553] Charles C. Ryrie, *The Holy Spirit* (Chicago, IL: Moody, 1965), 31

[554] Herbert Lockyer, *All about the Holy Spirit* (Peabody, MA: Hendrickson, 1995), 46.

[555] Paul Enns, *The Moody Handbook of Theology*, 250.

[556] Robert Morey, *The Trinity: Evidence and Issues*, 190-191.

The word translated "testified against" is וַתָּעַד which is a waw consecutive imperfect and means to bear witness, testify, or protest against someone. It is used of God (Psa 50:7; 81:8) as well as man (Gen 43:3; Deut 8:19). An impersonal force or power cannot bear witness, testify or protest anything.[557]

Ezekiel gives a very clear example of the personality of the Holy Spirit in Ezek 2:2; 8:3; 11:1. Here the Lord God tells Ezekiel to get up and then the "Spirit entered me." In the other two passages the "Spirit lifted me up." This is giving the activity of the Holy Spirit in His act of lifting up Ezekiel.[558] These previous verses cited serve as several examples to substantiate the personality of the Holy Spirit. Again, as Morey has stated, if the same evidence to confirm the fact of the personality of the Second Person of the tri-unity is used, then the Holy Spirit must be treated in the same manner.

Holy Spirit in Creation

Pache relates that the account of the creation is an allusion to the Trinity and indirectly to the Spirit. In Gen 1:1 *Elohim*, (discussed in chapter two as a plural noun) could be just as easily translated "In the beginning, the Gods created." Included with *Elohim* in verse 1 is verse 26 where God shows His plurality by referring to Himself with a plural personal pronoun.[559] The only other person of God that is mentioned is in Gen 1:2 where Moses says that God, the Spirit, hovered, moved or brooded over the face of the waters. Several Jewish and Christian authors attribute the "wind," as being the impersonal force from God. Towner makes a statement that "spirit" should not be capitalized because the Priestly (P) writers knew nothing about the Trinity.[560] Modern scholars using higher criticism have concluded that different authors using different documents composed the Pentateuch. This documentary hypothesis identified passage by supposed sources into the terms known today as Yahwistic (J); Elohistic (E), Deuteronomic (D), and Priestly (P), codes that were combined to form the Pentateuch. Gunkel is his book even divides his table of contents to reflect this view: The primeval History according to J, then primeval History in P, Abraham Legends of J and E.[561] These are completely fictitious authors that liberal theologians have concocted to explain the Old Testament in secular terms and remove the supernatural aspect of the Inspiration of Scripture. They have lost sight of the fact that God is the author of the Bible and He wrote through the agency of man. His Word was written exactly as He wanted it written, when He wrote it and by whom He said wrote it. The net result is that by 1890 this new secular approach had rejected the Mosaic authorship to the Pentateuch, except for conservative biblical scholars who hold to verbal, plenary

---

[557] Robert Morey, *The Trinity: Evidence and Issues*, 191-192.
[558] Millard J. Erickson, *Christian Theology*, 2nd Ed.,882.
[559] Rene Pache, *The Person and Work of the Holy Spirit* (Chicago, IL: Moody, 1954), 29.
[560] W. Sibley Towner, *Westminster Bible Companion: Genesis* (Louisville, KY: Westminster John Knox Press, 2001), 17.
[561] Hermann Gunkel, *Mercer Library of Biblical Studies: Genesis* (Macon, GA: Mercer University Press, 1997), contents.

inspiration of the Scriptures.[562] It was not the Priestly (P) authors that wrote Gen 1:2, but God wrote it through Moses, and God knows His own nature, and it is the conclusion of this author that Moses did too. So Towner comment of the "spirit" to void a reference to the Holy Spirit in creation is not consistent with the Word of God.

In Returning back to Gen 1:2 Hildebrandt refers to Rabbi Zlotowitz who states "and the divine presence hovered upon the surface of the water."[563] Zlotowitz argues that the "Spirit of God" was an impersonal force, not the "Holy Spirit," that was the active one in verse 2. Both Hildebrandt[564] and Allen Ross[565] recognize in verse 2 the personality of the Holy Spirit in creation. They refer to Deut 32:11 in relation to the Spirit who moved upon the waters. Hildebrandt disagrees with the Jewish Rabbi Zlotowitz who wants to suppress the thought of the personality of God in Gen 1:2. Wood makes the following statement in affirming the personality of the Holy Spirit:

> There are several Scripture passages that speak of the Holy Spirit's having had a part in the creative work. The most significant is Genesis 1:2, "And the Spirit of God moved upon the face of the water." The important word here is moved (*merahapeth*). The Hebrew form is a piel participle, connoting continued action. The thought in view is well illustrated in Deuteronomy 32:11, where the only other piel form of the word in the Old Testament is found. In this passage God's care of Israel in the wilderness is likened to an eagle fluttering over her young in providing for them. The idea of the word in Genesis 1:2, then, is that the Holy Spirit "fluttered over," "took care of," "moved upon" the chaotic state of the world in the interest of bringing order and design. Since the indication comes immediately before the description of the six-day creative activity, the implication is that the work of the six days was performed by the Spirit.[566]

Walvoord states that all the host of heaven was made by the Holy Spirit (Psa 33:6). He expresses the creative act as a beautiful picture painted of the heavens being garnished by the Holy Spirit (Job 26:13). These heavens that the Holy Spirit has made "declare the glory of God" (Psa 19:1). The heavens that the Holy Spirit had created have a distinctive characteristic of being designed to bring glory to the Father and Son. It is understood from the New Covenant in John 16:13-14 that the Holy Spirit does not glorify Himself but brings glory to the Son. Walvoord sums up his statement on the Holy Spirit as His active part in creation by saying:

> The work of the Holy Spirit ever bears this characteristic, as it reflects the glory of God, the Holy Spirit not being in the foreground.

---

[562] Alexander and Baker, *Dictionary of the Old Testament Pentateuch*, 61-62.

[563] Rabbi M. Zlotowitz, *Bereishis: Genesis* (Brooklyn, NY: Mesorah Press, 1986), 1:38.

[564] Hilderbrandt, *An Old Testament Theology of the Spirit of God*, 36.

[565] Allen P. Ross, *Creation & Blessing: Genesis* (Grand Rapids: Baker, 1988), 107.

[566] Leon J. Wood, *The Holy Spirit in the Old Testament*, 30.

In the work of creation itself, then, the Holy Spirit is revealed to have a distinct character of operation. He brings order to creation; He is the Giver of life; and shapes creation to achieve it significant purpose of bringing all glory to God.[567]

Walvoord states that even the term *Elohim* implies a work not done by one person but all the members of the triune God.[568] So when Gen 1:1 speaks of God creating, it involves all the God-head as the Son is involved in creation in Isa 48:13 and Zech 12:1. Solomon, in Ecclesiastes 12:1, also implies that all the members of the triune God were involved in creation and are to be remembered. Walvoord then proceeds to reference Isa 40:12-14 to show that the Spirit is revealed as the creator by implication:

> The Holy Spirit is described as the untaught, uncounselled, and omnipotent God, who without need of instruction or assistance measured the waters, the heavens, the dust of the earth, and the mountains. His intimate connection with the plan and management of the universe is apparent.[569]

Since *Elohim* created the universe and the earth, R. A. Torrey continues the argument that the *Elohim* is plural, which includes the Father, Son and Holy Spirit in creation. He states the following in relation to *Elohim* which adds further information to chapter two and implies the Holy Spirit, as well as the Father and Son in creation, was *Elohim*:

> Why did the Hebrews, with their unquestionable and intense monotheism, use a plural name for God? This was the question that puzzled the Hebrew grammarians and lexicographers of the past, and the best explanation that they could arrive at was the plural of God here used was 'the pluralis majestatis,' that is, the plural of majesty. But this explanation is entirely inadequate. To say nothing of the fact that the pluralis majestatis in the Old Testament is a figure of very doubtful occurrence – I have not been able to find any place in the Old Testament where it is clear that the pluralis majestatis is used – but in addition to that, even if it were true that the pluralis majestatis does occur in the Old Testament, there is another explanation for the use of a plural name for God that is far nearer at hand and far more adequate and satisfactory, and that is, that the Hebrew inspired writers used a plural name for God, in spite of their intense monotheism, because there is a plurality of person in the one Godhead.[570]

Even though Torrey does not speak specifically of the Holy Spirit, he is dealing with the whole of the triune God in the word *Elohim*, which includes the Holy Spirit. So whether dealing with the passages in Gen 1:2, 26; Deut 32:11; Job 26:13; or Psa 19:1 or with the name of God (*Elohim*), the Holy Spirit was involved in the creation of the world.

---

[567] John F. Walvoord, *The Holy Spirit*, 42.
[568] John F. Walvoord, *The Holy Spirit*, 39.
[569] John F. Walvoord, *The Holy Spirit*, 37-38.
[570] R. A. Torrey, *The Holy Spirit* (New York: Revell, 1927), 21-22.

Finally, the great evangelist of the 20th century, Billy Graham, states that the Holy Spirit was involved in creation by tying together Job 33:4 with Gen 2:7:

> When God 'formed man of dust from the ground' (Gen 2:7), the Holy Spirit was involved. We learn this indirectly in Job 33:4, 'The Spirit of God has made me, and the breath of the Almighty gives me life.' A play on words here shows how intimately God's Spirit and our breath are related: both 'Spirit' and breath' are from the same Hebrew word.[571]

There are numerous references in the *Tanakh* that specifically state, and others that strongly imply, that the Holy Spirit who was involved in creation was a person.

Holy Spirit is Distinct from the Father and Son

In previous chapters it was shown that the Messenger (Angel) of the *Yahweh* was distinct from *Yahweh* and yet *Elohim*. The *Shechinah* was distinct from *Yahweh*, and yet His presence was the presence of *Elohim* or *Yahweh*. Also, it was seen that even *Yahweh* was distinct from *Yahweh*! All of these were the representation of the Son being distinct from the Father.

Now the next logical step is to distinguish the Holy Spirit from both the Father and the Son. David, the Psalmist, in Psa 143:10 gave the distinctiveness of the Holy Spirit:

> Teach me to do thy will; for thou art my God: thy spirit is good; lead me into the land of uprightness.

Here David is asking the Spirit to lead him in righteousness as the Spirit indwells and guides him.[572]

In Haggai 2:1-9, the one who is speaking is *Yahweh*. Yet in verse 5 *Yahweh* speaks as the covenant maker with Israel, whom He brought out of Egypt. He speaks to the fact that his Spirit abode among them. According to Cooper, the Holy Spirit came and dwelt in Israel when the Lord God, through the angel of His presence, delivered her, making the Holy Spirit distinct from the one who made the covenant with them.[573]

In Neh 9:20 the Holy Spirit is given to the people by God to instruct them. This verse shows two aspects of his person: first, He is distinct from the Lord, and secondly, He teaches, which only a person can do.

Using Isa 48:16, Cooper shows the distinctiveness between all three members of the tri-unity. Cooper makes the following statement:

---

[571] Billy Graham, *The Holy Spirit* (Waco, TX: Word, 1978), 25.
[572] J. Barton Payne, *The Theology of the Older Testament*, 174.
[573] David L. Cooper, *The God of Israel*, 80.

Along with the Messiah, God sends His spirit. The latter here is as much a person as the Creator, whom God dispatches to the earth.[574]

In Isaiah 61:1, the passage that *Yeshua* read in the Nazareth synagogue (Luke 4:16-30), also points out that the "Servant" has been anointed by *Yahweh* for a distinct ministry "to preach the good tidings" and that the "Spirit of the LORD" is upon Him. In Isa 63:7-10 the distinction of the Holy Spirit from the other members of the tri-unity is clear. In verse 7 the LORD is referenced and the Messenger (Angel) of His Presences is referenced in verse 9. These two personalities are distinct from the Holy Spirit in verse 10. Cooper makes the following observation:

> We must also remember Jehovah made His Holy Spirit to dwell in the midst of Israel and that later she rebelled again Him and grieved Him. Thus the Holy Spirit is recognized as God and as being separate and distinct from the Lord Jehovah.[575]

The distinction is continued in verse 14 where it says that "the Spirit of the LORD gave them rest." So Isaiah 63 presents the distinction of the personalities of the tri-unity. In concluding this section, Feinberg states that even though the *Tanakh* does not explain how the God-head is identical and different, it does show the tri-unity of God in his following statement:

> In light of this evidence, it is hard to think that the Spirit of God or Holy Spirit is less than divine. Moreover, several passages cited distinguish him from *Yahweh*, so the Holy Spirit is somehow both identical and distinct from the Lord. The respects in which he is identical and different are not explained in the OT, but a fairly straightforward reading of the OT about the Spirit of God suggests that there is plurality in the Godhead. Moreover, attributes and actions that could only be true of God are attributed to the Holy Spirit."[576]

Holy Spirit: Coming upon and Indwelling

There is a difference and often a confusion of the ministry of the Holy Spirit in relation to how He ministered to human beings then and today. What will be observed is that the Holy Spirit functioned differently with Old Testament saints then with New Covenant saints. Several things need to be noted about the ministry of the Holy Spirit under the dispensation of Law. Pache brings out two distinctions: First, "the Spirit is not given to all" and second, "the Spirit was temporarily given, and could be withdrawn."[577] Ryrie states it a little differently when he gives three divisions that are related to the nature of the Holy Spirit's work. First, "the Spirit was in certain ones,"

---

[574] David L. Cooper, The God of Israel, 117.
[575] David L. Cooper, *The God of Israel*, 84-85.
[576] John S. Feinberg, *No One Like Him*, 454-455.
[577] Rene Pache, *The Person and Work of the Holy Spirit*, 30.

which is illustrated with the Spirit of God in Joseph and Daniel. Second, "the Spirit is said to have come upon many" as illustrated in the book of Judges (chapters 3, 6, 11, 13-15) and 1 Samuel (10) (Saul). Third, "the Spirit is said to have filled some" as recorded with Bezaleel (Exod 31:3; 35:31).[578] Ryrie summarizes his three previous statements:

> What do these examples indicate? Simply that, although the Spirit did indwell men of Old Testament times, it was a selective ministry, both in regard to whom He indwelt and for how long.[579]

What should be understood is that the Spirit's activity of coming upon, or in, or filling, had nothing to do with the person or his/her spirituality. Walvoord also sees the Holy Spirit in this light when he says:

> "It will be noted, first, that the coming of the spirit to indwell individuals has no apparent relation to spiritual qualities."[580]

It is important to understand that the Holy Spirit's ministry was selective as to who He came upon, in, or filled to accomplish the specific tasks or purposes that He desired. Walvoord and Payne both speak of the Holy Spirit indwelling believers, but Walvoord clarifies it by saying:

> "Only a few were indwelt by the Holy Spirit, and these were known for their distinctive gift, were sought out as leaders and prophets, and were usually marked men."[581]

David, in his confession of his sin in Psa 51:11, pleads with the Lord not to remove His Holy Spirit from him. David remembered vividly what happened to Saul. Because of his sin and lack of repentance, the Holy Spirit had been removed from him (1 Sam 16:14). So the fact was that the Holy Spirit could come and leave, totally unlike the ministry of the Holy Spirit in the New Covenant (Jn 14:17). The Holy Spirit came upon people for specific tasks. Wood states once that task was completed, He would leave:

> The Spirit came upon the persons involved for the activity concerned and then left them when that activity had been completed.[582]

The empowering presence of the Holy Spirit upon a person for a specific task was the norm during the Old Testament period.[583] Different aspects of the Holy Spirit's ministry of empowering will come out clearly as the different individuals in the *Tanakh* are viewed.

---

[578] Charles C. Ryrie, *The Holy Spirit*, 41-42.
[579] Charles C. Ryrie, *The Holy Spirit*, 42.
[580] John F. Walvoord, *The Holy Spirit*, 72.
[581] John F. Walvoord, *The Holy Spirit*, 72.
[582] Leon J. Wood, *The Holy Spirit in the Old Testament*, 43
[583] Willem A. VanGemeren, *Dictionary of Old Testament Theological and Exegesis*, 3:1076.

It appears that the Holy Spirit had a broader ministry then is generally recognized. Walter Kaiser expresses that the Holy Spirit also regenerated people in the Old Testament as referenced in Jesus' conversation with Nicodemus in John 3:3-10.[584] The Holy Spirit's had a ministry among Old Testament saints, but little attention has been given to that aspect of the Holy Spirit's Old Testament ministry.

Holy Spirit's Ministry to Individuals in the *Tanakh*

In the forthcoming examples of the Holy Spirit's ministry to Old Testament believers, it will be observed that the Holy Spirit came upon, filled, indwelt, and left because of sin or the completion of a task. (Those aspects will be underlined.)

Bezaleel:

Feinberg points out that in Exodus 31:2-3 God <u>filled</u> Bezaleel to do the work of an artisan as he prepared the Tabernacle:

> "In wisdom, in understand, and in knowledge and in all craftsmanship, to make artistic designs for work in gold, in silver and in bronze, and in the cutting of stones for setting, and in the carving of wood that he may work in all kinds of craftsmanship."

So as an artisan, in the construction of the Tabernacle, Bezaleel was enabled, by the Holy Spirit, to do and complete the task laid out before him. Moses concurs with what God said in Exodus 35:31.[585]

Unnamed Tailors:

In Exod 28:3 God tells Moses that the tailor had been <u>endowed with the Spirit of wisdom</u> to make all the High Priestly garments.[586]

> "And you shall make holy garments for Aaron your brother, for glory and for beauty. And you shall speak to all the skillful persons <u>whom I have endowed with the Spirit of wisdom</u>, that they make Aaron's garments to consecrate him, that he may minister as priest to Me. And these are the garments which they shall make: a breast piece and an ephod and a robe and a tunic of checkered work, a turban and a sash, and they shall make holy garments for Aaron your brother and his sons, that he may minister as priest to Me."

---

[584] Walter C. Kaiser, *The Christian and the "Old" Testament* (Pasadena, CA: William Carey Library, 1998), 223-224.
[585] John S. Feinberg, *No One Like Him*, 454.
[586] John F. Walvoord, *The Holy Spirit*, 71.

Seventy elders:

In Numbers 11:17, 25 the LORD told Moses that He will take some of the Spirit that he has and place it <u>upon the seventy elders</u> so they can bear the burden of the people with him.

> Then I will come down and speak with you there, and I will take of the Spirit who is <u>upon you</u>, and will put Him <u>upon them</u>; and they shall bear the burden of the people with you, so that you shall not bear it all alone.

> Then the LORD came down in the cloud and spoke to him; and He took of the Spirit who was <u>upon him</u> and placed Him <u>upon the seventy elders</u>. And it came about that when the Spirit rested upon them, they prophesied.

So Moses gathers the elders together, in obedience to God, for the partial transference of the Spirit to the elders. Hildebrandt gives added information to this movement of the Spirit as some of the Spirit is transferred from Moses to the 70 elders:

> Moses gathers the seventy elders in obedience to *Yahweh's* direction so that *Yahweh* could "take" from the *ruah* on him and bestow some of the *ruah* on each of the elders. The verb *asal* indicates the "withholding" of a portion of the *ruah* that is on Moses for his leadership duties and is then distributed among the elders for their new responsibilities. The term emphasizes the great endowment of Spirit on Moses and is conceived of materially and quantitatively.[587]

The immediate consequence of the *ruah* resting on the seventy elders was their spontaneous expression of "prophesying." In verse 29 two of the elders continued to prophesy and Joshua objected. But Moses responded by saying he wished all of the Lord's people were prophets and that the LORD would put His Spirit <u>upon them</u>. What is immediately apparent was that the Spirit is distinct from *Yahweh*, and that He is personal in giving divine judicial advice in His guidance of Israel.[588]

Balaam:

There is one non-Israelite example of the Holy Spirit coming upon a false prophet who knew the God of Israel (Num 22:8-35). Balaam was from Mesopotamia (Deut 23:4) and, according to the *Tanakh*, his reputation was that whoever he blessed would be blessed, and whom ever he cursed would be cursed (Num 22:6). Balak, King of Moab, called for Balaam to curse Israel. In Num 23:5 the Scriptures say that the LORD put the words in Balaam's mouth and he could only speak what God put in his mouth. Then in Num 24:2 the Scriptures distinctly say "and the Spirit of God <u>came upon him</u>." So Balaam was unable to curse Israel because the Spirit of God came <u>upon him</u> and he had to bless Israel.[589]

---

[587] Wilf Hildebrandt, *An Old Testament Theology of the Spirit of God*, 157.
[588] J. Barton Payne, *The Theology of the Older Testament*, 173.
[589] Leon J. Wood, *The Holy Spirit in the Old Testament*, 44.

> And Balaam lifted up his eyes and saw Israel camping tribe by tribe; and the Spirit of God <u>came upon him</u>.

This is a difficult passage in that Balaam was not a genuine prophet but rather a diviner. Yet He knew God but did not follow God. This passage shows God covenantal protection of Israel in taking over Balaam's mouth.[590]

Joshua:

> So the LORD said to Moses, take Joshua the son of Nun, a man <u>in whom is the Spirit</u>, and lay your hand on him. Number 27:18

Joshua was prepared by the Spirit of God to be the successor of Moses and to lead Israel into the Promised Land. He was a man of God, <u>filled with the Spirit of wisdom</u> (Deut 34:9), to do a very difficult job to lead Israel and conquer the Land.

In entering the period of the judges, the Holy Spirit came upon the judges for the purpose of delivering Israel from its oppressors after they repented of following other gods. Four judges are specifically mentioned as having the "Spirit of the LORD come upon" them. They were Othniel, Gideon, Jephthah and Samson. Several authors, such as Wood,[591] Hildebrandt,[592] Lockyer,[593] Walvoord,[594] Erickson,[595] Butler,[596] and Enns,[597] state that the Spirit, as a person, came upon the judges as they delivered Israel. Morey in referring to Othniel, states that the Spirit came upon him and instructed him or enabled him. Only a person can instruct or enable judges, not a force or power.[598]

Othniel:

> Othniel the son of Kenaz, Caleb's younger brother. And the Spirit of the LORD <u>came upon him</u>, and he judged Israel.   Judges 3:9-10

Block, in His discussion on the first judge, Othniel, refers to the Spirit of God, calling Him a member of the Trinity, but at the same time Block seems to want to make Him a power or force rather then a distinct person. However, the above authors distinctly imply the Spirit of God as a person coming upon Othniel and enabling him to have victory over the enemy. Block's statement on the personality of the Holy Spirit is confusing because of his statement that the Holy Spirit is an extension of the LORD's personality:

---

[590] Herbert Lockyer, *All About the Holy Spirit*, 55.
[591] Leon J. Wood, *The Holy Spirit*, 25, 53-55. Also see: Leon J. Wood, *Distressing Days of the Judges* (Grand Rapids, MI: Zondervan, 1975), 161-171, 201-233, 278-340.
[592] Wilf Hildebrandt, *The Holy Spirit in the Old Testament*, 114-117.
[593] Herbert Lockyer, *All About the Holy Spirit*, 55.
[594] John F. Walvoord, *The Holy Spirit*, 71, 74.
[595] Millard J. Erickson, *Christian Theology*, 2nd Ed, 884.
[596] J. Glentworth Butler, *Butler's Bible Works*, 3:179, 210, 230, 237.
[597] Paul Enns, *The Moody Handbook of Theology*, 260-261.
[598] Robert Morey, *The Trinity: Evidence and Issues*, 192.

Similarly, the Spirit of God is the agency/agent through which God's will is exercised, whether it be in creation, his dispensing of life, his guidance and providential care, the revelation of his will, his renewal of unregenerate hearts, or his sealing of his covenant people as his own. The Spirit of God is not a self-existent agent operating independently but 'an extension of the LORD's personality,' the third member of the Trinity, by which God exercises influence over the world.[599]

Block's statement is unclear. Does he see the 'Spirit of God' here as a distinct person from the Father, or is he making the 'Spirit of God' simply as an "extension" of, rather than distinct from, God?

Gideon:

> So the <u>Spirit of the LORD came upon</u> Gideon; and he blew the trumpet, and the Abiezrites were called together to follow him.   Judges 6:34 KJV

What is significant about Gideon is that he was very hesitant to become the "valiant warrior," as the Messenger (Angel) of *Yahweh* called him in verse 12. He questioned God about the "wondrous deeds" He preformed in the past (v. 13). His excuse, in verse 14, showed his reluctance and low position in his father's house. Then in verse 17 he asks for a sign because of his timidity in pulling down the altar of Baal by night because of the fear of his father's household and the town's people. Then in verse 36 Gideon made the request for the fleece. His faith was not strong. But nestled between all this is the statement in verse 34: "The spirit of the LORD enveloped" or came upon him. The Holy Spirit's personal presence came upon Gideon as He gave him divine enablement to blow the shofar and begin to muster the men for battle.[600] Block makes an interesting statement as to the response of the people to Gideon:

> This raises an extremely important question: Why are Gideon's clansmen, tribes-men, and countrymen so ready to respond to him? Are they impressed with his leadership ability or his courage? Do they recognize him as the "valiant warrior," whom the messenger of *Yahweh* had addressed in v. 12? Not if one may judge from the expressed perception of his standing within his own family and tribe (v. 15) when God calls him to military leadership or from the trepidation with which he destroyed the Baal cult site in the preceding account (v. 31). From the succeeding narrative of the dew and the fleece (vv. 36-40) it seems that nothing has changed internally or personally. Gideon remains hesitant. Juxtaposed with a text that portrays Gideon doing all he can to avoid a leadership role, the answer must lie in the opening clause of v. 34: the Spirit of

---

[599] Daniel I. Block, *The New American Commentary: Judges, Ruth.* (vol. 6. Nashville: Broadman & Holman, 1999), 6:154-155.
[600] John F. Walvoord and Ray B. Zuck, *The Bible Knowledge Commentary: Old Testament* (Wheaton, IL: Victor Books, 1985), 393.

Yahweh "clothed" Gideon. This idiom expresses in more dramatic form the notion expressed earlier in 3:10: "The Spirit of the LORD came upon Othniel," that is the Spirit took possession of the man.[601]

What is obvious is that the Spirit of the LORD that came upon him caused him to become the "valiant warrior," and that the people flocked to him to fight the Midianites.

Jephthah:

> Then the <u>Spirit of the LORD came upon</u> Jephthah, and he passed over Gilead, and Manasseh, and passed over Mizpah of Gilead, and from Mizpah of Gilead he passed over unto the children of Ammon.   Judges 11:29 KJV

This statement of Scripture is the same as that of Othniel and Gideon. The Spirit of the LORD came upon him, as in this case, upon Jephthah. There seems to be three general ways this passage is viewed by authors: First, some authors, as Grudem,[602] Wolf,[603] and Keil and Delitzsch,[604] acknowledge that the Spirit of the LORD did come upon Jephthah, but they did not interact with the passage in relation to the Holy Spirit. Second, others, as Garstang,[605] and Schneider,[606] do not even refer to the Spirit of the LORD in their discussion of Jephthah. Lastly, some authors, as McCann,[607] state that Jephthah "looks worse than bad" while Soggin[608] states that this section of Scripture on Jephthah was a later interpretation so as to make Jephthah a major judge rather than a minor judge. McCann and Soggin both have a tendency to discredit the person and judgeship of Jephthah.

This passage on Jephthah, in reference to the "Spirit of the LORD," is a neglected area by many authors. This author believes the passage is too challenging, thus neglected, so it is passed over due to the Spirit of the LORD coming upon him and the problem with Jephthah's daughter. Yet, God found the events of this judge's life worthy of mention in Hebrews 11:32, even with this problematic passage. The simple question that must be asked is: If the Holy Spirit came upon the others that have been previously mentioned in this chapter, wouldn't it be equally true in relationship to Jephthah's judgeship?

---

[601] Block, *The New American Commentary: Judges, Ruth*, 6:271-272.

[602] Wayne Grudem, *Systematic Theology*, 636.

[603] Herbert Wolf. *The Expositor's Bible Commentary* (12 vols. Grand Rapids: Zondervan, 1992), 3:455.

[604] C. F. Keil and F. Delitzsch, *Commentary on the Old Testament*, 2:384.

[605] John Garstang, *The Foundations of Bible History: Joshua Judges* (Grand Rapids: Kregel, 1978), 329-333.

[606] Tammi J. Schneider, *Berit Olam: Studies in Hebrew Narrative and Poetry, Judges* (Collegeville, MN: The Liturgical Press, 2000), 169-183.

[607] J. Clinton McCann, *Interpretation: A Bible Commentary for Teaching and Preaching: Judges* (Louisville, KY: John Knox Press, 2002), 85.

[608] J. Alberto Soggin, *The Old Testament Library: Judges*, (trans. John Bowden; Philadelphia: Westminster, 1981), 206-207.

Samson:

> And the <u>Spirit of the LORD began to stir</u> him in Mahaneh-dan, between Zorah and Eshtaol. Judges 13:25

> And the <u>Spirit of the LORD came upon him</u> mightily, so that he tore him as one tears a kid though he had nothing in his hand; but he did not tell his father and mother what he had done. Judges 14:6

> Then the <u>Spirit of the LORD came upon him</u> mightily, and he went down to Ashkelon and killed thirty of them and took their spoil, and gave the changes of clothes to those who told the riddle. And his anger burned, and he went up to his father's house. Judges 14:19

> When he came to Lehi, the Philistines shouted as they met him. An<u>d the Spirit of the LORD came upon him</u> mightily so that the ropes that were on his arms were as flax that is burned with fire, and his bonds dropped from his hands. And he found a fresh jawbone of a donkey, so he reached out and took it and killed a thousand men with it.   Judges 15:14-15

The ministry of the Holy Spirit in the life of Samson is unique to the Judges. Four times the Spirit of the LORD comes upon Samson as God uses him in judging the Philistines.   Only with Gideon (6:11-22) and Samson (13:3-23) is the Messenger (Angel) of *Yahweh* involved in their lives. Only with the promise and birth of Samson is the Messenger (Angel) of *Yahweh* involved with his birth. Each of the four judges mentioned in this section had a special empowerment to carry out God's assigned tasks. Because Samson was designated as a Nazirite (13:14), it seems that the Holy Spirit came upon him until Delilah cut his hair (16:18-20). The Holy Spirit came upon him on several occasions, with special empowerment, as illustrated by these verses in Judg 13:25; 14:6, 19; 15:14-15.

Samson is also unique among Israel's judges in that God instructed him to fight the Philistines alone rather than to raise an army. On four occasions he received a special enablement for a major display of strength.[609] *Yahweh*'s active participation with Israel is seen with the involvement of the Messenger (Angel) of *Yahweh* as well as the Holy Spirit coming upon these individuals when the nation repented and called for deliverance.[610]

It should also be noted that respected scholars as such Woods,[611] Walvoord and Zuck[612] refer to the Spirit of the LORD as the Holy Spirit. Most authors do not make that specific designation in relationship to the Spirit passages in Judges. This design-

---

[609] Leon J. Wood, *The Holy Spirit in the Old Testament*, 55.
[610] Wilf Hildebrandt, *An Old Testament Theology of the Spirit of God*, 117.
[611] Leon J. Wood, *Distressing Days of the Judges* (Grand Rapids: Zondervan, 1975), 311-312.
[612] John F. Walvoord, *The Bible Knowledge Commentary: Old Testament*, 404.

ation of the Holy Spirit is important because the Jewish response is that the Spirit is God's Spirit, not a distinct member of the Godhead. The lack of designation is expressed frequently by Schneider when she says, of the Spirit of the LORD, that He was "moved by the spirit of the deity."[613]

Elohim specifies and clarifies by showing a distinction by denoting God as a plurality. Hence, when the Hebrew Scriptures refer to the Spirit of *Yahweh*, or the Spirit of God, or by the statement that the Spirit of the LORD came upon an individual, the *Tanakh* is referring to the Holy Spirit, the Third Person of the Godhead of *Elohim*.

One final note on Samson and the ministry of the Holy Spirit in his life, even though Samson was anointed as a judge, there were periods of godless disobedience in his life. Both the personal and official blessedness of the Spirit were removed. This is not an issue of keeping or losing personal salvation, then or now, but of being anointed for high office or specific skillful tasks.

Saul:

> And the <u>Spirit of the LORD will come upon thee</u>, and thou shalt prophesy with them, and shalt be turn into another man.   I Sam 10:6   KJV

> When they came to the hill there, behold, a group of prophets met him; and the <u>Spirit of God came upon him</u> mightily, so that he prophesied among them.   1 Sam 10:10   KJV

> And the <u>Spirit of God came upon Saul</u> when he heard those tidings, and his Anger was kindled greatly.   I Sam 11:6   KJV

There are four basic passages that speak of the Spirit of God in relationship to Saul. Three references are found in I Sam 10 and 11 and one in chapter 16, which refers to both Saul and David. The first reference is a prophecy by Samuel that the Spirit of the LORD would come upon Saul and make him into a different man. The second reference is the recorded fulfillment of Samuel's words to Saul. Samuel gives Saul three signs that will confirm God's choice of him as king. The last one is the most significant because when the Spirit of God comes upon Saul, it caused him to prophesy with a band of prophets. Hildebrandt makes this comment in connection to Saul prophetic experience and *Yahweh*'s confirmation of him as the first king:

> The act of prophesying by Saul and the band of prophets is to be distinguished from that of prophetic inspiration, which conveys a message to the recipient. The ecstatic element indicates an encounter with the *ruah yhwh* that brings about external manifestations in additions to verbal utterances. In this instance, the fulfillment of the three signs would confirm that *Yahweh* is with Saul.[614]

---

[613] Tammi J Schneider, *Berit Olam: Judges*, 202.
[614] Wilf Hildebrandt, *An Old Testament Theology of the Spirit of God*, 120.

The Spirit of God came upon Saul, as with the judges, to equip him to fulfill the task of being king. Walvoord and Zuck affirm that the Spirit of God came upon Saul to equip him because he was inexperienced and unlettered and unable to assume kingly responsibilities in much the same way that the judges did before him.[615] Barber concurs and continues the same idea when he says:

> It seems most likely that God gave to Saul that which he lacked by training and heredity. He provided him with the inner disposition to fulfill the tasks of a king. He equipped him, as He had done the judges, so that Saul would be able to deliver his people from those who sought to oppress them. When the transitory enthusiasm of his meeting with the prophets passed, it left Saul with a certain inner sense that could not be satisfied without further communion with the Lord.[616]

So the coming of the Spirit of God upon Saul was not only to let him know that God was with him but was also to equip him for his task as king.

One other point that Bergen brings out is the contrast between the use of the terms "Spirit of God" and the "Spirit of the LORD." He observes that elsewhere in the *Tanakh*, when the Holy Spirit came upon an individual, it states that the Spirit of the LORD came upon them. However, here and only one other place does it say that the "Spirit of God" came upon him. Even though both terms refer to the same person of God, the Spirit of God is used only with one other person, Balaam. The reason for God's choice of words is not clear, but as Balaam was unfaithful to God, Saul was also unfaithful.[617] Bergen's observation is interesting but not valid. For the "Spirit of God" also came upon others such as: Bezaleel in Exod 31:2-3, Azariah, a prophet, who gave a warning to Asa in 2 Chr 15:1 and Zechariah, the priest, in 2 Chr 24:20. Bergen's statement is inconclusive because two people acted in disobedience, two people in obedience, and another, an artisan, prepared the tabernacle.

When the Spirit of God came upon Saul it was permanent because of his office. It was temporary with the other judges, because there ministry was limited in scope with the possible exception of Samson. The 1 Samuel passage indicates that had Saul not sinned with his incomplete obedience (1 Sam 16) but had remained faithful, the Spirit would have remained with Saul through out his life as king.[618] The permanence of the Holy Spirit upon Saul is also noted by McCarter in his remarks on this section:

> Divine spirit follows immediately upon the anointing and remains 'from that day forward.' Moreover, as we are about to discover, *Yahweh*'s spirit has departed from Saul (16:14).[619]

[615] John F. Walvoord and Roy Zuck, *The Bible Knowledge Commentary: Old Testament*, 441.

[616] Cyril J. Barber, *The Books of Samuel*. (vol. 1. Neptune, NJ: Loizeaux, 1994), 116.

[617] Robert D. Bergen, *The New American Commentary: 1 and 2 Samuel* (21 vols. Nashville: Broadman and Holman, 2002), 7:136.

[618] Leon J. Wood, *The Holy Spirit in the Old Testament*, 62.

[619] P. Kyle McCarter, Jr. *The Anchor Bible: I Samuel* (vol. 8. Garden City, NY: Doubleday, 1980), 8:276.

David and Saul:

> Then Samuel took the horn of oil and anointed him in the midst of his brothers; and the <u>Spirit of the LORD came mightily upon</u> David from that day forward. And Samuel arose and went to Ramah.
>
> Now the <u>Spirit of the LORD departed from Saul</u>, and an evil spirit from the LORD terrorized him.   1 Sam 16:13-14

What is seen here is that the Holy Spirit came upon Saul and was with him up to 1 Sam 16:14. Then the Lord sent an evil spirit to terrorize him because God had now rejected Saul and had Samuel anoint David to be king. These two events occurred in close sequence to each other. Once the Holy Spirit came upon David, the Holy Spirit left Saul. When the Holy Spirit left Saul, it did not mean that he was unsaved, but rather that the enabling power of God left him and was given to David.[620]

David:

> The <u>Spirit of the LORD spoke by me</u> and his word was on my tongue. The God of Israel said, The Rock of Israel spoke to me.   2 Sam 23:2-3a
>
> Do not cast me away from thy presence, and <u>do not take thy Holy Spirit from me</u>.   Psa 51:11

In 1 Samuel 16 it was observed that the Spirit of the LORD came upon David and was with him throughout his lifetime. That is seen by two things: first, the Holy Spirit spoke by David and second, the Holy Spirit's words were on his tongue. Bergen speaks of David as being in the passive role as the Holy Spirit spoke through him as he makes the following observation:

> Thus David has now been portrayed throughout the books of Samuel as king, priest, and prophet. ... Since David, the first member of Israel's royal messianic line, functioned in these three roles, it seems appropriate that Jesus the Messiah should not only be depicted by the New Testament writers as inheriting these roles but superseding David's accomplishments in them. He did not choose this role but accepted it when 'the Spirit of the Lord spoke through him. David's role was essentially passive in this event. When his spoke, it was the Lord's 'word' not his own- that was on his 'tongue.'[621]

Youngblood makes the observation that as God, He spoke through the mouth of Balaam (Num 24:2, 4), and the Spirit of the LORD spoke through David. Youngblood makes the following connection with *Yeshua*:

---

[620] Ronald F. Youngblood, *The Expositor's Bible Commentary*, 3:688.
[621] Robert D. Bergen, *The New American Commentary: 1, 2 Samuel*, 465-466.

That David spoke 'by the Spirit' on another occasion is affirmed by Jesus himself (Matt 22:43), and David's use of the phrase 'spoke through' represents a clear claim to divine inspiration. David was conscious of the fact that the 'word' of the Lord was on his 'tongue' and that the mighty 'Rock of Israel' had spoken to him.[622]

Youngblood was referring to Psalm 110:1, where David said, "The LORD said unto my Lord, Sit thou at my right hand, until I make thine enemies thy footstool." It is clearly presented by David that the Holy Spirit, who is distinct from *Yahweh*, spoke to and through him.

Also, it can be observed that David pleaded with the Lord (Psa 51:11) not to take his Holy Spirit from him. David wanted the presence of God with him to guide him and enable him as King of Israel. David also remembered very clearly what happened to Saul because of his sin. David wanted to walk righteously before his God as his Psalms so aptly speak.

Micah:

On the other hand I am <u>filled</u> with power – With the Spirit of the LORD.

Micah 3:8

In this verse Micah, a contemporary of Isaiah in the 8th century BCE, spoke of himself as being <u>filled with the Spirit of the LORD</u>. He traces the power of his prophetic ministry to the Holy Spirit.[623] Just as Bezaleel was filled with the Spirit, so was Micah. This filling of the Holy Spirit equipped Micah to deal with the corruption among the leaders of Israel (3:1-3; 7:1-4) and among the priest and prophets themselves (2:6, 11; 3:5-7).[624]

Isaiah:

And as for Me, this is My covenant with them, says the LORD: '<u>My spirit which is upon you,</u> and My words which I have put in your mouth, shall not depart from your mouth, nor from the mouth of your offspring, nor from the mouth of your offspring's offspring,' says the LORD 'from now and forever.'

Isaiah 59:21

This verse is connected to three themes in the book of Isaiah, as well as Jeremiah and Ezekiel, the New Covenant of Jeremiah, Messiah and the Holy Spirit. Walter Kaiser connects the "My covenant" in the above verse to the New Covenant of Jeremiah 31.[625]

[622] Ronald F. Youngblood, *The Expositor's Bible Commentary*, 3:1082.
[623] John F. Walvoord, *the Holy Spirit*, 50.
[624] Wilf Hildebrandt, *an Old Testament Theology of the Spirit of God*, 190-191.
[625] Walter C. Kaiser, *Toward an Old Testament Theology*, 231.

Motyer also connects the Isa 59:21 passage with the ministry of the Servant of the LORD in the servant passages of Isaiah.[626] Enns connects the fulfillment of the New Covenant to the return of the Messiah and the forgiveness of Israel.[627] Wolf connects the covenant with the Servant of the Lord and relates it to the New Covenant.[628]

The fact is that Isa 59:21 pertains to Israel's future where the New Covenant is God's future blessing on Israel, even though they grieved His Holy Spirit (63:10). The Holy Spirit was grieved and turned away. But the New Covenant speaks of the pouring out of God's Spirit (44:3). But in Jer 31:31-37, which was connected to Isa 59:21, is a promise by God, through His New Covenant, that "My spirit" will be upon them and "My words" will be put in their mouths and will not depart from them from generation to generation even "from now and forever." So in Isaiah 59:21 God promises His spirit would come upon them, that His words will be in their mouths, and all will come to pass in the New Covenant and through the Messiah, the Servant of the LORD. Christians recognize that the New Covenant is the indwelling of the Holy Spirit in the lives of believers, both Jew and Gentile. But this New Covenant will not be totally fulfilled until Israel embraces *Yeshua* as her own personal Messiah and trusts in Him.

Ezekiel:

> And as He spoke to me the Spirit entered me and set me on my feet; and I heard Him speaking to me.
> Ezek 2:2

> And He stretched out the form of a hand and caught me by a lock of my head; and *the Spirit lifted me up* between earth and heaven and brought me in the visions of God to Jerusalem, to the entrance of the north gate of the inner court, where the seat of the idol of jealousy, which provokes to jealousy, was located.
> Ezek 8:3;

> Moreover, the Spirit lifted me up and brought me to the east gate of the LORD's house which faced eastward. And behold, there were twenty-five men at the entrance of the gate, and among them I saw Jaazaniah son of Azzzur and Pelatiah son of Benaiah, leaders of the people.
> Ezek 11:1

> And the Spirit lifted me up and brought me in a vision by the Spirit of God to the exiles in Chaldea. So the vision that I had seen left me.
> Ezek 11:24

> The Hand of the LORD was upon me, and He brought me out by the Spirit of the LORD and set me down in the middle of the valley; and it was full of bones.
> Ezek 37:1[629]

---

[626] J. Alec Motyer, *The Prophecy of Isaiah* (Downers Grove, IL: InterVarsity, 1993), 492.

[627] Paul Enns, *The Moody Handbook of Theology*, 68.

[628] Herbert M. Wolf, *Interpreting Isaiah*, 235.

[629] All of the Ezekiel verses are taken from NASV

Most authors do not interact with the plurality of God that is present in these passages. In all these passages there is a plurality of persons involved with Ezekiel and his visions. It is disheartening to notice that scholars, such as Feinberg[630] and Cooper,[631] do not interact with the Spirit that is so prevalent in these passages. In fact, Taylor states that according to Ezek 2:2, the Spirit is "spiritual energy" and not a person.[632] Yet, these passages clearly indicate two members of the God-head arise out of these passages. In looking at the description in Ezek 1:26, God is appearing in a human form. In fact, Alexander refers to this section of Scripture as a "theophany,"[633] God appearing in human form. Paralleling these verses highlights the personalities in each of these verses:

Ezekiel 2:2	"a figure with the appearance of a man" (1:26) "Spirit entered me and set me on my feet"
Ezekiel 8:3	"a likeness as the appearance of a man" (8:2) "the Spirit lifted me up between heaven and earth"
Ezekiel 11:1	"And He spoke to the man clothed in linen" (10:2) "the Spirit lifted me up and brought me to the east gate"
Ezekiel 11:24	"Thus says the Lord God" (11:16-17) "And the Spirit lifted me up and brought me in a vision by the Spirit of God"
Ezekiel 37:1	"The hand of the LORD was upon me and He brought me" "by the Spirit of the LORD and set me down"

In each instance and in each verse, or immediate context, there are two personalities engaged with Ezekiel. This author believes that the one who was in the appearance of a man is a theophany of the Second Person of the God-head. The other personality, who is continually called the Spirit, is the Third Person of the God-head, the Holy Spirit. Cooke makes the following remarks along the same lines:

This was no messenger, no angel. As at the inaugural vision, so now, it is Jehovah Himself in human form, glowing with supernatural splendour, who appears to the prophet, and speaks to him, and announces the hour of visitation. … The distinction between the hand of Jehovah and the spirit seems to be that the one gave the impression of a visible, the other of an invisible agency: the

---

[630] Charles Lee Feinberg, *The Prophecy of Ezekiel: The Glory of the Lord* (Chicago: Moody, 1969).

[631] Lamar Eugene Cooper, Sr. *The New American Commentary: Ezekiel* (vol. 17. Nashville: Broadman and Holman, 1994).

[632] John B. Taylor, *Ezekiel* (Downers Grove: InterVarsity, 1974), 61.

[633] Ralph H. Alexander, *The Expositor's Bible Commentary: Ezekiel* (vol. 6. Grand Rapids: Zondervan, 1986), 6:761.

hand appeared to grasp the prophet by the forelock, the spirit impelled his movement.[634]

In each of these passages there is a clear distinction between the theophany of God (appearance of a man) and the Spirit of God. These two persons are addressed and treated as being distinct persons.

Inspiration of the Scriptures

The word "inspiration" comes from the Latin Vulgate Bible in which the verb "inspire" appears in 2 Tim 3:16 and 2 Pet 1:21. However, the word inspiration in the Greek is actually used only once in 2 Timothy to translate the word *theopneustos*. *Theopneustos*, which means "God-breathed" emphasizes the exhalation of God. Spiration would be more accurate since it emphasizes that Scripture is the product of the breath of God. The Scriptures are not something breathed *into* by God. Rather, the Scriptures have been breathed *out* by God.[635]

The Greek word that is used for the English word "Scripture" is *graphe*, which simply means "writing."[636] The written Word of God was given by God, and it was recorded in writing as He willed. The writings that He wanted preserved as Scripture have become what is called today, *The Bible*.

Inspiration and how is it to be understood in the Hebrew Scriptures, as well as the New Covenant, is important to understand. Walvoord lays out a clear statement as to the meaning of inspiration:

> That God so supernaturally directed the writers of Scripture that without
> excluding their human intelligence, their individuality, their literary style, their
> personal feelings, or any other human factor, His own complete and coherent
> message to man was recorded in perfect accuracy, the very words of Scripture
> bearing the authority of divine authorship. Nothing less than a plenary and
> verbal inspiration will satisfy the demands of the Scripture themselves and give
> to faith the confidence in the Word of God which is essential to faith and life.[637]

Geisler also gives the same kind of definition of inspiration as Walvoord:

> Inspiration is the supernatural operation of the Holy Spirit, who through the
> different personalities and literary styles of the chosen human authors invested
> the very words of the original books of Holy Scripture, alone and in their
> entirety, as the very Word of God without error in all that they teach or imply

---

[634] G. A. Cooke, *The International Critical Commentary: The Book of Ezekiel*, (Edinburgh: T. & T. Clark, 1936), 89-91.
[635] Paul Enns, *The Moody Handbook of Theology*, 160.
[636] Paul Enns, *The Moody Handbook of Theology*, 153.
[637] John F. Walvoord, *The Holy Spirit*, 58.

(including history and science), and the Bible is thereby the infallible rule and final authority for faith and practice of all believers.[638]

God worked with individual personalities and literary styles so that when the Word of God was given to human authors, there was an absence of any formal argument to prove the inspiration of their writings because none was deemed necessary. The character of the Scriptures themselves were sufficient evidence for both the authors and the readers.

The term inspiration makes other declarations as expressed by Geisler and Nix.

(1) The claim of inspiration has several other characteristics that need to be mentioned. First, inspiration is verbal, meaning that it "extends to the very words of Scripture" (Exod 24:4; Isa 8:1; 30:8).

(2) Inspiration makes the Scripture unbreakable or infallible (Psa 82; John 10:35).

(3) The Scriptures are irrevocable, meaning that they cannot be changed and will be fulfilled (Matt 5:18; Luke 16:17; 24:44).

(4) Inspiration makes the Scriptures the final authority (Matt 4:4, 7, 10). Nothing will supersede the written word of God.

(5) Inspiration is plenary, meaning that it is full, complete, extending to every part[639] (2 Tim 3:16).

There is one thing that needs to be made clear concerning the work of the Holy Spirit in inspiration. The Holy Spirit did not inspire men, but inspired his Word. Gray makes the distinction in the work on the Holy Spirit when he says:

When we speak of the Holy Spirit coming upon the men in order to the composition of the books, it should be further understood that the object is not the inspiration of the men but the books – not the writers but the writings. It terminates upon the record, in other words, and not upon the human instrument who made it.[640]

The more we think upon it the more we must be convinced that men unaided by the Spirit of God could neither have conceived, nor put together, nor preserved in its integrity that precious deposit known as the Sacred Oracles.[641]

---

[638] Norman Geisler, *Systematic Theology*, 1:241.

[639] Norman L. Geisler and William E. Nix, *A General Introduction to the Bible* (Chicago: Moody, 1968), 48-51.

[640] James M. Gray, *The Fundamentals* (Reprinted without alteration or abridgment from the original four volume edition issued by the Bible Institute of Los Angeles in 1917. Grand Rapids: Baker, 1980), 2:11.

[641] James M. Gray, *The Fundamentals*, 2:18-19.

There are two key verses in the New Covenant that clearly point to the inspiration of the *Tanakh*. Paul states that "all Scripture is given by inspiration of God" in 2 Timothy (3:16) and attributes inspiration of the *Tanakh* to the ministry of the Holy Spirit. Peter affirms in 2 Pet 1:20-21 (to Jewish believers in Messiah who had been scattered in the Diaspora) that the writings of the *Tanakh* did not come from the will or intellect of man but "man spake from God, being moved by the Holy Spirit."[642]

The writers of the *Tanakh* when referring to the Hebrew Scriptures as the authoritative Word of God, give their testimony and bore witness to their divine inspiration: the Law (Exod 20:1; 32:16; Lev. 27:34; Num 36:13) and the Prophets (Josh 24:26-27; 1 Sam 3:18-19; Isa 1:1-2; Jer 1:1-2; Ezek 1:3).[643]

A valid point needs to be injected here on a particular Jewish consideration of what is inspired. Jewish rabbis treat the Oral Law (Talmud) as equal to Scripture, although they would say that they don't. The Talmud has become their primary source of interpretation of Scripture. They ignore the Scriptures that refer to Moses writing down all that God gave him (Exod 24:4; Deut 31:9, 24; Josh 24:26).[644] This Oral Law is the source of all rabbinic authority and not the written Word of God. The children of Israel did not vow to keep the Oral Law. They made a commitment to *Yahweh* to keep the written law of God. Exod 24:3-7 rules out a fictitious Oral Law as being given to Moses, then to Joshua, the Judges and on to the Prophets. The Oral Law is fictitious because nowhere in the whole of the *Tanakh* is there even a glimmer, let alone a clear statement, of this uniquely Jewish position about the Oral Law (Talmud) as been given by God or as being divinely authoritative. Oral Law has become an "idol" of words by the Rabbis because the Jewish people bow to its authority, rather than the authority of the Written Word of God (which is what they vowed to keep), that *Elohim* has over and over again confirmed to His Scriptures. The Oral Law has no confirmation by God in the *Tanakh*. Verbal Inspiration deals with the very words of God that He so carefully gave and preserved in His Word (see appendix #3). The Oral Law is nothing more than the commentaries of the rabbis, their interpretations of the *Tanakh*.

The New Covenant uses the phrase "it is written" over 90 times.[645] Jesus described this written word as that which "comes out of the mouth of God" (Matt 4:4). So important were the exact words of God that Jeremiah (26:2) was told:

---

[642] James M. Gray, *The Fundamentals*, 2:20.

[643] Floyd H. Barackman, *Practical Christian Theology*, 27.

[644] Oral Law: Judaism states that Moses received two laws, one written and one oral. Now Judaism will not call the Oral Law the word of God. But the authority placed upon the Oral Law practically places the Oral Law on equal footing and greater then the written law of God given to Moses. For Rabbis will not interpret the Written Law without studying the oral law with cannot be substantiated any where in the entire *Tanakh*. The actual origin of the Oral Law occurred after the return from captivity. There was a need to read the Word of God in Hebrew in Nehemiah 8:8, then translate it into Aramaic and then applied to daily life. Then the generation after Ezra, they began to expand it by adding man made rules and regulation to each of the 613 written laws of Moses and giving it equal and greatly authority then the Scriptures themselves.

[645] Norman Geisler, *Systematic Theology*, 1:236.

This is what the LORD says: Stand in the courtyard of the Lord's house and speak to all the people of the towns of Judah who come to worship in the house of the LORD. Tell them everything I command you; do not omit a word."

Other New Covenant testimony of the *Tanakh* comes from *Yeshua* as a witness to divine inspiration.

(1) *Yeshua* recognized the whole of the *Tanakh* (John 5:39' Luke 24:44-46) and its three divisions (Mark 7:8-13; Matt 13:13-14; John 10:34-35).

(2) *Yeshua* made reference to 14 books of the *Tanakh*: Genesis (Mark 10:6-8), Exodus (Luke 18:20), Numbers (John 3:14), Leviticus and Deuteronomy (Luke 10:26-28), I Sam (Mark 2:25), I Kings (Matt 12:42), Psalms (Mark 12:10), Isaiah (Luke 4:17-21), Daniel (Matt 24:15), Hosea (Matt 9:13), Jonah (Matt 12:40), Zechariah (Matt 26:31), and Malachi (Matt 11:10).

(3) *Yeshua* believed in the historicity of persons, such as Abel (Luke 11:51), Noah and the Flood (Matt 24:37-39), Moses (John 3:14), David (Luke 20:41), Jonah and the fish (Matt 12:40), God's creation of man and the divine institution of marriage (Matt 19:4-7), and the prophet Daniel (Matt 24:15).

(4) *Yeshua* submitted Himself to the authority of the Hebrew Scriptures (Matt 5:17; 26:54; Luke 18:31).

(5) *Yeshua* had complete trust in the writings and teachings of the *Tanakh*. This is indicated by His appeal to them for God's will when He was tempted (Matt 4:4, 7, 10), His referring to God's statement regarding marriage (Matt 19:4-6), and His argument for the doctrine of the resurrection (Matt 22:29-32).

(6) *Yeshua* declared that the Scriptures could not be broken (John 10:35). In context, the Lord said that the Scriptures (Psa 82:6), which He identified as the Word of God, could not be annulled as though its declarations were untrue.[646]

The inspiration of the Holy Spirit is clearly seen in the New Covenant. But how is it seen in the Hebrew Scriptures? In the Hebrew Scriptures there are two phrases that are literally used thousands of times. These key phrases are: "Thus saith the Lord" and "The Word of the Lord came unto, both of which distinctly refer to the inspiration of the Scriptures.[647] Waterhouse makes that following observation:

Statements from the Law and the Prophets assert not only that the Old Testament is divine revelation, but, more specifically, that the words were at times given by God and at other times guided by God. This is verbal inspiration.[648]

---

[646] Floyd H. Barackman, *Practical Christian Theology*, 27.
[647] Steven W. Waterhouse, *Not By Bread Alone: An Outlined Guide to Bible Doctrine* (Amarillo, TX: Westcliff Press, 2000), 4.
[648] Steven W. Waterhouse, *Not By Bread Alone: An Outlined Guide to Bible Doctrine*, 4.

Waterhouse goes on to quote references from the Hebrew Scriptures to show that God indeed spoke and guided the human authors of Scripture (Deut 18:18; 34:10; 2 Sam 23:1-2; Isa 8:11, 20, 59:21; Jer 1:9; 15:16; 30:2; Ezek 3:1-4).[649] By closely observing 2 Sam 23:2 and Isaiah 59:21, both David and Isaiah express the fact that the Holy Spirit spoke through them:

> The Spirit of the LORD spake by me, and his word was in my tongue. KJV

> As for me, this is my covenant with them, saith the LORD; My spirit that is upon thee, and my words which I have put in thy mouth.… KJV

Here the Holy Spirit is clearly seen as the one who is speaking through David and Isaiah in the *Tanakh*. Geisler continues by expressing phrases, such as "God said" (Gen 1:3, 6), "the Word of the LORD came to me" (Jer 34:1; Ezek 30:1), which are found hundreds of times in the Hebrew Scriptures. Geisler states:

> These reveal beyond question that the writer is claiming to give the very Word of God. In the book of Leviticus alone there are some 66 occurrences of phrases like "the LORD spoke unto Moses" (1:1; 4:1; 5:14; 6:1, 8, 19; 7:22).[650]

God used words and expected those words to be used exactly as He instructed. Using them otherwise is a direct violation of verbal inspiration. This simply means that words were inspired, God's Word, not God's thoughts or dynamic equivalents which is so popular today in our modern translations and paraphrases. It is God's Word, rather than inspired thoughts, that man is held accountable for (Exod 24:3-7; Deut 18:18; 2 Sam 23:2; Isa 59:21; 2 Chr 34:14; Zech 7:12). Geisler strongly affirms that Scriptures were not man's words or thoughts, but God's Word:

> So it wasn't simply God's message that men were free to state in their words; the very choice of words was from God. … Sometimes we are reminded that even the tense of verbs are stressed by God.[651]

Inspiration usually has two other descriptive words to help clarify the meaning of inspiration. They are the words "verbal" and "plenary." Here plenary inspiration will be briefly discussed. Inspiration, in being verbal, extends to every word as being inspired. Plenary further defines the term inspiration as "extending to every part of the words and all they teach or imply."[652] Barackman further conveys that verbal extends to each word of Scripture and "to the grammatical form of each word," as well as speaking of plenary inspiration as not just the words but the equality of the words:

---

[649] Steven W. Waterhouse, *Not By Bread Alone: An Outlined Guide to Bible Doctrine*, 4.
[650] Norman Geisler, *Systematic Theology*, 1:234.
[651] Norman Geisler, *Systematic Theology*, 1:236
[652] Norman Geisler, *Systematic Theology*, 1:236.

Plenary Inspiration means that every part of the sixty-six canonical books of the Bible was a product of divine inspiration to an equal degree (2 Tim 3:16).[653]

Plenary inspiration simply means that all Scripture is equally inspired of God. However, Judaism, as they deduce from Num 12:5-8, see three levels of inspiration: The Law (Torah) as the most inspired, then the Prophets, while still inspired, but to a lesser degree then the Torah and lastly, the Writings, while still inspired but to a lesser degree than the Law and the Prophets.

Methods of Revelation

When speaking of Divine Revelation in connection with the Bible, the word "revelation" is derived from the Greek word *apokalupsis*, which means "disclosure" or "unveiling,"[654] which signified that God unveiled Himself to mankind through His written Word and through theophanies of Himself. If God did not disclose or unveil Himself to man, without revelation, man would have no idea as to what God is like or how man could interact with Him. Horne gives a clear meaning of revelation in his following comments:

> That act of God whereby he discloses himself or communicates truth to the mind, whereby he makes manifest to his creatures that which could not be known in any other way. The revelation may occur in a single, instantaneous act, or it may extend over a long period of time; and this communication of himself and his truth may be perceived by the human mind in varying degrees of fullness.[655]

The Holy Spirit is also involved in revelation of God as is expressed in the following statement by Walvoord:

> The most prominent means of revelation is that of the spoken word. "Thus saith Jehovah" is found in hundreds of instances in the Old Testament. A comparison of such passages as Isa 6:1-10 and Act 8:25 will demonstrate that the Holy Spirit is the person of the Trinity speaking in these instances. While the Old Testament used "Jehovah" and "Lord" as the speaker, the New Testament uses the title, Holy Spirit.[656]

In a broader use of the term revelation, God revealed Himself through creation, history, and in the Scriptures and the conscience of man. In general revelation God revealed Himself in history and nature, while in "special" revelation God revealed Himself in the Scriptures and in His Son.[657]

---

[653] Floyd H. Barackman, *Practical Christian Theology*, 25
[654] Paul Enns, *The Moody Handbook of Theology*, 155.
[655] Henry C. Thiessen, *Lectures in Systematic Theology*, 7.
[656] John F. Walvoord, *The Holy Spirit*, 50-51.
[657] Tenney, Merrill C. *Zondervan Pictorial Encyclopedia of the Bible*, 5:86.

OT and NT comparisons of the Holy Spirit

Throughout the Hebrew Scriptures there are times when the reader may not be able to determine that the one speaking is the person of the Holy Spirit. Although this section is not an argument for the personality of the Holy Spirit from the *Tanakh*, this argument does show how the Apostles in the first century C.E. understood the ministry of the Holy Spirit in the *Tanakh*.

There are five verses taken from the *Tanakh*, by these New Covenant writers, that show the writers of the New Covenant understood them to refer to the Holy Spirit. Matthew and John Mark spoke of the statements of *Yeshua*, Peter just before the feast of Succoth (Pentecost), Paul when speaking to the Jewish leadership in Rome and the unknown author of Hebrews who writes to the suffering Jewish believers who lived in the Land. Each passage will be briefly discussed supporting the contention that these writers understood the Holy Spirit to be present and active in the Hebrew Scriptures.

Psalm 110:1 with Matthew 22:42-44:

> The LORD said to my Lord, 'Sit at My right hand while I make your enemies your footstool.'

> While the Pharisees were gathered together, Jesus asked them, saying, what think ye of Christ (Messiah)? Whose son is he? They say unto him, The Son of David. He saith unto them, How then doth David in the spirit call him Lord, Saying, the LORD said unto my Lord, Sit thou on my right hand, till I make thine enemies thy footstool?

Here, according to Ryrie, *Yeshua* asks the Pharisees a question concerning Psalm 110:1. *Yeshua*, at this point, attributes to the Holy Spirit divine authorship of that Psalm of David.[658] Then Psa 110:1 is tied in with David's powerful statement of 2 Sam 23:2-3 where David states that "the Spirit of the LORD spoke by me," connecting that with David's statement with Psalm 22, a Messianic Psalm. Walvoord points out from Mark 12:36 the same incident when David spoke by the Holy Spirit, thus attributing inspiration to the Holy Spirit.[659]

Psa 41:9[10] with Acts 1:16:

> My ally in whom I trusted, even he who shares my bread, has been utterly false to me. (Psa 41:9[10])

> Yea, mine own familiar friend, in whom I trusted, which did eat of my bread, Hath Lifted up his heel against me. (Psa 41:9) KJV

---

[658] Charles C. Ryrie, *The Holy Spirit*, 36.
[659] John F. Walvoord, *The Holy Spirit*, 60.

> Men and brethren, this scripture must need have been fulfilled which the Holy Spirit by the mouth of David spake before concerning Judas, which was guide to them that took Jesus.　　　　(Acts 1:16)

Here again Peter gives testimony to the Holy Spirit as the authority of the word of David concerning Judas who betrayed *Yeshua*.

Isaiah 6:9-10 with Acts 28:25-27:

> And He said, 'Go, say to that people: Hear, indeed, but do not understand; See, indeed, but do not grasp. Dull that people's mind, stop its ear, and seal it eyes – lest, seeing with its eyes and hearing with it ears, it also grasp with it mind, and repent and save itself.

> And when they agreed not among themselves, they departed, after that Paul had spoken one word, Well spake the Holy Spirit by Isaiah the prophet unto our fathers, Saying, Go unto this people, and say, hearing ye shall hear, and shall not understand; and seeing ye shall see, and not perceive: For the heart of this people is waxed gross, and their ears are dull of hearing, and their eyes have they closed; lest they should see with their eyes, and hear with their ears, and understand with their heart, and should be converted, and I should heal them.

In the above passage, Paul ascribes to the Holy Spirit the words of Isaiah, a prophet 700 years before Messiah.

Psalm 95:9-11 with Hebrews 3:7-11

> When your fathers put Me to the test, tried Me, though they had seen My deeds. Forty years I was provoked by that generation; I thought, 'they are a senseless people; they would not know My ways.' Concerning them I swore in anger, 'they shall never come to My resting-place!'

> Wherefore as the Holy Spirit saith, today if ye will hear his voice, harden not your hearts, as in the provocation, in the day of temptation in the wilderness: When your fathers tempted me, proved me, and saw my works forty years. Wherefore I was grieved with that generation, and said, they do always err in their heart; and they have not known my ways. So I sware in my wrath, they shall not enter into my rest.

Here again the unknown author of Hebrews relates to his brethren concerning the hearts of the wilderness generation and attributed the words of the Psalmist to the Holy Spirit.

Jeremiah 31:33 with Hebrews 10:15-16:

> But such is the covenant I will make with the House of Israel after these days –
> Declares the LORD: I will put My teaching into their inmost being and inscribe
> it upon hearts. Then I will be their God, and they shall be My people.
>
> Whereof the Holy Spirit also is a witness to us: for after that he had said before,
> This is the covenant that I will make with them after those days, saith the
> LORD I will put my laws into their hearts, and in their minds will I write them.

Once again the unknown Jewish believer takes the New Covenant reference in Jeremiah 31 and ascribes the New Covenant that was given as being authored by the Holy Spirit.

These references of the Holy Spirit do not come from the *Tanakh*. The New Covenant writers understood that the Holy Spirit was responsible for the inspiration of the Hebrew Scriptures.

New Covenant

The Holy Spirit has a role in the New Covenant of Jeremiah 31 as can be seen in several assorted verses from the *Tanakh*, which clarify the Holy Spirit's involvement. Pache, in using these verses, makes four points in relation to the Holy Spirit coming upon mankind.

(1) The Holy Spirit will be poured out upon all flesh according to Joel 2:28-29. We see the beginnings of that in Acts 2:16-17 when the Holy Spirit was poured out on the 120 in the upper room.[660] Even though the fulfillment of this prophecy on the coming of the Holy Spirit is still future, it is a reference from the *Tanakh*. This is also a reference to the pouring out of the Holy Spirit in Isa 44:3 and Ezek 39:29. All three of these verses relate to the same event when His Spirit is poured out upon Israel.

(2) The Holy Spirit that is given in the New Covenant according to Isa 59:21 will remain forever.

(3) In Ezek 36:26-27; 37:14 it is very clear that the Holy Spirit will be placed within Israel. God through the Holy Spirit will give them a new heart and the stony heart will be removed and they will be placed in the Land. Also tie that together with I Cor 3:16 where the indwelling Holy Spirit makes us a temple to the living God.

---

[660] Joel 2:28-29: See Manuscript # 134 of Dr. Arnold Fruchtenbaum called *"How the New Testament Quotes the Old Testament*. See www.Ariel.org for Ariel Ministries in Tustin, CA

(4) It is clear that the Holy Spirit will rest upon the Messiah without measure as Isa 11:2; 42:1; 61:1 indicate.[661]

Enns addresses another vital issue that *Yeshua*, in all likelihood, was referring to John 3:10 in connection to Ezekiel 36. Enns continues by saying that the Holy Spirit, in Ezek 11:19; 36:25-27, is a promise by God to regenerate Israel during the Millennium.[662] These passages from the *Tanakh*, and *Yeshua*'s discussion with Nicodemus, suggest that the Old Testament believers should have been aware of the work of regeneration by the Holy Spirit.

If the New Covenant was to be used, it would be very simple to substantiate the personality of the Holy Spirit because Matthew, Mark, Luke, John, Paul, and Peter's writings are full of references to the Holy Spirit. In the Hebrew Scriptures alone, it must be remembered, as with the Second Person of the Godhead, that Scripture is progressive revelation. God did not choose to reveal everything about Himself at the start. That is equally true of the Third Person of the God-head. At the beginning of this chapter it was expressed that it is difficult to distinguish between the two because God Himself is pure Spirit. So how does one make a distinction between God the Father's Spirit and the Holy Spirit? It will be remembered that at the beginning of this chapter this very question was asked. In the New Covenant the personality of the Holy Spirit is clearly expressed by the authors. His person is clearly defined and separated from the other members of the triune God. But in the *Tanakh* that pattern is not followed. Rarely is there an expression that relates directly to the Holy Spirit as a person. However, what is clearly seen in the *Tanakh* is the action or movement of the Holy Spirit, which makes it difficult to show His personhood. This means that the personhood of the Holy Spirit has been seen, but only to a limited degree in the *Tanakh*. The Spirit, in the Hebrew Scriptures, can be grieved (Gen 6:3; Isa 63:10) and is distinct from God the Father and God the Son (Isa 48:16). The *Tanakh* implies the personhood of the Holy Spirit, but the New Covenant fully lays out the personality of the Third Person of the Godhead.

---

[661] Rene Pache, *The Person and Work of the Holy Spirit*, 34-35.
[662] Paul Enns, *The Moody Handbook of Theology*, 260.

CHAPTER 7

MESSIAH DIVINE?

In the *Tanakh* there are Scriptures written by Moses, David, Isaiah, Micah, Zechariah and the unknown author(s) of Samuel and Chronicles that clearly present the Messiah, the son of David as God!

However, in Judaism there are several views concerning the Messiah. Two of the most prominent will be addressed, in connection to who is Messiah, God or man? (1) Reform Judaism and Secular Jews do not believe that Messiah is a person but that a Messianic age will evolve and universal peace will come. A Messianic believer in Messiah reflects on that ideal:

> Messianism, which in the Bible is described as God's mighty interposition in human history, has become debased by contemporary Jewish spokesmen in something of a socio-economic program to be achieved by man alone by way of progressive, evolutionary fulfillment. The prophetic teachings concerning the day of judgment in which God will put an end to history as we know it are completely disregarded.[663]

As can be clearly seen, there is no personal Messiah involved at all in Secular and Reform Judaism's ideology. (2) Orthodox Judaism clearly believes that Messiah is a person, but they do not regard that person as God.[664] Ultra-orthodox Hasidim believe that, in the future, two Messiahs will come, due to the obvious portions of Scripture that point to two types of Messiahs. They identify the two as: (1) Messiah ben Joseph, who will come, suffer, and die (the suffering servant), and (2) and Messiah ben David, who will come and reign as king physically in Jerusalem.[665] A Jewish believer in *Yeshua*, the Messiah, relayed the following incident after being in an Orthodox Hasidic home in Brooklyn for Shabbat. The men sitting around the table were pounding their fists while singing songs with the words, "We want *Mashiach* now, we want *Mashiach* now." They were obviously acting out their fervent desire for the Messiah to come and fulfill the promise of God to Abraham. They obviously did not believe that the Messiah had already come in the person of Jesus (*Yeshua*) Christ (*ha Mashiach* or Messiah).

The term *Mashiach*, a Hebrew word meaning "anointed one," denotes two ideas of consecration and endowment of any object or person. The term appears 39 times in the Hebrew Scriptures and originally was used of the "anointed priest" (Lev 4:3, 4) and of kings when God referred to them as "my anointed" (1 Sam 2:35), "your anointed" (Ps 84:9), and "his anointed" (1 Sam 12:3, 5). By the time of the exile and post-exilic period, *Mashiach* had narrowed its meaning to the one who would fulfill the promises

---

[663] Arthur W. Kac. *The Spiritual Dilemma of the Jewish People; Its Cause and Cure* (Grand Rapids: Baker, 1983), 26-27.

[664] Jacobs, *A Jewish Theology*, 293.

[665] Joseph Klausner. *The Messianic Idea In Israel* (New York: Macmillan, 1955), 11, 519-531.

to Abraham and bring in the Kingdom and fulfill the covenant to David. So *Mashiach*, or Messiah, became the term for the long awaited promised one who would bring in the Kingdom spoken of by the Prophets.[666] In Dan 9:26 the Scripture says that before the destruction of the city (Jerusalem) occurs, the "anointed" (מָשִׁיחַ) will be cut off. That verse uses the term Messiah which history acknowledges that *Yeshua* was put to death 40 years prior to the destruction of the "city" and the "sanctuary."

A clear understanding of the actual verses depends on the interpretation of two important Hebrew words: (1) עוֹלָם or *olam* and (2) עַד or *'ad*.[667] Both of these words are translated in the English text as "eternal," "eternity," "everlasting," "for ever," and "ever and ever," "age or ancient."[668] In English such terms project beyond the end of time. However, in the Hebrew there is no word that expresses the English concept of "eternal." Therefore, to understand the term in English, a reader needs to know what the word meant in the Hebrew language then and how was it used.

Olam עוֹלָם

The first word *olam* (עוֹלָם) means "long duration, antiquity, futurity."[669] *Olam* is divided into two groups with numerous sections. It deals with time in the past, as well as indefinite futurity with many sub-headings. However, the majority of references deal with man's life, a dynasty, laws that are no longer in use as the Mosaic Law. The term *olam* deals with families and relationships with nations or an age. What is obvious is that the term *olam* in the *Tanakh* is confined to time, except for God who is outside of time. So *olam*, when used in connection with God, indicates that eternity is to be understood when used of Him. Schoonhoven expresses it this way:

> The OT has no special term for "eternity" that can be contrasted with a term denoting "temporality." The Hebrew word most often used to express "eternity" is *olam*. It is the same word that expresses duration of time, and it designates eternity only in such statements as "from *olam*" and "until *olam*" (Psa 90:2).[670]

The term *olam* is a very elastic term for time, stretching from a portion of time in man's life, to his whole life right through to a period of time that could be to the end of an age or time period. Schoonhoven's explanation is that:

> When viewed from the vantage point of the Bible, eternity is a term that includes temporal relations. Eternity is time stretching endlessly forward and

---

[666] James Smith. *The Promised Messiah* (Nashville: Nelson, 1993), 1-4.

[667] Botterweck, Ringgren, and Fabry. *Theological Dictionary of the Old Testament*, 10:456, 530

[668] Robert Young. *Analytical Concordance to the Bible* (22nd Edition, Grand Rapids: Eerdmans, n.d.), 310-312.

[669] Francis Brown, S. R. Driver and Charles A. Briggs, *A Hebrew and English Lexicon of the Old Testament* (Oxford: Clarendon Press, n.d.), 761-763.

[670] Geoffrey W. Bromiley. *The International Standard Bible Encyclopedia* (4 vols. Grand Rapids: Eerdmans, 1982), 2:162.

backward, with the result that time itself must be regarded as a segment of eternity.[671]

Because God is outside of time, He is not governed by time. So *olam* refers to man's relationship to other men, nations, or to God for a period of time, whether that time is a man's lifetime or an age. The exception is when the reference is to God, as He is not bound by time. Below are some passages of how *olam* is used "generally to point to something that seems long ago, but rarely, if ever, refers to a limitless past:"

Gen 6:4	"Those were the mighty men who were of old" written from Moses' point in time.
Deut 32:7	to the time of one's elder
I Sam 27:8	"ancient times"
Isa 51:9	"days of old, the generations of long ago"
Isa 58:12	Rebuild the "ancient ruins," a future prophecy, what they will do in relationship to their past.
Isa 63:9	"carried them all the days of old"
Jer 6:16	"ancient paths" where the good way is and walk in it
Jer 18:15	"ancient paths" they (Israel) have forgotten me and do not walk in my paths
Jer 28:8	prophets before me and you, from "ancient times"
Ezek 36:2	"ancient high places" (ASV)
Micah 7:14	"as in the days of old"
Mal 3:4	"as in the days of old and as in former years"
Job 22:15	"ancient path" which wicked men trod
Prov 22:28	"ancient boundary" that your fathers have set
Ezra 4:15	[Aramaic] "have incited revolt within it in past days"
Ezra 4:19	[Aramaic] "that the city has risen up against the kings in past days"[672]

Although *Olam* is not only used of the past, the majority of the time it is used of some future period. It refers to the future of limited duration or conditions that will exist continuously throughout a limited period of time, often a single lifetime. The following two examples express that position:

"as long as one lives" (a slave for life) Exod 21:16 (Deut 15:17; I Sam 27:12)
"May my lord King David live forever" 1 Kgs 1:31 (Neh 2:3; 'Dan 2:4)[673]

Arnold Fruchtenbaum, speaking in relation to the Sabbath being kept "forever," states that the word is used within time:

---

[671] Geoffrey W. Bromiley. *The international Standard Bible Encyclopedia*, 163.

[672] Harris, Archer, and Waltke, *Theological Wordbook of the Old Testament*, 2:672-673.

[673] Botterweck, Ringgren, and Fabry. *Theological Dictionary of the Old Testament*, 10:535-536.

While the English terms tends to carry concepts of eternity, this is not the meaning of the Hebrew words themselves. Classical Hebrew had no word that actually meant "eternal." The Hebrew term for "forever" (*olam*) means "long duration," "antiquity," or "futurity." The Hebrew terms basically mean "until the end of a period of time." What that period of time is must be determined by the context of related passages. The period of time may have been to the end of a man's life, or an age, or dispensation, but not "forever" in the sense of eternity. This is very clear from examining the usage of the same terminology in other passages.[674]

Fruchtenbaum further asserts that *olam* does not usually mean eternity but definitely refers to a period of time with different lengths of time involved:

> To focus on the meaning of the term forever, what does this really mean in classical Hebrew? First, the Hebrew word is *olam*. The word itself simply means "long duration," "antiquity," "futurity" or "until the end of a period of time." That period of time is determined by the context. Sometimes it is the length of a man's life, sometimes it is an age and sometimes it is a dispensation. Second, there are two Hebrew forms of *olam*. One is *le-olam*, which means "unto an age." The second form is *ad-olam*, which means "until an age." However, neither of these forms carry the English meaning of "forever." Though it was translated that way in English, the Hebrew does not carry the concept of eternity as the English word "forever" does.

> Third, the word *olam*, *le olam* or *ad-olam*, sometimes means only up to the end of a man's life. For example, it is used in Exodus 14:13 of someone's lifetime. It is used in Exodus 21:6, Leviticus 25:46, and Deut 15:17 of a slave's life. In 1 Sam 1:22 and 2:35, it is used of Samuel's life. First Samuel 20:23 speaks of the lifetime of David and Jonathan. First Samuel 27:12; 28:2 and 1 Chr 28:4 uses the word of David's lifetime. While the English reads, "forever," obviously from the context it does not mean forever in the sense of eternity, but only forever up to the end of the person's life.

> Fourth, *olam* sometimes means only an age or dispensation. For example, Deut 23:3 uses the term "forever," but it limits the term "forever" as only ten generations long. It obviously carries the concept of an age here. In 2 Chr 7:16 it is used only for the period of the first temple. So, again, the word "forever" in Hebrew does not mean eternal, it means up to the end of a period of time which could either be a man's life or an age or a dispensation.

> Fifth, the same word for "forever" is used of certain ceremonial facets of the Mosaic Law which everyone agrees has ended with the coming of Christ. For example, the same word "forever" is used of the kindling of the tabernacle lamp stands (Ex 27:20; Lev 24:3): it is used of the ceremony of the showbread (Lev

---

[674] Arnold G. Fruchtenbaum, *The Sabbath: Manuscript # 176* (Tustin, CA: Ariel Ministries, 1991), 18.

24:8); it is used of the service of the brazen laver (Ex 30:21); is used of the Levitical priesthood and Levitical garments (Ex28:43; 40:15; Lev 6:18; 10:9; Num 10:8; 18:23; 25:13; Deut 18:5; 1 Chr 15:2; 23:13); it is used of the sacrificial system, including the sacrifices and offerings (Ex 29:28; Lev 7:34, 36; 10:15; Num 15:15; 18:8, 11, 19; 19:10); it is used of the Day of Atonement sacrifice (Lev 16:34); and, it is used of the red heifer offering (Num 19:10). It is used of all of these ceremonial facets that everybody agrees has been done away with in Christ. [675]

Within all these references, the term *olam*, eternity is conceptualized from the perspective of man—not God, who according to the prophets, dwells in heaven and is outside of time and unlimited by space as pointed out by Vos. God, with the character of immutability, is outside of time, separated from time and not governed by time. Vos states:

> That the prophets represent God as dwelling in heaven, unlimited by space, and yet they also say that He dwells in Zion and that Canaan is His land. . . . The same relation applied as between Jehovah and time. In popular language, such as the prophets use, eternity can only be expressed in terms of time, although in reality it lies altogether above time."[676]

In his book, *On the Eternity of God*, Charnock does not use the Hebrew word *olam* to lay out the differences between time and eternity, for eternity is before and after time:

> Time hath a continual succession . . . We must conceive of eternity contrary to the notion of time; as the nature of time consists in the succession of parts , so the nature of eternity in an infinite immutable duration. . . . So eternity is the duration of his essence; and when we say God is eternal, we exclude from him all possibility of beginning and ending, all flux and change. As the essences of God cannot be bounded by any place, so it is not to be limited by any time; as it is his immensity to be everywhere, so it is his eternity to be always. . . . His duration is as endless as his essence is boundless: he always was and always will be, and will no more have an end than he had a beginning; and this is an excellency belonging to the Supreme Being. . . . Time began with the foundation of the world; but God being before time, could have no beginning in time. Before the beginning of creation, and the beginning of time, there could be nothing but eternity; . . .for as between the Creator and creatures there is no medium, so between time and eternity there is no medium.[677]

---

[675] Fruchtenbaum. *The Sabbath*, Manuscript #176, 18-19.

[676] Geerhardus Vos. *Biblical Theology, Old and New Testaments* (Grand Rapids: Eerdmans, 1948), 263.

[677] Steven Charnock. *Existence and Attributes of God* (Grand Rapids: Baker, 1996), 1:280-282. For some additional information see: L. Thomas Holdcroft, The Doctrine of God (Oakland, CA: Western Book Company, 19780, 21-23.

Charnock's whole chapter on the eternity of God is very worthwhile reading and meditating upon. Several other authors, such as Botterweck,[678] VanGemeren,[679] and Harris[680] also lay out some excellent material on the word *olam*.

So what is the conclusion in relation to the word *olam* and how it is to be understood in the *Tanakh*? Fruchtenbaum gives the clearest and simplest answer when he states that the context determines just how *olam* is to be understood.[681] The understanding of *olam*, in reference to man and/or to God, will be determined by its context. That context will determine whether *olam* is in the framework of time or whether *olam* in relation to God and His nature, essence and character as being outside of time, eternal. The following are two examples of *olam* being used in reference to God and carries with it the English concept of eternity:

> No longer shall you need the sun for light by day, nor the shining of the moon for radiance [by night]; for the LORD shall be your light everlasting, your God shall be your glory.
>
> Your sun shall set no more, your moon no more withdraw; for the LORD shall be a light to you forever, and your days of mourning shall be ended.
>
> Isaiah 60:19-20

In this passage Isaiah states that there will be no more need for the sun and moon for the *Shechinah* of God will be your light. Webb,[682] Wolf,[683] and Young[684] refer to Rev 21:23 (22:5) where John (*Yochanan*) states that after the destruction of the heavens and earth, and the new heavens and earth are in place, God's glory with be their light. Here something beyond the physical earth and time are in view in connection with God's *Shechinah* light. Psalm 119:89 states, "The LORD exists forever; your word stands firm in heaven," meaning that the Word of God is settled in heaven, a place outside of the limits of earth and time. This verse declares that the Word of God is in the eternal heavens. According to Leupold, the Word of God which comes from the eternal Lord of the heavens has its abiding resting place and will, like them, endure forever.[685]

While *olam* is predominately used in the context of time, it is also used outside of time in reference to God. So where *olam* is used of man and his relationship to others, whether other people or nations, it has a time context. Yet throughout the *Tanakh*, *olam*, when in context with God, has an eternal perspective beyond time.

---

[678] Botterweck, Ringgren, and Fabry. *Theological Dictionary of the Old Testament*, 10:531-545.
[679] Willem A. VanGemeren. *Dictionary of Old Testament Theology & Exegesis*, 3:345-350.
[680] Harris, Archer and Waltke. *Theological Wordbook of the Old Testament*, 2:672-673.
[681] Fruchtenbaum, *The Sabbath: Manuscript #176*, 18.
[682] Webb, *The Message of Isaiah*, 231.
[683] Wolf. *Interpreting Isaiah*, 238.
[684] Young, *The Book of Isaiah*, 3:455.
[685] Leupold, *Exposition of Psalm*, 842.

The second word for eternity is עַד which means "perpetuity."[686] The word perpetuity reflects both time and eternity. This Hebrew word refers to "past time" and "future time." In past time it is referenced only twice as the "ancient mountains" in Hab 3:6 and in relation to the wicked in Job 20:4.[687] The other references refer to future time and deals with things earthbound or time-related, except with reference to God. עַד is used 48 times in the *Tanakh*: 29 times in Psalm, 8 times in Isaiah, twice in each of Micah, Job, and Proverbs and once in Ezek 15:18, Amos 1:11, Hab 3:6, Dan 12:3 and 1 Chr 28:9.[688] In these 48 references *ad* is used 19 times in conjunction with *olam*[689] as in Isa 45:17 (*olam*/everlasting; *ad*/without end), Ex 15:18 (*olam*/for ever; *ad*/ever), and Dan 12:3 (*olam*/forever; *ad*/ever).

Brown, Driver and Briggs, in reference to עַד or *ad*, have two groupings of usages: (1) to past time as reflected in the above paragraph. (2) To future time as reflected in "for ever" as during a lifetime, of a king, or of things, or of "the continuous existence of nations" as well as "divine existence."[690] In the future sense, עַד "always denotes the unforeseeable future," which does not necessarily imply eternity. However, when עַד is applied to God, it does imply eternity or everlasting.[691] Like *olam*, *ad* must be understood and interpreted within the context in which it is given. It must be understood that time is only a segment of eternity, and God is outside of time.

Since no Hebrew word independently reflects eternity by itself, *olam* and *ad* reflect time, because time is only a part of eternity. God lives outside of time; He made time. Hence, He is not bound by time. But when *olam* and *ad* are used of God, in relation to His being, it is understood to be a reference to eternity, beyond time. Therefore, interpreting *olam* and *ad* requires the context and related passages to determine whether it is bound by time and whether it reflects eternity.

First Coming Messianic References

The English words "eternity," "everlasting" and "for ever" play a critical role in the understanding of these First Coming Messianic references. But first, in Genesis 12, 13, 15, 17, and 22, God makes a covenant called the Abrahamic Covenant which is

---

[686] Brown, Driver and Briggs. *A Hebrew and English Lexicon of the Old Testament*, 723.

[687] Harris, Archer, and Waltke, *Theological Wordbook of the Old Testament*, 2:645.

[688] Jenni, Theological *Lexicon of the Old Testament*, 2:837.

[689] Harris, Archer, and Waltke, *Theological Wordbook of the Old Testament*, 2:645.

[690] Brown, Driver, and Briggs, *A Hebrew and English Lexicon of the Old Testament*, 723.

[691] Harris, Archer, and Waltke, *Theological Wordbook of the Old Testament*, 2:645.

recognized as an eternal covenant.[692] Deuteronomy 30 is not only a promise of a Land Covenant[693] to be given to Abraham and to his descendents, (Gen 15:4-5, 18) but it is also an eternal covenant.[694] This is also critical in understanding the situation today in Israel. God is in the process of regathering Israel, as Deuteronomy 30 denotes, the fulfilling of His covenant to Abraham. Several years ago this author read a quote that is significant and well worth pondering:

> The most central portion of all Scripture is the Abrahamic Covenant;
> everything else is commentary on it. (source unknown)

Not only did God make an eternal covenant with Abraham and enlarge it to Israel in the Land Covenant, He also made an eternal covenant with David. These three covenants are eternal, and minimally last through future time, or "long duration," until time and history close. The Hebrew Scripture reveals nothing beyond the Messianic Kingdom that is promised to Abraham and to David's eternal son. Only in the New Covenant, in the book of Revelation, is further revelation given, about an eternal state. In dealing with the Davidic Covenant, there is an extremely strong indication that there is something here that has an eternal reference to the end of time into eternity. The coming verses will show that the promises of an eternal God, who is working to fulfill them through the eternal Son, who is the eternal son of David.

In this section there are several First Coming Messianic references (2 Sam 7:11-16; 1 Chron 17:11-14; Isa 9:6-7; Micah 5:2) that use the term *olam* or *ad*. How are these verses to be understood when referring to the Messiah? These verses are very important because Judaism often recognizes them as messianic, even when the messianic person appears to be divine. Yet while rabbis recognize these verses as messianic, they will not embrace the idea that Messiah can be God. To them it is completely inconceivable that God would incarnate Himself as flesh and dwell among men.

Despite Judaism's disclaimers, the divinity of the Messiah is clearly indicated in two distinct categories of Hebrew Scriptures. The first involves passages in which *olam* is used. Second are passages that are recognized as Messianic, where *Yahweh* is speaking of Himself, and what happened to Him was experienced only by the Second Person of the tri-unity.

What has been established is that *olam* and *ad* play a significant role in understanding the eternal aspect of the Abrahamic, Land, and Davidic Covenants, as well as the First Coming References of the Messiah that have direct bearing on those covenants and promises given by the prophets. But before these verses are discussed,

---

[692] Arnold G. Fruchtenbaum, *Israelology: The Missing Link in Systematic Theology* (Tustin, CA: Ariel Ministries Press, 1994), 334

[693] Land Covenant: Traditionally the Land Covenant has been called the "Palestinian Covenant." But to avoid confusion with the Palestinian Covenant that is in the PLO charter, which calls for the destruction of Israel, Land Covenant is being used to identify the Covenant that God made with Israel in Deut 30.

[694] Fruchtenbaum, *Israelology: The Missing Link in Systematic Theology*, 572-581.

one other observation is in order in relation to Gen 3:15. This passage is commonly called the protevangelium, meaning that it is the prototype for the Christian gospel.[695] There is something that must be said about this verse that draws attention to the nature and essence of the seed of the woman as is related to the promise given by God to Satan concerning his undoing. First the verse:

> And I will put enmity between thee and the woman, and between thy seed and her seed; it shall bruise thy head, and thou shalt bruise his heel.

It is commonly recognized that Satan, originally called "Lucifer, son of the morning (Isa 14:12)," was most likely a very beautiful creature (Ezek 28:13). In Ezek 28:14 (16) he is called "the anointed Cherub that covereth." Apparently, the Cherubim were the "guardian and proclaimer of God's glorious presence and holiness."[696] Cherubim seem to be the highest rank among the angels and also the closest to the presence of God.[697] Unger confirms Shower's statement:

> He is the highest and most exalted of heaven's beings, who became Satan when he led a celestial revolt that spread to myriads of the angelic beings."[698]

Satan, as a covering cherub, may have been one of the most powerful angels that God had created. So if the seed of the woman were just a man, he could not have touched Satan. This verse strongly indicates that the seed of the woman would have to be equal to, or greater than, Satan himself in order to defeat him. If that were the case, then the seed of the woman would be the incarnation of God in flesh. It would have been impossible for this prophecy, given to Satan, to be fulfilled without "the seed of the woman" minimally being a supernatural person. This passage by itself does not necessarily establish that God, in human flesh, is the "seed of the woman," however, Eve understood it that way in Gen 4:1. But by the time the last prophet has come, this is the only possibility.

Messiah Divine!

A significant place to start is an examination of the Davidic Covenant given in I Chr 17:10-14 and 2 Sam 7:11-16. Significance of this covenant hinges on the direct relationship between the Davidic Covenant and the passages given by the Prophets equating this physical son of David with the Messiah as God. Why are there two references to the Davidic Covenant? They are not totally the same. They are different, and yet they have tremendous similarities. Observe the two passages with the personages, differences and similarities involved.

---

[695] Mathews, *New American Commentary: Genesis 1:1-11:26*, 247.

[696] C. Fred Dickason, *Angels: Elect and Evil* (Chicago: Moody, 1975), 128.

[697] Renald Showers, *Those Invisible Spirits Called Angels*, (Bellmawr, NJ: Friends of Israel Gospel Ministry, 1997), 27-28.

[698] Merrill F. Unger, *Biblical Demonology* (Wheaton: Scripture Press, 1952), 15

2 Samuel 7 and 1 Chronicles 17

2 Samuel 7:11-16	1 Chronicles 17:10-14
Olam House or Dynasty	*Olam* House or Dynasty
Olam Kingdom	*Olam* Kingdom
Olam Throne	*Olam* Throne
If he sins – chasten	No sin or chastening mentioned
Solomon in view	Some one beyond Solomon in view
	Olam Son

Fruchtenbaum makes the following observation of these two passages of Scripture as to the differences and similarities:

> The parallel passage in 1 Chr 17:10b-14 is very similar, yet there are significant differences. In 2 Samuel the son is immediate; in 1 Chronicles he is distant. In 2 Samuel the son is a sinner; in 1 Chronicles there is no mention of sin. In 2 Samuel the reference is to Solomon; in 1 Chronicles the reference is to Messiah.
>
> The three promises of 2 Samuel are repeated here, but a fourth is also added: an eternal son. 'I will settle him in my house forever.' David's line will eventually culminate in the birth of an eternal Person whose eternality will guarantee David's dynasty, kingdom and throne forever.[699]

Olam is used three times both in the Chronicles and Samuel passages. These passages cannot be read without an understanding that God is making a perpetual covenant with David. This covenant will last through time and eternity because of the aspect brought out in the Chronicles passage concerning an eternity son, who is the Messiah.

What Ethan, the Ezrahite, who was in Solomon's court (1 Kgs 4:30-31) wrote about David in Psalm 89, is significant. He wrote after the time of David and during Solomon's reign, giving important confirmation and understanding as to the interpretation of the Davidic Covenant. Look at some of the following verses:

> v. 3-4 [4-5] I have made a covenant with My chosen one; I have sworn to My servant David; I will establish your offspring forever, I will confirm your throne for all generations. Selah.

> v. 29 [30] I will establish his line forever, his throne, as long as the heavens last.

> vs. 34-37 [35-38] I will not violate My covenant, or change what I have uttered. I have sworn by My holiness, once and for all; I will not be false to David. His line shall continue forever, his throne, as the sun before Me, as the moon, established forever, and enduring witness in the sky. Selah

---

[699] Fruchtenbaum. *Messianic Christology*, 79.

v. 51 [52] How your enemies, O LORD, have flung abuse, abuse at Your anointed at every step.

These statements of Scripture, by the hand of Ethan the Ezrahite, are clear and unmistakable. This Davidic Covenant is viewed by Ethan under the Inspiration of Scripture as being "for ever." The word "anointed," in verse 51, is the Hebrew word *Mashiach*, from which Messiah comes. The connection that Ethan makes with the Davidic Covenant and his use of *Mashiach* is significant.

One other dimension is the Jer 22:24-30 passage which appeared to threaten the "for ever" implications of the Davidic Covenant. This passage needs to be brought into view as to its direct relationship between Solomon and his kingly line which was cursed by God in Jer 22:24-30. *Yeshua*, in the New Covenant, could not get his right to rule from his stepfather, Joseph. *Yeshua* was of the Davidic line through *Miriam* (Mary), but there were many sons of David in the first century C.E. The New Covenant book of Luke gives the right to rule by God Himself in Luke 1:32 to *Yeshua*:

> He shall be great, and shall be called the Son of the Highest: and the Lord God shall give unto him the throne of his father David.

Nathan told David that his house, throne and kingdom would be secure because one of his sons would be the eternal Son of God, whose incarnation would place him physically in the house of David.

There is another significant verse from the New Covenant that deals directly with the Davidic Covenant. *Yeshua*, near the end of His ministry, asked the Pharisees a question as to who the Messiah would be. But they could not, and would not, answer. That answer was not acceptable to them. Matthew 22:41-46 *Yeshua* refers to Psalm 110:1:

> While the Pharisees were gathered together, *Yeshua* asked them, saying, What think ye of Messiah? Whose son is he? They say unto him, The Son of David. He saith unto them, how then doth David in spirit call him Lord, saying, The LORD said unto my Lord, sit thou on my right hand, till I make thine enemies thy footstool? If David then called him Lord, how is he his son? And no man was able to answer him a word, neither durst [dare] any man from that day forth ask him any more questions.

The answer to the question, "If David then called him Lord, how is he his son," was obviously, God. However, the Pharisees would not answer it.

Olam, in the 1 Chronicles account, points out clearly that a son of the sons of David would reign on his throne for *olam*. Once again the context definitely points to *olam* as the end of time. When Ethan, in Psa 89, adds his understanding to the original passage, it becomes even clearer that the one who is settled by God, in His house and in

His kingdom, shall be established and reign on the throne of David beyond the end of time into eternity, forevermore. Last, the curse of Jeremiah 22 totally disqualifies any descendent of Solomon from ever being King over Israel from the throne of David.

Isaiah 9:6-7

> For unto us a child is born, unto us a son is given: and the government shall be upon his shoulder: and his name shall be called Wonderful, Counselor, the mighty God, the Everlasting Father, The Prince of Peace.
>
> Of the increase of his government and peace there shall be no end, upon the throne of David, and upon his kingdom, to order it, and to establish it with judgment and with justice from henceforth even for ever. The zeal of the LORD of hosts will perform this. (KJV)

There are seven observations about this verse that point to this child being uniquely different than anyone else born.

First, the verse makes clear that God names a child promised in Isa 9:6-7. Human parents name a child because they like the sound of the name. Some parents name a child because of the biblical meaning or because of the biblical character of the person that bore that name. But they have absolutely no idea whether or not their child will live up to that name. Not so with God. When He names a child He does so from His omniscience, knowing that the name He gives will exactly fit the character and purpose of that child. Therefore, the names given for Messiah, the child that will be born in Isaiah 9, are a description of His character. Of the five descriptions given to Him, three of them are used only of God. Notice also that in verse 7 this person is directly tied to the throne of David. Who was this child? Jewish scholars teach that the "child" to be born was Hezekiah, a contemporary of Isaiah.[700] Cohen also argues that unlike his father Ahaz, who was a vassal to Assyria, Hezekiah was not a vassal. But Cohen's reasoning is not even logical. Hezekiah, King of Judah, led a vassal state under the Assyrians until he rebelled. Sennacherib then descends upon Judah and totally destroys 46 major cities and the "Oriental Institute Cylinder" which gives the account of Sennacherib's campaign against Judah and Jerusalem:

> As for himself (Hezekiah), like a bird in a cage is his royal city Jerusalem, I shut (him) up.[701]

2 Kings 18-20 makes it clear that Judah was a vassal state under Hezekiah's leadership. In fact, Hezekiah stripped the temple of its gold and silver to try to get Assyria to stop attacking Judah. That does not sound like he could be the "child" as Cohen tries to state or the "Wonderful" or the "Mighty God," let alone the "everlasting Father." Hezekiah, according to biblical history, did not have the character of any of these names.

---

[700] A. Cohen, *The Soncino Chumash, Isaiah* (New York: The Soncino Press, 1983), 44.
[701] Joseph P. Free and Howard F. Vos, *Archaeology and the Bible History* (Grand Rapids: Zondervan, 1992), 180-181.

Second, the word "wonderful" (Isa 9:6) in this passage is כֶּלֶא or *pele*, a variant of the Hebrew root word פָּלָא (*pala*).[702] Albertz states that the verb occurs 78 time and means "to be wondrous" or "to fulfill" (a vow) "or to separate."[703] Albertz also states that:

> In the large, major category of its usage, . . . it indicates an event that a person, judging by the customary and the expected, finds extraordinary, impossible, even wonderful. *Pele* never hinges on the phenomenon as such but includes both the unexpected event as well as one's astonished reaction to it. . . . The wonder, the astonishment, includes the recognition of the limits of one's own power to conceptualize and comprehend.[704]

This word "wonderful" is used in the context of something that is beyond human knowledge or ability as is stated by Conrad:

> The texts all deal with extraordinary phenomena, transcending the power of knowledge and imagination. . . . In fact, the texts do not deal with circumstances presented simply as being extraordinary, but rather with certain goals impossible for humans to attain by their own devices or with actions and events directed toward them or affecting them that they are nevertheless unable to influence. In other words, they deal with acts and effects transcending human knowledge and imagination and hence above all transcending the powers of human agency. . . . Primarily, the observation is made concerning a line that human beings cannot cross but that can be crossed from the other side. The word group thus also marks the contrast between the finitude of what is possible on one side of the line and infinite range of what is possible on the other side. . . but for the most part it applies to superhuman forces and powers, especially to God. The texts are concerned above all with the insurmountable contrast between what is possible for human beings and what is possible for God.[705]

What becomes rather obvious is that, even though *pele* is used of God rather than man, the context of v. 6 definitely links the word to God as well as a child that will bear all governmental responsibility and will sit on the throne of David. This verse states that a child will be born who will govern from the throne of David, and his name is Wonderful (*pele*) God Himself. Clearly, this one will be God in flesh reigning on the throne of David.

Third, the name "Mighty God" (Isa 9:6) is even more perplexing concerning the Jewish dilemma of its dual reference to God and to a child. Jewish people do not believe the Messiah will be God, and yet here is a child that will be born in order to reign on the throne of David, and "his name shall be called . . . the mighty God." Yet

---

[702] Botterweck, Ringgren, and Fabry, *Theological Dictionary of the Old Testament*, 11:534.

[703] Jenni, *Theological Lexicon of the Old Testament*, 2:982.

[704] Jenni, *Theological Lexicon of the Old Testament*, 2:982.

[705] Botterweck, Ringgren, and Fabry, *Theological Dictionary of the Old Testament*, 11:534-535.

Jer 32:18 states, "The Great, the Mighty God, the LORD of host, is his name." Even in the Jewish Study Bible, Jer 32:18 does not remove its meaning: "O Great and mighty God whose name is the LORD of Hosts." No Jewish person is going to question or doubt that the statement in Jeremiah is the LORD God Almighty Himself. So how can the same truth be denied in Isa 9:6, that speaks of a child who would be born whose name is *El gibbor* (God almighty)? Isaiah 10:21 also refers to Israel returning to the "Mighty God." God is consistent with His word, even if man is not. It is tremendously inconsistent to say that the Jeremiah 32 and Isaiah 10 passages refer to God and the Isaiah 9:6 passage does not.

Fourth, the "Everlasting" as in Everlasting Father in Isa 9:6 is the Hebrew word עַד (*ad*) which means duration or perpetuity. This is a reference to God as the Father who is their guardian and protector. Fruchtenbaum notes that Isa 9:6 can be compared to Isa 63:16 which says; "thou, O LORD, art our Father; our Redeemer from everlasting is thy name."[706] Here the word *olam*, rather than *ad*, is used, but both refer to eternity as unto the end of time and into eternity when used in reference to God. Also Isa 63:16 states that "LORD," "Father," and "Redeemer" are from everlasting and so is His name, even as Isa 9:6 refers to the child to be born, that His name will be called Everlasting Father.

Fifth, is the description in v. 7 "no end" and is the Hebrew word אֵין־קֵץ. Although Jenni claims that this word for end is "distributed throughout the entire Old Testament," he makes no reference to Isa 9:7.[707] Also Talmon, on writing on the word קֵץ, does not reference Isa 9:7, but he does divide the meaning and usage of the word into four groups: (1) end as in lifetime, (2) end as a period of time, (3) end as a historical period and (4) eschatology.[708] Isaiah states that this child that will be born, and of His government there will be "no end" to its increase and peace. That seems to be self-explanatory. This usage seems to be unique because the other usages do reference a specific period of time, where "no end" in this passage has something in view beyond time. Hill and Matties show the usage of "end" as theological as in divine judgment (Gen 6:13), "end of time" and "end of human history" (Dan 8:17, 19; 11:40; 12:4, 6) and even "end of wrongdoing" (Ezek 21:25, 29 [30, 34]). But because of the אֵין (no), the verse is stating that "a time of peace without end is expected."[709] So the אֵין gives it the opposite meaning, no ending, as is referenced by Brown, Driver and Briggs.[710] Coppes very clearly shows that difference with the word אֵין (no) when he states: "Contrariwise, the Messiah's kingdom will know no end."[711] Clearly this word אֵין (no) is used not in a time frame but in the sense of eternity. Clearly the Messianic Kingdom referenced in v. 7 will have no end.

---

[706] Fruchtenbaum, *Messianic Christology*, 40.

[707] Jenni, *Theological Lexicon of the Old Testament*, 3:1154.

[708] Botterweck, Ringgren, and Fabry, *Theological Dictionary of the Old Testament*, 13:82-83.

[709] VanGemeren, *Dictionary of Old Testament Theology & Exegesis*, 3:955.

[710] Brown, Driver, and Briggs, *A Hebrew and English Lexicon of the Old Testament*, 892.

[711] Harris, Archer, and Waltke, *Theological Wordbook of the Old Testament*, 2:809.

Jewish scholars recognize the enduring kingdom, but do not acknowledge that the Messiah will reign forever, but that God is reigning forever. The first paragraph is a comparison between Moses and Messiah ben David. Moses brought the people of the Exodus to the entrance of the Promised Land and Messiah ben David brings them to the kingdom. The following quote coming from the *Messiah Text* will be viewed in four parts:

> With the death of <u>Moses, the earthly career of Israel's first Redeemer</u> comes to an end. In the Other World, of course, he continues to keep a watchful eye on his people, continues to intercede in their behalf. <u>Messiah ben David, too, nears the end of his ministry with his victory over the armies of Gog and Magog and over their satanic master Armilus, whom he kills with the breath of his mouth.</u> This latter detail, incidentally, is an eloquent indication of the kind of victory Jewish legend envisaged would be achieved by the Messiah. There was to be first of all, a holocaustal sequence of wars, myriads would be killed in actual combat, or by earthquakes and other great cataclysms, but the greatest of victories, that over Armilus himself, the evil incarnate, would be a spiritual one: his annihilation would be brought about by breath from the pure mouth of the Son of David, the elect of God, the Messiah.[712]

What is so interesting in this section is that the Messiah ben David will bring them in the kingdom, the enemy is defeated, but then he fades away into obscurity. Their premise is there must be two messiahs, of which neither is divine, rather than seeing one Messiah who comes on two separate occasions.

> This greatest feat of the Messiah is, at one and the same time, also his last one. Just as Moses had brought the Children of Israel to the threshold of the Promised Land and then died, so the Messiah leads them to victory over Gog and Magog, culminating in the elimination of Armilus, <u>and then fades away, disappears from the scene. Nothing more is heard about him except some very vague and generalized statements to the effect that he would continue to rule over his people for an indeterminate period.</u> In all the great events which follow the victory over Armilus, the Messiah plays no role whatsoever.[713]

To the Jewish rabbis the Messiah fades away into obscurity, while God the Father takes central stage in Jerusalem as the King and rules over the earth as the Son of David. That makes the Scriptures null and void! Messiah must rule according to Moses, Ethan, Isaiah, Micah, Jeremiah, Daniel, and Zechariah. It is so heartbreaking because of Judaism blindness in seeing the multiple occasions where God shows Himself as a plurality (tri-unity), they mishandle or misinterpret the *Tanakh* because their premise is faulty.

---

[712] Raphael Patai, *The Messiah Texts* (Detroit: Wayne State University Press, 1979), xxxiii-xxxiv.
[713] Patai, *The Messiah Texts*, xxxiv. Underlining is this author's.

We know, or at least we are led to believe, that he is present at the Resurrection of the dead, at the Last Judgment, at the Messianic banquet, at the House of Study of the future in which the new, Messianic, Tora will be taught, but if he is, no mention is made of his presence and he plays no role at all. In all those great occurrences and processes it is God, the Holy one, blessed be He, who Himself takes the central place on the stage. It is God who resuscitates the dead, who judges the pious and the wicked, who sits with the saintly at the great feast, who pours wine into their cups, who entertains them by dancing before them, who teaches them the new Tora, and who received the homage of the entire rejuvenated, reformed and sanctified world. Where is the Messiah in all this? We are told nothing of him, and were it not that in the earlier phases of the Messianic myth we were assured that he would, after the ultimate victory, reign in Jerusalem as the Prince of Peace, we would not even suspect that he is present.[714]

Their conclusion is that just as Moses is a type of Messiah, both redeemers, and neither has a part in the Promise Land or in the Kingdom.

Thus, and in this primarily, the Messiah proves to be essentially a Moses figure, and Moses to be the accurate prefiguration of the Messiah. Both are Redeemers, but neither of them has a part in the great era to whose threshold they lead their people at the price of their lifeblood.[715]

Both the beginning and ending of this statement compare from the *Messiah Text*, Moses and Messiah as redeemers who do not enter the Promise. This parallel with Moses comes from the Torah in Deut 18:15-18 which speaks of a prophet like unto Moses. In the middle of the quote it refers to the Messiah that "fades away" as follows:

And then fades away, disappears from the scene. Nothing more is heard about him except some very vague and generalized statements to the effect that he would continue to rule over his people for an indeterminate period.

Instead of the Messiah reigning, they see God the Father reigning in Jerusalem. Considering what has been seen in all of the previous chapters of this study, God is a tri-unity. *Yeshua*, who is the Messiah, is the one on record in the *Tanakh* as the one ruling from Jerusalem during the Kingdom. It was also seen in those previous chapters that, without question, the plurality (tri-unity) of God is in the Hebrew Scriptures. The Scripture makes clear simple statements about who the Messiah is. But as in Judaism, if their basic premise is wrong, that the Messiah cannot be God because God is one, He is missed. He does not fade away because He is God Almighty who will reign in Jerusalem as was promised to David. God the Father is not a descendent of David, but God the Son is clearly understood from Psa 110:1, even understood by the Pharisees in *Yeshua*'s day.

---

[714] Patai, *The Messiah Texts*, xxxiv-xxxv. Underlining is this author's.
[715] Patai, *The Messiah Texts*, xxxiv-xxxv. Underlining is this author's.

The words "no end" are very significant in Isa 9:7. These words are even more significant when the descriptions of the child to be born in v. 6 are placed along side the fact that this child's kingdom and peace will have "no end."   God's kingdom will be ruled by God incarnate in the person of Messiah. Although Isaiah, in 9:6-7 underscores that very powerful statement concerning the person of Messiah who was to be born, he adds even more.

Sixth, the statement "upon the throne of David" (Isa 9:7) has a direct connection to the Davidic Covenant which was given 300 years early. This One, who will be human and yet is "Wonderful" (*pele*), the "mighty God," and the "everlasting Father," has a dual nature, and is the fulfillment of the covenant promises to Abraham and to David. The promises to both will be fulfilled when this One, the God/man, actually reigns from the throne of David in Jerusalem, and His kingdom will have "no end."

Seventh is the statement concerning the kingdom that says "hence forth even for ever (Isa 9:7)." The point is that a child would be born who would be God Himself. He will personally fulfill His promise to Abraham, to Israel and to David. As stated previously, His kingdom it will have "no end." Isaiah re-affirms that the Messianic person will personally reign on the throne as said from "hence forth even for ever (עוֹלָם – olam)."

Micah 5:2

> But thou, Beth-lehem Ephratah, though thou be little among the thousands of Judah, yet out of thee shall he come forth unto me that is to be ruler in Israel; whose goings forth have been from of old, from everlasting.   (KJV)

This verse is understood among Christians not only to give the birthplace of the Messiah but also His eternality.   Jewish scholars likewise recognize this passage as being Messianic.   In fact, "all ancient Jewish interpreters regarded the ruler as the Messiah." [716] Barker goes on to comment that the Targums also favor the Messianic interpretation of the prophecy. Goldman adds a divisive twist to the interpretation by stating that this passage refers to the House of David that originated in Bethlehem. Goldman quotes David Altschul who reflects his view:

> Not that the Messiah will be born in Bethlehem, but that is his origin of old, through David, will be Bethlehem. [717]

The above statement is very convenient. The Jewish people today do not know what tribe they are from, let alone if a future Messiah would come if he could prove he was a descendent from the house of David. The fact is that if the Messiah would appear

---

[716] Kenneth L. Barker, *The New American Commentary: Micah* (21 vols. Nashville: Broadman, 1998), 97.

[717] S. Goldman, *The Soncino Books of the Bible: The Twelve Prophets* (New York: Soncino Press, 1994), 175

today, he could not prove that he was from the line of David because the Jewish people do not know their tribal origin. They know only that they are Jewish.

Hengstenberg gives a response to the Jewish authors who argue that Messiah does not have to be born in Bethlehem. That is a convenient belief for them because Jewish people today do not know their tribal ancestry, plus today (2005) it is doubtful if any Jewish people even live in Bethlehem:

> The reference to the Messiah was, at all times, not the private opinion of a few scholars, but was publicly received, and acknowledged with perfect unanimity. As respects the time of Christ, this is obvious from Matt 2:5. According to that passage, the whole Sanhedrin, when officially interrogated as to the birth-place of he Messiah, supposed this explanation to be the only correct one. But if this proof required a corroboration, it might be derived from John 7:41-42. In that passage, several who erroneously supposed Christ to be a native of Galilee, objected to His being Messiah on the ground that Scripture says [the Messiah was to be born in Bethlehem.][718]

Hengstenberg makes it completely clear that the Messiah was to be born in Bethlehem, and that is exactly what the Jewish leadership understood when Herod inquired of the Messiah's place of birth (Matt 2:4-8).

There are two primary phrases that need to be studied: (1) "whose goings forth have been from old" and (2) "from everlasting." These are important because Jewish scholars state that Messiah is not eternal, and is created by the Father.[719] So do these phrases reflect eternity or just ancient? Barker points out that there are two possible readings of the text. One says, "whose origins are from of old, from ancient time," which does not necessitate being eternal. He reflects their understanding in the following quote:

> Those who prefer the main text that the expression *mime olam* refers to the ancient "origins" of the Messiah in the line of David. . . . The stress is on the "origins" of the future Davidic ruler in the Davidic town of Bethlehem. . . . The Davidic roots of the coming ruler are emphasized by the prophet Micah. . . . Certainly the deity and eternality of the Messiah are still plainly taught in other passages.[720]

An NIV footnote provides an alternative rendering: "whose goings out are from of old, from days of eternity." Many prefer the reading in the NIV footnote rather than the main text because of the use of the word "eternity." Eternity, or *olam*, when used of God has eternity in view, but when used of man has only time in view. Jewish authors would like the main text interpretation because it falls in line with Goldman's argument that Messiah is only eternal in the mind of God:

---

[718] Hengstenberg, *Christology of the Old Testament*, 1: 491.
[719] Patai, *The Messiah Texts*, 16-17, 19.
[720] Barker, *The New American Commentary*: Micah, 97-98.

That "goings forth" reflect lineage, and "from ancient days" is taken to mean that the Messiah existed in the mind of God from time immemorial, as part of the creator's plan at the inception of the universe."[721]

If Micah 5:2 were the only Messianic reference, these arguments might carry more weight. But with all the preparation by God in preparing His people for the Messiah through the words of Moses and the Prophets, plus all the plural references to God, this view is difficult to accept. In the following statements, the reality of the eternality of the Messiah is more in line with the theme and content of the *Tanakh* and Micah. It was noted at the beginning of this chapter that the word *olam* can carry two concepts, time and eternity. *Olam*, when used in conjunction with God, who is not confined and bound by time, and lives outside of space, refers to His eternality. The following author points to two perspectives, one by Jewish and liberal Christian scholars and the other by believers who take this passage with all that the *Tanakh* has to say and that what this reference (Micah 5:2) states is that the Messiah is eternal:

> "Goings forth;" "from of old;" "from everlasting". The Jewish rabbis in the Christian era refer these words either to the naming of the Messiah's name in eternity or to the idea of the Messiah existing in God's mind before the creation of the world. Rationalistic interpreters of the early nineteenth century generally adopted these interpretations. Modern Jewish and Protestant interpreters generally refer "from of old," "from everlasting," to the time of the rise of the Davidic dynasty.[722]

Here Laetsch points not just to Micah 5:2 but to the many references that would not have special significance just in tracing your lineage back to Abraham or Adam:

> Yet a lineage dating back to ancient times could not possibly have served as a special characteristic of the future Ruler. Every descendant of David and even of Abraham and Adam could trace his lineage back to creation. Nor can the words denote "the many preparations made by God from the earliest times in prophecy and history for the founding of the Messianic kingdom." For the words speak not of the founding of a kingdom, nor of the preparations for such a kingdom, nor of the prophecies of the going forth of the Ruler. The prophet here speaks of the goings forth and of the birth of a future Ruler.[723]

Laetsch points out the Jewish view as well as the modern rationalistic interpretations of Protestants and Jewish interpreters.   He gives a logical augmentation for viewing Messiah as eternal, before time, but without using the word *olam*. Feinberg, a Jewish believer, makes the following statement that the use of words in verse 2 is the strongest possible for infinite duration and preexistence of the Messiah:

---

[721] Goldman, *The Soncino Books of the Bible: The Twelve Prophets*, 175.
[722] Theodore Laetsch, *The Minor Prophets* (St Louis: Concordia, 1956), 272.
[723] Laetsch, *The Minor Prophets*, 272.

These goings forth were in creation, in His appearances to the patriarchs and throughout the Old Testament history of redemption. The phrases of this text are the strongest possible statement of infinite duration in the Hebrew language (Psa 90:2; Prov 8:22-23). The preexistence of the Messiah is being taught here, as well as His active participation in ancient times in the purposes of God.[724]

Henderson observes that Micah is speaking of one who is eternal and has been active in the affairs of man in the past:

His goings forth, when he created the world, and appeared to Moses and the patriarchs, and revealed to them the Divine will.[725]

In discussing the concept that the Messiah is eternal, Hailey considers the verse with the same idea but with a different approach:

From here would come the one through whom the "former dominion" would be restored. "Whose goings forth are from of old, from everlasting" indicates more than that He descends from an ancient lineage; it relates Him to God, the eternal One. His rule reaches back into eternity. The priests and scribes of Herod's day recognized that the Messiah would be born in Bethlehem.[726]

Barnes points out that the Messiah did not come forth from Bethlehem, but that His going forth was from eternity:

Whose goings forth have been *from of old, from everlasting*, lit. *from the days of eternity. Going forth* is opposed *to going forth; a going forth out of* Bethlehem, to *a going forth from eternity; a going forth*, which then was still to come, (the Prophet says, shall go forth) to a *going forth* which had been long ago, not from the world but from the beginning, not in the days of time, but *from the days of eternity*.[727]

Lastly, Kaiser refers to the Hebrew word *olam* and the fact that, when used in conjunction with God, it refers to eternity:

But this Ruler was not a recent creation, for even though He would be born in Bethlehem, He had existed from eternity. When the Hebrew word for "everlasting" olam, is used in connection with God, it can only mean "from eternity on" (Psa 25:6; 90:2). That can be its only meaning here if the Ruler is none other than the Son of God, the Messiah.[728]

---

[724] Charles L. Feinberg, *The Minor Prophets* (Chicago: Moody, 1951), 173.

[725] Ebenezer Henderson, *Thornapple Commentaries: The Twelve Minor Prophets* (Grand Rapids: Baker, 1980), 249.

[726] Homer Hailey, *The Minor Prophets* (Grand Rapids: Baker, 1972), 209.

[727] Albert Barnes, *Barnes Notes: Minor Prophets* (2 vols. Grand Rapids: Baker, 1950), 2:70.

[728] Kaiser, *The Communicator's Commentary*: Micah-Malachi, 64.

See, a time is coming, declares the LORD, when I will raise up a true branch of David's line. He shall reign as king and shall prosper, and he shall do what is just and right in the land. In his days Judah shall be delivered and Israel shall dwell secure. And this is the name by which he shall be called: The LORD is our Vindicator.

Behold, the days come, saith the LORD, that I will raise unto David a righteous Branch, and a King shall reign and prosper, and shall execute judgment and justice in the earth. In his days Judah shall be saved, and Israel shall dwell safely: and this is his name whereby he shall be called, THE LORD IS OUR RIGHTEOUSNESS. (KJV)

In this passage it is necessary to understand both the historical and spiritual climate of Judah. To briefly summarize, Judah had a series of wicked kings (Ahaz, Manasseh, and Amon) whose reigns totaled around 75 years full of wickedness and apostasy by the Kings and the people. In fact, Manasseh reigned for 55 years and was the most wicked of all the Kings of Judah (2 Kgs 21; 23:26-27; 24:3-4; 2 Chron 34:23-25; Jer 15:4). The spiritual condition of Judah was very poor. Assyria was the world power but had a growing concern about the rise of Babylonians. Josiah was a very righteous king and instituted a revival, but it was only a surface movement. After Josiah, the righteous king, was killed in 609 B.C., each of his three sons would reign in turn on the throne, plus a grandson. These three sons and grandson were all wicked, and Judah quickly lapsed back into sin and idolatry (Ezek 8-11). The common denominator is that these last four kings, who came to the throne in a short span of 12 years, did evil in the sight of the LORD and provided an unstable and insecure kingdom of Judah. The spiritual state of Judah was absolute rebellion against God as 2 Kings 23:30 – 25:30; 2 Chron 36, Ezek 8-11 and other passages would bear out. Jeremiah was the prophet of God in Jerusalem.

(1) Jaohaz, the middle son of Josiah, was crowned king by Judah at the age of 23. He did evil in the sight of the LORD (2 Kgs 23:31-32), and after three months he was deposed by Egypt and taken there in exile.

(2) Eliakim, the firstborn, was 25 years old when Pharaoh Necho of Egypt renamed him Jehoiakim and appointed him as King over Judah. He did evil in the sight of the LORD (2 Kgs 23:37), reigned for 11 years and died.

(3) Jehoiachin, the 18 year old son of Jehoiakim reigned only 3 months before Nebuchadnezzar invaded rebellious Judah and took them into captivity. He also states that he did evil in the sight of the LORD (2 Kgs 24:9).

(4) Mattaniah was the third son of Josiah and was 21when he was appointed king by Nebuchadnezzar. Nebuchadnezzar changed his name to Zedekiah. Zedekiah did evil in the sight of the LORD (2 Kgs 24:19) as well as

rebelling against Babylon in his 11th year. So Babylon came again and destroyed Judah, Jerusalem and the Temple. Zedekiah's sons were put to death before his eyes, and then he was blinded for life.[729]

With this spiritual and historical background in view, there are two significant portions of Scripture in Jeremiah 22 and 23 which had a direct bearing on Judah, both then and in the distant future, one of judgment and the other of Promise. In Jer 22:24-30 *Yahweh* curses Coniah or Jehioachin the king and his descendents, in a dogmatic statement that in the future not one of them would ever again reign on the throne of David.[730] When Coniah was deposed, his Uncle Zedekiah was made king. The kings of Judah were so wicked, especially Coniah, that God, through the prophet, makes a dogmatic unalterable decree against Coniah and his descendents. In leading up to Jer 23:5-6 *Yahweh* declares this: "Woe to the shepherds who are destroying and scattering the sheep of my pasture!" These evil kings, and the ones before them, have destroyed God's people, and God is about to deal with them and the people for their sins. God's promise in vs. 5-6 is not a new promise but a clarification of the Davidic Covenant concerning a good Shepherd. *Yeshua* draws from Ezekiel 34 and Zechariah 11 as he refers to Himself as the Good Shepherd in John 10:11. This was not just an illustration, He was referencing back to the *Tanakh*.[731]

The first item in v. 5 to draw attention is the phrase "When I will raise up a true branch of David's line" and that He will "reign as king and shall prosper, and he shall do what is just and right in the land." Fruchtenbaum draws from the following comment that the Messiah will be a descendent of David:

> The kingship of Messiah is yet to come, but this verse clearly speaks of Messiah as a descendent of David and thus stresses His humanity.[732]

The one thing that rings clear, whether in Judaism or Christianity, the understanding of this verse is that it speaks of a human descendent of David that will be king and shepherd over his people Israel. Keil and Delitzsch affirm that the one who is "raised up" is "my servant David:"

> Neither of these sayings can be spoken of a series of kings. Besides, we have the passages Jer 30:9; Ezek 34:23; 37:24, where the servant to be raised up to David by Jehovah is called "my servant David."[733]

In the beginning of 23:5, Jeremiah says, "See, a time is coming." That phrase is a common expression for the Messianic era as in Jeremiah 31:27-34.[734] Jeremiah

---

[729] Leon Wood. *A Survey of Israel's History* (Grand Rapids: Zondervan, 1970), 370-376.

[730] Davidic Kingly line: David had several sons, the most famous being Solomon. But Solomon's line is the subject of Jer. 22:24-30. Another lesser known son was Nathan who is not involved in the curse. Messiah could not come from Solomon's line, but Nathan's line was not involved in the curse of Coniah.

[731] Robert Davidson, *The Daily Study Bible Series: Jeremiah and Lamentations* (Philadelphia: Westminster, 1985), 25.

[732] Fruchtenbaum, *Messianic Christology*, 62.

[733] Keil and Delitzsch, *Commentary on the Old Testament*, 8:350.

proceeds to use that phrase three times, emphasizing the Messianic era (vs. 27, 29, 31 – KJV "Behold, the days come"). The last usage in Jer 31:31, is the promise of the New Covenant which started at Pentecost and will not be fulfilled until the end of the tribulation when Israel says concerning Messiah *Yeshua*, "Blessed is he that cometh in the name of the Lord" (Psa 118:26; Matt 23:39). Clearly, these references verify that the Messiah is a true human being.[735]

The Messiah, whose human descent is through David's line, will reign in three descriptive ways, "righteously," "wisely," and "just." The Messiah who will reign "righteously," "wisely" and "just" is in stark contrast to the reign of Coniah and the curse placed upon his descendents in Jer 22:24-30,[736] as well as the bad shepherds, the kings, priests and other leaders in Jer 23:1. Both Huey[737] and Davidson[738] point out an even sharper contrast between the meaning of Zedekiah's name, "the Lord our righteousness," and his reign, which was unlike the promised reign of the "righteous Branch" in his following comment:

> This message was most likely delivered during the reign of King Zedekiah. His name means the Lord is righteous or the Lord is my righteousness. The name of the new ruler was intended as a repudiation of Zedekiah. He will be an exact opposite of rulers such as Zedekiah and Jehoiakim. He will be called "the Lord Our Righteousness." The name of this coming ruler implies that a time will come when all the people will acknowledge the Lord as the only source of righteousness.[739]

The word for "Branch" is the Hebrew word "*Zemach*," which is never used to denote a twig but to indicate a sprout growing directly out from the root of the original tree forming a new second tree.[740] This "Branch" will be righteous by nature, not an acquired righteousness. Feinberg clarifies that this reference to the Branch, which is called "THE LORD OUR RIGHTEOUSNESS," is used symbolically of the Messiah. It is not being used horticulturally but is used as a technical term for the Messiah as Feinberg explains its usage:

> It is clear that the term "Branch" is symbolic of the Messiah because the adjective modifying it is a quality of persons and not plants. The shoot or sprout is a scion of the stock of David. "Branch" has a collective meaning when used horticulturally but not when used symbolically. "Branch," . . . a Technical Term in the Prophets.[741]

---

[734] Laetsch, *Bible Commentary*: Jeremiah, 189.

[735] Laetsch, *Bible Commentary*: Jeremiah, 190.

[736] Walvoord and Zuck, *The Bible Knowledge commentary: Old Testament*, 1158.

[737] F. B. Huey, *Bible Study Commentary: Jeremiah* (Grand Rapids: Zondervan, 1981), 77.

[738] Robert Davidson, *The Daily Study Bible Series*: Jeremiah and Lamentations, 25.

[739] F. B. Huey, *The New American Commentary: Jeremiah, Lamentations* (Nashville: Broadman, 1993), 212.

[740] Laetsch, *Bible Commentary*: Jeremiah, 190.

[741] Charles L. Feinberg, *Jeremiah* (Grand Rapids: Zondervan, 1982), 162.

This term, "the BRANCH" in the post-exilic times, became a technical term for the expected ideal king as noted by the prophet Zechariah (3:8; 6:12).[742] Interestingly, Jeremiah was not the first to use the term "Branch," for Isaiah had used it (Isa 11:1-2) a hundred years before Jeremiah.

All this groundwork from verse 5, as to the humanity and righteousness of the future son of David, leads up to verses 6. Two items in verse 6 needs to be discussed: first "his name" and "whereby he shall be called, THE LORD OUR RIGHTEOUS-NESS." When *Adonai Elohim* states the name of the son of David, it becomes clear that God is using this name because He knows the nature and essence of the future son of David, the Messiah:

> We must not overlook the unusual manner in which this name is introduced. The Lord does not merely say: His name is or shall be, nor: Call Him, nor: Call His name, nor: This shall He be called. He uses a phraseology unique in the entire Old Testament, occurring only here. "And this (is) His name which one shall call Him." That is not idle redundancy. Two facts of greatest importance are stressed. The first one: "This (is) His name. Name, as used here by the Lord, is not a mere label or tag, but designates the very nature, the essence and being of the Branch. And secondly, He expresses His will that mankind should know this *Zemach* and acknowledge Him and call Him by that name, given to Him by the Lord God of Hosts, which describes to us His inmost essence, as Jehovah Himself knows and understands it.[743]

The individual's name in Jer 23:5, "THE LORD OUR RIGHTEOUSNESS" is God. This man who will be the Messiah, who will be the Righteous Branch and will be raised up unto David, is the LORD. This man's name, by the very mouth of *Adonai Elohim*, is "THE LORD OUR RIGHTEOUSNESS." This Messiah is the God/man. Fruchtenbaum notes that even sources from rabbinic writings support that conclusion:

> In the Midrash on Proverbs 19:21 (200 – 500 A. D.) it says: "Rabbi Hunah said Eight names are given to the Messiah which are: Yinnon, Shiloh, David, Menachem, Jehovah, Justi de Nostra, Tsemmach, Elias."[744]

Notice the fifth name and seventh name from the quote just cited, Jehovah, coming from Jer 23:6 and *Tzemmach* or Branch based on Jer 23:5. Observe three other references quoted from rabbinic sources:

> In the Midrash on Lamentation 1:16, it says, "What is the name of Messiah?" Rav Ava Ben Kahanna said, "Jehovah is his name and this is proved by, this is his name [quoting Jeremiah 23:6]."

---

[742] J. A. Thompson, *The New International Commentary on the Old Testament: The Book of Jeremiah* (Grand Rapids: Eerdmans, 1980), 489.
[743] Laetsch, *Bible Commentary: Jeremiah*, 195.
[744] Fruchtenbaum, *Messianic Christology*, 62.

Clearly, the name of the Messiah in this Midrash quotation sees the Messiah as Jehovah the LORD OUR RIGHTEOUSNESS.

> In the Talmud (Babba Bathra Tractate 75b) it says: Shmuel ben Nachman said in the name of Rabbi Yohanan, "the following three will be named with the name of the Holy One blessed by he – the upright, as it is said, [quotes Isa 43:7], the Messiah, as it is written and this is his name whereby he shall be called THE LORD OUR RIGHTEOUSNESS [quoting Jeremiah 23:6]."

In this tractate of the Talmud, one Rabbi using the source authority of another Rabbi, clearly sees the Messiah as the LORD, for that is His name.

> In the Midrash on Psalm 21:1 it says: God calls King Messiah by his own name, but what is his name? The answer is "Jehovah is a man of war (Exod 15:3)" and concerning Messiah we read "Jehovah our righteousness this is his name."[745]

When all of the factors are laid out from Jer 23:5-6, along with the ancient Jewish commentary on the verse, the Messiah, the promised one of Israel, is the physical son of David. God not only shows the humanity of the Messiah but that His name is to be called "THE LORD OUR RIGHTEOUSNESS." This leaves no doubt that the Messiah is God incarnate, who came in the person of *Yeshua* of Nazareth.

Psalm 110:1-7

> The LORD said to my Lord, "sit thou at my right hand, while I make your enemies your footstool."

> The LORD will stretch forth from Zion your mighty scepter; hold sway over your enemies!

> Your people come forward willingly on your day of battle. In majestic holiness, from the womb, from the dawn, yours was the dew of youth.
> The LORD has sworn and will not relent, "You are a priest forever, a rightful king by My decree."

> The Lord is at your right hand. He crushes kings in the day of His anger.

> He works judgment upon the nations, heaping up bodies, crushing heads far and wide.

> He drinks from the stream on his way; therefore he holds his head high.

> This Psalm is one of the most fascinating Psalms in the *Tanakh* because of how *Yeshua* used it, and how it relates to the equality of David's Lord with the LORD. There are four observations in this passage that need to be investigated. First, David's

---

[745] Fruchtenbaum, *Messianic Christology*, 62-63.

son is his lord. Second, this lord has enemies. Third, this Psalm ties together two positions that are forbidden in the biblical Judaism. The kings of Israel (Judah) were not to be priests, yet in this Psalm the future reigning son of David is portrayed as a priest after the order of Melchizedek. This is unusual for a son of David, of the Tribe of Judah, to be king and priest. When King Uzziah tried to officiate in a high priestly function, God smote him with leprosy (2 Chron 26:16-21). Fourth, this Psalm is quoted in the New Covenant more times than any other passage from the Hebrew Scriptures. The Jewish response to this verse is very sharp and clear as Rabbi Singer explains that this Psalm cannot refer to *Yeshua*:

> Psalm 110 represents one of the New Testament's most stunning, yet clever mistranslations of the Jewish scriptures. Moreover, the confusion created by the Christianization of this verse was further perpetuated and promulgated by numerous Christian translators of the Bible as well. . . . The story of the church's tampering with Psalm 110 is so old that it begins in the Christian canon itself.[746]

Rabbi Singer, an anti-missionary for the Jewish people, makes some serious charges against the Christian interpretation of Psalm 110. However, in Michael Brown's book, it will be observed that Singer's problem is not with Christians but with the Jewish translators themselves. When translating the Greek Septuagint (LXX) from the Hebrew Scriptures, their usage of the Greek word for lord, *kyrios* lays at the heart of controversy.[747] A part of this lengthy argument will be discussed later in this chapter.

The Psalm 110 passage is used 14 times by the New Covenant writers--more than any other portion of the Hebrew Scriptures. Wilson states that this verse, in each case, refers to *Yeshua*. *Yeshua* uses Psalm 110:1 with authority against the Pharisees, affirming that it was written by David under the inspiration of the Holy Spirit.[748] Echoing Wilson, Mays asserts that it is used more than any other reference from the *Tanakh* in reference to *Yeshua* (Matt 22:44; Mark 14:62; 16:19; Luke 22:69; Acts 2:34-35; 7:55; Rom 8:34; Eph 1:20; Col 3:1; Heb 1:3, 13; 8:1; 10:12; 1 Pet 3:22).[749]

Previously it was mentioned that four areas needed to be studied in reference to this verse: (1) David's son is his lord, (2) this lord has enemies, (3) this Psalm ties together two positions, kingship and the priesthood, (4) this Psalm is referenced in the New Covenant more than any other passage from the *Tanakh*. The fourth point was observed first and now the three remaining will each be taken separately and discussed as listed.

In the first argument David writes Psalm 110:1 as being an oracle of *Yahweh*! David states the following: "The LORD said to my lord." Philips is correct in seeing

---

[746] Tovia Singer, http://www.OutReachJudaism.org/psalm110.html.

[747] Michael Brown, *Answering Jewish Objections to Jesus: Messianic Prophecy Objections* (Grand Rapids: Baker, 2003), 133-145.

[748] T. Ernest Wilson, *The Messianic Psalms* (Neptune, NJ: Loizeaux, 1978), 126.

[749] James L. Mays, *Interpretation: Psalms* (Louisville: John Knox Press, 1989), 350.

God as two distinct personalities, but his statement is too rash and abrupt. He gives no information as to how he arrived at his conclusion:

> Hebrew and Gentile scholars translate it the following way: "God said unto my God." This is very significant and revealing, for it presents two personalities: God number one and God number two. God number one spoke to God number two and said, "Sit thou at my right hand until I make thine enemies thy footstool."[750]

Hebrew scholars? Phillips cannot mean Jewish Hebrew scholars because no Jewish scholar would make such rash and abrupt acknowledgement concerning God. Phillips does not explain how he arrived at his statement; he just makes it. Rabbi Singer has a valued point on the words for God which some versions give misleading translations by using two Lords, as representing two Gods.[751] Searching eight of nine popular versions confirms that only one of them replicates the emphasis of the original Hebrew. The King James Version uses "LORD" and "Lord" in that order. The problem of how "Lord" is used lies in the Greek Septuagint (LXX). In the Greek, "lord," "Lord," or "LORD" are all *kyrios*, which is translated lord or Lord in the New Covenant. However, in the Hebrew text the first LORD is Israel's personal name for God, whereas *adon* simply means "lord" or "master," not generally referring to God. Johnson states that *adon* is used 334 times (Gen 18:12; 19:2; Ruth 2:13; 1 Sam 1:15), 300 of which directly refer to a human lord and master. Only 30 times is the word used "of the divine Lord/Master, as in a divine title (Exod 34:23; Deut 10:17)."[752] If the first six words of Psa 110:1 (The LORD said unto my Lord) are only considered, it could very easily be seen as *Yahweh* speaking to the Messiah. But those first six words would not necessitate the "lord" (*adon*) being God. However, those six words are not isolated but are connected to "Sit at My right hand," and that changes the whole prospective of the verse. That is a personal invitation by *Yahweh* for the Messiah to sit on the very throne of *Yahweh* at his right hand. Fruchtenbaum states that in the ancient Near East in Old Testament times, when a host king entertained a visiting king from another country, he would place him on his right side (1 Kgs 2:19). This act of the host king was making a statement that the visiting king was his equal.[753] Keil and Delitzsch affirm that conclusion:

> The conclusion to be drawn from this Psalm must have been felt by the Pharisees themselves, that the Messiah, because the Son of David and Lord at the same time, was of human and at the same time of superhuman nature; that it was therefore in accordance with Scripture if this Jesus, who represented Himself to be the predicted Christ, should as such profess to be the Son of God and of divine nature.[754]

---

[750] O. E. Phillips, *Exploring the Messianic Psalms* (Philadelphia: Hebrew Christian Fellowship, 1967), 274.

[751] Tovia Singer, http://www.OutReachJudaism.org/psalm110.html.

[752] VanGemeren, *Dictionary of Old Testament Theology & Exegesis*,1:257.

[753] Fruchtenbaum, *Messianic Christology*, 88.

[754] Keil and Delitzsch, *Commentary on the Old Testament: Psalms*, 5:185.

A mere mortal will never sit on God's right hand. Angels don't even sit at God's right hand. So whoever the Messiah is, God Himself is making a statement that this physical seed of David is *Yahweh*'s equal. No human father, if he has any pride as a man, would ever call his physical son lord! *Yahweh*'s invitation for an earthly monarch to sit on His right hand is momentous and even stupendous for the Hebrew mind. That is an understatement. The invitation between *Yahweh* and this future lord of David's "shows an exceptional degree of intimacy between God and this "new" monarch."[755] Phillips is correct in his statement that there are two God's even though it does need to be tempered with explanation.

The second argument *Yahweh* states are that "while I make your enemies your footstool." Phillips issues a very valued statement concerning who are the enemies of God, and who is the son of David. When and where did God and His enemies ever have the acquaintance to meet each other to become enemies:

> God number two has some enemies . . . On further reflection, we realize that the enemies of God number two could not have been His enemies without knowing Him and having had some dealings with Him. The natural thought that comes to us is, who are these enemies? And when did they have an acquaintance with each other, and why did they become enemies?[756]

When will his enemies become the footstool of a king? When the enemies were defeated, the ancient practice of a victorious king was to symbolically place his foot on the neck of the defeated enemy who was lying on the ground. Smith refers to that very action as the practice of the ancient Near East:

> The allusion is to the custom of conquerors placing their feet upon the necks of the captured enemies as a symbolic token of total victory (Josh 10:24).[757]

Lay,[758] Pritchard[759] and Howard[760] affirm Smith's statement by also referencing Josh 10:24 as a biblical example of placing one's foot on the neck of the defeated enemy. *Yahweh* is saying that David's physical Lord, the Messiah, is invited to sit on His right hand because this son of David is His equal and He is going to make Messiah's enemies His footstool, and you will reign over them. That verse is a powerful statement to show David's Lord is indeed the Lord, equal with the Father and that He will reign from David's throne over all the earth.

The last argument is the forbidden area of intertwining the offices of the king and the priesthood. A king could be a prophet but not a high priest (Num 16:40; 18:7).

---

[755] Samuel Terrien, *Critical Eerdmans Commentary: The Psalms* (Grand Rapids: Eerdmans, 2003), 752.
[756] O. E. Phillips, *Exploring the Messianic Psalms* (Philadelphia: Hebrew Christian Fellowship, 1967), 275.
[757] Smith, *The Promised Messiah*, 187.
[758] Bromiley, *The International Standard Bible Encyclopedia*, 2:332.
[759] James B. Pritchard, *The Ancient Near East in Pictures* (Princeton, NJ: Princeton University Press, 1954), 285.
[760] David M. Howard, *The New American Commentary: Joshua*, 254.

A high priest could be a prophet, but not a king. Merrill,[761] Smith[762] and Geisler[763] express that these two offices were never to be combined in the same person, yet *Yeshua* will be King of Israel and also be a priest. The answer is not complex, for *Yeshua* was born of the house of David, the tribe of Judah, which would disqualify Him from serving in a priestly function under the Law. However, according to Psa 110:4, this son of David, the Messiah, will serve as a priest-king even though God forbid that kind of dual role in the Mosaic Law. This son of David will not be a priest through the tribe of Levi, for David (and the author of the book of Hebrews) compares Him to a different High Priestly order "after the order of Melchizedek," who was not Jewish, but Canaanite. There is absolutely no way a mere human being of the house of David, of the tribe of Judah, could be a priest or Levite at the same time unless His priestly function came from a different order. The order of Melchizedek is a type of His High Priestly order. While this son of David is of the tribe of Judah, His origin is eternal and Melchizedek is described as being "without father, without mother, without descent, having neither beginning of days, nor end of life" as Heb 7:1-3 clearly states. Messiah, after the "order of Melchizedek," lays out the premise that the Mosaic Law has been discontinued because the Messiah is a priest and king, which simply means the Law cannot be in force during the dispensation of Grace, otherwise known as the Church age. Fruchtenbaum gives insight on this situation:

> The Law of Moses laid down that all priests had to be of the tribe of Levi and that kings had to be of the tribe of Judah. In order for this prophecy to be fulfilled, therefore, it is clear that it will be necessary for the Law of Moses and the Levitical Order to be moved.
>
> The New Testament (Hebrews 7:11-18) clearly teaches that with the death of Jesus, the Law of Moses was rendered inoperative by His fulfillment of it and was replaced with the Law of Christ. Under the new law of Christ, the Order of Melchizedek is instituted in place of the Levitical Order; therefore, Messiah is indeed a priest and a king. Verse 4 states that Messiah's priesthood and kingship will be eternal.[764]

These four arguments clarify that Psalm 110 is a unique Psalm that was used by *Yeshua* to silence the Pharisees and for the writers of Scripture to show that He is the Lord of all.

Daniel 9:24-27

> Seventy weeks are determined upon thy people and upon thy holy city to finish the transgression, and to make an end of sins, and to make reconciliation for

[761] Eugene H. Merrill, *Kingdom of Priests* (Grand Rapids: Baker, 1987), 377.

[762] William Smith, *Old Testament History* (Joplin, MO: College Press, 1970), 639.

[763] Norman L. Geisler, *A Popular Survey of the Old Testament* (Grand Rapids: Baker, 1977), 155.

[764] Fruchtenbaum, *Messianic Christology*, 89.

iniquity, and to bring in everlasting righteousness, and to seal up the vision and prophesy, and to anoint the most holy.

Know therefore and understand, *that* from the going forth of the commandment to restore and to build Jerusalem unto the Messiah the Prince *shall be* seven weeks, and threescore and two weeks: the street shall be built again, and the wall, even in troublous times.

And after threescore and two weeks shall Messiah be cut off, but not for himself: and the people of the prince that shall come shall destroy the city and the sanctuary; and the end thereof *shall be* with a flood, and unto the end of the war desolations are determined.

And he shall confirm the covenant with many for one week: and in the midst of the week he shall cause the sacrifice and the oblation to cease, and for the over-spreading of abominations he shall make it desolate, even until the consumm-ation, and that determined shall be poured upon the desolate.   KJV

In a personal conversation this author had with a Jewish believer, she stated that her rabbi said this passage was forbidden to study. She resented that, and as a result she read and studied it and God had opened her eyes to see that if the Messiah is in this passage, then He had already come. The result of her investigation of this passage, and other passages, had brought her to a saving knowledge of her Messiah, *Yeshua*. What is so powerful and convincing about this passage that rabbis do not want Jewish people to study it?

Other Christian scholars see this passage differently than is historically under-stood. Surprisingly, authors such as Goldingay,[765] Charles,[766] and Towner,[767] state that this passage was fulfilled during the time of the Maccabees (171 - 164 B.C.E). One problem with this view is that they state that Onias III was the "anointed one" who is cut off. [768] He was the legitimate high priest at the time when Antiochus IV took over Israel from the Ptolemy's of Egypt, but Onias III had no spiritual impact on Judah at that time. By subtracting the 69 "weeks" or 483 years from 536 B.C as the starting date, the cutting off of the Messiah would be approximately 73 B.C., and that is almost 100 years after the Maccabean Revolt. To those scholars this passage is not to be understood as the promise of the coming of the Messiah to Israel as in *Yeshua*, who was put to death or "cut off." Nor do those same scholars see it as referring to the destruction of the city of Jerusalem and the Temple. This is liberal higher criticism at its "best." The biggest problem between the position that liberal higher critics take and the historical position is, when do the 70 weeks begin? Was the starting date 536 B.C.E. or approximately 444 B.C.E. with the decree of Artaxerxes? The purpose of this

---

[765] John E. Goldingay, *Word Biblical Commentary: Daniel* (Dallas: Word Books, 1989), 30:266-268.
[766] R. H. Charles, *A Critical and Exegetical Commentary on the Book of Daniel* (Oxford: Clarendon Press, 1929), 246-247.
[767] W. Sibley Towner, *Interpretation: Daniel* (Atlanta: John Knox Press, 1984), 140-144.
[768] Towner, *Interpretation: Daniel*, 144.

book is to substantiate the tri-unity of God, and in this particular passage, to examine the place of the Messiah in prophetic history, not to spend a multitude of pages showing why fundamental Christianity holds to 444 B.C.E. Sir Robert Anderson has written a whole book just dealing with this 444 B.C.E. dating of this prophecy and its fulfillment in *Yeshua*.[769] His writing does not need to be reduplicated.

There are two things that need to be observed concerning Dan 9:24-27: First, Jewish scholars today generally do not view this text as referencing the first century and especially does not refer to *Yeshua*. Second, it is to show that this prophecy of Messiah, the destruction of Jerusalem and the Temple had a direct bearing on the deity of the Messiah from the standpoint of Christians.

Michael Brown quotes portions of Rashi, the respected Rabbi (1040-1105) of the 11th Century, from northern France[770] whose commentaries are included in the Talmud. To summarize Rashi's understanding and interpretation of Dan 9:24-27, Brown makes the following comments from Rashi: that the "anointed one" was the Judean King Agrippa, who was ruling at the time of the rebellion and destruction of Jerusalem and the Temple. Rashi interprets the "prince" as Titus, the Roman General, who flooded the Land with Roman legions. What Rashi does is place the "anointed one" in the first century before the destruction--in the same century at *Yeshua*. Rashi ultimately does point to the Messiah and his reign, but his identification is misplaced to the wrong people. In terms of God's purposes the death of King Agrippa had absolutely no impact on his people Israel.[771] As far as the identification of the "prince" as being General Titus, that is impossible. Titus never made a 7 year (70th week) covenant with rebellious Israel, plus grammatically the "he" in verse 27 does not refer to Messiah but to a future "prince" that will come offering Israel a 7 year covenant, as Fruchtenbaum explains:

> The pronoun 'he' in verse 27 goes back to its nearest antecedent in verse 26, which is not the Messiah but "the prince who is to come." This "prince" has been a topic of Daniel's earlier prophecies in chapters 7-8. This political leader is better known to Christians as the Antichrist.[772]

So the "prince" is neither General Titus nor the Messiah, but the future Antichrist. That reality has startled more than one Jewish person. For example, when Rachmiel Frydland, a young orthodox man, was confronted by a German missionary in pre-World War II Poland, with the Messiah, using Dan 9:24-27. He states that as he looked through rabbinic commentaries, they were saying the same thing that Rashi stated centuries before.[773]

---

[769] Sir Robert Anderson, *The Coming Prince* (Grand Rapids: Kregel, 1967), 1-304.

[770] Robinson, *Essential Judaism*, 300-301.

[771] Brown, *Answering Jewish Objections*, 3:86-92

[772] Fruchtenbaum, *Messianic Christology*, 98.

[773] Rachmiel Frydland, *When Being Jewish Was A Crime* (Nashville: Nelson, 1978), 72-73.

The reason why the rabbis have forbidden the reading and studying of Dan 9:24-27, is because after the rejection of *Yeshua* as Messiah, rabbis over the centuries tried to figure out the time of the Messiah's coming and in the process had accepted many false messiahs, as is stated by Frydland:

> The Jewish people rarely study the Book of Daniel because many rabbinic Jews were misled attempting to interpret Daniel's cryptic "time." Some were led so far astray that they came to believe in false messiahs, and therefore Talmudic Jews frowned on students who studied Daniel with a view of finding out the time of the Messiah. However, religious Jews knew that this book revealed more about Messiah than any other book.[774]

His statement is absolutely true, for the Jewish people over the centuries, in trying to determine the time of the Messiah's coming, have followed 46 false messiahs.[775]

The impact of the 70 weeks of Dan 9:24-27 in determining whether they reference the Messiah as divine will also be studied. These four verses will be observed in connection to the subject at hand. In verse 24 the Seventy Weeks that are determined need to be understood because of the confusion that has arisen over the centuries as to the meaning of the term weeks:

> Many English versions have translated the phrase to read seventy "weeks." But this translation is not totally accurate and has caused some confusion about the meaning of the passage. Most Jews know the Hebrew for "weeks" because of the observance of the Feast of Weeks, and that Hebrew word is *Shavuot*. However, the word that appears here in the Hebrew text is *shavuim*, which means "sevens." This word refers to a "seven" of anything with the context determining the content of the "seven." It is similar to the English word "dozen," which means twelve of anything based upon the context.[776]

The second item to be observed is the word "people." God's message is being relayed through Gabriel to Daniel to the Jewish people, not the Church. These three authors, Fruchtenbaum,[777] Lang[778] and Feinberg,[779] among many others, identify six things in verse 24 that are determined upon "your people and your holy city." Feinberg lists them as follows:

> During those seventy weeks of years, the great works to be accomplished were: first, "to finish the transgression;" second, "to make an end of sin;" third, "to make atonement for iniquity;" fourth, "to bring in everlasting righteousness;"

---

[774] Frydland, *When Being Jewish Was a Crime*, 72.

[775] Smith, *The Promised Messiah*, 470-474.

[776] Fruchtenbaum, *Messianic Christology*, 94-95.

[777] Fruchtenbaum, *Messianic Christology*, 95-96.

[778] G. H. Lang, *The Histories and Prophecies of Daniel* (Grand Rapids: Kregel, 1940), 130-131.

[779] Charles Lee Feinberg, *Daniel: The Kingdom of the Lord* (Winona Lake, IN: BMH Books, 1981), 127.

fifth, "to seal up vision and prophecy;" and sixth, "to anoint the most holy place."[780]

These six areas are divided into two classes. The first three are concerned with the removal of sin, and the second three deal with bringing in righteousness. Walvoord points out that the first class all deal with sin named three ways: transgression, sin and iniquity.[781] Each one of these phrases needs to be looked at individually. Fruchtenbaum states that the words "to finish," means "to restrain firmly," "to restrain completely," or "to bring to completion," while the word "transgression" is a very strong word for sin and means literally "to rebel." Also, in the Hebrew this word is with a definite article: "the transgression" or "the rebellion" indicates that some specific act of rebellion is finally going to be finished:

> The point is that some specific act of rebellion is finally going to be completely restrained and brought to an end. This act of rebellion or transgression is to come under complete control so that it will no longer flourish. Israel's apostasy is now to be firmly restrained in keeping with a similar prediction in Isa 59:20. Specifically, this is the rejection of the Messiah as dealt with in Isa 52:13-53:12.[782]

This understanding of "the transgression" lends credence to Renald Showers' assertion that Israel has committed a particular transgression:

> With the word "the" in this context, it refers to the Jew's specific sin of rebellion against the rule of God. This rebellion was the root sin which prompted all of Israel's other sins. Gabriel was saying that Israel would not stop its rebellion against God's rule until these 490 years would run their course. In agreement with this, other scriptures indicate that Israel will not repent, turn to God and be saved until the second coming of Christ at the end of these 490 years (Zech 12:10-13:1; Rom 11:25-27).[783]

Showers clearly established the fact, with scriptural references, that Israel has been in a state of rebellion against God and against His Messiah, and will continue to do so until Messiah comes the second time. As was seen in the previous chapters in this study, *Yeshua* was very active as the God of Israel, and He was the ultimate Theophany of God in flesh evidenced in such passages as Isa 9:6-7; 48:12-16; 50:1-7; Mic 5:2. In other words, Walvoord adds to Showers' argument by stating that Israel's rebellion will only come to an end when "the transgression" is finished.

---

[780] Feinberg, *Daniel: The Kingdom of the Lord*, 127.

[781] John F. Walvoord, *Daniel: The Key To Prophetic Revelation* (Chicago: Moody, 1971), 221.

[782] Fruchtenbaum, *Messianic Christology*, 95.

[783] Renald Showers, *The Most High God* (West Collingswood, NJ: The Friends of Israel Gospel Ministry, 1982), 118.

187

The expression is derived from the *piel* verb form of the root *kala* meaning "to finish" in the sense of bringing to an end.[784]

The second phrase of six in Dan 9:24 is "to make an end of sins." This word is a more general word for transgressions that Israel has and is committing toward their God. The word "sin" also carries the idea of "missing the mark," as an arrow would miss its intended mark. Miller expresses the word and concept as follows:

> "To put an end to sin" may either be translated *tamam*, "be complete, come to an end, finish," or *hatam*, "to seal, affix a seal, or seal up." Either translation would make sense and have basically the same meaning, for "sealing up" sin would be tantamount to putting an end to it. Yet "to put an end to" would fit the context better, a reading most scholars and translations accept.[785]

Accordingly, the transgression of Israel as they rebelled against *Yahweh* and His Messiah at His coming, all of these and future individual acts of sins will be sealed up, end or be finished. The way God intends to deal with the sins and transgression of Israel will be through atonement.

The third phrase of six in Dan 9:24 is "to make atonement for iniquity." The Hebrew word translated "to make atonement" is *kaphar*. This word has the same root meaning as the word *kippur*, as in Yom Kippur, the Day of Atonement. In fact, this atonement is the means that God will use "to finish the transgression" and "to make an end of sins." The word "iniquity" refers to the inward sin or what Christian theologians term the "sin nature." But that term "sin nature" would not be known in Judaism or accepted by them. The phrase that would be known to them is *yetzer hara* -- "the evil inclination."[786] Fruchtenbaum expresses what the atonement is for and how the nation of Israel will be reconciled with their God:

> The third purpose of the Seventy Sevens is: to make reconciliation for iniquity. The Hebrew word for reconciliation is a word that means "to make an atonement." This is the means by which the first and second purposes will be accomplished. The means by which Israel's national sin of rejecting the Messiah will be removed and the means by which her daily sins will be removed is by an atonement.
>
> The third purpose is to make atonement specifically for iniquity. The word iniquity refers to the sin nature. The program of the Seventy Sevens is a cleansing of Israel that will include the removal of all three things; first, the national sin of rejecting His Messiahship; second, sinning daily; and third, dealing with the sin nature itself.[787]

---

[784] Walvoord, *Daniel: The Key to Prophetic Revelation*, 221.
[785] Stephen Miller, *The New American Commentary: Daniel* (Nashville, Broadman, 2003), 260.
[786] Fruchtenbaum, *Messianic Christology*, 96.
[787] Arnold Fruchtenbaum, *The Footsteps of the Messiah* (Tustin, CA: Ariel Ministries Press, 2003), 192.

Miller states in a brief summary of Dan 9:24 that sin will be ended and transgression finished, for this would all be accomplished through *Yeshua*'s atonement for humanity's sin by the Messiah's substitutionary death upon the cross at Calvary. His blood was to be the atonement, or the covering for sin, reflected in this verse.[788]

These three purposes to "finish the transgression," "make an end of sins," and "make reconciliation for iniquity," will deal with sin and the cleansing of Israel, who is today in a state of rebellion. Lang further states that this atonement for iniquity will be expiated by sacrifice.[789] These same three purposes mentioned at the beginning of this paragraph will bring about the three other remaining purposes. God will deal with the sin issue of Israel, as well as all of mankind, through the Messiah. The fourth phrase of the six (first of the second group) purposes will be to "bring in everlasting righteousness." Feinberg expresses that the atonement will be necessary to bring righteousness to Israel:

> He would first provide a basis on which men can become righteous, and then He
> will set up on earth an eternal kingdom of righteousness. Salvation and
> righteousness are in fact, the chief characteristics of Messiah's coming rule on
> earth (Isa 45:17; 51:6-8; Jer 33:14-16).[790]

Showers illustrates that in the past, Israel had revivals but fell again into sin. That righteousness was only temporary, but this future righteousness will be permanent:

> In the past, as the result of periodic revivals, Israel had experienced righteous-
> ness. However, that righteousness was temporary, for eventually the nation
> rebelled against God again. But when Israel repents and believes in Jesus Christ
> at His second coming, they will never rebel against God again (Jer 31:31-34;
> Ezek 36:22-32). It will be given righteousness that will last forever.[791]

This righteousness will be permanent, but when does this future righteousness come? The first three purposes (Dan 9:24a) and the atonement for transgression, sin and iniquity are tied to sacrifice, and that atoning sacrifice will bring in righteousness. That Messianic person bringing in righteousness is the righteous BRANCH of Jer 23:5-6 who is called the LORD OUR RIGHTEOUSNESS. In Dan 9:24, one of the purposes of the Seventy Sevens is "to bring in everlasting righteousness." Fruchtenbaum states that the word translated everlasting is the word *olam* and should be understood as being "age" and not "eternity."

> This could be more literally translated "to bring in an age of righteousness,"
> since the Hebrew *olam* is better translated as "age" rather than as "everlasting."
> This age of righteousness is to be the Messianic Kingdom spoken of in the
> Prophets (Isa 1:26; 11:2-5; 32:17; Jer 23:5-6; 33:15-18). It is this very age that

---

[788] Miller, *The New American Commentary: Daniel*, 260.
[789] Lang, *The Histories and Prophecies of Daniel*, 131.
[790] Feinberg, *Daniel: The Kingdom of the Lord*, 127.
[791] Showers, *The Most High God*, 118-119.

Daniel had been expecting to see established after the 70 years of captivity, but now he is told that that will only be after the 490 year period of the Seventy Sevens.[792]

The phrase "to bring in everlasting righteousness" is connected in the immediate context to the Messianic Kingdom and not in the context of eternity. The book of Revelation in the New Covenant states that after this righteousness is brought in for the Messianic Kingdom, it will then go into the new order of the New Heavens, New Earth and the New Jerusalem for eternity (Rev 21-22), but the immediate context in Daniel only has the Kingdom in view.

The fifth phrase of six is "to seal up vision and prophecy" (Dan 9:24). In Genesis 3 when sin came into the world, prophecy was introduced by God Himself in verse 15 as the method that He would use to reveal His plan of redemption from sin to mankind. Sin will be removed from Israel as referenced in the first half of Dan 9:24. There will be no further need for prophecy and visions for sin will no longer be an issue. [793] Hence, "vision and prophecy" will be sealed up and removed in the future Messianic Kingdom. The actual Hebrew word *hatam* means to "seal, affix seal, seal up."[794] Showers' adds some additional insights as to future completion of the "seal[ing] up [of] the vision and prophecy":

> The thrust of this phrase seems to be as follows: revelation that comes through vision or prophecy no longer has to be of concern to people once that revelation has been fulfilled. The vision of prophecy can be sealed up in the sense of being laid aside from the realm of active concern. The word translated "to seal up" is the same word which was translated "to make an end" in the phrase "to make an end of sins" earlier in this verse. It would appear that there is an intended relationship between the two phrases. That relationship is as follows: when Israel will make an end of its daily sins at the end of the 490 years, then all revelation that came through vision and prophecy concerning God's chastening of Israel can be sealed up. The people of Israel will no longer have to be concerned about that revelation, for all the foretold chastening will have been fulfilled. Since their sins which caused chastening will have ended, there will be no further need for chastening.[795]

When transgression, sin and iniquity are removed (Lev 26:40-42; Jer 3:11-18; Hos 5:15) by the atoning work of Messiah (Isa 53), and the Jewish nation calls on Him (Ps 80:1, 15-17; Dan 7:13 with Matt 26:64) and believes on Him, the Second Coming will occur (Psa 118:26; Matt 23:39). According to the New Covenant of Jeremiah 31 and Ezekiel 36, there will be no need for visions and prophecy because Israel will be saved and walking in His statutes.

---

[792] Fruchtenbaum, *Messianic Christology*, 96.
[793] Lang, *The Histories and Prophecies of Daniel*, 132.
[794] Miller, *The New American Commentary: Daniel*, 261.
[795] Showers, *The Most High God*, 119.

The last phrase of the six is "to anoint the most Holy (place)." This is the anointing of the millennial temple (Ezekiel 40-48). In other words, after transgression, sin and iniquity are removed by the anointing sacrifice of the Messiah and all sin, as it relates to Israel, will be put away and the millennial temple will be anointed.[796] The term "anointed" here is *Masah*, "to anoint" which means "to consecrate for religious service."[797]

Daniel 9:24 clearly shows that something supernatural will happen in regard to Israel and their sin in relationship to their God. That relationship between God and Israel is connected by two opposites: First, Israel's sin which keeps them in the state of rebellion. Second, in making reconciliation for iniquity, the sacrifice for sin will bring righteousness; visions and prophecy will come to an end and the temple consecrated, all culminating in the Messiah Himself. The Messiah is interwoven throughout verse 24, as well as verses 25-27. In verse 26 only two words will be analyzed because of the impact they have on *Yeshua* in His First Coming: "Messiah" and being "cut off."

The term Messiah in the *Tanakh* denotes two ideas, one of consecration and endowment of either an individual, such as with Saul, David and priests, or an object such as the Tabernacle, the altar and laver. Messiah comes from the Hebrew word משח and is pronounced *mashiach* "anointed one," and occurs 39 times[798] in the Hebrew Scriptures.[799] Smith does not place the Daniel passage in with the listing of references (footnote 776), but Young's Concordance does,[800] as well as Oswalt, who states that the term Messiah developed in its understanding to focus in a person:

> This existence of the concept of "The Anointed One" in its own right, over and above the more narrowly prescribed historical functions of prophet, priest, and king, undoubtedly contributed to the rise of the concept of the eschatological Anointed One, the Messiah. Within the canon of the OT there are only two unambiguous references to this figure, both in Dan 9:25, 26. Here Daniel predicts a time in the future when the Anointed One, who may well be the Most Holy who is anointed in 9:24, will appear and then be cut off with nothing.[801]

This term Messiah developed into the understanding of a Messianic person in Jewish thinking from very early times, especially during the exile and post-exilic period. Oswalt expresses the fact that these two references in Dan 9:25-26 are without a doubt a reference to the Messiah. The Jewish rabbis, from the post-exilic period into the time of *Yeshua*, had good reason to see Daniel 9 as a reference and a time table for the coming

---

[796] Feinberg, *Daniel: The Kingdom of the Lord*, 128.
[797] Miller, *The New American Commentary: Daniel*, 261.
[798] **Saul** - 1 Sam 12:3, 5; 24:6, 10; 26:9, 11, 16, 23; 2 Sam 1:14, 16, 21; **David** – 2 Sam 19:21; 22:51; 23:1; Ps 18:51; 20:6; 28:8; **Priest** – Lev 4:3, 5, 16; 6:22; **Reigning King** – Lam 4:20; Ps 84:9; 89:38; **Patriarchs** – Ps 105:15; 1 Chron 16:22; **Solomon** – 2 Chron 6:42; **Prospective King** – 1 Sam 16:6; **Cyrus** – Isa 45:1; **Messiah** – 1 Sam 2:10, 35; Ps 2:2; 89:51; 132:10; Hab 3:13 and Dan 9:25-26.
[799] Smith, *The Promised Messiah*, 1-3.
[800] Young, *Young's Analytical Concordance to the Bible*, 39.
[801] VanGemeren, *Dictionary of Old Testament & Exegesis*, 2:1126.

of the Messianic person. Rabbi Silver agrees that the Messianic expectation was very high during the second quarter of the first century C.E. in the following statement:

> Prior to the First Century (C.E.) the messianic interest was not excessive. . . . The First Century, however, especially the generation before the destruction [of the Second Temple] witnessed a remarkable outburst of Messianic emotional-ism. This is to be attributed, as we shall see, not to an intensification of Roman persecution, but to the prevalent belief induced by the popular chronology of that day that the age was on the threshold of the Millennium . . . When Jesus came into Galilee, 'spreading the gospel of the Kingdom of God and saying the 'time is fulfilled' and the Kingdom of God is at hand, 'he was voicing the opinion universally held that … the chronological fact which inflamed the Messianic hope rather than the Roman persecutions … Jesus appeared in the procuratorship of Pontius Pilate (26-36 C.E.) … It seems likely, therefore, that in the mind of the people the Millennium was to begin around the years 30 C.E. Be it remembered that it is not the Messiah who brings about the Millennium. It is the inevitable advent of the Millennium which carries along with it the Messiah and his appointed activities. The Messiah was expected around the second quarter of the First Century C.E. because the Millennium was at hand. Prior to that time he was not expected, because according to the chronology of the day the Millennium was still considerably removed.[802]

It is significant that a rabbi would acknowledge the time of the coming of the expected Messiah, even recognize *Yeshua*'s presence historically and yet miss *Yeshua* as the promised Messiah. These verses in Dan 9:25-26 are very significant, powerful and forceful in unambiguously pinpointing the time of the Messiah's coming. Even Moses, in a more general sense, spoke of the time of the Messiah in Gen 49:10. The words "scepter will not depart from Judah until" he comes whose right it is,[803] clearly shows that Messiah's tribal identity must be present. Judah and all the other tribes lost their tribal identity when the Romans destroyed the Temple in 70 C.E. This simply means that in order for the Jewish people to identify the Messiah, and even identify the tribal identity, the Messiah had to come before the destruction of the Temple because the genealogical records of the families and tribes were kept in the temple. Both Moses and Daniel predicted the time of the coming of the Messiah, but Daniel was more precise in regard to time and purpose of the Messiah's coming.   This one, the Messiah, would deal with the transgressions, sin and iniquity of the people by His sacrifice or anointing work at Calvary.

The last words to be discussed in Dan 9:26 is "cut off." Examples of the term "cut off" are defined as follows: (1) as cutting off part of the body as the head or hands, (2) or the cutting off of the foreskin in the act of circumcision, (3) or the cutting down of trees, idols, to cut out or to eliminate, to kill or to cut (make) a covenant.[804] The

---

[802] Rabbi Abba Hillel Silver, *A History of Messianic Speculation in Israel*, (New York: Macmillan, 1927), 5-7

[803] Compare the words in Gen 49:10 with Ezek 21:27. [Shiloh is not in the Genesis text]

[804] Harris, Archer, and Waltke, *Theological Wordbook of the Old Testament*, 1:456.

Messiah, in the context of Daniel 9, is viewed as being killed in the prophetic future. A violent death is seen by Walvoord,[805] Miller,[806] Lang,[807] Showers[808] and Fruchtenbaum.[809] Walvoord states the verb rendered "to cut off" means to "destroy, to kill" and makes reference to Gen 9:11, Deut 20:20, Jer 11:19, Ps 37:9. Miller relates the phrase "cut off" to the crucifixion of *Yeshua*. Lang relates the phrase "cut off" to the Passover sacrifice in the month of Nisan. Although Lang and Feinberg[810] suggest that Artaxerxes issued the decree in the month of Nisan, neither one has it documented. Showers connects the words "cut off" with the death penalty (Lev 7:20, 21, 25, 27) and with reference to a violent death (1 Sam 17:51; Obad 9; Nah 3:15). Being "cut off" is obviously a separation of body parts, foreskin, or the severing of a tree from its trunk. But it is also used in reference to death, a violet death. The context of Dan 9:24-27 would lead very strongly to a death by execution, as the Romans did on their crosses.

This passage in Daniel 9 becomes quite powerful in that Israel's transgression, sin, and iniquity, are reconciled, and Israel will experience real righteousness for the first time through Jeremiah's New Covenant. The Millennial temple is anointed, and there is an end to Israel's sins. Therefore, there is no further need for vision and prophecy, because all of the elements in Dan 9:24-27 are focused in the Messiah, who was "cut off" in death as the substitutionary sacrifice for sin and was literally the "anointed one" who would and did come 483 years after the decree of Artaxerxes. A tremendous amount of power and time is compressed into 4 verses.

Isaiah 7-12

This portion of Isaiah is a unit and is called the "Book of Immanuel." Within the "Book of Immanuel," where Immanuel is referenced three times in Isa 7:14, 8:8, 10, there are three strategic portions of Scripture. Immanuel is the one born of a virgin in Isa 7:14. Isaiah states that this child which would be born would have some unique names for a human being and will reign from his father David's throne in Isa 9:6-7. Later Isaiah states that this one will be from the "stem of Jesse" and that "the spirit of the LORD" rests upon Him in Isaiah 11:1-2. The impact of the "Book of Immanuel" is significant, and that is where attention needs to be focused.

The person who will be born of a virgin in chapter 7 is called Immanuel, which means "God with us." So the virgin who will conceive and bear a son who will be "God with us!" For a further discussion on this section of Scripture, see Fruchtenbaum's work on Isaiah 7.[811]

---

[805] Walvoord, *Daniel: The Key To Prophetic Revelation*, 229.

[806] Miller, *New American Commentary: Daniel*, 267.

[807] Lang, *The Histories and Prophecies of Daniel*, 134.

[808] Showers, *The Most High God*, 125.

[809] Fruchtenbaum, *Messianic Christology*, 97.

[810] Feinberg, *Daniel: The Kingdom of the Lord*, 130.

[811] Fruchtenbaum, *Messianic Christology*, 32-37.

Once again Immanuel is referenced in Isa 8:8, 10 which leads up to another well known passage in Isa 9:6-7. Here that virgin-born son, who is "God with us," is called names that only God is called ("wonderful" or "pele," "mighty God," and the "everlasting Father"), as was already observed earlier in this chapter under the section called Isa. 9:6-7. This Immanuel will be God/man and will reign on the throne of David, His father, forever because He is eternal.

In Isaiah 11:1-2 a further description is given of Immanuel or "God with us." Verse one identifies the humanity of Immanuel, and He is presented through the metaphor of Him coming from the stem of Jesse, a Branch growing out of his roots. This passage is echoed by two other passages, Jer 23:5-6 where the Branch is called "the LORD OUR RIGHTEOUSNESS," the Branch is "God with us." Also, in Isa 61:1 the Messiah is anointed by "the Spirit of the LORD God" and "the spirit of the Lord shall rest upon Him" in seven different manifestations as Isa 11:2 clearly states.

The Book of Immanuel has some tremendous portions of Scripture that speak of the one who is "God with us" as the God/man who was virgin-born, a son of David, who is also "Wonderful," "mighty God" and "everlasting Father." What a significant section of Scripture Isaiah 7-12 is as it presents "God with us."

Isaiah 50:1a, 4-6

Thus said the Lord:

The Lord God hath given me the tongue of the learned, that I should know how to speak a word in season to him that is weary: he wakeneth morning by morning, he wakeneth mine ear to hear as a learned.

The Lord God hath opened mine ear, and I was not rebellious, neither turned away back.

I gave my back to the smiters, and my cheeks to them that plucked off the hair: I hid not my face from shame and spitting.   KJV

In relation to this verse and other verses in the *Tanakh*, a valid question can be asked. Who in history does this passage of Scripture describe? There can only be one answer: *Yeshua* of Nazareth. In v. 1 *Yahweh* is speaking, but then in v. 4 *Yahweh* states that the Lord (*Adonai*) God (*Elohim*) did something. Here are two personalities, *Yahweh* and the Lord God, Who is who? The answer comes in v. 6 where *Yahweh* gives a description of Himself:

I offered my back to the floggers and my cheeks to those who tore out my hair. I did not hide my face from insult and spittle.

194

When did *Yahweh*, in history, give His back to the floggers or smiters? When did *Yahweh*, in history, allow his beard to be pulled from His face? When, in history, did *Yahweh* permit Himself to be shamed and spat upon? Before the answer is given, there are two points as to the personalities observed. First, there are two personalities represented here as God: *Yahweh* and the Lord God. Second, *Yahweh* allowed men to afflict Him with such beatings, shame and spitting. The identity of *Yahweh* and what happened to Him is what happened to *Yeshua* who is the exact image of the Father, at His trial before the Sanhedrin and before the Romans.

Isaiah is clearly presenting that a son will be born of a virgin and He will be "God with us." He will be born from the stem of Jesse of the house of David and He will reign on David's throne forever. This one who is to reign on David's throne forever is named by God as "Wonderful," "almighty God" and the "everlasting Father." He is introduced as the Servant of the Lord in chapters 42, 49 and 50 of Isaiah. This is the promised Messiah, the God/man repeatedly promised ever since Gen 3:15.

Isaiah 52:13 – 53:12

Isaiah 53 introduces the suffering servant. The identity of the suffering servant brings controversy between Jewish and Christian adherences. Who is this Servant? Some Jewish scholars point to Isaiah, but predominately to Israel as fulfilling the suffering Servant passage. This argument and the reasoning behind the rabbis changing their historic understanding were brought out by Victor Buksbazen, a Jewish believer in Messiah.[812] If a Jewish person is asked to read this passage and to identify the person, he or she invariably will say, upon reading Isaiah 53, that this passage comes from the Christian Bible (New Testament) and that this passage refers to Jesus. What a surprise it is for them when they realize that this passage comes from their own prophet Isaiah, and they themselves have identified *Yeshua* as the Suffering Servant. Isaiah 53 is not a passage of scripture known by most Jewish people because it is forbidden by the rabbis to be read, and it is never read in the synagogue services. Rabbis in synagogue services end their reading at Isa 52:12 and pick up again at the beginning of Isaiah 54. That was not always the case as Rabbi Moshe Alshekh of the 16th century states:

> [Our] Rabbis with one voice, accept and affirm the opinion that the prophet is speaking of king Messiah.[813]

There are many things that could be presented in this passage to show that this is *Yeshua*. For a fuller treatment of this passage there are numerous books that deal with each verse in depth as indicated in the footnote below.[814] One point that needs to be

---

[812] Victor Buksbazen, *The Prophet Isaiah* (Collingswood, NJ: Spearhead Press, 1971), 2:400-404.

[813] Rachmiel Frydland, *What the Rabbis Know About the Messiah* (Cincinnati, OH: Messianic Publishing Co, 1991), 53.

[814] Arnold G. Fruchtenbaum, *Jesus of a Jew* (Tustin, CA: Ariel Ministries Press, 1981); David Baron, *The Servant of Jehovah* (Jerusalem: Keren Ahvah Meshihit, 2000); Victor Buksbazen, *Isaiah's Messiah* (Bellmawr, NJ: Friends of Israel Gospel Ministry, 2002).

brought out in this passage is to identify *Yeshua* as the Suffering Servant, the identities of the speaker and the one who he is speaking about must be determined. What will be addressed here are the personal pronouns in Isaiah 53 and to whom these pronouns refer to in this chapter.

The most common Jewish interpretation of Isaiah 53 is that it refers to Israel, for the nation of Israel is the servant of the Lord. This interpretation was given by Rashi, an 11th century rabbi. However, his contemporary, Maimonides, a rabbi from Egypt, took issue with Rashi. This interpretation did not become popular until the 1800s when Protestant missionaries began to use it with great success in sharing the Gospel of Messiah with the Jewish people in Europe.[815]

In Isa 53:2-7, a large number of pronouns are used. In these verses the pronoun "he" (used 12 times), "him" (used 7 times), and "his" (used 3 times) refer to the person who is the subject of this chapter. These 22 pronouns ("he" "him" and "his"), within the space of six verses, all point to this person and describe him. Then in the same verses numerous other pronouns "we," (8 times), "our," (6 times), and "us" (once) refer to someone else 15 different times. When totaling all of the pronouns used in these six verses, there are 37 personal pronouns.

A close examination of the text gives strong evidence that these pronouns, "we" "our" and "us" cannot be referring to God for God is not a sinner who has iniquities. These pronouns refer to Israel because they are sinners with iniquities. The "he," "him," and "his" clearly refer to the Servant of the Lord who is the Messiah because the description cannot possibly be referring to Israel. If the suffering servant were Israel, then verse 8 would mean that Israel was "cut off," executed, or dead. Also if Isaiah 53 is Israel, then who is the term "for the transgression of my people was he stricken," referring to? Israel just does not fit! But when the person of *Yeshua* is placed in the context of Isaiah 53, and the sins and iniquities of Israel were laid upon him, that fits the context and the passage. In history, when Isaiah 53 is read, who does this passage fit? The answer is *Yeshua*.

Zechariah 11:12-14; 12:10; 13:7

These next three passages are all connected and should be approached as a unit, because each one presents *Yahweh* as experiencing something that only a human being could experience. There are some key words in these passages, and they are tied together around one person, the Messiah: "Shepherd," "pierced," "My Shepherd" and "My Associate." In Zech 11:12-14, 12:10, the question is who, in history, do these passages describe? There is not a lack of material as to the Messianic references to *Yeshua* on these passages. Numerous scholars agree on the God/man aspect and see

---

[815] Fruchtenbaum, *Messianic Christology*, 54. This whole section in Fruchtenbaum's book is very interesting and valuable (pp. 53-59.)

Yeshua as the central person fulfilling these passages: Baron,[816] Feinberg,[817] Fruchtenbaum,[818] Brown,[819] Unger,[820] Merrill,[821] Kaiser,[822] Hartman,[823] and Barrett.[824]

The Jewish interpretation is to distance themselves from anything that would even hint of *Yeshua* being the fulfillment of these passages because they do not believe in the tri-unity of God. These verses have had to be dealt with by the Rabbis to suppress the obvious prophecies of *Yeshua* the Messiah as being *Yahweh*. These will be referenced just a little later as each passage is dealt with separately.

Zechariah 11:12-13

> And I said unto them, If ye think good, give me my price; and if not, forbear. So they weighed for my price thirty pieces of silver.
>
> And the LORD said unto me, cast it unto the potter: a goodly price that I was prised at of them. And I took the thirty pieces of silver, and cast them to the potter in the house of the LORD.

Zechariah 11:4-14 speaks of the good "Shepherd" that ministers to the flock of Israel, but his leadership is not wanted by the "flock" or "people" of Israel. First, in 11:4, Zechariah speaking for God, refers to God as *Yahweh* my *Elohim* (LORD my God). The first person pronouns appear 19 times in these verses, three times; in v. 6, five times in v. 7, once in v. 8, twice in v. 9, three times in v. 10, and once each in vs. 12 and 14. The backdrop of this passage is that Zechariah is to act out the part of the shepherd for the LORD. *Yahweh* also took two staves called Beauty (10) and Bands (v. 14) and cut them asunder, breaking His covenant with the nations and between Israel and Judah. Because of Israel's rejection of His leadership as the good "Shepherd," *Yahweh*, the "Shepherd" asks them for His wages.

Before the wages issue is dealt with, it needs to be determined who the "Shepherd" is in Zechariah. On the surface the "Shepherd" appears to be *Yahweh* and it is. However, the picture that the "Shepherd" describes concerning His wages leads to an additional conclusion. David Baron adds some valuable insight as to the identity of

---

[816] Baron, *The Visions and Prophecies of Zechariah*, 379-380, 403-404, 437-440, 447-449, 474-477.

[817] Charles L. Feinberg, *God Remembers: A Study of the Book of Zechariah* (New York: American Board of Missions to the Jews, 1965), 208-209, 229-231,244-246.

[818] Fruchtenbaum, *Messianic Christology*, 67-74.

[819] Brown, *Answering Jewish Objections*, 3:37-38, 149-151.

[820] Merrill F. Unger, *Zechariah: Prophet of Messiah's Glory* (Grand Rapids: Zondervan, 1963), 199, 216-217, 230-232.

[821] Eugene H. Merrill, *An Exegetical Commentary: Haggai, Zechariah, Malachi*, 297-298, 320-321, 335-336.

[822] Kaiser, *The Communicators Commentary: Micah – Malachi*, 394-395, 405-406, 413.

[823] Fred Hartman, *Zechariah: Israel's Messenger of the Messiah's Triumph* (Bellmawr, NJ: Friends of Israel Gospel Ministry, 1994), 111-112, 129.

[824] Michael Barrett, *Beginning at Moses* (Greenville, SC: Ambassador-Emerald Int'l, 2001), 236-237.

the "Shepherd" who is also addressed as *Yahweh*. What is discovered is that *Yahweh* is *Yeshua*:

> But it practically comes to much the same thing, whether we regard the prophet as representing in his actions as shepherd, Jehovah, or more directly the Messiah, for the coming of the Messiah is often spoken of in the Old Testament as the coming of Jehovah. In Ezek 34 for instance, Jehovah Himself is represented, in His capacity as the true Shepherd of Israel, as seeking, saving, strengthening, healing, and satisfying His people; but as we read on in that chapter we become aware that it is not Jehovah directly who is going to do all this, but immediately through the Messiah. "And I will set them up one shepherd over them, and He shall feed them even My servant David; He shall feed them, and He shall be their shepherd" (Ezek 34:23) namely, the true David, the Messiah as the Jews themselves have always rightly interpreted this passage.[825]

The Shepherd is none other that *Yeshua*, the Good Shepherd (John 10:11). This will also be seen shortly as the rest of this passage is studied. The good Shepherd asks for His wages. He did not give a demand, but asked for a voluntary response: "If you are satisfied, pay me my wages; if not, don't." The good Shepherd was not looking for money but for spiritual qualities or spiritual fruit. Feinberg and Baron make similar observations concerning the wages that the good Shepherd desired:

> He was requesting of them fruitage from His ministry, such as piety, godly fear, devotion, and love and they gave Him instead that which was far worse than a direct refusal (Matt 21:33-41).[826]

> The wages which He actually sought from them for all His Shepherd care, was, as the commentators rightly understand, the spiritual fruit of His labours – repentance, faith, true heart piety, humble obedience and grateful love. This is brought out clearly in the Lord's parable of the Vineyard, which is Israel, to whom He first sent His servants, and then His own son, "that He might receive the fruits of it."[827]

But the Jewish leadership considered His entire ministry to them as worthless, and what they offered Him was an insult. Their response of 30 pieces of silver was a statement, not just an act of payment for services rendered. Their act of payment for how they viewed His ministry to them was that He was totally unworthy and worthless in their sight.[828] Giving the good "Shepherd" 30 pieces of silver, their statement was that He was worth no more than a dead slave (Exod 21:32).

What needs to be observed is that *Yahweh*, in Zech 11:4-14, was valued by the Jewish leadership as nothing more than a dead slave. Neither God the Father nor God

---

[825] Baron, *The Visions and Prophecies of Zechariah*, 380.
[826] Feinberg, *God Remembers: A Study of the Book of Zechariah*, 209.
[827] Baron, *The Visions and Prophecies of Zechariah*, 403.
[828] Hartman, *Zechariah: Israel's Messenger of the Messiah's Triumph*, 111.

the Holy Spirit took on humanity. So They could never be betrayed or valued for 30 pieces of silver for Their services to them as a "Shepherd." Only God the son, the Messiah, the son of David, the Branch, and the good Shepherd was valued for 30 pieces of silver. These verses show that *Yahweh*, in this passage, must have become a man in order to be betrayed in such a manner. This may not have been evident to the Jewish people before *Yeshua*'s coming, but after the death, burial, resurrection and ascension of *Yeshua* there is only one man in history, the God/man, that fits this description.

Zechariah 12:10

> And I will pour upon the house of David, and upon the inhabitants of Jerusalem, the spirit of grace and of supplications: and they shall look upon me whom they have pierced, and they shall mourn for him, as one mourneth for his only son, and shall be in bitterness for him, as one that is in bitterness for his firstborn.
>
> KJV

Zechariah 12:10 is another powerful statement because *Yahweh* states that something happened to Him that could only be experienced by human beings; He was pierced. So that the identity of the person speaking in verse 10 can be verified, the speaker needs to be identified so that there is no confusion. By paying close attention to these first person pronouns it clarifies the identity of the person is verse 10. The person speaking in verses 1 and 4 identifies Himself as *Yahweh* (LORD). Then He uses the first person pronouns in v. 2, "I will make Jerusalem," v. 3, "In that day will I make," v. 4, twice, "I will smite" and "I will open mine eyes," v. 6, "I will make the governors," and v. 9, "I will seek to destroy," all referring to the speaker *Yahweh*. Notice also that the speaker from verse one claims to be the creator of the heavens and earth, just as the one who called Jacob, and identified Himself as the "first and the last" in Isa 48:13, 16. In Zech 12:10, *Yahweh* states that "I will pour upon the house of David," and then continues with his powerful statement, "and they shall look upon me whom they have pierced." *Yahweh* is referring to a time when He was physical pierced, but that is impossible because Rabbinic Judaism believes that God is pure spirit and cannot, in anyway, become a man. Yet, here *Yahweh* distinctly states that He was pierced, and the text does not call it to be read in a metaphorical sense. The literal sense of the verse is obvious. *Yeshua*, the Messiah, the God/man was pierced on Mt. Calvary, as the atonement (Dan 9:24-25), the sin offering (Isa 53:10) for the sins of the world.

The Jewish response is to divert the natural meaning of Zech 12:10 away from any possibility of it implying that *Yeshua* could be the God/man promised by God from the very beginning when sin entered the world in Genesis 3 (15). Brown references two Jewish interpretations of this text where they try to say that the "evil inclination" was pierced, or that the people of Israel will weep over Messiah ben Joseph being slain in the last Great War. These interpretations are not consistent with the text as Jewish scholars attempt to avoid having to admit that *Yeshua* is speaking in Zech 12:10:

> Zechariah 12:10 is discussed in the Talmud in b. Sukkah 55a. The verse - read with a singular, not plural, subject – is first interpreted to mean that it is the evil

inclination (i.e., the sinful tendency in man) that was slain, and the people wept when they saw how easily it could have been overcome. The second interpretation states that the people wept over Messiah son of Joseph who was slain fighting in the last great war (i.e., the last great future war) for his people, after which Messiah son of David asked God to raise him from the dead, and his request was granted. From this we learn two significant points: (1) The Hebrew was understood to be speaking of an individual person or thing, not of a plural subject (in other words, the one who was pierced through and slain, not those who were pierced through and slain); and (2) there was an ancient Jewish tradition interpreting the text in terms of a Messianic figure who died and then was raised from the dead.[829]

Brown's point is that the text is speaking of an individual and not something collective as the "evil inclination." Brown's other point is that the text is speaking of the Messiah, but not just a mere man called Messiah ben Joseph. What the Jewish scholars do recognize in their interpretation is that the Messiah will be killed, they just miss identify who the Messiah is. The text is speaking of an individual and not something collective. Now in the same mental frame of reference, consider the translation given in the *Jewish Study Bible* for Zechariah 12:10 as they divert attention away from the Hebrew text, which clearly states "and they look upon me whom they have pierced." They rephrase it to say that Israel will lament to God for those who are slain:

> But I will fill the House of David and the inhabitants of Jerusalem with a spirit of pity and compassion; and <u>they shall lament to Me about those who are slain, wailing over them as over a favorite son</u> and showing bitter grief as over a first-born.

Kaiser also quotes this reference from the *Jewish Study Bible* as well as quoting from the 1896 Jewish translation:

> And they [i.e., the house of David and the inhabitants of Jerusalem] shall look up to Me because of Him whom they [i.e., the nations which came up against Jerusalem] have pierced."[830]

In the first quote (underlined), Jewish scholars have made two changes: First they removed the word "pierced" and inserted "slain." Second, they change the wording from "look upon me" to "lament to me." These changes effectively remove the intent of what Zechariah was saying by removing the meaning in the verse that *Yahweh* was pierced, and that they would look upon Him. Whereas, the second quote (immediate above) implies that the nations pierced, in Jewish interpretation, Messiah ben Joseph. If the passage is read naturally without the preconception of the interpreter, then Messiah *Yeshua* is in view.

---

[829] Brown, *Answering Jewish Objections*, 148-149.
[830] Kaiser, *The Communicator's Commentary: Micah – Malachi*, 405-406.

Next, the word "pierced" is a powerful word if kept within its context. This word "pierced" or דָּקַר (*daqaru*) is used 11 times in the Hebrew text (Num 25:8; Judg 9:54; 1 Sam 31:4; 1 Chron 10:4; Isa 13:15; Jer 37:10; 51:4; Lam 4:9; Zech 13:3) meaning to "pierce" or "thrust through".[831] Almost all references to being pierced in the *Jewish Study Bible* are all rendered as being "pierced through." So there is no doubt as to the meaning of this word in the text of this passage and its fulfillment in the crucifixion when *Yeshua* was pierced with the Roman spear (John 19:34), which is what Zech 12:10 references. Rabbinic Judaism believes that Messiah is not God, so the rabbis speak of two completely human Messiahs in the form of Messiah ben Joseph (suffering Messiah) and Messiah ben David (reigning Messiah) to try and avoid the obvious reference in Zech 12:10 that the Scriptures present the Messiah as the God/man. But if the text, as given in Zech 12:10, is taken for what it says, two messiahs are not needed, because the same Messiah comes twice with two different purposes. The main issue for Jewish scholars is how to resolve the changing of the pronouns that God used of Himself, from "Me" to "Him" in this passage.[832] This shift in the pronouns goes from *Yahweh* as first person, "Me," to the one who is mourned for in the third person, as "Him." The lament for *Yahweh* who was pierced through, is viewed from *Yahweh*'s perspective as "Me," whereas the "Him" is viewed from a future generation of Jewish people who will recognize *Yahweh* as "Him" the one they were responsible for piercing. The answer to the problem of the pronouns is a matter of viewpoint as both Barrett and Merrill express:

> The shift in pronouns from the first to the third person testifies to the distinctive association. That God would send His perfect representative, His Son, was the great message of hope.[833]

> From YHWH's viewpoint it is "Me" that is the focus; from the standpoint of the people it is "Him." Such a transition from one person to another is not at all uncommon in Hebrew composition, especially in poetic and prophetic language.[834]

Yahweh, who is the obvious speaker in this passage, is the Messiah, the One who was physically pierced with a sword, the one for whom Israel will mourn for bitterly. Kaiser mentions there is only one possible example of that kind of mourning in the biblical account which was the death of King Josiah in 2 Kgs 23:29 and 2 Chron 35:25.[835] Zechariah 12:10 states that Israel will weep for "Him" bitterly as one mourns for his only son, because to that future generation, *Yahweh* will be recognized as *Yeshua* who came as the Messiah 20 centuries ago. The word "only" is the Hebrew word *yachid* (discussed in chapter four).

---

[831] Unger, *Zechariah: Prophet of Messiah's Glory*, 216.
[832] Kaiser, *The Communicator's Commentary: Micah – Malachi*, 406.
[833] Barrett, *Beginning at Moses*, 237.
[834] Merrill, *An Exegetical Commentary: Haggai, Zechariah, Malachi*, 320.
[835] Kaiser, *The Communicator's Commentary: Micah – Malachi*, 407.

As can be clearly seen in Zech 12:10, *Yahweh* will pour on the house of David and Jerusalem the spirit of grace and supplication. He would be physically pierced and Israel will some day mourn for Him greatly. This is one of the most gut-wrenching passages in Scripture, when the Jewish people realize that *Yeshua* was indeed the Messiah, God incarnate. They will weep and mourn, for they will then realize that all their fathers before them who worshipped *Yahweh* or *ha Shem*[836] with zeal were literally rejecting the one they said they worshipped. The last public words of *Yeshua* bring together the person Messiah and *Yahweh* in Matt 23:37 as he speaks as *Yahweh*:

> O Jerusalem, Jerusalem, thou that killest the prophets, and stonest them which are sent unto thee, how often would I have gathered they children together, even as a hen gathereth her chickens under her wings, and ye would not!

Zechariah 13:7

> Awake, O sword, against my shepherd, and against the man that is my fellow, saith the LORD of hosts: smite the shepherd, and the sheep shall be scattered: and I will turn mine hand upon the little ones.

Finally Zech 13:7 is a very potent reference in connection to God the Father and God the Son being equals. There are numerous words such as "sword," "man," "My shepherd" and "My associate" in this verse. Each one needs to be dealt with individually, and then within the context to see that *Yahweh* takes complete responsibility for the "sword" to be used against His shepherd and His associate, the Messiah.

First, the speaker is clearly "the LORD of hosts, *Yahweh*. However, in this verse the speaker is not the Messiah as in Zech 12:10 and 11:4-14.

The "sword," is told to awaken against "My shepherd." *Yahweh* is telling the sword to awaken against His Shepherd, the good Shepherd of chapter 11. The "sword" is a valid personification of the instrument of death and is instructed to move against the Shepherd, who is addressed as being "My shepherd."[837]

The second term "My shepherd" is the same shepherd of Zech 11:4-14, who is the personal Shepherd of *Yahweh*, "My shepherd." The term "Shepherd" also indicates that this is no ordinary shepherd but a particular Shepherd, "My shepherd."

The third and fourth words are "man" that is "My associate" or mine equal. The Hebrew word is עֲמִית or *"amith,"* which means "associate, fellow, relation,"[838] and is

---

[836] Ha Shem: Simply means "the Name." Because of Jewish sensitivity to the use of God's name, many Jewish people will avoid using the name of *Yahweh*, and insert *ha Shem* in its place.

[837] Kaiser, *The Communicator's Commentary: Micah – Malachi*, 413.

[838] Harris, Archer and Waltke, *Theological Wordbook of the Old Testament*, 2:675.

used in the *Tanakh* 11 times in Leviticus except this one in Zech 13:7.[839] How does this word "*amith*" or "associate" relate to man and to *Yahweh* in this verse? First, the associate is a man, a human being that *Yahweh* designates as His associate. The word associate, as it is used in Leviticus, is a general term for "fellowman." Unger defines it as:

> The Hebrew word employed, *amith*, is used to denote persons associated together under common love for the enjoyment of common rights and privileges.[840]

In Leviticus "*amith*" or "associate" is used as a neighbor who is their equal. Here in Zechariah, God is calling His shepherd, His associate or His equal. Kaiser expresses that concept in this statement:

> This Shepherd is One who is side by side with, or the equal of, the Lord! The term "associate" (or companion) is used to refer to those who are close neighbors or close companions (Lev 6:2; 18:20; 19:15). The equality that such a relationship brings to mind is the equality with God claimed by Jesus in John 10:30 and 14:9. The Shepherd's close association with the Lord strengthens the case for identifying him as the Shepherd of 11:4-14 and the One who was pierced in 12:10.[841]

What has been established is that *Yahweh* has a man who is His Associate or equal. He then instructs a weapon of death (sword) to be against His Shepherd or Associate. It is no coincidence that chapter 11 speaks of a good Shepherd who is paid 30 pieces of silver for his leadership among His people, as an insult. This Shepherd is the one who was pierced in Zech 12:10, and the one to whom the nation of Israel will look upon in the future. This Shepherd is a man, just as other Messianic prophecies predicted. But this man is also God, as Messianic prophecies predicted. Now this Shepherd, the man who is *Yahweh*'s equal, is having a sword instructed to be against Him.

The last phrase in Zech 13:7 states "smite the shepherd" or kill the shepherd. Here *Yahweh* is instructing the sword to kill the Shepherd. It is not without significance that a sword is used even as it was on *Yeshua* who was given wages (an insult) for His ministry as the good Shepherd in Zech 11:12-13. It is also significant that his death would come by being pierced and that a future generation will mourn for Him as Zech 12:10 clear states. The word for "pierced" in Zech 12:10 is the same word used in Zech 13:3 where parents of a false prophet are to pierce their son or "thrust him through." This verse shows how all of these passages are connected together in Zechariah chapters 11 and 12 with 13 in the same person. Also, it is important not to miss Zech 9:9, which *Yeshua* fulfilled on his entrance into Jerusalem a week before Passover. All

---

[839] Kohlenberger III and Swanson, *Hebrew English Concordance to the Old Testament*, 1241-1242.
[840] Unger, *Zechariah: Prophet of Messiah's Glory*, 232.
[841] Kaiser, *The Communicator's Commentary: Micah – Malachi*, 413.

of these verses as seen contain a wealth of information concerning God working with Israel and the Messiah, His shepherd.

The responsibility for killing Christ or the Messiah, needs to be examined. The Jewish people have taken the brunt of this for centuries by being called "Christ Killers." Let's set the record straight from a biblical prospective. The Jewish people were instruments in seeing Messiah killed, but so were the Romans. *Yeshua*, in Matthew 12, spells out very clearly that it was that generation, and not future generations, that was guilty of rejecting Him. All the hideous acts against the Jewish people have been inspired by Satan, who used ignorant "Christians" to keep the Jewish people from receiving the Gospel. Barrett and Kaiser express the same idea in this quote:

> The sword is told, "Strike the Shepherd." This accords with what Isaiah taught: "Yet it pleased the LORD to bruise Him" (Isa 53:10). Thus Jesus was delivered up in accordance with the definite plan of God, although it is the men who did the deed who are culpable for what they did (Acts 2:23).[842]

> Although Zechariah 12:10 indicates that unbelievers were responsible for piercing the Messiah, 13:7 squelches any notion that Messiah's death was anything other than the eternal purposes of God. Zechariah advances Isaiah's announcement that it was God's pleasure or purpose to bruise the Servant (Isaiah 53:10) by revealing that Christ's execution was God's command.[843]

This subject of who is responsible for killing Messiah must be dealt with biblically. God the Father takes full responsibility for the death of Messiah and as Isa 53:10 clearly states, "if he was willing to be the guilt offering." The sins of the world were placed on Jesus, on the cross, and the world stands guilty of his death, as being the free agent which committed the act. Jewish people have been persecuted for centuries for "killing Christ" by "Christians." But bear in mind that without His volunteer death, there is no resurrection and no eternal life. The human race is completely helpless and lost in their sins, with absolutely no power to remedy the situation. Yes, the Jewish people and the Romans of the first century were the instruments that God used, yet God takes full responsibility. The Jewish people are no more "Christ's Killers" than any other person from among the nations.

The impact of the tri-unity of God and the purpose of the Messiah's two comings are inseparable in understanding the redemptive purposes of God in two areas: first that the plurality of God is taught throughout the pages of the *Tanakh* and that God would have to become man to redeem mankind from his sins, and second that the Messiah is God and will come twice, once to redeem the world from the curse of sin and again to redeem Israel and fulfill the promises made to Abraham in the future coming for the Kingdom. The Key factor is that God is a tri-unity who revealed Himself through the Messenger of *Yahweh*, and His Holy Spirit coming upon man is critical in comprehending the ministry of Messiah as given in the *Tanakh*. No one

---

[842] Kaiser, *The Communicator's Commentary: Micah – Malachi*, 413.
[843] Barrett, *Beginning at Moses*, 237.

should even pretend to know or understand just how *Elohim* is plural and how He works within His person. What is known is that the *Tanakh* as well as the New Covenant presents God operating in a triune form.

Finally, Josh McDowell in reference to the chances of one "man" fulfilling the major prophecies of the First Coming of Messiah was all but mathematically impossible. For Jesus Christ to fulfill eight of the major prophecies concerning His first coming was 1 to the 17th power, or 1 to 100,000,000,000,000,000.[844] The eight prophecies are as follows: (1) Born in Bethlehem – Micah 5:2; (2) Preceded by a messenger – Isa 40:3; (3) Entering Jerusalem on a donkey – Zech 9:9; (4) Betrayed by a friend – Ps 41:9 and hands and feet pierced – Psa 22:16; (5) Sold out for 30 pieces of silver – Zech 11:12; (6) Money to be thrown into God's house – Zech 11:12 and price given for potter's field – Zech 11:13; (7) Dumb before His accusers – Isa 53:7; (8) Crucified with thieves.[845] The probability that a single man could fulfill 48 of the first coming references is 10 to the 157th power.[846] The probability of one man fulfilling these prophecies of Messiah's first coming is beyond question and absolute miracle of God.

This chapter has demonstrated that *Yeshua* is divine. He is the God/man that God promises, from the time of the fall in Genesis 3:15 right up through the prophet Zechariah. The Scriptures are clear that *Yeshua* is both God and man, who will reign on the throne of David, and will fulfill the promises to Abraham, Isaac and Jacob, to the Nation of Israel, to David, all in the New Covenant of Jeremiah.

---

[844] McDowell, *Evidence That Demands a Verdict*, 1:167.
[845] Josh McDowell, *Evidence That Demands a Verdict* (Nashville: Nelson, 1979), 1:141-166.
[846] McDowell, *Evidence That Demands a Verdict*, 1:167.

CHAPTER 8

SUMMARY

This author recognizes that above everything else "all scripture is given by inspiration of God." The utmost point to be advanced is that the Scriptures, including the *Tanakh* and New Covenant, are God's revelation of Himself. God had authors, such as Moses, use words to best describe His nature and character to human beings who could not have known Him at all unless He revealed Himself to them.

The purpose of this study was to analyze Jewish teaching that the plurality of God is not inherent in the Hebrew Scriptures. Therefore, research was confined to the context of the *Tanakh*. As a Christian committed to the tri-unity of God, this writer's goal was to determine whether it is possible to substantiate that doctrine solely from the Hebrew Scriptures. After intense study and analysis, the conclusion is that the plurality (tri-unity) of God is unquestionably presented in the *Tanakh*. That conclusion is possible because, as Paul asserts, the *Tanakh* is the inspired word of God (2 Tim 3:16) used to reveal Himself to mankind through human authors.

As demonstrated in chapter two, God's names reflect His character and nature, unlike human beings who cannot look down through the life of their children when they are born. Names are chosen that sound good, or parents name their child envisioning what they would like their child's character to be. But whether the name and character of the child is compatible to his future life is totally unforeseen to earthly parents. However, God knows His nature, character and who He is. Michael Barrett expresses the practice of naming children well and that God is capable of doing so with perfect knowledge of Himself:

> The point is that we use names without necessarily thinking about what the name means. That, however, was not the case for the writers of Scriptures. Names, particularly and especially the names of God, were never used haphazardly or casually in the Scripture. Names conveyed something about the nature or character of the one so named. "Thou shalt call his name JESUS: for he shall save his people from their sins" (Matt 1:21). That "Jesus" means "Jehovah saves" is certainly a significant statement given the purpose of the Savior's being born. What God called Himself was always an important means of His revealing Himself.[847]

When God used terms such as *Elohim*, *Eloah*, *Elah*, *El*, *Adonai* and *Yahweh* to describe Himself, He did so with an intended meaning for the reader. God chose to violate Hebrew grammar by using the plural noun "*Elohim*" with a singular verb "create" in Gen 1:1. This was so readers would recognize that God revealed Himself as one God (which the singular verb would affirm), but also that He showed Himself as a plurality

---

[847] Michael P. V. Barrett, *Beginning At Moses*, 24.

(which the plural noun would affirm). God using *Elohim* 2350 times to refer to Himself in the plural was not a mistake. God, who is one and a plurality, is not the author of confusion, so why are the very people He has revealed Himself to so unable to see the multitude of plural references He has made? This author believes that if God were one, then He would have used *El, Elah,* or *Eloah* in the singular so that mankind would not be confused. However, if God is a tri-unity then the plural noun *Elohim* makes absolute logical sense.

The fact remains that God did use the plural noun *Elohim* with singular verbs. Coupled with that God used, on several occasions, His personal name *YHVH* (*Yahweh* – LORD), which is a singular noun, not plural, in the *Tanakh* to refer to two *Yahwehs* which again reveals plurality. God chose words to describe Himself in the plural which is what confuses readers. As a human being and a singular being, readers are confused by God referring to Himself in both singular and plural ways and sometimes with the same combination of names as *Elohim* (plural) and *Yahweh* (singular). Added to that God, Himself and others, refer to Him as Lord (*Adonai*), which again is a plural description of Him. Judaism has taken that plural form (*Adonai*) and they used it to replace the personal name for God, which is singular. God shows Himself to be a plural compound unity, while at the same time confirming the fact that He is "one." All of these facts and references to *Elohim, Yahweh* and *Adonai* show a significant number of times that God chose to represent Himself as a plural, while being "one" as discussed in this book. Here is a brief summary: (1) uses of *Elohim* as the true God - 2350 times; (2) two *Yahwehs* - 4 times; (3) uses of Lord when used with God - 449 times; (4) combination of *Elohim* and *Yahweh* - 930 times; (5) uses of two *Elohims* - 1 time. Those usages of God, which He prompted the writers of Scripture to use of Himself, should not be overlooked or interpreted in ways that God by inspiration did not intend. Those usages amount to a significant amount of plural references in the Hebrew Scriptures.

In chapter three, the theophanies of God, of the Messenger (Angel) of *Yahweh* and the *Shechinah* Glory of God, further build the case for the plurality of God. The Messenger (Angel) of *Yahweh* and the *Shechinah* of God are, without question, God yet are distinct from God. However, the fact and presence of these theophanies of God give great difficulty to Jewish scholars who attempt to explain away the significance of these passages throughout the *Tanakh*. These appearances of God before man are a precursor to the incarnation of God in the New Covenant. These passages are generally held in common by Christians as the pre-incarnate Messiah, the Second Person of the Godhead. Barrett alone lists 25 references to the Messenger (Angel) of *Yahweh*.[848] Here again is a substantial number of references that lay a strong foundation for the plurality (or tri-unity) of God.

In chapter four the term *echad* in the *Shema* makes the point that God is "one" but also that oneness is made up as a compound or complex unity. The word *echad* is used 970 times throughout the *Tanakh*. Minimally, this word for "one" is in a plural

---

[848] Barrett, *Beginning At Moses*, 160-162.

context of others being involved. Some of these references relate specifically to a compound or complex unity. If Jewish scholars want to use *echad* to show oneness as to only one, their usage of *echad* does not accomplish that.

Chapter five deals with passages which have four types of plural descriptions of God and as a group are difficult to ignore. First, there are the plural personal pronouns in Genesis and Isaiah where God uses all His significant names of Himself, affirming plurality. Second, there are plural verbs with the plural noun *Elohim* that also point to the plurality of God. This is important because usually God uses the plural noun (*Elohim*) and a singular verb to show plurality and unity. Whereas in the four references cited, God has chosen to use the plural noun with plural verbs. On the one hand, the plural noun with the singular verb departs from the pattern of Hebrew grammar. On the other hand, the plural noun and plural verb are in harmony with Hebrew grammar. Once again God affirms that He is one God with a plurality of persons. Third, plural descriptions of Himself by the writers of Scripture affirm His plurality with plural modifiers of God. Fourth, there are three references in Isaiah that not only show plurality but also the tri-unity of God. Since God cannot make mistakes in the writing of His revelation of Himself to man, this is another significant amount of passages that shows not only His plurality but the tri-unity of God in the *Tanakh*. One or two passages in the *Tanakh* would prove absolutely nothing, but when dealing with the amount of references cited in this study, it becomes an overwhelming weight to affirm God's plurality.

In Chapter six the tri-unity of God becomes visible when the person of the Holy Spirit is included in the plurality of God in the *Tanakh*. As was demonstrated the Holy Spirit is not as visible in the *Tanakh* as in the New Covenant. It is harder to see Him in the Hebrew Scriptures. It is harder because in the *Tanakh*, the Holy Spirit works as the active power of God. However, it was also seen from other passages that His personality is not removed from the pages of the *Tanakh*. He is never really given a name in either testaments, but his personality, character and ministry are present in the *Tanakh*.

The Hebrew Scriptures do reveal His personality by being involved in creation, being grieved, or being impatient, and that He can testify or give witness against rebellious Israel. All these aspects of His personality have been born out in chapter six. Also His ministry has been seen to be different in the *Tanakh* than in the New Covenant. For in the *Tanakh* He came upon people to guide them, as with Saul and David, and to equip artisans, to accomplish specific tasks in the making of the Tabernacle and High Priestly garments. He came upon others like the judges to deliver the people. Isaiah alone is the prophet who couples together all three members of the tri-unity in the God-head as three distinct persons (Isa 42:1, 48:16, 61:1, 63:7-14), all operating as God throughout the *Tanakh*.

So once again the Hebrew Scriptures add more evidence to strengthen support for the triune God. Even though it is the deeds of the Holy Spirit that are predominate, personality still comes through confirming Him as part of the unity of God, the triune God.

Chapter seven gives unquestioned evidence to the fact that Messiah is divine. It has substantiated that the Messiah is God and not just a man. The understanding of the English terms: forever, everlasting, and eternity became so helpful in understanding the usage of *olam* in connection with the Messiah. His divinity becomes so clear in passages such as 1 Chron 7, Isa 9, Micah 5:2, Jer 23:5-6, Psa 110:1, Dan 9:24-27. As these passages are added, the evidence to the triune nature of God continues to build an insurmountable weight of evidence in substantiating the tri-unity of God in the *Tanakh*.

One the very first page of the book, Rabbi Greenberg was quoted. In summary he compared Judaism's and Christianity's belief in the oneness of God and that they are not compatible with each other. He spoke of the "overwhelming testimony" of the Bible that it speaks only of a monotheistic God. That what ever Christians call monotheism it is not the monotheism of Judaism. After going through all the Hebrew Scriptures and analyzing a multitude of passages. It becomes clear that the *Tanakh* points without question to the plurality (tri-unity) of God. In summarizing his words from the context of the *Tanakh*, the testimony of the Hebrew Bible flies in the face of Judaism to explain that God isn't a triune God.

The whole tone of Scripture when read as God gave it clearly supports the plurality and tri-unity of God. It is only when man entangles himself with the liberal humanistic thought that Christian scholars attempt to rewrite Scripture to suit their personal humanistic philosophy or pseudo-Christian bias. Throughout this study, the question has been asked, have Christian scholars abandoned the Doctrine of the Triune God in the Hebrew Scriptures to Rabbinic thought. The reality is that Christian scholars have abandoned this doctrine not because of Rabbinic teaching, but because of the secular humanism that has infiltrated the church of the last 200 years or so. Wilson points out that the church, up until modern times (the 1700's), saw the plurality and tri-unity of God in the Hebrew Scriptures.[849] What made the difference? It is this author's opinion that secular humanistic thought could not accept the supernatural aspect of the Word of God. Modern humanistic thinkers had to find natural ways to get around the obvious intent of Scripture. Erickson speaks of this humanism as modernism:

> Basically, modernism retained the conception of the world but removed its supernatural or at least extranatural basis. Thus, the vertical dualism was replaced by a horizontal dualism, in which the meaning or cause was found within or behind the natural world, rather than beyond or above it. The pattern of history is to be found within it rather than beyond it. Events are explained in terms of the social realities that cause them, rather than in terms of the purpose of a transcendent God.

---

[849] Wilson, *Our Father Abraham*, 54-55.

Modernism has been essentially humanistic. The human being is the center of reality, and in a sense everything exists for the sake of the human. In an earlier period, God had been thought of as the central and supreme object of value.[850]

A good example of humanism, or modern thinking, is expressed by Parkes. Even though he has some very valuable insights in the Jewish world of Paul's day, he does not see anything trinitarian in Paul or the *Tanakh*:

> His double experience of the atonement compelled him to think of Jesus Christ as more than human. But into what category was he then to place him? For as a Jew he recognized only one being to whom the category divine was fully applicable, and that was God himself. Paul was not a trinitarian; he had not the resources which were to be made available by several centuries of hammering on the anvil of both experience and philosophic thought. For him Jesus was never equal to God; whatever of divinity was to be ascribed to him was to be so ascribed because God had willed and planned it thus.[851]

> Undoubtedly the early Church was puzzled as to who Jesus was. . . . The experience which they had undergone was an emotional and not an intellectual one. . . . It is only as we understand this that we can appreciate the profound bewilderment which the Christian message caused in Jewish circles, and even among Jewish adherents of the new faith.[852]

As a scholar Parkes has some very interesting information on the early first century Jewish church which was surrounded by rabbinic Judaism's beliefs and concepts. It seems strange that anyone would say that Paul was not a trinitarian, but that is the context of Parkes' statement. He does not refer nor allude to Paul before his salvation but only after his conversion experience on the Damascus road. This author's view is that Parkes' views are not consistent with the teachings of Scripture. This humanistic modern thought sounds just like many rabbis who, not from humanistic reasons but for religious reasons, reject the plurality of God. Modern humanistic thought has infected many Christian scholars in not accepting God's word but find humanistic reasons that leave out God and the supernatural. However, contrary to Parkes, the teaching of Paul and all the other New Covenant writers clearly taught and understood the triune God from the *Tanakh* long before it was hammered out by experience and philosophic thought in the Nicean Council in 325 C.E. A careful observation of first century Jewish believers in Messiah *Yeshua* clarifies one basic concept: these believers had no problem moving from absolute monotheism to monotheism with three persons making up that unity of God as a complex unity. Buswell expresses it clearly:

> In the section in which we called attention to the unity of God as taught
> in the New Testament, several passages were cited in which the divine

---

[850] Millard J. Erickson, *Christian Theology* (2nd ed. Grand Rapids, Baker Books, 1998), 161, 163.
[851] James Parkes, *The Foundations of Judaism and Christianity* (Chicago: Quadrangle Books, 1960), 219-220.
[852] Parkes, *The Foundations of Judaism and Christianity*, 215.

unity is strongly affirmed, in direct conjunction with equally strong references to the deity of Jesus Christ. These passages are remarkable in that they contain no hint that the New Testament writers were at all conscious of any problem in the conjunction of these two ideas. That one God is complex in His being, and so subsists that there are personal distinctions within the Godhead, was no problem for the first century Christians.[853]

It appears that many Christian scholars have abandoned the doctrine of the tri-unity of the Godhead in the Hebrew Scriptures not primarily to the unbelief of rabbinic scholars, but to the unbelief of humanistic "Christian" secularists who use the unbelief of "higher criticism" to reinterpret God.

This author sees three valuable benefits in having an understanding of the character and nature of God in the Hebrew Scriptures as shown in the plurality of the Godhead. With a clear, practical and balanced understanding of the character and nature of God in the *Tanakh*, the Church today would be better equipped for living and witnessing for their Saviour and Lord. First, having a practical understanding of the plurality of God in the *Tanakh* has been sadly neglected by the Church in America. The Church today primarily has a New Testament understanding of the character and nature of God. Second, this material on the plurality of God in the Hebrew Scriptures, is not only valuable in witnessing to Jewish people but also in witnessing to anyone who depreciates Christ, such as the cults. Third, it produces a better understanding of the Second Person of the Godhead as to His character of holiness, righteousness and justice, demonstrated in the Hebrew Scriptures. Understanding the plurality of God from the *Tanakh* is important because the Church teaches that God is immutable (Mal 3:6), and as a consequence has done Jesus a disservice by presenting a lopsided view in relation to the character of God. The Church has depressed the holiness, righteousness and justice of Jesus, who was very active in the Hebrew Scriptures as the Second Person of *Elohim*. At the same time, the Church has elevated the love of God totally out of proportion to the other characteristics of Jesus. *Yeshua* demonstrated His love by coming as the "Servant of the LORD" (Isa 42) and becoming the Lamb that God would provide (Gen 22:8) the substitutionary sacrifice for the sins of the world. Thus, the Church today has an imbalanced view of the person of Christ, lacking fear, reverence, awe and commitment to the Almighty God who is the active sustainer of the universe (Col 1:18).

However, with this lack of understanding as to the plurality (and tri-unity) of God in the *Tanakh*, it negatively impacts evangelizing the Jewish people by discouraging them and keeping them from recognizing *Yeshua* as their Messiah (Hos 5:15; Matt 23:39). Ultimately they must believe the plurality (and tri-unity) of God and embrace that plural unity. Without believing in the oneness and plurality of God, that Jesus is God, they will continue to reject Him as their Messiah and remain lost in their sins. Zechariah 12:10 is one of the most gut-wrenching verses in Scriptures: "They shall mourn for him, as one mourneth for his only son." When the Jewish nation calls

---

[853] Buswell, *A Systematic Theology of the Christian Religion*, 120.

for the One sitting on the Father's right hand (Ps 80:17) and they realize that He is *Yeshua* (Jesus), the Messiah whom they rejected almost 2,000 years earlier, they will weep bitterly. Why? Because they and their fathers and their fathers' fathers had been rejecting the very one in whom they said they trusted.

In closing, Matt 23:39 *Yeshua* made His last public statement to the Jewish nation, that they will not see Him again until they say the following words, "Blessed is he that cometh in the name of the Lord." The rabbis say that when the Messiah comes they are to greet Him with these words. In fact only four days earlier in Matt 21:9 they used these words as He entered Jerusalem riding on the donkey (Zech 9:9). But the statement was not accepted because the nation had already rejected Him by attributing to Him and all the works He had done by the power of the Holy Spirit, that He did so by the power of Beelzebub, the prince of the devils (Matt 12:23-24). So the unpardonable sin, which was a national or corporate sin, was committed, and until He is recognized for who He is, God incarnate, the Messiah of Israel, the suffering servant and the King of Kings, and they call for Him to come, the Jewish nation will not see His face. The plurality of God is at the heart of Jewish evangelism, and being able to defend it from the Hebrew Scriptures is essential.

One final encouragement to Christians, God has given the responsibility to each believer to share the gospel of Messiah to the world. The Believing church sends thousand of missionaries to every corner of the earth and to as many unreached people groups as possible. Many believers and more mission agencies have forgotten about God's chosen people, through whom every believer owes everything. The church in past history has been the biggest obstacle for Jewish people to come to faith in Messiah Jesus. The church over the span of 1800 years has been the largest anti-Semitic group in the world. Because of the churches unbiblical treatment of Jewish people, they have become harder and more resistant to the gospel of Messiah. Keep in mind the Abrahamic Covenant, that if Israel is blessed, then the one who blesses Israel will be blessed. It is the conviction of this author that worldwide missions would see more fruit for its labor if Missions agencies, and individual believers, would revisit the Jewish people and once again share the Gospel with the Jew first. Stan Telchin, a Jewish believer in Messiah, has said that the greatest act of anti-Semitism that the church could commit is to withhold the Gospel of Messiah from the Jewish people.[854]

---

[854] Stan Telchin, *Messianic Judaism IS NOT Christianity* (Grand Rapids: Chosen Books, 2004),

Appendix 1

HOW TO BECOME ONE WITH G-D

To Be Reconciled To G-d

It is my prayer that upon reading this book your heart has been stirred as you recognized Jesus of Nazareth as the incarnation of G-d, He is *Hashem*.   It has been demonstrated throughout this book that He is G-d Almighty, *Yahweh*, the Messenger (Angel) of *Yahweh*, the Son of David who sits at the right hand of G-d, the One for whom the Father will make His enemies His footstool (Psa 110:1).

Below is a group of verses referred to as the Jerusalem Road to lead you into embracing the Messiah, the Son of David, *Yeshua*, as your Saviour from sin. I know you do not consider yourself a great sinner. But consider in your *Tanakh* the G-d of your fathers Abraham, Isaac and Jacob, Who is absolutely Holy, pure, and totally separated from sin. Open your Scripture and study His character and how He originally gave His covenant people, your fathers, sacrifices and priests to mediate between them and Himself. What was the need for the sacrifices and why did your fathers need a mediator to act on their behalf before G-d in His temple? It is because they where sinners and needed a substitute to take *Hashem*'s wrath for their sins. That is what the sacrificial system was all about.

To sin against G-d is simply man's disobedience against His Law and against *Hashem* Himself. You may call it the "evil inclination," but whatever you call it, it is simply missing the mark of His holiness. In *Hashem*'s eyes little acts of sin are just as much sin as murder. Sinful things that you think or hide in your heart, even if you do not do them physically, are sins in *Hashem*'s eyes. If you in your mind, or your heart have lusted after a woman, you have committed adultery in your heart before *Hashem*. Ladies if you coveted something that is your neighbors, and want it to the point that you will obtain it at most any cost, G-d judges that as sin. Notice that in neither of these examples was the act literally committed, yet *Hashem* views your hearts from which wrong, evil, or sin comes from. Listen to the words of *Yeshua* from the New Testament:

> But those things which proceed out of the mouth come forth from the heart; and they defile the man. For out of the heart proceed evil thoughts, murders, adulteries, fornication, thefts, false witness, blasphemies.   Matthew 15:18-19

Also the New Testament book that was written to Jewish believers in Messiah in the first century of the Common Era reflects the penetration of the Word of *Hashem*:

> For the word of God is quick, and powerful, and sharper than any two-edged sword, piercing even to the dividing asunder of the soul and spirit, and of the joints and marrow, and is a discerner of the thoughts and intents of the heart.
>
> Neither is there any creature that is not manifest in his sight: but all things are naked and open unto the eyes of him with whom we have to do. Hebrews 4:12-13.

That verse is simply stating that the Scriptures are like a double edged sword and can pierce into the spiritual part of man (soul and spirit), as well as the physical part of man (joints and marrow). It can even discern the very thoughts you think and the motivation behind them before you ever do them.

Nearly 2000 years ago *Hashem* allowed Rome to destroy the Holy City and the Holy Temple, just as He allowed Babylon centuries before to destroy Jerusalem and Solomon's Temple. When G-d destroyed Jerusalem the first time, He gave Israel prophets, like Jeremiah, Ezekiel, and Daniel. He also gave them prophets after the return, like Haggai, Zephaniah, Zechariah, and Malachi. G-d destroyed Jerusalem because of the sin of His covenant people, Israel. Notice that there has not been from Judaism's perspective a prophet to Israel since Malachi who lived 2400 years ago. Now if the sacrificial system was *Hashem*'s picture of His Holy demands and man's complete inability to keep His laws, why did G-d remove the sacrificial system which was absolutely necessary, and why did He not replace it or even give a prophet with a word from *Hashem*? Or did He give a prophet (Deut 18:15-18), in the person of His Son (Psa 2:7-12; Prov 30:4), the Suffering Servant of Isaiah 53, the Servant of the LORD? In Rabbinic Judaism today, how do you get rid of your sins biblically? Rabbis have made substitutions, but not on *Hashem*'s authority, only on theirs. Since your eternal destiny is at stake, whose word is more important, the Rabbis, or *Hashem* Himself through His Word? That is a question you must ask yourself. Who is my spiritual authority, Rabbis or *Hashem*? *Hashem* loves you with an everlasting Love!

> The LORD did not set his love upon you, nor choose you, because ye were more in number than any people; for ye were the fewest of all people: But because the LORD loved you, and because he would keep the oath which he had sworn unto your fathers.
>   Deuteronomy 7:7-8

> For thus says the LORD of hosts, "After glory He has sent me against the nations which plunder you, for he who touches YOU, touches the apple of His eye.
>   Zechariah 2:8

Search the Scriptures, ask the G-d of you fathers to show you what He has written in His Word that your prophets recorded for Him concerning His Son, your Messiah, the Son of David, the King of Israel, and your substitutary sacrifice for your sin.

The Jerusalem Road
1. "There is none without sin"

- Psalm 14:3

    They are all gone aside, they are all together become filthy: there is none that doeth good, not one.

- Psalm 51:5

    Behold, I was shapen in iniquity; and in sin did my mother conceive me.

- Isaiah 53:6

    All we like sheep have gone astray; we have turned every one to his own way; and the LORD hath laid on him the iniquity of us all.

- Jeremiah 17:9

    The heart is deceitful above all things, and desperately wicked: who can know it?

- Isaiah 59:1-2

    Behold, the LORD's hand is not shortened, that it cannot save; neither his ear heavy, that it cannot hear:

    But your iniquities have separated between you and your God, and your sins have hid his face from you, that he will not hear.

- Ecclesiastes 7:20

    For there is not a just man upon earth, that doeth good, and sinneth not.

2. Good deeds cannot purify

- Isaiah 64:6

    But we are all as an unclean thing, and all our righteousness are as filthy rags; and we all do fade as a leaf; and our iniquities, like the wind, have taken us away.

- Habakkuk 2:4

    Behold, his soul which is lifted up is not upright in him: but the just shall live by his faith.

- Jeremiah 18:20

    Shall evil be recompensed for good? For they have digged a pit for my soul. Remember that I stood before thee to speak good for them, and to turn away they wrath from them.

217

3. God requires a blood sacrifice

- Leviticus 17:11

  > For the life of the flesh is in the blood: and I have given it to you upon the altar to make an atonement for your souls: for it is the blood that maketh an atonement for the soul.

4. Apply the blood of the Messiah

- Exodus 12:21-23

  > Then Moses called for all the elders of Israel, and said unto them, Draw out and take you a lamb according to your families and kill the Passover.
  >
  > And ye shall take a bunch of hyssop, and dip it in the blood that is in the bason and strike the lintel and the two side posts with the blood that is in the bason; and none of you shall go out at the door of his house until morning.
  >
  > For the LORD will pass through to smite the Egyptians; and when he seeth the blood upon the lintel, and on the two side posts, the LORD will Passover the door, and will not suffer the destroyer to come in unto your houses to smite you.

- Leviticus 16:15-19

  > Then shall he kill the goat of the sin-offering, that is for the people, and bring his blood within the vail, and do with that blood as he did with the blood of the bullock, and sprinkle it upon the mercy seat, and before the mercy seat:
  >
  > And he shall make an atonement for the holy place, because of the uncleanness of the children of Israel, and because of their transgressions in all their sins: and so shall he do for the tabernacle of the congregation, that remaineth among them in the midst of their uncleanness.
  >
  > And there shall be no man in the tabernacle of the congregation when he goeth in to make an atonement in the holy place, until he come out, and have make an atonement for himself, and for his household, and for all the congregation of Israel.
  >
  > And he shall go out unto the altar that is before the LORD, and make an atonement for it; and shall take of the blood of the bullock, and of the blood of the goat, and put it upon the horns of the altar round about.

And he shall sprinkle of the blood upon it with his finger seven
times, and cleanse it, and hallow it from the uncleanness of the
children of Israel.

- Daniel 9:26

    And after threescore and two weeks shall Messiah be cut off, but
    not for himself: and the people of the prince that shall come shall
    destroy the city and the sanctuary; and the end thereof shall be
    with a flood, and unto the end of the war desolations are
    determined.

- Hebrews 9:12

    Neither by the blood of goats and calves, but by his own blood he
    entered in once into the holy place, having obtained eternal
    redemption for us.

5. Safety and refuge in God's Messiah

- Psalm 2:12

    Kiss the Son, lest he be angry, and ye perish from the way, when
    his wrath is kindled but a little. Blessed are all they that put their
    trust in him.

- Psalm 51:13

    Then will I teach transgressors thy ways; and sinner shall be
    converted unto thee.

"Who is this Messiah?"

- He was born of a virgin – Isaiah 7:14

    Therefore the Lord himself shall give you a sign; Behold, a virgin
    shall conceive, and bear a son, and shall call his name Immanuel.

- Born in Bethlehem – Micah 5:2

    But thou, Beth-lehem Ephratah, though thou be little among the
    thousands of Judah, yet out of thee shall he come forth unto me
    that is to be ruler in Israel; whose goings forth have been from of
    old, from everlasting.

- Slain for our sins – Isaiah 53:5-6

    But he was wounded for our transgressions, he was bruised for
    our iniquities: the chastisement of our peace was upon him; and
    with his stripes we are healed.

    All we like sheep have gone astray; we have turned every one to
    his own way; and the LORD hath laid on him the iniquity of us
    all.

219

- Resurrected -- Psalm 16:10, Daniel 12:2

  > For thou will not leave my soul in hell; neither wilt thou suffer thine Holy One to see corruption.

  > And many of them that sleep in the dust of the earth shall awake, some to everlasting life, and some to shame and everlasting contempt.

Isaiah Avenue
1. Sinners Before God -- Isaiah 64:5-6
2. Separation From God -- Isaiah 59:1-2
3. Salvation in God -- Isaiah 53:6
4. Saviour is God -- Isaiah 9:5-6
5. Stayed Upon God -- Isaiah 26:3

   > Thou wilt keep him in perfect peace, whose mind is stayed on thee: because he trusteth in thee.

ALL MEN ARE SINNERS

I Kings 8:46

> If they sin against thee, (for there is no man that sinneth not), and thou be angry with them, and deliver them to the enemy, so that they carry them away captives unto the land of the enemy, for or near;

Ecclesiastes 7:20

> For there is not a just man upon earth, that doeth good, and sinneth not.

Psalm 14:1-3

> The fool hath said in his heart, there is no God. They are corrupt, they have done abominable works, there is none that doeth good. The LORD looked down from heaven upon the children of men, to if thee were any That did understand, and seek God. They are all gone aside, they are all together become filthy: there is none that doeth Good, no, not one.

Psalm 53:2-3

> God looked down from heaven upon the children of men, to see if there were any that did understand, that did seek God. Every one of them is gone back: they are altogether become filthy; there is none that doeth good, no, not one.

Psalm 130:3

> If thou, LORD, shouldest mark iniquities, O Lord, who shall stand?

Isaiah 64:6

But we are all as an unclean thing, and all our righteousnesses are as filthy rags and we all do fade as a leaf; and our iniquities, like the wind, have taken us away.

Jeremiah 17:9

The heart is deceitful above all things, and desperately wicked: who can know it?

SIN SEPARATES US FROM G-D

Job 15:14-16

What is man, that he should be clean? And he which is born of a woman, that he should be righteous? Behold, he putteth no trust in his saints; yea, the heavens are not clean in his sight. How much more abominable and fifty is man, which drinketh iniquity like water?

Isaiah 59:2

But your iniquities have separated between you and your God, and your sins have hid his face from you, that he will not hear.

THE PENALTY OF SIN IS DEATH

Jeremiah 31:30

But every one shall die for his own iniquity.

Ezekiel 18:4, 20

Behold, all souls are mine; as the soul of the father, so also the soul of the son is mine: the soul that sinneth, it shall die.

The soul that sinneth, it shall die. The son shall not bear the iniquity of the father, neither shall the father bear the iniquity of the son: the righteousness of the righteous shall be upon him, and the wickedness of the wicked shall be upon him.

Daniel 12:2

And many of them that sleep in the dust of the earth shall awake, some to everlasting life, and some to shame and everlasting contempt.

GOD PUNISHES FOR DISOBEDIENCE

Jeremiah 6:19-20

> Hear, O earth: behold, I will bring evil upon this people, *even the fruit of their thoughts*, because they have not hearkened unto my words, nor to my law, but rejected it. (Italics added for emphasis)

RESULTS OF DISOBEDIENCE

Jeremiah 5
(read this length section)

Joshua 23:14-16

> And, behold, this day I am going the way of all the earth: and ye know in all your hearts and in all your souls, that not one thing hath failed of all the good things which the LORD your God spake concerning you; all are come to pass unto you, and not one thing hath failed thereof.
>
> Therefore it shall come to pass, that as all good thing are come upon you, which the LORD your God promised you; so shall the LORD bring upon you all evil things, until he have destroyed you from off this good land which the LORD your God hath given you.
>
> When ye have transgressed the covenant of the LORD your God, which he commanded you, and have gone and served other gods, and bowed yourselves to them; then shall the anger of the LORD be kindled against you, and ye shall perish quickly from off the good land which he hath given unto you.

Deuteronomy 4:23-40

Deuteronomy 28

MEN MUST TURN FROM SIN

Ezekiel 33:10-11

> Therefore, O thou son of man, speak unto the house of Israel; Thus ye speak, saying, If our transgressions and our sins be upon us, and we pine (rotting) away in them, how should we then live (survive)? Say unto them, As I live, saith the Lord God, I have no pleasure in the death of The wicked; but that the wicked turn from his way and live: turn ye, turn ye from your evil ways; for why will ye die, O house of Israel?

Hosea 14:1

Return, O Israel, unto the Lord thy God; for thou hast stumbled in thine iniquity.

INABILITY TO REDEEM OR CLEANSE OUR HEARTS

Psalm 49:7

None of them can be any means redeem his brother, nor give to God a ransom for him

Proverbs 20:9

Who can say, I have made my heart clean, I am pure from my sin?

Jeremiah 2:22

For though thou was thee with nitre, and take thee much soap, yet thine iniquity is marked before me, saith the Lord God.

WE NEED A MEDIATOR and REDEEMER

Isaiah 59:16, 20

"And he saw that there was no man, and wondered that there was no intercessor: therefore his arm brought salvation unto them; and his righteousness, it sustained him."

"And the Redeemer shall come to Zion, and unto them that turn from transgression in Jacob, saith the LORD."

BLOOD NEEDED FOR REMISSION OF SIN

Exodus 12:13

And the blood shall be to you for a token upon the houses where ye are; and when I see the blood, I will pass over you, and the plague shall not be upon you to make an atonement for your souls; for it is the blood that maketh an atonement for the soul.

Leviticus 17:11

For the life of the flesh is in the blood; and I have given it to you upon the altar to make an atonement for your souls; for it is the blood that maketh an atonement for the soul.

A CIRCUMCISED HEART IS NEEDED

Deuteronomy 10:12-17

And now, Israel, what doth the LORD thy God require of thee, but to fear the LORD they god, to walk in all his ways, and to love him, and to serve the LORD they god with all thy heart and with all they soul,

To keep the commandments of the LORD, and his statutes, which I command thee this day for thy good?

Behold, the heaven and the heaven of heavens is the LORD's thy God, the earth also, with all that therein is.

Only the LORD had a delight in thy fathers to love them, and he chose their seed after them, even you above all people, as it is this day.

Circumcise therefore the foreskin of your heart, and be no more stiffnecked.

For the LORD your God is God of gods, and Lord of lords, a great God, a might, and a terrible, which regardeth not persons, nor taketh reward.

Deuteronomy 30:6

And the Lord thy God will circumcise thine heart, and the heart of they seed, to love the Lord thy God with all thine heart, and with all thy soul, that thou mayest live.

Leviticus 26:40-42

If they shall confess their iniquity and the iniquity of their fathers, with their trespass which they trespassed against me, and that also they have walked contrary unto me;

and that I also have walked contrary unto them and have brought them into the land of their enemies; if then their uncircumcised hearts be humbled, and they then accept of the punishment of their iniquity:

Then will I remember my covenant with Jacob, and also my covenant with Isaac, and also my covenant with Abraham will I remember; And I will remember the land.

Jeremiah 4:4

Circumcise yourselves to the Lord, and take away the foreskins of your heart, ye men of Judah and inhabitants of Jerusalem: lest my fury come forth like fire, and burn that none can quench it, because of the evil of your doings.

Jeremiah 6:9, 10

Thus saith the Lord of hosts, they shall thoroughly glean the remnant of Israel as a vine: turn back thine hand as a grape gathered in the baskets.

To whom shall I speak, and give warning, that they may hear? Behold their ear is uncircumcised, and they cannot hearken: behold, the word of the Lord is unto them a reproach; they have no delight in it.

Jeremiah 9:25

Egypt, and Judah, and Edom, and the children of Ammon, and Moab, and all that are in the utmost corners, that dwell in the wilderness: for all these nations are uncircumcised, and all the house of Israel are uncircumcised in the heart.

YOU MUST BE CONVERTED

Psalm 51:15

Then will I teach transgressors thy ways; and sinners shall be converted unto thee.

Isaiah 6:10

Make the heart of this people fat, and make their ears heavy, and shut their eyes; lest they see with their eyes, and hear with their ears, and understand with their hearts, and convert, and be healed.

THERE WILL BE A RESURRECTION

Daniel 12:2

And many of them that sleep in the dust of the earth shall awaken some to everlasting life and some to shame and everlasting contempt.

Job 19:25-26

For I know that my Redeemer liveth, and that he shall stand at the latter day upon the earth, and after they have thus destroyed my skin yet from my flesh shall I see God.

Psalm 49:16

But God will redeem my soul from the power of the grave: for he shall revive me.

Isaiah 25:8

He (Messiah) will destroy death forever and the Lord God will wipe away from off all faces; and the rebuke of his people shall he take away from off all the earth, for the Lord hath spoken it.

Isaiah 26:19

> Thy dead men shall live, together with my dead body shall they rise.

Hosea 13:14

> I will ransom them from the power of the grave; I will redeem them from death: O death, where are thy plagues? O grave, where is thy destruction?

Personal Invitation

Both the Hebrew Scripture and the New Covenant (Testament) present Jesus (*Yeshua*) as being equal with the Father (John 10:30). He became flesh and dwelt among us (John 1:14) and according to the Fathers plan, His Son, the Messiah, the Son of David was the final sacrifice for our sins which took place on the Feast of Passover. He was the perfect Unleavened Bread that came down from heaven (John 6:28-51). He then arose from the dead on the Feast of First Fruits (John 20:1), on the first day of the week becoming the first fruits of the resurrection (1 Corinthians 15:20-26). He ascending and was seated on the Father's right hand to make intercession for us and will return in the future to restore Israel and fulfill the promises to Abraham, Isaac and Jacob. Go to the Father and confess that you're a sinner, separated from Him, and acknowledging that Jesus is your saviour from sin, your redeemer. Asking Him to come into your heart and life as your Messiah and Lord.

John 1:12

> But as many as received him (*Yeshua*), to them gave he the power to become the sons of God, even to them that believe on his name.

John 3:16-17, 36

> For God so loved the world, that he gave his only begotten Son, that whosoever believeth in him should not perish, but have everlasting life
>
> For God sent not his Son into the world to condemn the world; but that the world through him might be saved.
>
> He that believeth on the Son hath everlasting life: and he that believeth not the Son shall not see life; but the wrath of God abideth on him.

Acts 4:12

> Neither is there salvation in any other: for there is none other name under heaven given among men, whereby we must be saved.

Romans 3:23

> For all have sinned, and come short of the glory of God

Romans 5:8

But God commendeth his love toward us, in that while we were yet sinners, Messiah died for us.

Romans 6:23

For the wages of sin is death; but the gift of God is eternal life through *Yeshua* Messiah our Lord.

Philippians 2:5-11

Let this mind be in you, which was also in Messiah *Yeshua*:

Who, being in the form of God, thought it not robbery to be equal with God:

But made of himself of no reputation, and took upon him the form of a servant, and was made in the likeness of men:

And being found in fashion as a man, he humbled himself, and became obedient unto death, even the death of the cross.

Wherefore God also hath highly exalted him, and given him a name which is above every name:

That at the name of *Yeshua* every knee should bow, of things in heaven, and things in the earth, and things under the earth;

And that every tongue should confess that *Yeshua* Messiah is Lord, to the glory of God the Father.

Colossians 2:9-11

For in him dwelleth all the fullness of the Godhead bodily.

And ye are complete in him, which is the head of all principality and power:

In whom also ye are circumcised with the circumcision made without hands, in putting off the body of sins of the flesh by the circumcision of Messiah:

Hebrews 1:1-3

God, who at sundry times and in different manners spake in time past unto the fathers by the prophets,

Hath in these last days spoken unto us by his Son, whom he hath appointed heir of all things, by whom also he made the worlds;

Who being the brightness of his glory, and the express image of his person, and upholding all things by the word of his power, when he had by himself purged our sins, sat down on the right hand of the Majesty on high.

Hebrews 10:10-18

By the which will we are sanctified through the offering of the body of *Yeshua* Messiah once for all.

And every priest standeth daily ministering and offering oftentimes the same sacrifices, which can never take away sins:

But this man, after he had offered one sacrifice for sin forever, sat down on the right hand of God;

From hence forth expecting till his enemies be made his footstool.

For by one offering he hath perfected forever them that are sanctified.

Whereof the Holy Spirit also is a witness to us: for after that he had said before,

This is the covenant that I will make with them after those days, saith the Lord, I will put my laws into their hearts, and in their minds will I write them;

And their sins and iniquities will I remember no more.

Now where remission of these is, there is not more offering for sin.

Appendix 2

Moses' Use of *Echad* in the *Torah*

This section will demonstrate the plurality of *echad* as Moses used it in the Torah. There are 382 references scattered throughout his writings. The Hebrew word *echad* is translated as "one". There are three ways that scholars say *echad* is used: (1) *Echad* used as a unity, more than two things coming together in a unity of one, (2) *Echad* used in relationship to other things or persons but not as a compound unity, (3) *Echad* used to indicate the separateness or individuality of a person or thing. The third grouping is then divided into three parts: (a) first part denotes one standing by itself, (b) second part, called a "cardinal one" as Joshua enumerates the kings that he defeated in conquering the Land, (c) and an ordinal number expressed by the first of the week or month as in Exod 40:17.

Jewish rabbis believe that the *echad*, in the *Shema* of Deut 6:4 (see chapter four), is an absolute one with absolutely no suggestion or hint of a plurality. In order to demonstrate the usage of *echad*, all the references of *echad* listed below show how this word is used and understood by Moses. It is my desire that Jewish people understand that the *echad* within the *Shema*, which is the cornerstone of their faith, that they see and understand that *echad* is consistently used in a plural context in all three divisions listed above.

As a Christian, this author was surprised to discover that the word for "one" in the *Shema* was not always a "one of unity." Forced by the evidence that has been observed, this author has revised his understanding of *echad*. The first division above, the unity of more than one thing, is less frequently used (34 times) of any of the other usages of the word *echad*. The second usage appears quite frequently (172 times). That usage is a context of plurality, not necessarily unity. It was also observed in the third section that even though a particular "one" is being referenced (176 times), it is also very often used in the context of plurality. It is never used as an absolute one like *yachid*, which is only "one" with absolutely no reference to plurality. Moses in his usage of *echad* used this word almost exclusively within a plural context. God is viewed in Judaism as "one" alone, and they would have people believe that *echad* is only "one," but that just does not fit the context of *echad* and how Moses used it.

Notice on the extended chart, in the first column are the scriptural references, in the second column are the quotations in which *echad* is found, and the third, fourth and fifth columns show the three areas of the third section mentioned above: (a) First *echad* denotes unity of one, (b) second denotes one is the context of plurality and (c) third, one as an individual one. In these quotations *echad* is italicized, and if the *echad* is translated with another word besides one, that is italicized as well.

After going through all 382 references, there is only one conclusion that a student of the Scriptures can come to: *echad* is not generally used as a unity of one, but in most instances it is used in the context of plurality. Clearly, Deut 6:4 evidences a plural context: "Hear, O Israel, the LORD our God, LORD is one." The plural context is *elohenu* which is translated "our God(s)." *Elohim* is the plural form for God as was discussed in chapter two, and *elohenu* is translated "our God(s)." Moses was stating that *Yahweh* was their God(s), emphasizing God as a one of unity and as one within a plurality. Moses knew that at his disposal were the singular forms for God, like *El* or *Eloah* (*Elah* was not used until the time of the exile and post-exilic period), and yet he chose to use the plural form. According to rabbis, if *Yahweh* is "one," then Moses surely confused the issue when he used *echad* in Deut 6:4 to describe God. But if God chose to represent Himself as a plurality -- as He did so frequently throughout the *Tanakh* -- then the plural word *elohim* is correct, and the plural usage of *echad* is also correct.

In using the Hebrew Scripture published by assorted Jewish publishers, it should be noted that most often they treat *echad* the same way as translated in the King James Version or the New American Standard Version. Even passages that view *echad* within a plural context are also viewed in a plural context in their translations. So Judaism does understand that in Deut 6:4 *echad* is not an absolute one because Jewish scholars also translate *echad* as one in a plural context.

In investigating the usage of *echad* in different Jewish translations to see how they viewed *echad* in the Torah, the observation can clearly be seen that *echad* is used the same way as in the Christian bibles. The chart that follows this section there are asterisks preceding some of the verses that this author has checked in the following copies of the Hebrew Scriptures; The Jewish Study Bible,[855] The Soncino Chumash,[856] The Harkavy Version,[857] The Pentateuch and Haftorahs,[858] Friedman's Commentary on the Torah,[859] The Holy Scriptures according to the Masoretic Text,[860] and the Isaac Leeser Version.[861] In going through the references of *echad* in all the Hebrew/English editions listed above, *echad* was used consistently the same way as in the KJV and the ASV.

It is quite apparent that *echad* is primarily used in a plural context throughout the writings of Moses. That plural usage implies that *echad* is a unity of one, but even more so a plurality and is not used as an absolute one.

[855] Berlin and Brettler, *The Jewish Study Bible*.

[856] Cohen, *The Soncino Chumash: The Five Books of Moses with Haphtaroth*.

[857] Alexander Harkavy, *The Twenty-Four Books of the Old Testament* (2 vols. New York: Hebrew Publishing Co, 1916).

[858] Hertz, *The Pentateuch and Haftorahs*.

[859] Friedman, *Commentary on the Torah* (San Francisco: Harper Collins Publishers, 2001).

[860] The Jewish Publication Society, *The Holy Scriptures: According to the Masoretic Text* (Philadelphia: Jewish Publication Society, 1917).

[861] Isaac Leeser, *The Twenty-Four Books of the Holy Bible* (New York: Hebrew Publishing Co).

References of *Echad* in the Torah

GENESIS

Gen 1:5	And the evening and the morning were the **echad-first** day.
*Gen 1:9	God said, Let the waters under the heaven to be gathered unto **echad** place,
*Gen 2:11	The name of the **echad-first** is the Pishon;
*Gen 2:21	and he slept: and he took **echad** of his ribs, and closed up the
*Gen 2:24	and shall cleave unto his wife: and they shall be **echad** flesh.
*Gen 3:22	Behold, the man is become as **echad** of us, to know good and evil:
*Gen 4:19	the name of the **echad** (was) Adah, and the name of the other Zillah
Gen 8:5	on the **echad-first** (day) of the month,
Gen 8:13	And it came to pass in the six hundredth and **echad-first** year,
Gen 8:13	in the **echad-first** month,
*Gen 10:25	And unto Eber were born two sons: the name of **echad** (was) Peleg
*Gen 11:1	And the whole earth was of **echad** language,
*Gen 11:1	and of **echad** speech.
*Gen 11:6	Behold, the people (is) **echad,**
*Gen 11:6	and they have all **echad** language;
*Gen 19:9	This **echad** came in to sojourn, and he will needs be a judge:
*Gen 21:15	and she cast the child under **echad** of the shrubs.
*Gen 22:2	a burnt-offering upon **echad** of the mountains which I will tell thee of.
Gen 26:10	**echad** of the people might lightly have lien with thy wife,
Gen 27:38	Hast thou but **echad** blessing, my father?
Gen 27:45	why should I be deprived also of you both in **echad** day?
Gen 32:8	If Esau come to the **echad** company, and smite it,
Gen 33:13	and if men should overdrive them **echad** day, all the flock will die.
Gen 34:16	and we will dwell with you, and we will become **echad** people.
Gen 34:22	to be **echad** people, if every male among us be circumcised,
Gen 37:20	and let us slay him, and cast him into **echad-some** pit,
Gen 40:5	each man his dream in **echad** night,
Gen 41:5	and behold, seven ears of corn came up upon **echad** stalk,
Gen 41:11	And we dreamed a dream in **echad** night, I and he;
Gen 41:22	and behold, seven ears came up in **echad** stalk, full and good:
Gen 41:25	The dream of Pharaoh (is) **echad**: God hath shewed Pharaoh
Gen 41:26	and the seven good ears (are) seven years: the dream (is) **echad**.
Gen 42:11	We (are) all **echad** man's sons: we (are) true (men),
Gen 42:13	twelve brethren, the sons of **echad** man in the land of Canaan;
Gen 42:13	the youngest is this day with our father, and **echad** is not.
Gen 42:16	Send **echad** of you, and let him fetch your brother
Gen 42:19	If ye (be) true (men), let **echad** of your brethren be bound in the house
Gen 42:27	And as **echad** of them opened his sack to give his ass
Gen 42:32	We (be) twelve brethren, sons of our father; **echad** (is) not,
Gen 42:33	leave **echad** of your brethren (here) with me
Gen 44:28	And the **echad** went out from me, and I said,
Gen 48:22	Moreover I have given to thee **echad** portion above thy brethren,
Gen 49:16	Dan shall judge his people, as **echad** of the tribes of Israel.

EXODUS

*Ex 1:15	Hebrew midwives, of which the name of the **echad** (was) Shiphrah

*Ex 8:31	removed the swarms of (flies) from Pharaoh, . . . Remained not **echad**
Ex 9:6	but of the cattle of the children of Israel died not **echad.**
Ex 9:7	And Pharaoh sent, and, behold, there was not **echad** of the cattle
Ex 10:19	there remained not **echad** locust in all the coasts of Egypt.
Ex 11:1	Yet will I bring **echad** plague more upon Pharaoh,
Ex 12:18	until the **echad** and twentieth day of the month at even,
Ex 12:46	In **echad** house shall it be eaten; thou shalt not carry forth
Ex 12:49	**Echad** law shall be to him that is hometown,
Ex 14:28	there remained not so much as **echad** of them.
Ex 16:22	they gathered twice as much bread, two omers for **echad** (man)
Ex 16:33	Take **echad-a** pot, and put a omer full of manna therein,
*Ex 17:12	and Aaron and Hur stayed up his hands, the **echad** on the echad side
*Ex 17:12	the echad on the **echad** side, and the other on the other side;
Ex 18:3	of which the name of the **echad** (was) Gershom;
Ex 18:4	And the name of the **other-echad** (was) Eliezer;
Ex 23:29	I will not drive them out from before thee in **echad** year;
*Ex 24:3	and all the people answered with **echad** voice,
Ex 25:12	and two rings shall be in the **echad** side of it,
*Ex 25:19	And make *echad* cherub on the **echad** end,
*Ex 25:19	and the **echad-other** cherub on the other end:
Ex 25:32	three branches of the candlestick out of the **echad** side,
Ex 25:33	with a knop and a flower in **echad** branch;
Ex 25:33	and three bowls made like almonds in the **echad-other** branch,
Ex 25:36	all it (shall be) **echad** beaten work (of) pure gold.
*Ex 26:2	The length of **echad** curtain shall be eight and twenty cubits,
*Ex 26:2	and the breadth of **echad** curtain four cubits:
*Ex 26:2	and every **echad** of the curtains shall have echad measure
Ex 26:2	and every echad of the curtains shall have **echad** measure
Ex 26:4	And thou shalt make loops of blue upon the edge of the **echad** curtain
Ex 26:5	Fifty loops shalt thou make in the **echad** curtain,
Ex 26:8	The length of **echad** curtain (shall be) thirty cubits,
Ex 26:8	and the breadth of **echad** curtain four cubits:
Ex 26:8	and the eleven curtains (shall be all) of **echad** measure.
*Ex 26:10	And thou shalt make fifty loops on the edge of the **echad** curtain
*Ex 26:11	and couple the tent together, that it may be **echad.**
Ex 26:16	and a cubit and a half (shall be) the breadth of **echad** board.
Ex 26:17	Two tenons (shall there be) in **echad** board,
Ex 26:19	two sockets under **echad** board for his two tenons,
Ex 26:21	And their forty sockets of silver; two sockets under **echad** board,
Ex 26:24	they shall be coupled together above the head of it unto **echad** ring
Ex 26:25	sixteen sockets; two sockets under **echad** board,
Ex 26:26	five for the boards of the **echad** side of the tabernacle,
Ex 27:9	the court of (fine) twined linen of a hundred cubits long for **echad** side:
Ex 28:10	Six of their names on **echad** stone
Ex 28:17	(even) four rows of stones: the **echad-first** shall be a sardius,
Ex 29:1	Take **echad** young bullock, and two rams without blemish,
Ex 29:3	and thou shalt put them into **echad** basket,
Ex 29:15	Thou shalt also take **echad** ram;
Ex 29:23	And **echad** loaf of bread
Ex 29:23	and **echad** cake of oiled bread,

Ex 29:23	and ***echad*** wafer out of the basket of the unleavened bread	
Ex 29:39	The ***echad*** lamb thou shalt offer in the morning	
Ex 29:40	And with the ***echad*** lamb a tenth deal of flour mingled with	
Ex 30:10	***echad-once*** in a year with the blood of the sin-offering of atonements:	
Ex 30:10	***echad-once*** in the year shall he make atonement upon it	
Ex 36:9	The length of ***echad*** curtain was twenty and eight cubits	
Ex 36:9	and the breadth of ***echad*** curtain four cubits:	
*Ex 36:10	And he coupled the five curtains ***echad*** unto another;	
Ex 36:11	And he made loops of blue on the edge of ***echad*** curtain	
*Ex 36:12	Fifty loops made he in ***echad*** curtain,	
*Ex 36:12	the loops held ***echad*** curtain to another.	
*Ex 36:13	fifty taches of gold, and coupled the curtains ***echad*** unto another	
*Ex 36:13	so it became ***echad*** tabernacle.	
Ex 36:15	The length of ***echad*** curtain was thirty cubits,	
Ex 36:15	and four cubits (was) the breadth of ***echad*** curtain:	
Ex 36:15	the eleven curtains (were) of ***echad*** size.	
*Ex 36:18	to couple the tent together, that it might be ***echad***	
Ex 36:21	and the breadth of a board ***echad*** cubit and a half	
Ex 36:22	***Echad*** board had two tenons,	
Ex 36:22	equally distant ***echad*** from another:	
Ex 36:24	two sockets under ***echad*** board for his two tenons,	
Ex 36:24	and two sockets under ***echad-another*** board for his two tenons.	
Ex 36:26	And their forty sockets of silver; two sockets under ***echad*** board,	
Ex 36:26	and two sockets under ***echad-another*** board.	
Ex 36:29	and coupled together at the head thereof, to ***echad*** ring:	
Ex 36:30	their sockets (were) 16 sockets of silver, under ***echad-every*** board	
Ex 36:31	five for the boards of the ***echad*** side of the tabernacle,	
Ex 37:3	even two rings upon the ***echad*** side of it,	
*Ex 37:8	***Echad*** cherub on the end on this side,	
*Ex 37:8	and ***echad-another*** cherub on the (other) end on that side:	
Ex 37:18	three branches of the candlestick out of the ***echad*** side thereof,	
Ex 37:19	Three bowls made after the fashion of almonds in ***echad*** branch,	
Ex 37:19	and three bowls made like almonds in ***echad-another*** branch,	
Ex 37:22	all of it (was) ***echad*** beaten work (of) pure gold.	
Ex 39:10	And they set in it four rows of stones: the ***echad*** (first) row	
Ex 40:2	On the ***echad-first*** day of the first month thou shalt set up	
Ex 40:17	on the ***echad-first*** day of the month, the tabernacle was reared up	

LEVITICUS

Lev 4:2	Speak unto the children of Israel, saying, If ***echad-a*** soul shall sin	
Lev 4:2	If echad-a soul shall sin through ignorance against ***echad-any*** of the	
Lev 4:2	commandments . . . and shall do against ***echad-any*** of them.	
Lev 4:13	and they have done (somewhat against) ***echad-any*** of the commandments	
Lev 4:22	When a ruler hath sinned, and done through ignorance (against) ***echad-any***	
Lev 4:27	And if ***echad*** of the common people sin through ignorance,	
Lev 4:27	while he doeth (somewhat against) ***echad-any*** of the commandments of the	
Lev 5:4	then he shall be guilty in ***echad*** of these	
Lev 5:5	And it shall be, when he shall be guilty in ***echad*** of these (things),	
Lev 5:7	unto the LORD, ***echad*** for a sin-offering	
Lev 5:7	and the ***echad-other*** for a burnt-offering.	

Lev 5:13	In this way the priest will make atonement for him for ***echad-any*** of these
*Lev 7:7	As their sin-offering (is), so is the trespass-offering: there is ***echad*** law
Lev 7:14	And of it he shall offer ***echad*** out of the whole oblation
Lev 8:26	he took ***echad*** unleavened cake
Lev 8:26	and ***echad-a*** cake of oiled bread,
Lev 8:26	and ***echad*** wafer, and put (them) on the fat
Lev 12:8	the ***echad*** burnt-offering,
Lev 12:8	and the ***echad-other*** for a sin-offering;
*Lev 13:2	then he shall be brought unto Aaron the priest, or unto ***echad*** of his sons
*Lev 14:5	And the priest shall command that ***echad*** of the birds be killed
Lev 14:10	and ***echad*** ewe lamb of the year without blemish,
Lev 14:10	mingled with oil, and ***echad*** log of oil.
Lev 14:21	then he shall take ***echad*** lamb (for) a trespass-offering to be waved,
Lev 14:21	to make an atonement for him, and ***echad*** tenth deal of fine flour
Lev 14:22	and the ***echad*** shall be a sin-offering
Lev 14:22	and the ***echad-other*** a burnt-offering.
*Lev 14:30	And he shall offer the ***echad*** of the turtledoves,
Lev 14:31	the ***echad*** (for) a sin-offering,
Lev 14:31	and the ***echad-other*** (for) a brunt-offering
Lev 14:50	And he shall kill the ***echad*** of the birds in an earthen vessel
Lev 15:15	the ***echad*** (for) a sin-offering,
Lev 15:15	and the ***echad-other*** (for) a burnt-offering;
Lev 15:30	And the priest shall offer the ***echad*** (for) a sin-offering,
Lev 15:30	and the ***echad-other*** (for) a burnt-offering;
Lev 16:5	two kids of the goats for a sin-offering, and ***echad*** ram for a burnt-offering
Lev 16:8	And Aaron shall cast lots upon the two goats: ***echad*** lot for the LORD,
Lev 16:8	and the ***echad-other*** lot for the scapegoat.
Lev 16:34	make an atonement for the children of Israel for all their sins ***echad*** a year,
Lev 22:28	ye shall not kill it and her young both in ***echad*** day.
Lev 23:18	seven lambs without blemish of the first year, the ***echad*** young bullock,
Lev 23:19	Then ye shall sacrifice ***echad*** kid of the goats for a sin-offering,
Lev 23:24	In the seventh month, in the ***echad*** (day) of the month,
Lev 24:5	two tenth deals shall be in ***echad*** cake.
*Lev 24:22	Ye shall have ***echad*** manner of law, as well for the stranger,
Lev 25:48	After that he is sold he may be redeemed again, ***echad*** of his brethren
Lev 26:26	ten women shall bake your bread in ***echad*** oven,

NUMBERS

Num 1:1	on the ***echad*** (day) of the second month, in the second year
Num 1:18	And they assembled all the congregation together on the ***echad*** (day) of the
Num 1:41	of the tribe of Asher, (were) forty and ***echad*** thousand and five hundred
*Num 1:44	(being) twelve men: each ***echad*** was for the house of his fathers.
Num 2:16	in the camp of Reuben (were) an 100,000 and 50 and ***echad*** thousand and
Num 2:28	and those that were numbered of them, (were) 40 and ***echad*** thousand
Num 6:11	And the priest shall offer the ***echad*** for a sin-offering,
Num 6:11	and the ***echad-other*** for a burnt-offering,
Num 6:14	he shall offer his offering unto the LORD, ***echad*** he lamb of the first year
Num 6:14	without blemish for a burnt-offering, and ***echad*** ewe lamb of the first year
Num 6:14	without blemish for a sin-offering, and ***echad*** ram without blemish
Num 6:19	and ***echad*** unleavened cake out of the basket

234

Num 6:19	and ***echad*** unleavened wafer,
Num 7:3	and twelve oxen; a wagon for two of the princes, and for each ***echad*** an ox:
*Num 7:11	They shall offer their offering, ***echad-each*** prince on this day,
Num 7:13	And his offering (was) ***echad*** silver charger,
Num 7:13	***echad*** silver bowl of seventy shekels,
Num 7:14	***Echad*** spoon of ten (shekels) of gold, full of incense:
Num 7:15	***Echad*** young bullock
Num 7:15	***echad*** ram,
Num 7:15	***echad*** lamb of the first year, for a burnt-offering:
Num 7:16	***Echad*** kid of the goats for a sin-offering:
Num 7:19	He offered (for) his offering ***echad*** silver charger,
Num 7:19	***echad*** silver bowl of seventy shekels, after the shekel of the sanctuary;
Num 7:20	***Echad*** spoon of gold of ten (shekels), full of incense:
Num 7:21	***Echad*** young bullock,
Num 7:21	***echad*** ram,
Num 7:21	***echad*** lamb of the first year, for a burnt-offering:
Num 7:22	***Echad*** kid of the goats for a sin-offering:
Num 7:25	His offering (was) ***echad*** silver charger, the weight whereof
Num 7:25	***Echad*** silver bowl of seventy shekels,
Num 7:26	***Echad*** golden spoon of ten (shekels), full of incense:
Num 7:27	***Echad*** young bullock
Num 7:27	***echad*** ram,
Num 7:27	***echad*** lamb of the first year, for a burnt-offering:
Num 7:28	***Echad*** kid of the goats for a sin-offering:
Num 7:31	His offering (was) ***echad*** silver charger, the weight whereof
Num 7:31	***echad*** silver bowl of seventy shekels, after the shekel of the sanctuary;
Num 7:32	***Echad*** golden spoon of ten (shekels), full of incense:
Num 7:33	***Echad*** young bullock,
Num 7:33	***echad*** ram,
Num 7:33	***echad*** lamb of the first year, for a burnt-offering:
Num 7:34	***Echad*** kid of the goats for a sin-offering:
Num 7:37	His offering (was) ***echad*** silver charger, the weight whereof
Num 7:37	***echad*** silver bowl of seventy shekels,
Num 7:38	***Echad*** golden spoon of ten (shekels), full of incense:
Num 7:39	***Echad*** young bullock
Num 7:39	***echad*** ram,
Num 7:39	***echad*** lamb of the first year, for a burnt-offering:
Num 7:40	***Echad*** kid of the goats for a sin-offering:
Num 7:43	His offering (was) ***echad*** silver charger, the weight whereof
Num 7:43	***echad*** silver bowl of seventy shekels, after the shekel of the sanctuary;
Num 7:44	***Echad*** golden spoon of ten (shekels), full of incense:
Num 7:45	***Echad*** young bullock
Num 7:45	***echad*** ram,
Num 7:45	***echad*** lamb of the first year, for a burnt-offering:
Num 7:46	***Echad*** kid of the goats for a sin-offering:
Num 7:49	His offering (was) ***echad*** silver charger, the weight whereof
Num 7:49	***echad*** silver bowl of seventy shekels, after the shekel of the sanctuary;
Num 7:50	***Echad*** golden spoon of ten (shekels), full of incense:
Num 7:51	***Echad*** young bullock
Num 7:51	***echad*** ram,

Num 7:51	*echad* lamb of the first year, for a burnt-offering:
Num 7:52	*Echad* kid of the goats for a sin-offering:
Num 7:55	His offering (was) *echad* silver charger, the weight whereof
Num 7:55	*echad* silver bowl of seventy shekels, after the shekel of the sanctuary;
Num 7:56	*Echad* golden spoon of ten (shekels), full of incense:
Num 7:57	*Echad* young bullock
Num 7:57	*echad* ram,
Num 7:57	*echad* lamb of the first year, for a burnt-offering:
Num 7:58	*Echad* kid of the goats for a sin-offering:
Num 7:61	His offering (was) *echad* silver charger, the weight whereof
Num 7:61	*echad* silver bowl of seventy shekels, after the shekel of the sanctuary;
Num 7:62	*Echad* golden spoon of ten (shekels), full of incense:
Num 7:63	*Echad* young bullock
Num 7:63	*echad* ram,
Num 7:63	*echad* lamb of the first year, for a burnt-offering:
Num 7:64	*Echad* kid of the goats for a sin-offering:
Num 7:67	His offering (was) *echad* silver charger, the weight whereof
Num 7:67	*echad* silver bowl of seventy shekels, after the shekel of the sanctuary;
Num 7:68	*Echad* golden spoon of ten (shekels), full of incense:
Num 7:69	*Echad* young bullock
Num 7:69	*echad* ram,
Num 7:69	*echad* lamb of the first year, for a burnt-offering:
Num 7:70	*Echad* kid of the goats for a sin-offering:
Num 7:73	His offering (was) *echad* silver charger, the weight whereof
Num 7:73	*echad* silver bowl of seventy shekels, after the shekel of the sanctuary;
Num 7:74	*Echad* golden spoon of ten (shekels), full of incense:
Num 7:75	*Echad* young bullock
Num 7:75	*echad* ram,
Num 7:75	*echad* lamb of the first year, for a burnt-offering:
Num 7:76	*Echad* kid of the goats for a sin-offering:
Num 7:79	His offering (was) *echad* silver charger, the weight whereof
Num 7:79	*echad* silver bowl of seventy shekels, after the shekel of the sanctuary;
Num 7:80	*Echad* golden spoon of ten (shekels), full of incense:
Num 7:81	*Echad* young bullock
Num 7:81	*echad* ram,
Num 7:81	*echad* lamb of the first year, for a burnt-offering:
Num 7:82	*Echad* kid of the goats for a sin-offering:
Num 7:85	His offering (was) *echad* silver charger, the weight whereof
Num 7:85	*echad* silver bowl of seventy shekels, after the shekel of the sanctuary;
Num 8:12	and thou shalt offer the *echad* (for) a sin-offering,
Num 8:12	and the *echad-other* for a burnt-offering, unto the LORD
Num 9:14	ye shall have *echad* ordinance, both for the stranger,
Num 10:4	And if they blow (but) with *echad* (trumpet), then the princes,
Num 11:19	Ye shall not eat *echad* day, nor two days, nor five days, neither ten days,
*Num 11:26	and the name of the *echad* (was) Eldad, and the name of the other Medad:
*Num 13:2	of every tribe of their fathers shall ye send *echad-a* man,
*Num 13:2	every *echad* a ruler among them.
*Num 13:23	and cut down from thence a branch with *echad* cluster of grapes,
Num 14:15	Now (if) thou shalt kill (all) this people as *echad* man,
Num 15:5	with a burnt-offering or sacrifice, for *echad* lamb.

Num 15:11	Thus shall it be done for **echad** bullock,
Num 15:11	or for **echad** ram,
Num 15:11	or for **echad-a** lamb,
Num 15:11	or **echad-a** kid.
Num 15:12	According to the number that ye shall prepare, so shall ye do to every **echad**
Num 15:15	**Echad** ordinance (shall be both) for you of the congregation,
*Num 15:16	**Echad** law and echad manner shall be for you,
*Num 15:16	**Echad** law and *echad* manner shall be for you,
Num 15:24	that all the congregation shall offer **echad** bullock for a burnt-offering,
Num 15:24	according to the manner, and **echad** kid of the goats for a sin-offering.
Num 15:27	And if **echad-any** soul sin through ignorance,
Num 15:29	Ye shall have **echad** law for him that sinneth through ignorance,
Num 16:15	I have not taken **echad** ass from them, neither have I hurt echad of them.
Num 16:15	I have not taken echad ass from them, neither have I hurt **echad** of them.
Num 16:22	O God, the God of the spirits of all flesh, shall **echad** man sin,
Num 17:3	for **echad** rod (shall be) for the head of the house of their fathers.
*Num 17:6	and every **echad** of their princes gave him a rod apiece,
*Num 17:6	each prince **echad**, according to their fathers' houses, (even) twelve rods:
Num 28:4	the **echad** lamb shalt thou offer in the morning
Num 28:7	drink-offering thereof (shall be) the fourth (part) of an hin for the **echad** lamb
Num 28:11	two young bullocks, and **echad** ram, seven lambs of the first year without
Num 28:12	mingled with oil, the **echad** bullock;
Num 28:12	mingled with oil, for **echad** ram;
Num 28:13	flour mingled with oil (for) a meat-offering unto **echad** lamb;
Num 28:15	And **echad** kid of the goats for a sin-offering unto the LORD shall be offered,
Num 28:19	two bullocks, and **echad** ram, and seven lambs of the first year:
Num 28:21	A several tenth deal shalt thou offer for **echad-every** lamb,
Num 28:22	and **echad** goat (for) a sin-offering, to make an atonement for you.
Num 28:27	two young bullocks, **echad** ram, seven lambs of the first year;
Num 28:28	three tenth deals unto **echad** bullock, two tenth deals unto echad ram,
Num 28:28	three tenth deals unto echad bullock, two tenth deals unto **echad** ram,
Num 28:29	A several tenth deal unto **echad** lamb, throughout the seven lambs;
Num 28:30	(And) **echad** kid of the goats, to make an atonement for you.
Num 29:1	And in the seventh month, on the **echad-first** (day) of the month,
Num 29:2	**echad** young bullock, echad ram, (and) seven lambs of the first year
Num 29:2	**echad** young bullock, *echad* ram, (and) seven lambs of the first year
Num 29:4	And **echad** tenth deal for echad lamb, throughout the seven lambs;
Num 29:4	And echad tenth deal for **echad** lamb, throughout the seven lambs;
Num 29:5	And **echad** kid of the goats (for) a sin-offering, to make an atonement for
Num 29:8	**echad** young bullock, echad ram, (and) seven lambs of the first year
Num 29:8	echad young bullock, **echad** ram, (and) seven lambs of the first year
Num 29:9	three tenth deals unto **echad** bullock, two tenth deals unto echad ram,
Num 29:9	three tenth deals unto echad bullock, two tenth deals unto **echad** ram,
Num 29:10	three tenth deals unto echad bullock, two tenth deals unto **echad** ram,
Num 29:11	**Echad** kid of the goats for a sin-offering:
Num 29:14	three tenth deals unto **echad-every** bullock of the thirteen bullocks,
Num 29:14	two tenth deals to **echad-each** ram of the two rams.
Num 29:15	And a several tenth to **echad-each** lamb of the fourteen lambs:
Num 29:16	And **echad** kid of the goats (for) a sin-offering,
Num 29:19	And **echad** kid of the goats (for) a sin-offering;

Num 29:22	And *echad* goat (for) a sin-offering, beside the continual burnt-offering,	
Num 29:25	And *echad* kid of the goats (for) a sin-offering, beside the continual	
Num 29:28	And *echad* goat (for) a sin-offering, beside the continual burnt-offering,	
Num 29:31	And *echad* goat (for) a sin-offering, beside the continual burnt-offering,	
Num 29:34	And *echad* goat (for) a sin-offering, beside the continual burnt-offering,	
Num 29:36	*echad* bullock, echad ram, seven lambs of the first year without blemish:	
Num 29:36	echad bullock, *echad* ram, seven lambs of the first year without blemish:	
Num 29:38	And *echad* goat (for) a sin-offering, beside the continual burnt-offering,	
Num 31:28	*echad* soul of five hundred, (both) of the persons, and of the beeves,	
Num 31:30	thou shalt take *echad* portion of fifty, of the persons, of the beeves,	
Num 31:47	Moses took *echad* portion of fifty, (both) of man and of beast,	
Num 33:38	in the *echad-first* (day) of the fifth month.	
*Num 34:18	ye shall take *echad* prince of every tribe, to divide the land by inheritance.	
*Num 34:18	Any ye shall take echad prince of *echad-every* tribe, to divide the land by	
Num 35:30	but *echad* witness shall not testify against any person (to cause him) to die.	
Num 36:3	And if they be married to any of the sons of the *echad* tribes of the children	
Num 36:8	shall be wife unto *echad* of the family of the tribe of her father,	

DEUTERONOMY

Deut 1:3	in the fortieth year, in the eleventh month, on the *echad-first* (day) of the	
*Deut 1:23	and I took twelve men of you *echad* of a tribe:	
Deut 4:42	and that fleeing unto *echad* of these cities he might live:	
Deut 6:4	Hear, O Israel: the LORD our God (is) *echad* LORD.	
*Deut 12:14	But in the place which the LORD shall choose in *echad* of thy tribes,	
*Deut 13:12	If thou shalt hear (say) in *echad* of thy cities,	
Deut 15:7	If there be among you a poor man of *echad* of thy brethren	
Deut 15:7	within *echad-any* of they gates in thy land,	
Deut 16:5	Thou mayest not sacrifice the passover with *echad-any* of thy gates,	
Deut 17:2	If there be found among you, within *echad-any* of thy gates	
Deut 17:6	(but) at the mouth of *echad* witness he shall not be put to death.	
*Deut 18:6	And if a Levite come from *echad-any* of thy gates out of all Israel,	
Deut 19:11	and smite him mortally that he die, and fleeth into *echad* of these cities:	
Deut 19:15	*Echad* witness shall not rise up again a man for any iniquity,	
Deut 21:15	If a man have two wives, *echad* beloved,	
Deut 21:15	and *echad-another* hated, and they have born him children,	
Deut 23:16	(even) among you, in that place which he shall choose in *echad* of thy gates,	
Deut 24:5	(but) he shall be free at home *echad* year, and shall cheer up his wife	
Deut 25:5	If brethren dwell together, and *echad* of them die, and have no child,	
Deut 25:11	men strive together one with another, and the wife of the *echad* draweth	
Deut 28:7	they shall come out against thee *echad* way, and flee before thee seven	
Deut 28:25	thou shalt go out *echad* way against them, and flee seven ways before	
Deut 28:55	So that he will not give to *echad-any* of them of the flesh of his children	
Deut 32:30	How should *echad* chase a thousand, and two put ten thousand to flight,	

Totals for individual columns: 34   172   176

Grand total of *echad* references in the Five Books of Moses: 382

Appendix 3

The Word:
Verbal Plenary Inspiration

The subject of Verbal Plenary Inspiration could easily fill a book; however, here in this context only one aspect will be viewed in relation to the spoken or written word of God. Chapter six (pp. 201, 207) defines Inspiration as well as the terms "verbal" and "plenary" so there is no need to address it again here. This is a challenge to both Christian and Jewish adherents to take another look at the doctrine of Inspiration.

The two purposes of this appendix are to draw attention to the Hebrew word(s) for the expression "the word of the Lord," or similar expressions like "it is written," that deal with the words of God that were given by God to the human authors and written in the Hebrew Scriptures. These two purposes are to draw the attention of Christians to how they interpret the word of God and to Jewish people concerning the Written Law versus the Oral Law.

The first purpose is to express the dire need in the 21st century for pastors and teachers to re-examine the doctrine of Inspiration as it is being presented in the church today. The believing church is quickly losing its biblical bearings as liberal scholars (higher criticism) have infected evangelical authors and translators who, as a result, are chipping away at this doctrine. They are aggressively flooding the "Christian" market place with books that reinterpret what God says into what they think God meant, or else they are giving the dynamitic equivalent to the words in the Bible (NIV, Living Bible, Good News, TNIV etc.) that God Himself inspired.

During a conversation with my writing coach[862] I discovered that the humanistic secular academic approach to all writings -- including Scripture -- is not the same today, in the postmodern world, as it was in previous years. She explained the new perspective: "the meaning lies – not in the text – but in the interpretation of the text." Fundamental Bible believers bristle at that statement because it undercuts their firmly held belief in verbal plenary inspiration of Scripture. The core of that postmodern perspective is a frontal attack on the very words that God used. Their implication is that all literature -- including the Scriptures -- is to be given over to the fallible mind of the humanistic secular person who wants to interpret all literature – including the Scriptures – the same way. Many contemporary evangelical authors have adopted that view in relation to Scripture, even though they claim a belief in the Inspiration of Scripture.

Robert Wilkin expresses deep concern that some evangelicals are broadening their view of Inspiration:

---

[862] In a private conversation with Dr. Elaine Huber

He [Wallace of Dallas Theological Seminary] suggested that the authors of the NT did not approach the reporting of history in the same way that current historians do. In order to interpret the NT correctly, we must be aware of this different approach. Practically speaking this brings into question the NT author's concern about historical accuracy in terms of the speaker, the location, the date, and the precise content of what was said.[863]

As Wilkin later points out that it is ludicrous to claim that the New Testament can contain historical inaccuracies and still be God-breathed, without error. God, who is the author, used words, precise words, to express His nature and His person to mankind. It is troubling to see evangelical authors saying and implying that the Scriptures can't be trusted with the facts in history and science. History has demonstrated that it is finite man who cannot be trusted, when he moves away from what God said to reinterpret what God said.

In the process evangelicals move believers away from "Thus saith the LORD" as the absolute final authority of Scripture. In their attempt to make the Scripture more readable to people, scholars have sacrificed one of the foundational doctrines of Scripture -- Inspiration. Unfortunately, 21st century evangelicals have taken it upon themselves to correct God's Word into what they think God meant. That is ludicrous -- that an unreliable, fallible man, a creature made by infallible God, would take it upon himself to correct the Creator and Author of His own word.

The second purpose is to invite Rabbis and Jewish people at large to reinvestigate the claims of *Hashem* that the words that He inspired, which He gave to Moses and the prophets were all written down. His word is supreme, not the writings of fallible men in their interpretations of the *Tanakh* in Talmud and other rabbinic commentaries. This next statement may be viewed as a harsh statement, but it is meant to be taken in love and to be thought through logically within the context of this book. Rabbinic Judaism has been the instrument to cause Jewish people to prostrate themselves before an idol, the god of the Oral Law, the one and only authoritative pillar of Rabbinic Judaism. Included in that call to investigate is the movement within Jewish believers of Messiah to lift up rabbinic practices and teaching in order to be more Jewish. The Hebrew Scriptures lifts up the Word of the LORD as being final to any opinion, theory or teaching of men. Nowhere in the Hebrew Scriptures did God even hint at another law, the Oral Law, running parallel to the Written Law. Where does God tell Jewish believers in Messiah to go back to rabbinic practices to be more Jewish? Jewish believers should be encouraged to read San Telchin's book, *Messianic Judaism IS NOT Christianity*. Judaism before the time of the destruction of Jerusalem and the Temple prefabricated the myth that *Hashem* gave two laws to Moses, the written and oral law. Nowhere in the writings of Moses or the prophets is there even a shred of evidence that *Hashem* did such a thing. The only possible reference to oral law in the Hebrew Scriptures is when the written law was read orally as Ezra did to the people (Neh 8:1-8).

---

[863] Robert N. Wilkin, "Toward a Narrow View of Ipsissima Vox," *JOTGES* 14, no. 26 (Spring 2001), 3-8.

Let this be a challenge to any Jewish rabbi or Jewish person to investigate for themselves the claims that *Hashem* makes concerning His own word. Your eternal destiny hinges on what *Hashem* said versus what the rabbi said that *Hashem* said. The two are different and even contradictory. Stop accepting the words of the rabbis blindly. You are the most intelligent, blessed people of the world, which is a by-product of the Abrahamic Covenant. Investigate *Hashem*'s word for yourself with the minds that *Hashem* gave you and open your minds and hearts to what *Hashem* said in His word.

Moses, the prophets and other unknown writers of the *Tanakh* used several words to express the concept of words and writing:

אָמֶר	emer (50)	words[864]
אִמְרָה	imra (36)	word, words, utterance[865]
דָבַר	dabar – v (1140)	said, speak, spoken, spoke, speaking, tell[866]
דָבָר	dabar – nm (1455)	word, words[867]
כָּתַב	katab – v (223)	written, write, wrote[868]
מִכְתָּב	miktab – nm (9)	writing[869]
פֶה	peh – nm (498)	mouth[870]

These Hebrew words which are generally translated as indicated in English word(s) refer to "words" that were spoken by *Hashem* directly or by *Hashem* through a human agent and "written down" by those human agents. These Hebrew words also refer to "words" spoken between mankind as well as directed from man to *Hashem*. "Writing" refers to several things: (1) "writing down" the very "words" that *Hashem* wanted in a book or scroll by the human agent, or whether *Hashem* to man, man to man, or man to *Hashem*, (2) *Hashem* personally has used "writing" as he wrote down the Ten Commandments with His finger, and (3) the word "mouth" refers to the "words" that come from the mouth, where they are formed and spoken. What is to be observed is that *Hashem* used "words" and "wrote down" the "words." *Hashem* did not give divine thoughts and leave it to the human agent to decide how to say or write His word. G-d the *Ruah HaKodesh* (Holy Spirit) so guided the authors of the "words" in such a way that *Hashem*'s "words" were spoken or "written down" without violating the personality and style of that particular human agent. If there is a conflict with some of the words that *Hashem* used, it is our lack of understanding, not *Hashem*'s inability to convey His word to us.

---

[864] Botterweck, Ringgren and Fabry. *Theological Dictionary of the Old Testament*, 1:343.
[865] Harris, Archer, and Waltke, Theological *Wordbook of the Old Testament*, 1:55.
[866] VanGemeren, *Dictionary of Old Testament Theology & Exegesis*, 1:912.
[867] VanGemeren, *Dictionary of Old Testament Theology & Exegesis*, 1:913.
[868] Botterweck, Ringgren and Fabry. *Theological Dictionary of the Old Testament*, 7:373.
[869] Harris, Archer, and Waltke, *Theological Wordbook of the Old Testament*, 1:458.
[870] Harris, Archer, and Waltke, *Theological Wordbook of the Old Testament*, 2:718.

Below is a chart with references concerning the "word," "words" or all the words "written" by G-d or *Hashem*. In the first column is a Scriptural reference and in the second column is an actual quote. This is not a complete list, but a sampling from the Hebrew Scriptures. The list is intended to demonstrate that words used of God or man mean just that, God used words to express Himself to his people. Words make up phrases and sentences to express what God wants the reader to understand. Words that *Hashem* used points out strongly that His words were *written down*. In fact Moses is very clear that he wrote down *all* the words of *Hashem*. The Scriptures are the verbal plenary inspired word of God, and man should not be tampering with, or altering His word, to suit their personal bias or to meet "Christian" marketing needs.

"The Word:" Verbal Plenary Inspiration

Genesis

Reference				
Gen 15:1	After these things the **word** of the LORD came unto Abram in a vision,	dabar		
Gen 15:4	And, behold, the **word** of the LORD came unto him, saying	dabar		

Exodus

Reference				
Exod 17:14	And the LORD said unto Moses, **Write** this for a memorial in a book,		katab	
Exod 19:6	These are the **words** which thou shalt speak unto the children of	dabar		
Exod 19:7	and laid before their faces all these **words** which the LORD commanded him.	dabar		
Exod 19:8	All that the LORD hath spoken we will do. And Moses returned the **words** of the people	dabar		
Exod 20:1	And God spake all these **words,** saying	dabar		
Exod 24:3	And Moses came and told the people **all the words** of the LORD . . . and said **all the words** which the LORD hath said will we do.	dabar		
Exod 24:4	And Moses **wrote all the words** of the LORD	dabar	katab	
Exod 24:8	behold the blood of the covenant, which the LORD hath made with you concerning **all the words**	dabar		
Exod 31:18	two tables of testimony, tables of stone, **written** with the finger of God	katab	katab	
Exod 32:16	tables were the work of God, and the **writing** was the **writing** of God,			miktab
Exod 33:4	And when the people heard these evil **tidings-words,**	dabar		
Exod 34:1	Hew thee two tables of stone like unto the first: and I will **write** upon these tables the **words** that were that were in the first tables	dabar	katab	
Exod 34:27	And the LORD said unto Moses, **Write** thou these **words:** for after the tenor of these words I have made a covenant with thee and with Israel	dabar	katab	
Exod 34:28	And he **wrote** upon the tables the **words** of the covenant, the ten commandments	dabar	katab	
Exod 35:1	These are the **words** which the LORD hath commanded,	dabar		
Exod 39:30	And they made the plate of the holy crown of pure gold, and **wrote** upon it a **writing,**		katab	miktab

Numbers

Reference				
Num 3:16	And Moses numbered them according to the **word** of the Lord,			peh
Num 3:51	according to the **word** of the LORD, as the LORD commanded			peh
Num 5:23	And the priest shall **write** these curses in a book,		katab	
Num 12:6	Hear now my **words:** If there be a prophet among you, I the LORD	dabar		
Num 15:31	Because he hath despised the **word** of the LORD, and hath broken his commandments	dabar		
Num 24:4	He hath said, which heard the **words** of God,			emer
Num 24:16	He hath said, which heard the **words** of God, and knew the knowledge of the most High,			emer
Num 33:2	And Moses **wrote** their goings out according to their journeys			peh

Deuteronomy

Reference				
Deut 1:1	These be the **words** which Moss spake unto all Israel on this side	dabar		
Deut 4:10	and I will make them hear my **words**, that they may learn to fear	dabar		
Deut 4:13	ten commandments and he **wrote** them upon two tables of stone		katab	
Deut 4:36	Out of heaven he made thee to hear his voice, . . . and thou heardest his **words** out of the midst of the fire	dabar		
Deut 5:5	I stood between the LORD and you at that time, to shew you the **word** of the LORD	dabar		

Deut 5:22	These **words** the LORD spake unto all the assembly in the mount out of the midst of the fire, of the cloud, and of the thick darkness, with a great voice and he added no more, and he **wrote** them in two tables of stone and delivered them unto me.	dabar	katab		
Deut 8:3	but by every **word** that preceedeth out of the **mouth** of the LORD doth man live.			peh	
Deut 9:23	then ye rebelled against the **commandment** of the LORD your God			peh	
Deut 10:4	And he **wrote** on the tables, according to the first **writing,** the ten commandments,		katab		miktab
Deut 11:18	Therefore shall ye lay up these my **words** in your heart and in your soul, and bind them for a sign upon your hand,	dabar			
Deut 11:20	And thou shalt **write** them upon the door posts of thine house,		katab		
Deut 17:18	And it shall be, when he sitteth upon the throne of his kingdom, that he shall **write** him a copy of this law in a book		katab		
Deut 17:19	that he may learn to fear the LORD his God, to keep all the **words** of this law and these statutes, to do them.	dabar			
Deut 18:18	and I will put my **words** in his **mouth** and he shall speak unto them	dabar		peh	
Deut 18:19	And it shall come to pass, that whosoever will not hearken unto my **words** which he shall speak in my name, I will require it of him.	dabar			
Deut 24:1	then let him **write** her a bill of divorcement,		katab		
Deut 24:3	if the latter husband hate her, and **write** her a bill of divorcement,		katab		
Deut 27:3	And thou shalt **write** upon them all the **words** of this law,	dabar	katab		
Deut 27:8	shalt **write** upon the stones all the **words** of this law very plainly.	dabar	katab		
Deut 27:26	Cursed be he that confirmeth not all the **words** of this law	dabar			
Deut 28:58	If thou wilt not observe to do **all the words** of this law that are **written** in this book	dabar	katab		
Deut 28:61	Also every sickness, and every plague, which is not **written** in the book of this law,		katab		
Deut 29:20	and all the curses that are **written** in this book shall lie upon him,		katab		
Deut 29:21	according to all the curses of the covenant that are **written** in this book of the law		katab		
Deut 29:27	to bring upon it all the curses that are **written** in this book		katab		
Deut 29:29	that we may do **all the words** of this law.	dabar			
Deut 30:10	to keep his commandments and his statutes which are **written** in this book of the law and his statutes which are written in this book		katab		
Deut 31:1	And Moses went and spake these **words** unto all Israel	dabar			
Deut 31:9	And Moses **wrote** this law, and delivered it unto the priests		katab		
Deut 31:12	that they may hear, and that they may learn, and fear the LORD your God, and observe to do **all the words** of this law.	dabar			
Deut 31:19	Now therefore **write** ye this song for you and teach it		katab		
Deut 31:22	Moses therefore **wrote** this song the same day, and taught it the children of Israel.		katab		
Deut 31:24	when Moses had made an end of **writing** the **words** of this law in a book, until they were finished	dabar	katab		
Deut 31:28	that I may speak these **words** in their ears, and call heaven and earth to record against them.	dabar			
Deut 31:30	And Moses spake in the ears of all the congregation of Israel the **words** of this song	dabar			
Deut 32:1	Give ear, O ye heavens, and I will **speak;** and hear, O earth, the **words** of my **mouth**	dabar	Emer	peh	
Deut 32:46	And he said unto them, Set your hearts unto all the **words** which I testify among you this day, which ye shall command your children to observe to do, all the **words** of this law.	dabar			

Joshua

Josh 1:8	This **book of the law** shall not depart out of thy **mouth,** . . . that thou mayest observe to do according to all that is **written** therein		katab	peh
Josh 1:13	Remember the **word** which Moses the servant of the LORD	dabar		
Josh 1:18	Whosoever he be that doth rebel against thy **commandment,** and will not hearken unto thy **words** in all that thou commandest him,	dabar		peh
Josh 3:9	And Joshua said unto the children of Israel, Come hither, and hear the **words** of the LORD your God.	dabar		
Josh 6:10	Ye shall not shout, nor make any noise with your voice, neither shall any **word** proceed	dabar		
Josh 8:31	As Moses the servant of the LORD commanded the children of Israel, as it is **written** in **the book of the law** of Moses,		katab	
Josh 8:32	And he **wrote** there upon the stone a copy of the law of Moses, which he **wrote** in the presence of the children of Israel.		katab	
Josh 8:34	And afterward he read all the **words** of the law, the blessings and cursings, according to all that is **written in the book of the law**	dabar	katab	
Josh 8:35	There was not a **word** of all that Moses commanded, which Joshua read not before all the congregation of Israel,	dabar		
Josh 10:13	Is not this **written** in the book of Jasher		katab	
Josh 18:4	and they shall rise, and go through the land, and **describe-write** it according to the		katab	
Josh 18:6	Ye shall therefore **describe-written** the land into seven parts saying go and walk through the land, and **describe-write** it and come again		katab	
Josh 18:9	And the men went and passed through the land, and **described-wrote** it by cities into seven parts in a book		katab	
Josh 23:6	Be ye therefore very courageous to keep and to do all that is **written in the book of the law** of Moses		katab	
Josh 24:26	And Joshua **wrote** these **words** in **the book of the law** of God,	dabar	katab	
Josh 24:27	for it hath heard all the **words** of the LORD which he spake unto us:			emer

Judges

Judg 11:11	and Jephthah uttered al his **words** before the LORD in Mizpeh	dabar

1 Samuel

1 Sam 3:1	And the **word** of the LORD was precious in those days;	dabar	
1 Sam 3:7	neither was the **word** of the LORD yet revealed unto him.	dabar	
1 Sam 10:25	Then Samuel told the people the manner of the kingdom, and **wrote** it in a book,		katab
1 Sam 15:10	Then came the **word** of the LORD unto Samuel, saying	dabar	
1 Sam 15:23	Because thou hast rejected the **word** of the LORD, he hath also rejected thee	dabar	

2 Samuel

2 Sam 1:18	behold, it is **written** in the book of Jasher		katab
2 Sam 7:4	that the **word** of the LORD came unto Nathan,	dabar	
2 Sam 7:17	According to all these **words,** and according to all this vision,	dabar	
2 Sam 11:14	And it came to pass in the morning that David **wrote** a letter to Joab,		katab
2 Sam 11:15	And he **wrote** in the letter, saying, Set ye Uriah in the forefront of the hottest battle,		katab
2 Sam 12:9	Wherefore hast thou despised the **commandment-word** of the LORD	dabar	
2 Sam 22:31	As for God, his way is perfect; the **word** of the LORD is tried: he is a buckler to all them		imra

2 Sam 24:11	when David was up in the morning, the **word** of the LORD came unto the prophet Gad	dabar	

1 Kings

1 Kgs 2:3	And keep the charge of the LORD thy God . . . as it is **written** in the law of Moses,		katab
1 Kgs 6:11	And the **word** of the LORD came to Solomon, saying	dabar	
1 Kgs 11:41	his wisdom, are they not **written** in the book of the acts of Solomon.		katab
1 Kgs 12:22	But the **word** of God came unto Shemaiah the man of God, saying,	dabar	
1 Kgs 13:1	there came a man of God out of Judah by the **word** of the LORD	dabar	
1 Kgs 13:2	And he cried against the altar in the **word** of the LORD	dabar	
1 Kgs 13:5	the sign which the man of God had given by the **word** of the LORD	dabar	
1 Kgs 13:9	For so was it charged me by the **word** of the LORD, saying	dabar	
1 Kgs 13:17	For it was said to me by the **word** of the LORD	dabar	
1 Kgs 13:20	as they sat at the table, that the **word** of the LORD came unto	dabar	
1 Kgs 13:26	the man of God, who was disobedient unto the **word** of the LORD:		peh
1 Kgs 13:32	For the saying which he cried by the **word** of the LORD against the altar in Beth-el	dabar	
1 Kgs 14:19	behold, they are **written** in the book of the chronicles of the kings		katab
1 Kgs 14:29	are they not **written** in the book of the chronicles of the kings of		katab
1 Kgs 15:29	according unto the **saying-word** of the LORD	dabar	
1 Kgs 16:1	Then the **word** of the LORD came to Jehu the son of Hanani	dabar	
1 Kgs 16:34	according to the **word** of the LORD, which he spake by Joshua	dabar	
1 Kgs 17:2	And the **word** of the LORD came unto him (Elijah), saying	dabar	
1 Kgs 18:1	that the **word** of the LORD came to Elijah	dabar	
1 Kgs 22:19	and he said (Micaiah), Hear thou therefore the **word** of the LORD	dabar	

2 Kings

2 Kgs 15:12	This was the **word** of the LORD which he spake unto Jehu	dabar	
2 Kgs 22:11	when the king had heard the **words** of the book of the law, concerning the **words** of this book that is found: . . . because our fathers have not hearkened unto the **words** of this book to do	dabar	
2 Kgs 22:13	according unto all that which is **written** concerning us.	dabar	katab
2 Kgs 22:16	even all the **words** of the book which the king of Judah hath read:	dabar	
2 Kgs 22:18	As touching the **words** which thou hast heard:	dabar	
2 Kgs 23:2	and he read in their ears all the **words** of the book of the covenant which was found in the house of the LORD	dabar	
2 Kgs 23:16	and polluted it, according to the **word** of the LORD which the man of God proclaimed, who proclaimed these **words**.	dabar	
2 Kgs 24:2	according to the **word** of the LORD, which he spake by his servant the prophets	dabar	

1 Chronicles

1 Chr 10:13	even against the **word** of the LORD, which he kept not,	dabar	
1 Chr 15:15	as Moses commanded according to the **word** of the LORD.	dabar	
1 Chr 16:15	Be ye mindful always of his covenant; the **word** which he commanded to a	dabar	
1 Chr 16:40	and to do according to all that is **written** in the law of the LORD, which he commanded		katab
1 Chr 17:3	that the **word** of God came to Nathan, saying	dabar	

2 Chronicles

2 Chr 6:17	Now then, O LORD God of Israel, let thy **word** be verified, which thou hast spoken	dabar		
2 Chr 10:15	for the cause was of God, that the LORD might perform his **word**, which he spake by the hand of Ahigah	dabar		
2 Chr 11:2	But the **word** of the LORD came to Shemaiah the man of God,	dabar		
2 Chr 11:4	And they obeyed the **words** of the LORD, and returned from going	dabar		
2 Chr 12:7	And when the LORD saw that they humbled themselves, the **word** of the Lord	dabar		
2 Chr 21:12	And there came a **writing** to him from Elijah the prophet,			miktab
2 Chr 23:18	as it is **written** in the law of Moses, with rejoicing and with singing,		katab	
2 Chr 25:4	But he slew not their children, but did as it is **written** in the law in the book of Moses		katab	
2 Chr 29:15	according to the commandment of the king, by the **words** of the LORD, to cleanse	dabar		
2 Chr 30:12	one heart to do the commandment of the king . . the princes by the **word** of the LORD	dabar		
2 Chr 31:3	as it is **written** in the law of the LORD		katab	
2 Chr 33:18	and the **words** of the seers that spake to him in the name of the LORD God of Israel behold, they are **written** in the book of the kings	dabar	katab	
2 Chr 34:19	when the king had heard the **words** of the law, that he rent his	dabar		
2 Chr 34:21	concerning the **words** of the book that is found . . . Because our fathers have not kept the **word** of the LORD, to do after all that is **written** in this book.	dabar	katab	
2 Chr 34:26	Thus saith the LORD God of Israel concerning the **words** which thou hast heard	dabar		
2 Chr 34:30	and he read in the ears all the **words** of the book of the covenant that was found in the	dabar		
2 Chr 34:31	to perform the **words** of the covenant which are **written** in this book.	dabar	katab	
2 Chr 35:4	according to the **writing** of David king of Israel, and according to the **writing** of Solomon		katab	miktab
2 Chr 35:12	to offer unto the LORD, as it is **written** in the book of Moses.		katab	
2 Chr 35:26	according to that which was **written** in the law of the LORD		katab	
2 Chr 36:16	But they mocked the messengers of God, and despised his **words**,	dabar		
2 Chr 36:21	To fulfill the **word** of the LORD by the **mouth** of Jeremiah,	dabar		peh
2 Chr 36:22	that the **word** of the LORD spoken by the **mouth** of Jeremiah might be accomplished, . . . the spirit of Cyrus king of Persia, that he made a proclamation throughout all his kingdom, and put it also in **writing**,	dabar	Peh	miktab

Ezra

Ezra 1:1	the fist year of Cyrus king of Persia, that the **word** of the LORD by the **mouth** of Jeremiah might be fulfilled, and put it also in **writing**,	dabar	peh	miktab
Ezra 3:2	as it is **written** in the law of Moses the man of God		katab	
Ezra 3:4	They kept also the feast of Tabernacles, as it is **written,**		katab	
Ezra 9:4	Then were assembled unto me every one that trembled at the **words** of the God of Israel	dabar		

Nehemiah

Neh 8:9	For all the people wept, when they heard the **words** of the law.	dabar	
Neh 8:12	because they had understood the **words** that were declared unto	dabar	
Neh 8:13	unto Ezra the scribe, even to understand the **words** of the law.	dabar	
Neh 8:14	And they found **written** in the law which the LORD had commanded		katab

Neh 10:34	to burn the altar of the LORD our God, as it is **written** in the law			katab	
Neh 10:36	the firstborn of our sons, and of our cattle, as it is **written** in the law,			katab	

Psalms

Psa 12:6	The **words** of the LORD are pure **words:** as silver tried in a furnace				imra
Psa 19:14	Let the **words** of my **mouth,** and the meditation of my heart,		emer	peh	
Psa 33:4	For the **word** of the LORD is right and all his works are done in truth.	dabar			
Psa 33:6	By the **word** of the LORD were the heaven made;	dabar			
Psa 107:11	Because they rebelled against the **words** of God,				emer
Psa 119:9	by taking heed thereto according to thy **word.**	dabar			
Psa 119:13	With my lips have I declared all the judgments of thy **mouth.**			peh	

Isaiah

Isa 1:1	Hear the **word** of the LORD, ye rulers of Sodom;	dabar			
Isa 1:20	devoured with the sword: for the **mouth** of the LORD hath spoken it.			peh	
Isa 2:3	and the **word** of the LORD from Jerusalem.	dabar			
Isa 5:24	and despised the **word** of the Holy One of Israel.				imra
Isa 8:1	Take thee a great roll, and **write** in it with a man's pen			katab	
Isa 30:8	Now go, **write** it before them in a table, and note it in a book,			katab	
Isa 38:4	Then the **word** of the LORD came to Isaiah:	dabar			
Isa 38:9	The **writing** of Hezekiah king of Judah, when he had been sick,				miktab
Isa 41:26	there is none that declareth, . . . that heareth your **words.**				emer
Isa 58:14	for the **mouth** of the LORD hath spoken it.			peh	
Isa 66:5	Hear the **word** of the LORD, ye that tremble at his **word;**	dabar			

Jeremiah

Jer 1:2	To whom the **word** of the LORD came in the days of Josiah	dabar			
Jer 1:9	the LORD said unto me, Behold, I have put my **words** in thy **mouth.**	dabar		peh	
Jer 2:1	Moreover the **word** of the LORD came to me, saying,	dabar			
Jer 6:10	behold, the **word** of the LORD is unto them a reproach;	dabar			
Jer 21:1	The **word** which came unto Jeremiah from the LORD,	dabar			
Jer 30:2	Thus speaketh the LORD God of Israel saying, **Write** thee all the **words** that I have spoken unto thee in a book	dabar	katab		
Jer 31:33	I will put my law in their inward parts, and **write** it in their hearts,		katab		
Jer 36:2	Take thee a roll of a book, and **write** therein all the **words** that I	dabar	katab		
Jer 36:4	Baruch **wrote** from the mouth of Jeremiah all the **words** of the LORD	dabar	katab		
Jer 36:6	Therefore go thou, and read in the roll, which thou hast **written** from my mouth, the **words** of the LORD in the ears of the people	dabar	Katab		
Jer 36:16	when they had heard all the **words,** they were afraid both one and other, and said . . . , We will surely tell the king of all these **words**.	dabar			
Jer 36:17	Tell us now, How didst thou **write** all these **words** at his mouth?	dabar	katab		
Jer 36:18	He pronounced all these **words** unto me with his mouth and I **wrote** them with ink	dabar	katab		
Jer 36:27	and the **words** which Baruch **wrote** at the mouth of Jeremiah,	dabar	katab		
Jer 45:1	The **word** that Jeremiah the prophet spake unto Baruch the son of Neriah, when he had **written** these **words** in a book	dabar	katab		

Lamentations

Lam 2:17	he hath fulfilled his **word** that he had commanded in the days of old:				imra
Lam 3:38	Out of the **mouth** of the most High proceedeth not evil and good?			peh	

Ezekiel

Ezek 1:3	The **word** of the LORD came expressly unto Ezekiel the priest,	dabar	
	And he spread it before me; and it was **written** within and without;		
Ezek 2:10	all my **words** that I shall speak unto thee receive in thine heart,	dabar	katab
Ezek 6:1	And the **word** of the LORD came unto me, saying	dabar	
Ezek 7:1	Moreover the **word** of the LORD came unto me, saying,	dabar	
Ezek 12:1	The **word** of the LORD also came unto me, saying	dabar	
Ezek 37:4	and say unto them, O ye dry bones, hear the **word** of the LORD	dabar	
Ezek 38:1	And the **word** of the LORD came unto me, saying,	dabar	

Daniel

Dan 9:2	whereof the **word** of the LORD came to Jeremiah the prophet,	dabar	
Dan 9:11	and the oath that is **written** in the law of Moses the servant of God		katab
Dan 9:13	As it **written** in the law of Moses,		katab

Hosea

Hos 1:1	The **word** of the LORD that came unto Hosea, the son of Beeri,	dabar	
Hos 6:5	I have slain them by the **words** of my **mouth:**	emer peh	

Joel

Joel 1:1	The **word** of the LORD that came to Joel the son of Pethuel.	dabar

Amos

Amos 3:1	Hear this **word** that the LORD hath spoken again you, O Children of	dabar

Jonah

Jonah 1:1	Now the **word** of the LORD came unto Jonah the son of Amittai,	dabar

Micah

Micah 1:1	The **word** of the LORD that came to Micah the Morasthite	dabar
Micah 4:4	for the mouth of the LORD of hosts hath **spoken** it.	peh

Zephaniah

Zeph 1:1	The **word** of the LORD which came unto Zephaniah the son	dabar

Haggai

Hag 1:1	came the **word** of the LORD by Haggai the prophet unto	dabar

Zechariah

Zech 1:1	second year of Darius, came the **word** of the LORD unto Zechariah,	dabar
Zech 8:18	And the **word** of the LORD of hosts came unto me, saying	dabar
Zech 12:1	The burden of the **word** of the LORD for Israel, saith the LORD,	dabar

Malachi

Mal 1:1	The burden of the **word** of the LORD to Israel by Malachi	dabar

Appendix 4

The Drift Away From the Bible
By Arthur W. Kac
From His book
The Spiritual Dilemma of the Jewish People

1. Works Versus Faith

The cessation of the sacrificial worship in the first century disrupted the divinely instituted approach to God. The Jewish followers of Jesus saw in this event indirect proof that the atoning death of the Messiah had made the continuation of the Old Testament sacrificial cult unnecessary. Having said no to the messianic claims of Jesus, Jewish religious leadership was hard put to find a theological explanation for the events of A.D. 70. The chief sin which brought about the destruction of the first Temple was idolatry. But there was no idolatry in the days of the second Temple. There is a passage in the Talmud which states that it was the sin of "hatred without a cause" which led to the destruction of the second Temple, because - it is explained – the sin of "hatred without a cause" is equivalent to the combined affect of the sins of idolatry, incest, and murder. It is quite possible that this represents an isolated opinion; otherwise it could have easily played into the hands of the followers of Jesus, especially in view of the fact that in the Gospel of John "hatred without a cause" is mentioned as one of the factors which led to the Jewish rejection of Jesus (John 15:25).

This only goes to show how the very existence of the Christian faith must have proved an embarrassment to religious Judaism. Having originated in the Holy Land and in the bosom of the Old Testament religion, Christianity looked upon itself as the goal to which the Old Testament pointed. It challenged religious Judaism to justify from the pages of the Old Testament its opposition to Jesus Christ.

Thus it was that under the combined influence of these two farreaching developments – that cessation of the Old Testament sacrificial worship and the Christian challenge – Judaism was steered in a direction away from the Bible. It is true that this rabbinic trend was in evidence even before A.D. 70. But the existence of the Temple cult with its powerful priesthood acted as a brake on this rabbinic trend. The cessation of the sacrificial worship removed the priesthood as an influential force from Jewish life. Rabbinism was thus left free to pursue its course.

And yet rabbinism fulfilled an important historical mission. With the loss of the Jewish national homeland a substitute had to be provided to safeguard Jewish nationality. Rabbinism produced this safeguard by creating a uniform religious way of life which served to cement unity between the Jewish communities dispersed all over the world.

Humanly speaking, rabbinism saved Jewish nationally from extinction. It built a spiritual fence around the Jew which together with the physical wall erected by the Gentiles around the ghetto served to seal the Jew off effectively from outside influence. This will explain the seemingly strange phenomenon that when the ghetto walls were removed following the Napoleonic wars and the Jew became exposed to the outside world the spiritual fence of rabbinism began to fall apart. This gave rise to the nineteenth century phase of the religious crisis which has lasted to this day and for which there appears to be no solution. The primary elements of the present phase of the religious crisis have their roots in the two events in Jewish life which took place in the first century – the cessation of the sacrificial cult and the emergence of the messianic movement of Jesus. The secondary elements of the present crisis are the end results of the anti-Biblical tendencies which, consciously or unconsciously, rabbinism pursued in its efforts to solve the first century phase of the religious crisis. The primary factors have been described above. We will now proceed with a discussion of the secondary factors of the present phase of the Jewish religious crisis.

If the reader will now turn to Part One of this study or the two periodicals which conducted the symposia, he will see that many of the participants stress the fact that Judaism favors deeds over faith;

> I do not regard Jewishness as primarily a matter of religious belief. The most profound and valuable insight of Judaic religion was, I believe, the ideal of universal justice. . . .

> Knowledge and action are paramount over faith.

> Torah and mitzvah – reverence for learning and the piety of the 'deed' of 'right action' – were the constant factors in Jewish existence.

> I find compelling in this ethic [of Judaism of the last 1,000 years] . . . its conviction that redemption lies within the grasp of any man, not through 'faith' but through his assumption of the responsibility of being his brother's keeper . . .

Notice also the following utterances culled from the other sources:

> Moreover, Judaism places the emphasis on practical religion rather than on dogma.

> Whereas Christianity emphasizes salvation by grace, Judaism stresses salvation through works.

Modern Jewish orthodoxy demands unquestioned adherence to the Law.

> It is not true, then, that Judaism is a 'religion of law' . . . It is law, pure and simple, accepted by the Jewish nation at Mount Sinai . . . Judaism, in contrast [to other religions], demands actions, irrespective of convictions . . . Judaism does

not – in the manner of religions – aim to gain acceptance by 'convincing' the individual but by giving him, as the member of a nation, historical self-consciousness . . . It is not faith, then, which redeems the Jew, but historical self-consciousness . . .

Though Liberal Judaism gave up belief in the divine origin of the Law, its position on the importance of the Law in Jewish religious life is the same as that of Orthodox Judaism, as seen from the following excerpts:

It is not so much what man's belief is, but how that belief expresses itself in conduct.

Faith in Judaism we are told by the same Rabbinical writer, is not a creed in the accepted sense of the word, but an adherence to a code of moral practice revealed to man.

All radiates from the Law, and from it all depends.

Only the right deed places man in the presence of God at all times and only it can be demanded of him at all times. Through it alone can man reach that deep inner unity with God, as well as that other unity with his fellow men. . . . Judaism also has its Word, but it is only one word – 'to do.'

This works-versus-faith attitude, which is so characteristic of present-day Judaism, is the final stage in the evolution of a religious trend. This trend had its inception in the beginning of the Christian era. It was Rabbinic Judaism's answer to the doctrinal position of the New Testament, epitomized in Paul's declaration that "by the works of the law shall no flesh be justified in his sight" (Rom 3:20). It led to the exaltation of the Law by rabbinism as seen from the following few but representative passages from Talmudic writings.

2. The Exaltation of the Torah

In its narrow sense Torah refers to the Law of Moses, or the written Law. In its broad sense "Torah" includes the whole of the Old Testament and also the so-called oral Law. By "oral law" is meant a body of rabbinic literature which we now call the Talmud. It consists of two parts, the Mishnah, which was compiled in written form at the end of the third century of the Christian era, and the Gemarah, which is a commentary on the Mishnah and was compiled toward the end of the fifth century. The name "oral law" is derived from the fact that for a long time it existed by virtue of oral transmission. Rabbinism taught that this oral Law was given to Moses by God at the same time as the written Law, and that from Moses this unwritten Law was passed on together with the written Law to Joshua; Joshua delivered it to the elders; the elders to the prophets; and the prophets passed this tradition on to the Men of the Great Assembly, a religious institution which is said to have arisen in the days of Ezra, in accordance with the record contained in Nehemiah, chapters 8 to 10. The Great Assembly, or as it is also called the Great Synagogue, is the ancestor of traditional Rabbinic Judaism.

> The Torah existed before the creation of the world.

> The Torah participated in the creation of the world. In creating the world God was guided by the Torah as an architect is guided by his blueprint when planning the construction of some edifice.

> The world was created for the sake of the Torah

> The Torah is Israel's Mediator

> The Torah is unchangeable. No other Moses will come to bring another Torah, for there is no other Torah left in Heaven

The anti-New Testament connotation of the above statement is evident when compared with the following passage in the Gospel of John:

> For the law was given by Moses, but grace and truth came by Jesus Christ (John 1:17).

In the third chapter of his letter to the Romans Paul discusses the matter of Abraham's justification by faith as recorded in the fifteenth chapter of Genesis. This statement in Genesis, that Abraham was considered righteous in the sight of God on the basis of his trust in God, is recorded before the Abrahamic Covenant was made and some time before the commandment of circumcision was given. To this the rabbinic answer was that the patriarchs observed the written and even the unwritten Law, notwithstanding the fact that the patriarchs lived centuries before the promulgation of the written law.

Side by side with the emphasis of present-day Judaism on work versus faith there is a tendency to divorce ethical conduct from religion or faith in God. To be sure, this tendency is not confined to Judaism alone.

> I have no quarrel with religion for others: I believe I have a strong sense of ethics and social responsibility without it.

One American rabbi states that Jews can no longer accept on intellectual grounds a belief in a personal God, He, therefore, calls for the creation of a Jewish humanism which would be concerned with God but with humanity. In a pamphlet seeking to explain the aims of the Jewish Reconstructionist movement, we are told that religion should not be viewed as a supernaturally revealed creed or code but rather as the affirmation of the worthwhileness of life. This is the extreme logical development of the idealization and idolization of ethical conduct. If man's salvation is determined by his conduct rather than by his relation to God, then man can save himself and God can be dispensed with. This tendency to separate man's ethical conduct from faith in God, or the Law from God, may be seen in the following Talmudic passages:

> Would that they [the Jewish people] would forsake Me but keep My Torah.

One of the Talmudic sages who represented a minority opinion in a discussion of a certain halachah (i.e. legal item) appealed to Heaven for a decision. The voice which came from Heaven in response to this appeal gave its support to the dissenting rabbi. But this heavenly decision was promptly set aside by the deliberating rabbis representing the majority opinion. This action was justified on the grounds that since the Torah was delivered by God to Israel, the consensus of rabbinic opinion carries more weight than a voice from Heaven.

The great Rabbi Hillel the Elder has for many centuries exerted a powerful influence on traditional Judaism. The story is told that a heathen asked him once to teach him the Law while standing on one foot; in other words, he wished Hillel to tell him what is the essence of the Jewish religion. The answer which Hillel gave is as follows:

> Do not do to your fellow that which is hateful to you. This is the whole Law.
> The rest is its interpretation.

Not a word about faith in God or man's relationship to God!

Of course, this exaltation of the Law by rabbinism is not quite in agreement with the teachings of the Old Testament. The Ten Commandments which represent the first body of laws given on Mount Sinai begin not with a commandment, but with a divine declaration. In this declaration God defines His relationship to Israel, based on what He has done for Israel, and not on what the Israelites have done for Him. "I am Jehovah thy God, who brought thee out of the land of Egypt, out of the house of bondage" (Exod 20:2).

As for Israel, she has broken the Law through her entire Biblical history: in the wilderness, and in the days of the first Temple. And since the Synagogue recognizes that the catastrophe of the year 70 [A.D.] was due to Israel's sinfulness, this means that Israel broke the Law in the days of the second Temple also.

Not only so, but Moses, Aaron, and their sister Miriam – these three under whose leadership the Exodus from Egypt had taken place – all failed before God in the wilderness. Aaron, Israel's first high priest, transgressed and was appointed to die in the wilderness and be buried there. His two sons died because of their sins. And Moses, who in the Old Testament stands nearer to God than any other human being, was not permitted to enter the promised land because of failure to comply with God's will, and he too was left to die in the wilderness. And it is this broken Sinai Covenant that God promised through Jeremiah to replace, and to replace it, not with another Covenant of Law but with a New Covenant of Grace [Jer 31:31-34]. Thus we can see that Paul stood on Old Testament ground when he declared that "by the works of the law shall no flesh be justified" (Rom 3:20).

3. The Downgrading of the Bible

Rabbinism was not unaware that its teachings were not always in harmony with the Bible. This may be seen from a reference in the Mishnah to the effect that important parts of Rabbinic law are like "mountains hanging by a hair," i.e., find little support in the Biblical text. Perhaps this awareness led to a gradual depreciation of the Bible, as seen from the following excerpts:

> The Rabbis have taught, that when Rabbi Eliezer was ill, his disciples came to visit him, and they said to him 'Rabbi, teach us the ways of life that we may merit eternal life.' His answer, among other things, was: 'Prevent your children from meditating.' That he referred to meditating upon Scripture is seen from Rashi's comment on this passage: 'Do not get your children accustomed to read the Bible too much, so that they may not be carried away by it.

> Our Rabbis taught, that to be engaged in the study of the Bible is neither good nor bad, but to be engaged in the study of the Mishnah is a good habit and it brings reward, while there is nothing better than the study of the Gemara.

> My son, give heed to the words of the Scribes rather than the words of the Law [i.e. the Law of Moses], for the words of the Law consist of positive and negative precepts [the transgression of which is not always a capital offense]; but whosoever transgresses any of the words of the Scribes is guilty of death.

> It is a more serious matter to contradict the word of the Scribes [Mishnah] than the words of the Law of Moses.

> He who interprets the Law [of Moses] not according to Halachah [i.e. in the manner of the rabbis], even though he possesses [the virtue of knowledge of] Torah and good deeds has no portion in the world to come.

This statement is attributed to Rabbi Eleazar. He was a member of the assembly at Yabneh which under the presidency of Rabbi Gamaliel was busy reconstructing Judaism following the cessation of the sacrificial cult. Rabbi Gamaliel was the one at whose request the test prayer, the so-called Birkat Haminim, was composed, which contained a curse upon heretics, mainly Hebrew Christians. Rabbi Eleazar's saying cited above belongs to the same circle of ideas and was probably aimed at Hebrew Christians, since at that time only Hebrew Christians were likely to interpret the Law of Moses not according to the Halachah.

> The [rabbinic] sage is more important than the prophet.

4. The Depersonalization of God

The Old Testament is frankly anthropomorphic, i.e., it ascribes to God human form or human qualities. By anthropopathism is meant the imputation to God of human feelings or emotions, such as love, anger, displeasure, etc. There is a rabbinic saying to the effect that the Torah speaks the language of man, i.e., in His effort to communicate with man God adopts human ways. This is certainly correct; there could be no divine revelation unless God condescended to use human means by which to make Himself and His will known to man. But this is not all. Biblical anthropopathism reflects a truth which is basic in Biblical theology, namely, that the same God who is everywhere, in, outside, and beyond His creation, is also the personal God of mankind.

The first definite attempt to weaken this Old Testament concept of a personal God may be seen in the Septuagint, which is the name of a Greek translation of the Old Testament made in Alexandria, Egypt. There is no agreement as to the exact date of the completion of this translation, but it is believed that the Pentateuch was translated first, about the middle of the third century before the Christian era, while the other parts of the Old Testament were translated at a later date. Alexandria had a large and prosperous Jewish Community, and the mother tongue of the Jews there was Greek. A great need was felt by the Alexandrian Jews to have the Bible, especially the Pentateuch which was read in the synagogues, in their own tongue. The elimination of many of the anthropomorphic expressions from the Greek Septuagint was prompted by a desire to adapt it to the Greek way of thinking of the Alexandrian Jews. The following are a few examples.

> And upon the nobles of the children of Israel he [God] laid not his hand (Hebrew)
> And of the elect of Israel not one uttered a dissenting voice (Septuagint)
> Exod 24:11

> And there I [God] will meet with thee (Hebrew)
> And thence I will be known to thee (Septuagint)   Exod 25:22

> And I [God] will dwell in the midst of the children of Israel (Hebrew)
> And I will be invoked by the Children of Israel (Septuagint) Ex. 29:45

> The eternal God is a dwelling-place (Hebrew)
> The power of God will protect thee (Septuagint)   Deut 33:27

The Septuagint reflects Greek influence and an effort to bring Old Testament ideas in accord with Greek philosophy. This development reached its climax in Philo, a Greek Jewish Philosopher, of Alexandria, who lived at the end of the first century before Christ and in the first half of the first century of the Christian era. In Philo's philosophy God became so transcendent that He practically became unknowable.

While rabbinism of the Aramaic-speaking Palestinian Jews had no need to harmonize Old Testament ideas with Greek thought, it, in time, was confronted with such a need by the challenge presented to it by the rise of the Christian faith. Targum Onkelos is the name of the Aramaic Translation of the Pentateuch which appeared among the Aramaic-speaking Jews of Palestine in the second century of the Christian era. From its very inception it has exercised considerable authority in traditional Judaism. To this day many Hebrew Bibles print the Targum Onkelos version alongside the Hebrew text of the Pentateuch. This Targum version shows a definite tendency to eliminate certain anthropomorphic ideas of the Hebrew text, impelled to do this by a necessity to counteract the doctrine of the Incarnation of the New Testament. The following are a few illustrations:

> And Jehovah went his way, as soon as he left off speaking to Abraham.
> (Hebrew)
> And the Glory of Jehovah departed when he had ceased to speak with Abraham
> (Targum)   Gen 18:33

> And, behold, Jehovah stood above it (Hebrew)
> And, behold, the Glory of Jehovah stood above it (Targum) Gen 28:13

> And, behold, I am with thee (Hebrew)
> And, behold, My Word shall be for thy help (Targum)   Gen 28:15

> I [Jehovah] have surely seen the affliction of my people that are in Egypt . . .; for
> I know their sorrows (Hebrew)
> The bondage of my people which is in Egypt is verily disclosed before Me. . .;
> for their afflictions are disclosed before Me (Targum) Ex 3:7

This last sentence deserves some comment. In the Hebrew text God states: "I know their sorrows." In the Targum their sorrows are merely disclosed before God. The "I know" in the Hebrew text does not refer to being aware of the afflictions of Israel. An Omniscient God would be expected to be aware of everything which transpires on this earth. The expression "I know" in the Hebrew version has the connotation of intimate knowledge, bordering on personal experience. We have here the beginning of one of the most precious teachings of the Bible, namely, that God identifies Himself with His people's joys and sorrows. This may be seen from the following passages:

> And his [God's] soul was grieved for the misery of Israel. Judg 10:16

> In all their afflictions he [God] was afflicted, and the angel of his
> presence saved them. Isaiah 63:9

This concept reaches its culmination in the teachings concerning the suffering Servant of Jehovah through whom God is willing to identify Himself with His people in their sins, sickness, and death (Isaiah 53).

To return now to the question of the depersonalization of God in rabbinic Judaism. The following statements in the *Universal Jewish Encyclopedia* are of importance.

> The doctrine of divine attributes played a great role in the Christian doctrine of the trinity; it was in connection with such theological discussions between Christians and Mohammedans that the Mutakallimum (Mohammedan rationalist theologians of the 8th and following centuries) developed the doctrine of divine attributes which is so important in medieval Jewish philosophy. The Jewish philosophers from Saadia to Albo (10th to 15th centuries) and beyond followed in the main the discussions of the Arabs.

> In Palestine and Babylonia, however, no progress [in the depersonalization of God] was made until the beginning of the philosophic movement with Saadia (10th cent.). From Saadia to Albo (15th cent.) the elimination of anthropomorphism was one of the motives of the doctrine of the attributes, and Maimonides (12th cent.) was not far behind Philo in insisting on the absolute transcendence of God . . . The modern Jewish view is the same as that of the philosophers.

5. The Depersonalization Of The Messiah

In the middle of the nineteenth century newly formed Liberal Judaism in Germany took steps to introduce certain important changes in the ritual of the Synagogue. Among other things it decided to delete from the Prayer Book all references to a national restoration of the Jews to Zion, as well as references to the coming of the Messiah. In place of "Redeemer" the word "Redemption" was substituted. For the first time in many centuries Jews in the emancipated countries of Western Europe began to feel at home in the countries of their birth or residence. The petitions for a national restoration to Palestine lost all meaning to them. Since the hope of national restoration to Zion and the coming of the Messiah are closely related in the Jewish religion, the idea of a Messiah was discarded along with the hope of national restoration. However, subsequent events proved how wrong Liberal Judaism was in taking this stand. With the exception of a small orthodox group the vast majority of Zionists have no belief in a Messiah, even though they have been busy promoting the national restoration of the Jewish people.

A second factor which impelled Liberal Judaism to give up belief in a Messiah was its desire to be in a better position to deal with the Christian challenge. Joseph Albo, a learned Spanish Jew (1380-1444), composed a work which he named *Ikarim* (Principles) in which he attempted to formulate the principles of Jewish belief. One of his chief objects was to prove to the Jewish people that theirs was the true religion while Christianity was a false religion. It is said that he felt that belief or nonbelief in a Messiah has no effect on the Jew's religious status. In fact, he is said, by implication at least, to have recommended that Jews give up belief in a Messiah, hoping thereby to cut the ground from underneath Christianity, where the person of the Messiah is at the heart of its faith. Liberal Judaism of the nineteenth century adopted this line of reasoning.

A third factor which had much to do with the discarding of the belief in a Messiah by Liberal Judaism was related to the general state of things in Europe of the nineteenth century. The great strides made in science, industry, education, and in the direction of attainment of democratic goals generated an atmosphere of optimism concerning human destiny. Man was believed to be essentially good. He was expected to receive from science all the power he needs; from education, all the knowledge he must have; from democracy, all the freedom he wants. The millennium was seen to be approaching, but it was a millennium which was indifferent to the actual spiritual state of man, a millennium without God.

It was tragic that German Jewry, the fountainhead of Liberal Judaism, should have seen in the prevailing state of affairs with its materialistic mood the fulfillment of Israel's mission of the messianic hope of the prophets of the Old Testament. The effect which that era had on the German Jews may be seen from the following excerpts from addresses made at the rabbinical conference, held at Frankfort-on-the-Main, Germany, in July, 1845.

One rabbi declared that:

> Everywhere the Jewish doctrine of the Messiah is fulfilling itself rapidly. Every-where the emancipation of mankind is being striven for so that a morally pure and holy life may be possible of being lived by man on this earth.

Another rabbi said that the conference,

> Should state that we are now entering upon the period of redemption. Freedom and virtue are spreading, the world is growing better.

Still another rabbi held that:

> In our days . . . the ideals of justice and the brotherhood of men have been so strengthened through the laws and institutions of modern states, that they can never again be shattered; we are witnessing an ever nearer approach of the establishment of the Kingdom of God on earth through the strivings of mankind.

About a century following the Frankfort conference German Jewry disappeared under the Nazi regime. Many of the German Jews who survived made their way to Palestine, there to help with the task of rebuilding the Jewish national homeland and thus fulfill the centuries-old Jewish hope which the grandfathers of these German refugees repudiated at the Frankfort conference.

One of the rabbis at the Frankfort conference, who tried unsuccessfully to stop the trend towards the elimination of the prayers for the coming of the Messiah, reminded his listeners that:

259

All great events in the world's history have been accomplished by great personalities; may we not then confidently expect that this greatest and highest consummation of all, the ushering in of religious harmony, peace and brotherhood will be accomplished through one sent of God?

This rabbi was certainly on Biblical ground, for the Old Testament knows of no messianic age without a messianic person, and no messianic program which leaves the human heart unregenerated.

6. Concluding Observations On The Cause Of the Jewish Spiritual Dilemma

The present religious crisis began in the nineteenth century. It came in the wake of the political emancipation of the Jewish communities in the countries of Western Europe. It is the nineteenth-century phase of the religious crisis which was precipitated when the destruction of the Temple in the year 70 caused the cessation of the sacrificial cult.

To appreciate the causal relationship between the termination of the sacrificial cult and the religious crisis one needs only to read the numerous detailed laws and instructions regarding the sacrificial worship as recorded in the Pentateuch. A continual offering was to be sacrificed in the Temple every day in the year, consisting of two lambs, one in the morning and one in the evening. Additional sacrifices were to be offered on the Sabbath day, on the first day of the month, and on the appointed festivals.

> It shall be a continual burnt-offering throughout your generations . . .
>
> Exod 29:42

When rabbinism realized that it might take a long time before the sacrificial worship would be restored, it reconstructed Judaism from a religion with sacrifices to a religion without sacrifices. Prayers were composed into which were incorporated certain portions from the Pentateuch dealing with the institution of the sacrifices. These were to be recited with the added petition that God would accept these recited prayers in place of the sacrifices.

But this was to be an interim measure, a stopgap as it were. The Prayer Book is replete with passages in which the Synagogue bemoans the cessation of the sacrificial worship, as seen from the following passage from the Musaph and Minchah prayers for the Day of Atonement.

> But we are sinners and trespassers.
> Wherewith shall our heavy iniquities be atoned for?
> The glory of the Temple has been removed from us,
> Since then there is no forgiveness or atonement for us.
> The burnt-offerings and sacrifices ceased,
> How shall we confront Him who dwells in the heavenlies?

If there is no atonement, whence shall help come for those tainted daily in sin, iniquity, and wickedness?

Accordingly, we find in the Prayer Book many heart-touching petitions for the speedy restoration of the sacrificial worship, as seen from the following excerpt:

> May it please Thee, Jehovah our God, and the God of our fathers, King of mercy, to have abundant compassion upon us and upon thy Sanctuary, and rebuild it speedily, and increase its glory . . . And lead us to Zion, Thy city, with singing, and with an everlasting joy to Jerusalem, the place of Thy Sanctuary; and there we shall offer before thee the sacrifices enjoined on us, the continual sacrifices according to their order, and the additional sacrifices according to their ordinance.

The Mishnah devotes one of it main six divisions to a detailed description of the rules and regulations which govern the Temple sacrifices. The pious Jews have for centuries studied and meditated over these Talmudic chapters, as if the Temple had never been destroyed.

When Palestine was devastated by Rome and the Jews dispersed, the Jewish people lost all knowledge of their genealogy. But there is one group of Jews who to this day have retained their genealogical connections with the past. These are the Jews who are descendants of the family of Aaron the high priest. The reason for this is twofold: First, these Aaronic Jews are duty-bound to pronounce the Aaronic benediction in the Synagogue on the regular festivals. Second, they are the means of preserving the priesthood for the day when the Temple cult will be reestablished.

If the State of Israel were to regain the Temple site, now in the hands of the tiny Arab state of Jordan, would the Jews rebuild the Temple and restore the sacrifices? The answer that is possible to give now is that the Temple would probably be rebuilt, but it is highly doubtful whether world Jewry would favor the reinstitution at this time of the sacrificial worship. And yet the fact remains that if the Old Testament revelation is God's last word to man, then there is no other way whereby a Jew who rejects the New Testament revelation can approach God except by way of the Old Testament sacrifices. This is the essence of the Jewish religious dilemma. The two horns of this dilemma are the rejection of Jesus Christ and the cessation of the sacrificial worship of the Old Testament. In its persistent efforts to get away from Jesus, Judaism was forced to move further and further away from the Old Testament. In the process of this movement away from the Bible many Jews lost faith in God's word, faith in a Messiah, faith in a hereafter and, finally, faith in God. This is the source of the spiritual conflict in the Jewish soul.

BIBLIOGRAPHY

Alexander, T. Desmond and David W. Baker. *Dictionary of the Old Testament Pentateuch*. Downers Grove, Ill: InterVarsity, 2003.

Alexander, Ralph H. *The Expositor's Bible Commentary: Ezekiel*. 12 vols. Grand Rapids: Zondervan, 1986.

Baker, Charles F. *A Dispensational Theology*. Grand Rapids: Grace Bible Publications, 1971.

Bancroft, Emery H. *Christian Theology*. Grand Rapids: Zondervan, 1964.

Barackman, Floyd H. *Practical Christian Theology*. 4th ed. Grand Rapids: Kregel, 1998.

Barber, Cyril J. *The Books of Samuel*. 2 Vols. Neptune, NJ: Loizeaux, 1994.

Barker, Kenneth. *The New American Commentary: Micah*. 21 vols. Nashville: Broadman, 1998.

Barnes, Albert. *Barnes' Notes: Minor Prophets*. 2 vols. Grand Rapids: Baker, 1950.

Baron, David. *The Visions and Prophecies of Zechariah*. Jerusalem: Keren Ahvah Meshihit, 2000.

Barrett, Michael P.V. *Beginning At Moses*. 2nd ed. Greenville, SC: Ambassador-Emerald International, 2001.

Benach, Henry. *Go To Learn*. Chattanooga: International Board of Jewish Missions, 1997.

Bergen, Robert D. *The New American Commentary: 1 and 2 Samuel*. 21 Vols. Nashville: Broadman, 2002.

Berger, David. *The Rebbe, The Messiah and the Scandal of Orthodox Indifference*. Portland: The Littman Library of Jewish Civilization, 2001.

Berlin, Adele, and Marc Zvi Brettler. *The Jewish Study Bible*. New York: Oxford University, 2004.

Berkhof, L. *Systematic Theology*. Grand Rapids: Eerdmans, 1941.

Block, Daniel I. *The New American Commentary: Judges, Ruth*. Nashville: Broadman and Holman, 1999.

Botterweck, G. Johannes, Helmer Ringgren and Heinz-Josef Fabry. *Theological Dictionary of the Old Testament*. Grand Rapids: Eerdmans, 1977.

Briggs, Charles A. *Messianic Prophecy*. Peabody, MA: Hendrickson, 1988

Briscoe, Stuart. *The Communicator's Commentary: Genesis*. Waco, TX: Word
 Books, 1987.

Bromiley, Geoffrey W. *The International Standard Bible Encyclopedia*. 4 vols. Grand
 Rapids: Eerdmans, 1988

Brown, Francis, S. R. Driver, and Charles A. Briggs. *A Hebrew and English Lexicon of
 the Old Testament*, Oxford: Clarendon, n.d.

Brown, Michael L. *Answering Jewish Objections to Jesus*. Vol. 2 of *Answering Jewish
 Objections*. Grand Rapids: Baker Books, 2000.

Brueggemann, Walter. *Theology of the Old Testament*. Minneapolis: Fortress
 Press, 1997.

Buksbazen, Victor. *The Prophet Isaiah*. 2 vols. Collingswood, NJ: Spearhead Press,
 1971.

Buswell, James Oliver. *A Systematic Theology of the Christian Religion*. Grand Rapids:
 Zondervan, 1962.

Butler, J Glentworth. *Butler's Bible Work*. 6 vols. New York: Funk & Wagnalls, 1889.

Buttrick, George Arthur. *The Interpreter's Bible*. Nashville: Abingdon, 1953.

Cassuto, U. *A Commentary on the Book of Genesis: Part one*. Jerusalem: Magnes, 1961.

Chafer, Lewis Sperry. *Systematic Theology*. 8 vols. Dallas: Dallas Seminary Press,
 1964

Charnock, Steven. *Existence and Attributes of God*. Grand Rapids: Baker, 1979.

Cohen, A. *The Soncino Chumash, Isaiah*. New York: The Soncino Press, 1983.

Cohen, A. *The Soncino Chumash, The Five Books of Moses with Haphtaroth*. New
 York: The Soncino Press, 1993.

Cohen, A. *The Soncino Chumash, The Twelve Prophets*. New York: Soncino Press,
 1994.

Cooke, G. A. *The International Critical Commentary: The Book of Ezekiel*. Edinburgh:
 T. & T. Clark, 1936.

Cooper, David L. *God's Gracious Provision for Man*. Los Angeles: Biblical
 Research Society, 1953.

Cooper, David L. *The God of Israel.* Los Angeles: Biblical Research Society, 1945.

Cooper, Lamar Eugene. *The New American Commentary: Ezekiel.* vol. 17. Nashville: Broadman and Holman, 1994.

Craigie, P. C. *The New International Commentary on the Old Testament, The Book of Deuteronomy.* Grand Rapids: Eerdmans, 1976.

Crenshaw, James. *The Old Testament Library, Ecclesiastes.* Philadelphia: Westminister Press, 1987.

Criswell, W.A. *The Criswell Study Bible.* Nashville: Nelson, 1979.

Dahood, Mitchell. *The Anchor Bible: Psalms 101-150.* Garden City, NY: Doubleday, 1970.

Dickason, C. Fred. *Angels: Elect and Evil.* Chicago: Moody, 1975.

Dockery, David S. *Biblical Illustrator, Monotheism in the Scriptures.* Nashville, TN: Sunday School Board of the Southern Baptist Convention, 1991.

Driver, S. R. *Westminster Commentaries, the Book of Genesis.* London: Methuen & Co. 1911.

Driver, S. R., A Plummer, and C. A. Briggs, eds. *The International Critical Commentary: Genesis.* Edinburgh: T & T Clark. 1930.

Dyrness, William. *Themes in Old Testament Theology.* Downers Grove: InterVarsity, 1977.

Enns, Paul. *The Moody Handbook of Theology.* Chicago: Moody Press, 1989.

Elwell, Walter A. *Evangelical Dictionary of Theology.* Grand Rapids: Baker Book House, 1984.

Erickson, Millard J. *Christian Theology.* 2nd ed. Grand Rapids: Baker Books, 1998.

Erickson, Millard J. *Introducing Christian Doctrine.* Grand Rapids: Baker, 1992.

Evans, William. *The Great Doctrines of the Bible.* Chicago: Moody, 1974.

Feinberg, Charles L. *God Remembers, A Study of the Book of Zechariah.* New York: American Board of Missions to the Jews, 1965.

Feinberg, Charles L. *The Prophecy of Ezekiel: The Glory of the Lord.* Chicago: Moody, 1969.

Feinberg, John S. *No One Like Him*. Wheaton: Crossway Books, 2001.

Fischer, John, "Yeshua: The Deity Debate." *Mishkan* issue 39 (2003): 20-28.

Free, Joseph P., Howard F. Vos. *Archaeology and the Bible History*. Grand Rapids: Zondervan, 1992.

Fruchtenbaum, Arnold. *Israelology, the Missing Link in Systematic Theology*. Tustin, CA: Ariel Ministries, 1993.

Fruchtenbaum, Arnold. *Genesis*. Tapes. Tustin, CA: Ariel Ministries, n.d.

Fruchtenbaum, Arnold. *Messianic Christology*. Tustin, CA: Ariel Ministries, 1998.

Fruchtenbaum, Arnold. *The Footsteps of Messiah*. Tustin, CA: Ariel Ministries, 2003.

Fruchtenbaum, Arnold. *The Sabbath, Manuscript #176*. Tustin, CA: Ariel Ministries, 1991.

Frydland, Rachmiel. *What the Rabbis Know About the Messiah*. Cincinnati, OH: Messianic Publishing Co, 1991

Frydland, Rachmiel. *When Being Jewish Was a Crime*. Nashville: Nelson, 1978.

Fuchs, Daniel. *Israel's Holy Days*. Neptune, NJ: Loizeaux Brothers, 1985.

Fuller, Reginald H. "The *Vestigia Trinitatis* in the Old Testament." Page 507 in *The Quest for Context and Meaning* Edited by Craig A. Evans and Shemaryahu Talmon. Leiden, Netherlands: Brill, 1997.

Garstang, John. *Joshua – Judges: Foundations of Bible History*. Grand Rapids: Kregel, 1978.

Geisler, Norman. *Systematic Theology*. 4 vols. Minneapolis: Bethany House, 2003.

Geisler, Norman L and William E. Nix. *A General Introduction to the Bible*. Chicago, IL: Moody Press, 1968.

Goldberg, Louis. *Our Jewish Friends*. Neptune, NJ: Loizeaux Brothers, 1983.

Gordis, Robert. *Koheleth, The Man and His World, A Study of Ecclesiastes*. New York: Schocken Books, 1968.

Graham, Billy. *The Holy Spirit*. Waco: Word, 1978.

Gray, James M. *The Fundamentals*. Grand Rapids: Baker, 1980.

Grudem, Wayne. *Systematic Theology.* Grand Rapids: Zondervan, 1994.

Gunkel, Hermann. *Mercer Library of Biblical Studies: Genesis.* Macon, GA: Mercer University Press, 1997.

Hailey, Homer. *The Minor Prophets.* Grand Rapids: Baker, 1972.

Harkavy, Alexander. *The Twenty-Four Books of the Old Testament.* 2 vols. New York: Hebrew Publishing Co, 1916.

Harris, R. Laird., Gleason L. Archer, Jr., and Bruce K. Waltke, eds., *Theological Wordbook of the Old Testament,* Chicago: Moody, 1981.

Hamilton, Victor P. *The New International Commentary on the Old Testament. Genesis Chapters 1-17.* Grand Rapids: Eerdmans, 1990.

Hamilton, Victor P. *The New International Commentary on the Old Testament.* Genesis Chapters 18-50. Grand Rapids: Eerdmans, 1990.

Harvey, Richard. "Jesus the Messiah in Messianic Jewish Thought: Emerging Christologies." *Mishkan* (issue 39, 2003): 4-19.

Hasel, Gerhard F. "The Meaning of "Let Us" in Genesis 1:26." *Andrews University Seminary Studies* 13 Spring (1975) 58-66.

Henderson, Ebenezer. *Thornapple Commentaries: The Twelve Minor Prophets.* Grand Rapids: Baker, 1980.

Hendren, Noam. "The Divine Unity and the Deity of Messiah." *Mishkan* (issue 39, 2003): 36-47.

Hengstenberg, E.W. *Christology of the Old Testament.* 4 vols. Grand Rapids: Kregel, 1956.

Hertz, J.H. *Pentateuch and Haftorahs.* London: Soncino Press, 1952.

Heydt, Henry J. *Studies in Jewish Evangelism.* New York: American Board to the Jews, 1951.

Hildebrandt, Wilf. *An Old Testament Theology of the Spirit of God.* Peabody, MA: Hendrickson, 1995.

Hill, Andrew E. and John H. Walton. *A Survey of the Old Testament,* Grand Rapids: Zondervan, 1991.

Hinson, David F. *Theology of the Old Testament.* London: Society for Promoting Christian Knowledge, 2001.

Hodge, Charles. *Systematic Theology*. 3 vols. Grand Rapids: Eerdmans, 1970.

House, Paul. *Old Testament Theology*. Downers Grove: InterVarsity, 1998.

Hubbard, David A. and Glenn W. Barker. *Word Biblical Commentary: Genesis 1-15*. 52 vols. Waco, Tex: Word Books, 1987.

Jacobs, Louis. *A Jewish Theology*. West Orange, NJ: Behrman House, Inc, 1973.

Jamieson, Robert, A. R. Fausset and David Brown. *A Commentary: Critical Experimental and Practical on the Old and New Testaments*. 6 vols. Grand Rapids: Eerdmans, 1945.

Janzen, J. Gerald. "On The Most Important Word In The Shema (Deuteronomy VI 4-5)." *Vetus testamentum* 37, no. 3 (1987): 280-300.

Jenni, Ernest and Claus Westermann. *Theological Lexicon of Old Testament*, Peabody, MA: Hendrickson, 1997.

Jocz, Jacob. "The Invisibility of God and the Incarnation." *Canadian Journal of Theology* (1958): 179-186.

Johnson, John J. "A New Testament Understanding of the Jewish Rejection of Jesus: Four Theologians on the Salvation of Israel." *Journal of the Evangelical Theological Society* (2000): 229-246.

Johnson, Paul. *A History of the Jews*. New York: HarperCollins, 1987.

Johnston, Patrick and Jason Mandryk. eds. *Operation World*, Waynesboro, GA: Paternoster USA, 2001.

Jukes, Andrew. *The Names of God*. Grand Rapids: Kregel, 1980.

Loewen, Jacob A. "The Names of God in the Old Testament." *The Bible Translator* 35, no. 2 (1984): 201-207.

Kac, Arthur W. *The Messiahship of Jesus*. Grand Rapids: Baker Book House, 1986.

Kac, Arthur W. The *Spiritual Dilemma of the Jewish People: Its Cause and Cure*. Grand Rapids: Baker, 1983.

Kaiser, Walter C. *The Communicator's Commentary*. Vol. 21 of *The Communicator's Commentary*. Waco, TX: Word Books, 1992.

Kaiser, Walter C. *The Messiah in the Old Testament*. Grand Rapids: Zondervan, 1995.

Kaiser, Walter C. *The Christian and the "Old" Testament*. Pasadena, CA: William Carey Library, 1998.

Kaiser, Walter C. *Toward an Old Testament Theology*. Grand Rapids: Zondervan, 1991.

Keil, C. F. and F. Delitzsch. *Commentary on the Old Testament*. Translated by James Martin. 10 vols. Grand Rapids: Eerdmans, 1973.

Kirkpatrick, A. F. *The Book of Psalms*. Cambridge: The University Press, 1914.

Klausner, Joseph. *The Messianic Idea In Israel*. New York: Macmillan, 1955.

Kohlenberger, John R., III. *The Interlinear NIV Hebrew-English Old Testament*. Grand Rapids: Zondervan, 1987.

Kohlenberger, John R., III. and James A Swanson. *The Hebrew English Concordance to the Old Testament*. Grand Rapids: Zondervan, 1998.

Laetsch, Theodore. *The Minor Prophets*. St. Louis: Concordia, 1956.

Lange, John Peter. *Lange's Commentary on the Holy Scriptures*. Translated by Philip Schaff. 12 vols. Grand Rapids: Zondervan, 1960.

Leupold, H. C. *Exposition of Genesis*. Grand Rapids: Baker Book House, 1942.

Leupold, H. C. *Exposition of Ecclesiastes*. Columbus, OH: Wartburg Press, 1952.

Leupold, H. C. *Exposition of The Psalms*. Grand Rapids: Baker Book House, 1959.

Livingston, G. Herbert. *The Pentateuch in Its Cultural Environment*. 2nd ed. Grand Rapids: Baker Book House, 1987.

Lockyer, Herbert. *All About the Holy Spirit*. Peabody: Hendrickson, 1995.

Lockyer, Herbert. *All The Divine Names and Titles in the Bible*. Grand Rapids: Zondervan, 1975.

Longman III, Tremper, *The New International Commentary on the Old Testament: Ecclesiastes*. Grand Rapids: Eerdmans, 1998.

Mathews, Kenneth. *The New American Commentary: Genesis 1:11:26*. 21 vols. Nashville: Broadman & Holman Publishers, 1996.

McCann, J. Clinton. *Interpretation, A Bible Commentary for Teaching and Preaching: Judges*. Louisville, KY: John Knox Press, 2002.

McCarter, P. Kyle, Jr. *The Anchor Bible: I Samuel*. vol. 8. Garden City, NY: Doubleday, 1980.

McConville, J. G. *Apollos Old Testament Commentary: Deuteronomy*. vol. 5. Downers Grove, IL, 2002.

McDowell, Josh. *Evidence That Demands a Verdict*. 2 vols. Nashville: Nelson, 1993.

Merrill, Eugene H. *The New American Commentary: Deuteronomy*. 21 vols. Nashville: Broadman & Holman Publishers, 1994.

Merrill, Eugene H. "Rashi, Nicholas de Lyra, and Christian Exegesis." *Westminster Theological Journal 38*, (Fall 1975): 66-79.

Miller, H. S. *General Biblical Introduction*. Houghton, NY: Word Bearers, 1960.

Moeller, Henry R. *The Legacy of Zion*. Grand Rapids: Baker, 1977.

Morey, Robert. *The Trinity: Evidence and Issues*. Grand Rapids: Word Publishers, 1996.

Morris, Henry M. *The Genesis Record*. Grand Rapids: Baker Book House, 1980.

Morris, Robert. *Anti-Missionary Arguments, The Trinity*. Irvine, CA: HaDavar Messianic Ministries,

Motyer, J. Alec. *The Prophecy of Isaiah*. Downers Grove, IL: InterVarsity, 1993.

Nachman, Moshe ben. *Ramban (Nachmanides), Commentary on the Torah – Genesis*. Translated by Chavel. New York: Shilo Publishing Inc.

Neusner, Jacob. *An Introduction to Judaism*. Louisville: Westminster/John Knox Press, 1991.

Neusner, Jacob and William Scott Green. *Dictionary of Judaism in the Biblical Period*. Peabody, MA: Hendrickson, 1999.

Nixon, Jim. "The Doctrine of the Trinity in the Old Testament." Th.M. thesis., Dallas Theological Seminary, 1974.

Ogden, Graham and Lynell Zogbo. *A Handbook On Ecclesiastes*. New York: United Bible Societies, 1997.

Oehler, Gustave Friedrich. *Theology of the Old Testament*. Grand Rapids: Zondervan, 1883.

Orr, James. *The International Standard Bible Encyclopedia*. 5 vols. Grand Rapids: Eerdmans, 1939.

Owens, John Joseph. *Analytical Key to the Old Testament*. Grand Rapids: Baker Book House, 1989.

Pache, Rene. *The Person and Work of the Holy Spirit*. Chicago: Moody, 1954.

Parkes, James. *The Foundations of Judaism and Christianity*. Chicago: Quadrangle Books, 1960.

Patai, Raphael. *The Messiah Texts*. Detroit: Wayne State University Press, 1979.

Payne, J. Barton. *The Theology of the Older Testament*. Grand Rapids: Zondervan, 1962.

Pfeiffer, Charles F. *Old Testament History*. Grand Rapids: Baker, 1973.

Preuss, Horst Dietrich. *Old Testament Theology*. 2 vols. Translated by Leo G. Perdue. Louisville: Westminster John Knox, 1995.

Pritchard, James B. *The Ancient Near East in Pictures*. Princeton, NJ: Princeton University Press, 1954.

Rendsburg, Gary. "Dual Personal Pronouns and Dual Verbs in Hebrew." *Jewish Quarterly Review* 73, no. 1 (July 1982): 38-58.

Reyburn, William D. and Euan McG. Fry. *A Handbook on Genesis*. New York: United Bible Societies, 1997.

Reymond, Robert L. *Jesus: Divine Messiah*. Ross-shire, Scotland: Mentor Imprint, 2003.

Reznick, Leibel. *The Holy Temple Revisited*. Northvale, NJ: Jason Aronson, Inc, 1993.

Robinson, George. *Essential Judaism*. New York: Pocket Books, 2000.

Root, Gerald. "A Critical Investigation of Deuteronomy 6:4." B.D. thesis., Grace Theological Seminary, 1964.

Rosenthal, Stanley. *One God or Three?* Bellmawr, NJ: Friends of Israel Gospel Ministry, 1978.

Ross, Allen P. *Creation & Blessing: Genesis*. Grand Rapids: Baker, 1988.

Ross, Allen P. *Introducing Biblical Hebrew*. Grand Rapids: Baker Academics, 2001.

Ryle, Herbert E. *Cambridge Bible, the Book of Genesis*. London: Cambridge University Press, 1914.

Ryrie, Charles Caldwell. *The Holy Spirit*. Chicago: Moody, 1965.

Sacchi, Paolo. *The History of the Second Temple Period*. Sheffield, England: Sheffield Academic Press, 2000.

Sailhamer, John H. *The Expositor's Bible Commentary: Genesis*. 12 vols. Grand Rapids: Zondervan, 1990.

Saucy, Robert L. *The Church in God's Program*. Chicago: Moody, 1972.

Schneider, Tammi J. *Berit Olam: Judges*. Collegeville, MN: Liturgical Press, 2000.

Schurer, Emil. *A History of the Jewish People in the Time of Jesus Christ*. 5 vols. Trans by John Macpherson. Peabody, MA: Hendrickson, 2003.

Scott, J. Julius. *Jewish Backgrounds of the New Testament*. Grand Rapids: Baker Books, 1995.

Schiffman, Michael. *Return of the Remnant*. Baltimore: Lederer, 1992.

Schultz, Samuel J. *The Old Testament Speaks*. New York: Harper & Row, 1970.

Shorrosh, Anis A. *Islam Revealed: A Christian Arab's View of Islam*. Nashville: Nelson, 1988.

Showers, Renald E. *There Really is a Difference*! Bellmawr, NJ: Friends of Israel Gospel Ministry, 1990.

Singer, Isidore. *The Jewish Encyclopedia*. New York: Funk and Wagnalls Co, 1906.

Sloan, W. W. *Between the Testaments*. Paterson, NJ: Littlefield, Adams & Co, 1964.

Slotki, I. W. A. *Isaiah*, New York: The Soncino Press, 1983.

Smith, Henry. *The Religion of Israel*. New York: Charles Scribner's Sons, 1914.

Smith, James. *The Promised Messiah*. Nashville: Thomas Nelson, 1993.

Smith, Payne. *Ellicott's Commentary on the Whole Bible*. 8 vols. Grand Rapids: Zondervan, 1954.

Smith, Ralph L. *Old Testament Theology, Its History, Method, and Message*. Nashville: Broadman & Holman, 1993.

Soggin, J. Alberto. *The Old Testament Library: Judges*. Translated by John Bowden. Philadelphia: Westminster, 1981.

Speiser, E. A. *The Anchor Bible: Genesis*. Garden City, NY: Doubleday & Company, 1964.

Steinberg, Milton. *Basic Judaism.* New York: Harvest/HBJ Book, 1947.

Stone, Nathan. *Names of God.* Chicago: Moody, 1944.

Strong, Augustus H. *Systematic Theology*, Westwood, NJ: Revell, 1907.

Tanenbaum, Marc H. and Marvin R. Wilson, A. James Rudin. *Evangelicals and Jews in Conversation on Scripture, Theology, and History*. Grand Rapids: Baker Book House, 1978.

Taylor, John B. *Ezekiel*. Downers Grove: InterVarsity, 1974

Telchin, Stanley. *Abandon*. Grand Rapids: Baker Book House, 1997.

Telchin, Stan. *Messianic Judaism IS NOT Christianity*, Grand Rapids: Chosen Books, 2004

Tenney, Merrill C. *The Zondervan Pictorial Encyclopedia of the Bible*. 5 vols. Grand Rapids: Zondervan Publishing House, 1975.

Thiessen, Henry C. *Lectures in Systematic Theology*. Grand Rapids: Eerdmans, 1979.

Thomas, Thomas A. "The Trinity in the Old Testament." Th.M. diss., Dallas Theological Seminary, 1952.

Torrey, R. A. *The Holy Spirit*. New York: Revell. 1927.

Torrey, R. A. and A. C. Dixon. *The Fundamentals*. Grand Rapids: Baker, 1980.

Towner, W. Sibley. *Interpretation: Daniel*. Atlanta: John Knox Press, 1984.

Towner, W. Sibley. *Westminster Bible Companion: Genesis* (Louisville, KY: Westminster John Knox Press, 2001.

Turner, Laurence A. *Genesis*. Sheffield, England: Sheffield Academic Press, 2000.

Unger, Merrill F. *Biblical Demonology*. Wheaton: Scripture Press, 1952.

VanGemeren, Willem A. *Dictionary of Old Testament Theology & Exegesis*, Grand Rapids: Zondervan, 1997.

Vine, W. E. *Isaiah*. Grand Rapids: Zondervan, 1946.

Vos, Geerhardus. *Biblical Theology, Old and New Testament*. Grand Rapids: Eerdmans, 1948.

Walvoord, John F. *Jesus Christ Our Lord*. Chicago: Moody Press, 1969.

Walvoord, John F. *The Holy Spirit*. Findlay, OH: Dunham Publishing, 1958.

Walvoord, John F. and Roy B. Zuck. *The Bible Knowledge Commentary: Old Testament*. Wheaton: Victor Books, 1985.

Warfield, Benjamin Breckinridge. *Biblical and Theological Studies*. Philadelphia: Presbyterian and Reformed Publishing, 1968.

Waterhouse, Steven W. *Not By Bread Alone: An Outlined Guide to Bible Doctrine*. Amarillo, TX: Westcliff Press, 2000.

Webb, Barry G. *The Message of Isaiah*. Downers Grove, IL: Inter-Varsity, 1996.

Weinfeld, Moshe. *The Anchor Bible: Deuteronomy 1-11*. New York: Doubleday, 1991.

Weiss-Rosmarin, Trude. *Judaism and Christianity, the Differences*. Middle Village: Jonathan David Publishers, Inc, 1997.

Westermann, Claus. *Genesis 1-11: A Continental Commentary*. Translated by John J. Scullion. Minneapolis: Fortress Press, 1994.

Whiston, William. *Josephus' Complete Works*. Grand Rapids: Kregel, 1978.

Wigram, George V. *The Englishman's Hebrew Concordance of the Old Testament*. Peabody, MA: Hendrickson Publishers, 1996.

Wilkin, Robert N. "Toward a Narrow View of Ipsissima Vox." *JOTGES* 14, no 26 (Spring 2001): 3-8.

Wilson, Marvin R. *Our Father Abraham*. Grand Rapids: Eerdmans, 1989.

Wolf, Herbert M. *Interpreting Isaiah*. Grand Rapids: Baker, 1985.

Wolf, Hebert M. *The Expositor's Bible Commentary: Judges*. 12 vol. Grand Rapids: Zondervan, 1992.

Wood, B. G. "Prophecy of Balaam Found In Jordan." *Bible and Spade* 6 (Autumn 1977): 121-124.

Wood, Leon J. *Distressing Days of the Judges*. Grand Rapids: Zondervan, 1975.

Wood, Leon J. *The Holy Spirit in the Old Testament*. Eugene, OR: Wipf and Stock, 1998.

Young, Edward. *The Book of Isaiah*. 3 vols. Grand Rapids: Eerdmans, 1972.

Young, Robert. *Analytical Concordance to the Bible*. Grand Rapids: Eerdmans, n.d.

Youngblood, Ronald. *The Book of Genesis*. 2nd ed. Eugene, OR: Wipf and Stock, 1999.

Youngblood, Ronald. *The Expositor's Bible Commentary*. 12 vols. Grand Rapids: Zondervan, 1992.

Youngblood, Ronald. *The Genesis Debate*. Nashville: Nelsons, 1986.

Zimmerli, Walter. *Ezekiel 1*. Philadelphia: Fortress, 1979.

Zlotowitz, Meir. *The Family Chumash Bereishis: Genesis*. Brooklyn: Mesorah Press, 1986.

Author Index

Author Index

Author Index

Author Index

Proper Names and Places

Aaron: 51, 62-63, 74, 132, 239, 246

Abel: 147

Abihu: 62

Abimelech: 10, 104-105

Abiram: 62

Abraham: 5-6, 10, 15, 21, 37-38, 40, 46-49, 52, 54-57, 60, 62, 104-105, 111, 114, 116, 126, 155-156, 162-163, 171, 173, 205, 213, 215, 224, 226, 233, 238, 242

Abraham Ibn Ezra: 39

Adam: 35, 42-44, 60, 173

Agrippa: 185

Ahaz: 166, 175

Ammon: 136, 225

Amon: 175

Amorites: 30, 55-56

Anointed One: 156, 185, 191-193

Antiochus IV: 185

Aramaic: 23, 59, 122, 146, 157, 241-242

Aristotle: 83-84

Armilus: 169

Artaxerxes: 193

Asa: 139

Ashkelon: 137

Assyria: 2, 57, 166-167, 175

Asterah: 50, 68

Azariah: 139

Baal: 7, 20, 30, 44, 50, 67-68, 73, 135-136

Babel: 35, 94, 96

Babylon(ian): 2, 98-99, 114, 176-176, 216, 243

Balaam: 10, 133-134, 139-141

Balak: 133

Bands: 197

Bar Kokhba: 6

Bathsheba: 74

Beauty: 197

Beelzebub: 213

Belshzzar: 64

Bethlehem: 5, 41, 171-172, 174-175, 205, 219

Bezaleel: 85, 131-132, 139, 141,

Bochim: 56

Branch: 175-179, 190, 194, 199

Caleb: 134

Canaan(ites): 20, 30, 50, 55-56, 74, 106, 118, 159, 183

Chaldea: 142

Christians (ity): 1, 3, 6-8, 12, 15, 28, 31, 48, 52-53, 59, 67-71, 73, 79, 83-84, 91, 97, 142, 171, 177, 180, 185-186, 204, 208, 210-213, 217, 231-232, 235-236, 240, 243

Coniah: 176-177

Cyrus: 114, 191

Daniel: 9, 23-24, 34, 64, 122, 131, 147, 170, 186, 187, 190, 191-193, 216

David: 4-6, 9, 27, 32, 37-38, 42-43, 64, 74-75, 85, 101, 123-125, 129, 131, 138, 140-141, 147-148, 150-151, 155-156, 158, 162-160, 171-173, 175-183, 191, 193-199, 200-202, 205, 209, 215-216, 226

Dathan: 62

Delilah: 137

Egypt(ian): 21, 30, 34, 44, 55-56, 61, 106, 118, 129, 175-176, 185, 196, 218, 225, 239, 241-242

El-bethel: 37, 105-106

Eliakim: 176

Elias: 179

Emmaus Road: 66

Ethan: 164-166, 169

Eshtaol: 137

Eve: 35, 42-44

Ezekiel: 9, 23, 63-64, 74, 83, 126, 141-143, 216

Ezra: 4, 9, 23, 39, 46, 57, 97, 232, 238

France: 185

Gabriel: 187

Gideon: 57, 134-137

Gilead: 136

Gog: 169

Golden, Moshe: 84

Haftorah: 100-101, 104-105, 230

Hagar: 10, 21, 57

Haggai: 9, 23, 216

Hezekiah: 57, 166-167

Hivites: 55-56

Proper Names and Places

House of David: 5, 32, 165, 171-172, 183, 195, 199-200, 202
Hunah, Rabbi: 179
Hur: 74

Immanuel: 193-194, 219
Isaac: 9, 24, 34-35, 40, 45-47, 50, 87, 112, 115, 117, 123-124, 141-142, 147-148, 151, 155, 160-161, 166, 168, 170-171, 178, 193-195, 204-205, 209, 215, 224, 226, 230
Israel: 2-4, 6-10, 13, 15-17, 20-24, 26-34, 36-37, 39-47, 49-53, 55, 57-64, 67, 71-76, 79-80, 82-85, 89, 95-96, 98-99, 103-104, 106, 108, 110, 112, 114-115, 117-118, 123-125, 127, 129-130, 133-134, 137, 140-141, 146, 148, 151, 157, 160-162, 166, 168-171, 175, 177, 179-181, 183, 185, 189, 193, 195-198, 200-205, 209, 213, 216, 230, 238-239, 241-242, 244, 246

Jaazaniah: 142
Jacob: 15, 21, 37-38, 40, 46, 48, 57, 106, 114, 125, 199, 205, 215, 223-224, 226
James: 70-71, 103
Jaohaz: 175
Jebusites: 55, 56
Jehoiachin: 176
Jehoiakim: 176-177
Jephthah: 134, 136-137
Jeremiah: 9, 23, 142, 147, 168, 170, 175, 177-178, 193, 205, 216
Jericho: 48, 57
Jerusalem: 6, 63, 111, 142, 155-156, 166, 169-171, 175-176, 184-185, 190, 199-200, 202, 204-205, 213, 215-216, 232, 246
Jesse: 125, 194-195
Jethro: 10
Job: 2, 24, 125, 134, 161
Jonathan: 158
John: 20, 59, 65, 71, 103, 116 153, 160
Jonah: 9, 21, 147
Jordan: 10, 246
Joseph: 131, 165
Josiah: 175-176, 202
Joshua: 2, 15, 40, 44, 48, 51-52, 57, 75, 85, 108-109, 133-134, 146, 229, 237

Judah: 2, 5, 31-33, 36, 74, 147, 166-167, 171, 175-176, 183, 185, 192, 198, 219, 246
Judah Ha-Nasi: 4

Kahanna, Rabbi: 179
Korah: 62
Kimchi: 97, 115

Judaism: 1, 3, 7, 12-13, 15-17, 19, 26-28, 43, 47-48, 67-71, 73, 78, 82, 97, 149, 155, 162, 170, 177, 180, 188, 204, 208, 210-211, 216, 229-230, 232, 235-240, 242-243, 245-246
Judas: 151
Jude: 70-71, 103

Lancaster School of the Bible: 81
Latin Vulgate Bible: 54, 144
Lehi: 137
Lucifer: 163
Luke: 20, 103, 153, 165
Luther: 70

Maccabees: 184-185
Magog: 169
Maimonides: 16, 83, 84, 101, 196
Mahaneh-dan: 137
Malachi: 23
Manasseh: 136, 175
Mark: 103, 150, 153
Mary: 165
Masoretic Text: 110, 230
Matthew: 103, 150, 153
Medes: 114
Melchizedek: 21, 180, 183
Messiah ben David: 155, 169, 200-201
Messiah ben Joseph: 155, 200-201
Mesopotamia: 133
Mattaniah: 176
Melchizedek: 21, 180, 183
Menachem: 5, 179
Micah: 9, 17, 114, 141, 155, 161, 170, 172-174
Millennium: 153, 192, 244
Miriam: 21, 62, 165, 239
Mizpah: 136
Moab(ites): 30, 133, 225

Proper Names and Places

Scripture Index

287

Subject Index

Subject Index

Emmanuel: see Immanuel

Eternal: 6, 17, 48, 68-70, 102, 156, 158-165, 172-174, 183-184, 189, 194, 204, 216, 219, 227, 233, 240-241

    Eternity: 17, 156, 164, 171, 173

    Everlasting: 17, 23, 37, 46, 160-162, 166-168, 171-175, 184, 187, 189-190, 194-195, 210, 219, 246

    Olam: 21, 156-164, 166, 168, 171-175, 190, 210

Etymology: 10, 20, 25, 46

Evangelical: see Theological

Evangelicalism:

Exile: see Time

Finger of God: 64-65, 219, 233

Fundamentalism: 12-14, 19, 30, 38, 50, 60, 76, 185, 271

Gentiles: 4, 6, 8, 32, 142, 181, 236, 111

Glory of God: see Shechinah

Godhead: 1, 4-5, 7, 9, 24, 28, 38, 55-56, 60-61, 65, 73, 78, 83, 89-91, 94, 99, 106-107, 112, 116, 128, 130, 138, 153, 208, 212, 227

God/man: 3, 7, 11, 44, 71, 103, 171, 178, 194-195, 197, 199-201, 205

god(s):

    Asherah (ot): 20, 50

    Baal (im): 7, 20, 30, 44, 50, 67-68, 73, 135

    Idolatry: 2, 44, 80, 175, 235

Grammatical Plural: see Plural of Majesty

Haftorah: 100-101, 104-105, 230

Heathen: see Pagan

Heavenly Council: see Plural of Majesty

Heavenly Court: see Plural of Majesty

Heavenly Host: see Plural of Majesty

Hebrew Scriptures: 1, 3-17, 19-27, 30-31, 33, 38-39, 41, 45, 52-54, 58-59, 63, 66, 71, 73-76, 78, 81-82, 84-85, 89, 96, 104, 107, 109, 114, 116-117, 119-121, 123, 138, 144, 146-148, 150-153, 155, 162, 170, 180, 191, 207-210, 212-213, 230-232, 234

Hellenism: 39, 59

Henotheism: 43-44

Holocaust: 6, 169

Holy Spirit: 7, 12, 16, 20, 48, 65-66, 69, 85, 115-121, 123-143, 145-154, 180, 199, 205, 209, 213, 228, 233

    Ruah haKodesh: 16, 233

        Breath: 12-13, 43, 102, 121-122, 129, 144, 169, 232

        Wind: 120-122, 124, 126, 217

    Spirit: 16, 28, 30, 38, 48, 67-69, 85, 91, 102, 114-135, 137-139, 141-144, 148, 150-154, 164, 199, 216

    Spirit of the LORD: 16, 117, 121, 123-125, 130, 134-141, 143, 148, 150, 194

        Empowering: 131, 137

        Endow: 114-115, 132-133, 155, 191

        Filled (ing): 59, 62-63, 85, 95, 131-132, 134, 141, 145, 200

        Indwell (t): 78, 129-132, 142, 153

        Upon: 85, 117, 124, 130-143, 145, 148, 153, 194, 209

    Spirit of God: 32, 77-78, 109, 119-121, 123, 125, 127, 129-131, 133-135, 138-139, 142-144, 146

Idolatry: see gods

Image: 32, 44, 53, 69, 87-91, 93, 97, 101-102, 111, 195, 228

Immanuel: 193-194

Incarnation: 15, 17, 43, 48, 51, 65, 67-68, 70, 163, 165, 208, 215, 242

Inspiration: 12-14, 20, 28, 30, 36, 82, 87, 92-93, 105, 108-109, 125-127, 138, 141, 144-150, 152, 165, 180, 207-208, 231-232

    Infallible: 12, 106, 145, 232

    Inspired: 12, 19, 30, 40-41, 106, 128, 145-146, 148-149, 204, 207, 231-232, 234

    Verbal Plenary: 12-14, 23, 28, 36, 40, 46, 82, 87, 92, 126, 138, 144-146, 148, 231,

Interpretation: 3, 11, 13-15, 17, 28, 30, 36, 71-72, 75-76, 79, 84, 89-90, 93, 96-98, 100-102, 105-106, 109, 136, 146, 156, 1645, 171, 173, 180, 185 196-197, 200-201, 231-232, 239

    Literal: 13, 27, 30, 35-37, 105, 109, 122, 199

Jewish Theologians: see Theologians

Subject Index

Subject Index

Subject Index

299

Subject Index